ADVANCE PRAISE FOR

INDIGENOUS RESURGENCE
in the CONTEMPORARY CARIBBEAN

"A collection of fourteen remarkably diverse and stimulating essays, this book represents a new milestone in scholarly research and writing about the Caribbean. These authors are not armchair specialists, but the people who have collected the evidence from first hand experience. They are the participant observers of indigenous population persistence, a phenomenon reluctantly recognized by many traditional scholars and regional governments. *Indigenous Resurgence* reports on the most recent and current data and concepts in a subject field that has assumed global significance, and sparks a variety of controversy."

Helen Hornbeck Tanner, Senior Research Fellow, The D'Arcy McNickle Center for American Indian History, The Newberry Library, Chicago

"The indigenous peoples of the Caribbean are widely supposed to have been extinct since shortly after Columbus's arrival in the area. Despite a huge loss of population, they never were extinct, just 'persisting in quiet remembrance,' as one contributor to this book memorably puts it, but over the last twenty-five years their presence has been increasingly felt. Now, at last, in this volume, we have a project that charts their resurgence in fourteen varied and fascinating chapters.

Expertly marshaled by editor Maximilian C. Forte, these chapters range across the entire Caribbean, from Cuba to Suriname, from the Dominican Republic to Belize, from Trinidad to Dominica. Their authors explain the various reasons for the growing contemporary understanding of indigenous survival in the Caribbean over the second half of the twentieth century: how colonial practices erased indigenous identities as a matter of political economy; how, in matching fashion, indigenous resistance often adopted the tactic of avoiding the state; how local creole practices (domestic and agricultural) are now being better understood as indigenous cultural survivals; and how the new understanding of descent given by DNA analysis has taken over from crude accountings of blood quanta. Contemporary indigenous identity has changed over five hundred years just as much as other cultural or ethnic identities have, and this book offers an excellent guide as to how transformation should be thought of as survival rather than loss.

The general cultural and intellectual climate has changed dramatically in recent years. There is now a better appreciation of the possibility of multiple personal identities relating to multiple ancestries, and censuses now tend to work through self-ascription rather than 'expert' opinion as to someone else's ethnicity. While some of the stigma of being indigenous in the Caribbean has disappeared over recent years, the actual advantages are still zero, so it's intriguing that some of the pride in being so has returned, or at least begun to become more public, as Caribbean indigenous peoples begin to draw on material and symbolic resources from a broader world culture in order to reproduce their indigeneity in some of the ways so well analyzed here. But there is more than just scholarly analysis: throughout this volume resonate the voices of three particular indigenous leaders, Panchito Ramírez Rojas (eastern Cuba), Ricardo Bharath Hernandez (Trinidad), and Joseph Palacio (Belize), all eloquently testifying to what survival and resurgence might really mean."

Peter Hulme, Professor of Literature, University of Essex

INDIGENOUS RESURGENCE
in the CONTEMPORARY CARIBBEAN

PETER LANG
New York • Washington, D.C./Baltimore • Bern
Frankfurt am Main • Berlin • Brussels • Vienna • Oxford

INDIGENOUS RESURGENCE
in the CONTEMPORARY CARIBBEAN

Amerindian Survival and Revival

EDITED BY
Maximilian C. Forte

PETER LANG
New York • Washington, D.C./Baltimore • Bern
Frankfurt am Main • Berlin • Brussels • Vienna • Oxford

Library of Congress Cataloging-in-Publication Data

Indigenous resurgence in the contemporary Caribbean: Amerindian survival
and revival / edited by Maximilian C. Forte.
p. cm.
Includes bibliographical references and index.
1. Indians of the West Indies—Ethnic identity. 2. Indians of the West Indies—
Social conditions. 3. Indians of the West Indies—Government relations.
4. Self-determination, National—Caribbean Area. I. Forte, Maximilian Christian.
F1619.3.E83I63   323.1197'0729—dc22   2005012816
ISBN 978-0-8204-7488-5

Bibliographic information published by **Die Deutsche Nationalbibliothek**.
Die Deutsche Nationalbibliothek lists this publication in the "Deutsche
Nationalbibliografie"; detailed bibliographic data are available
on the Internet at http://dnb.d-nb.de/.

Cover design by Lisa Barfield
Cover photo of Santo Lopez, elder of the Santa Rosa Carib Community, Arima, Trinidad
and Tobago. Photograph courtesy of the archives of the Santa Rosa Carib Community.
Taino cave drawings from the Dominican Republic are sketched renditions
by Maximilian Forte based on photographs provided by Lynne Guitar.

© 2006, 2012 Peter Lang Publishing, Inc., New York
29 Broadway, 18th floor, New York, NY 10006
www.peterlang.com

All rights reserved.
Reprint or reproduction, even partially, in all forms such as microfilm,
xerography, microfiche, microcard, and offset strictly prohibited.

CONTENTS

List of Figures ... ix

Chapter One. Introduction: The Dual Absences of Extinction and Marginality—What Difference Does an Indigenous Presence Make? ... 1
  MAXIMILIAN C. FORTE

PRESENCE: Contemporary Paths of Survival after the Myth of Extinction ... 19

Chapter Two. Taíno Survivals: Cacique Panchito, Caridad de los Indios, Cuba ... 21
  JOSÉ BARREIRO

Chapter Three. Ocama-Daca Taíno (Hear Me, I Am Taíno): Taíno Survival on Hispaniola, Focusing on the Dominican Republic ... 41
  LYNNE GUITAR, PEDRO FERBEL-AZCARATE, and JORGE ESTEVEZ

IDENTITIES: Articulating Indigenous Identities and Spaces in the Contemporary Caribbean ... 69

Chapter Four. Placing the Carib Model Village: The Carib Territory and Dominican Tourism ... 71
  KELVIN SMITH

Chapter Five. Land Ownership and the Construction of Carib Identity in St. Vincent ... 89
  PAUL TWINN

Chapter Six. "In This Place Where I Was Chief": History and Ritual in the Maintenance and Retrieval of Traditions in the Carib Community of Arima, Trinidad ... 107
  RICARDO BHARATH HERNANDEZ and MAXIMILIAN C. FORTE

RIGHTS: Indigenous Rights, International Conventions, and Current Legal Frameworks within the Circum-Caribbean 133

*Chapter Seven. "These Forests Have Always Been Ours":
Official and Amerindian Discourses on Guyana's Forest Estate* 135
  JANETTE BULKAN and ARIF BULKAN

*Chapter Eight. Indigenous and Tribal Peoples in Suriname:
A Human Rights Perspective* 155
  FERGUS MACKAY

NATION-STATE: Modern Incorporations and Challenges to Articulating and Organizing Aboriginality 175

Chapter Nine. Cultural Identity among Rural Garifuna Migrants in Belize City, Belize 177
  JOSEPH O. PALACIO

Chapter Ten. Disputing Aboriginality: French Amerindians in European Guiana 197
  GÉRARD COLLOMB

REGION: The Transnationalization of Caribbean Indigenous Resurgence 213

*Chapter Eleven. Looking at Ourselves in the Mirror:
The Caribbean Organization of Indigenous Peoples (COIP)* 215
  JOSEPH O. PALACIO

Chapter Twelve. A Bridge for the Journey: Trajectory of the Indigenous Legacies of the Caribbean Encounters, 1997–2003 235
  JOSÉ BARREIRO

*Chapter Thirteen. Searching for a Center in the Digital Ether:
Notes on the Indigenous Caribbean Resurgence on the Internet* 253
  MAXIMILIAN C. FORTE

*Chapter Fourteen. Conclusion. "Before, We Were Asleep:
Now We Must Awake from Our Sleep and Move Forward"* 271
  ARTHUR EINHORN

Contributors 287
Index 293

FIGURES

1	*Panchito Ramirez and José Barreiro, Cuba*	23
2	*Panchito Ramirez Conducts Tobacco Prayer, Cuba*	33
3	*Peeling Bitter Yucca, Dominican Republic*	57
4	*María De Los Santos, Cooking Casaba Bread, Dominican Republic*	57
5	*Gina Rodriguez, Taíno Heritage Art, Dominican Republic*	58
6	*Mural of Taíno Figure Slaying Columbus, Dominican Republic*	64
7	*Maintained Traditions: Julie Calderón, Sifting Cassava, Trinidad*	122
8	*Retained Traditions: Caribs in the Santa Rosa Festival, 1998, Trinidad*	123
9	*Travelers to Caridad de los Indios, Cuba*	249
10	*Houses at La Ranchería, Guantánamo, Cuba*	251

※ CHAPTER ONE ※

Introduction: The Dual Absences of Extinction and Marginality—What Difference Does an Indigenous Presence Make?

Maximilian C. Forte

> One debilitating consequence of the way in which the native Caribbean has been locked into an 'ethnographic present' of 1492, divorced from five-hundred years of turbulent history, has been that the present native population has usually been ignored: some seemingly authoritative accounts of the region even appear written in ignorance of the very existence of such a population.
> —Peter Hulme (1993, p. 214)

> Twenty five years ago it was widely assumed that indigenous peoples were dying out; that they were either being physically extinguished by disease and the savage onslaughts of the modern world or that they were abandoning their indigenous identities and disappearing into the mainstream of the societies that surrounded them. This assumption was quite wrong.
> —David Maybury-Lewis (1997)

> Reports of the death of indigenous cultures...have been exaggerated.
> —Marshall Sahlins (1999, p. i)

Indigenous peoples have been ever vanishing, almost as if disappearance was their predetermined historical role. The story of indigenous extinction is one the West tells itself about its own civilizational supremacy and cultural victory as the zenith of human achievement—indigenous people are always disappearing and declining. Why? They simply must, or the story will lose its power. It is an influential story, to be encountered in unexpected quarters. There I was in 1995, sitting around a table with other graduate students in Immanuel Wallerstein's seminar, "Introduction to Modern World-Systems Studies," at SUNY-Binghamton, the lone anthropology student in

"SOC 601." Wallerstein had just started to talk—briefly—about the Caribbean as the launching pad for European expansion. Then he added, "the native peoples of that region were simply *wiped out*," sweeping his hand off to the side. I felt uncomfortable. I had just returned that summer from my first meeting with members of the Carib community in Arima, Trinidad. Wallerstein is by no means alone in his belief. As an undergraduate in Latin American and Caribbean Studies, I never encountered a course on the indigenous peoples of the Caribbean, and I only briefly heard of "Caribs and Arawaks" in passing, leaving me with the impression that they must have simply passed away. Recent anthropological writings that emphasize the presence and reproduction of indigenous cultures that were previously alleged to be on their way out (see Sahlins, 1993, 1999), also stay well away from the Caribbean, focusing instead on the usual suspects: the Inuit, highlanders of Papua New Guinea, the Maya. These are the most likely candidates to be seen as "really" indigenous, indicative of Field's observation of "anthropologists' preference for describing the 'most Indian' sociocultural areas" (1994, p. 234).

Some orthodoxy gets the better of the best of us. Wallerstein was only reproducing what he must have felt was common knowledge. One might therefore also feel embarrassed for macro-perspectives that rarely bother themselves with examining local ethnographies, thereby passing vast generalizations that are sometimes not evidenced on the ground, putting lines through whole peoples, and placing check marks in the "capitalism rules" column. David Maybury-Lewis makes an observation above that I certainly agree with, except on one point: assumptions of extinction have been generated for much longer than the past 25 years. In the case of the Caribbean those assertions have been made for the better part of the past five centuries, and the passage of time that helps to make some ways of knowing more common does not necessarily make them wiser. One should also note that the last 25 years have seen a shift from writing about indigenous peoples in a state of decline, facing a future of assimilation, to perspectives on indigenous peoples engaged in resistance, facing a future of resurgence (Bruner, 1986, p. 4).

For all the assertions of actual or impending extinction and sociocultural irrelevance, what we witness "on the ground" presents us with other realities. States have recognized existing Carib communities in Dominica, St. Vincent, and Trinidad and Tobago. In some territories, nationalist intellectuals have hailed Amerindians as the bedrock of the modern nation, territorial ancestors whose struggle for freedom could readily be folded into the wider Caribbean quest for independence. From the late 1980s, indigenous bodies in Belize, St. Vincent, Dominica, Trinidad, and Guyana cooperated in the formation of the Caribbean Organization of Indigenous Peoples. In the Guyanas, indigenous federations have emerged to challenge the erosion of their resource base and to assert rights to their own cultural identities and traditions, often linking themselves to wider South American and Caribbean indigenous confederations. Regional indigenous gatherings have taken place on multiple occasions in St. Vincent, Trinidad, Guyana, Dominica, and Cuba. The news media in various territories of the Caribbean have focused greater attention than ever before on the existence and current situation of indigenous peoples. Indigenous governmental bodies in North America have built supportive networks of exchange with Caribbean Amerindian bodies, including Canada's Assembly of First Nations, the Assembly of Manitoba Chiefs, and the Federation of Saskatchewan Indian Nations. Agencies of the United Nations and the Organization of American States have recognized, supported, or otherwise worked with indigenous organizations in the region. The Internet has witnessed the growth of dozens of sites by and about contemporary indigenous peoples of the Caribbean. Many individuals are expressing a new pride in their indigenous ancestry as they broaden knowledge of their own family and cultural histories. Ethnographers have documented indigenous cultural survivals in numerous contemporary Caribbean cultural practices that have previously been taken for granted as simply "local," generically "creole," or of "unknown origins." In addition, there are more Caribbean indigenous scholars themselves, including Jose Barreiro and Joseph Palacio in this volume. Territories where, for generations, scholars and commentators had asserted the biological extermination of indigenous peoples have been shown to not only possess indigenous descendants, but that such descendants may in fact be in the majority, as in the case of Puerto Rico (see DRLAS, 2000; Kearns, 2003; Martinez Cruzado, 2002). Whether in terms of demography, symbolic meanings, cultural practices, political organization, or mere commemoration, the indigenous peoples of the Caribbean have, far from vanishing, become more visible than ever. The only way one can "miss" seeing them is by choosing not to look.

On many different levels we can speak of a *resurgence* of the indigenous in the Caribbean. The notion of resurgence will involve different meanings in different local contexts across the region. In some cases resurgence only exists as an expression of renewed interest by scholars in the indigenous peoples of the Caribbean, as they challenge their blinkered inattention to peoples who have never consented to the view that they either disappeared or were unimportant. Theses of extinction have been a hallmark of island Caribbean historiography more than is the case with the mainland. On the other hand, challenges to notions of disappearance, efforts to resist political and economic marginalization, the formation of new regional organizations, and the recent growth in a committed body of scholarship focused on these issues, collectively produce resurgence. In all cases, contemporary indigenous peoples of the Caribbean refuse to be measured by the relics of their past or to be treated condescendingly as mute testimonials to a disappearing history, or a history of disappearance.

What "We" Have Been Missing

The Caribbean is a remarkable place, a central place. At one and the same time, the Caribbean was present at the birth of world capitalism and the birth of two modern narratives that have since been applied to other parts of the world: extinction and cannibalism (see Hulme, 1992). This volume focuses on the former theme, under the heading of "absence"—absence as perceived through the lens of extinction or marginality: indigenous island populations as extinct, and mainland indigenous populations as marginal and on their way to meet the fate of their island precursors (at least, from an orthodox view point, which we collectively challenge). Fourteen contributors from three continents, including four indigenous representatives, collaborate here to provide a survey-like overview of the contemporary situation of indigenous peoples in the Caribbean and they analyze some of the challenges they face in making their identities present and their societies viable.

If the Caribbean is a central place in some respects, it is "out of place" in much of anthropology for being too novel, too hybrid, too discontinuous, not indigenous enough. As one anthropologist opined, "depicted today as uncertain, variegated, and unfinished—as creole—the world seems to have found its emblem in the Caribbean" (Khan, 2001, p. 271). The Caribbean has thus been typecast as the zone of "impurity," of permanent "artificiality," a place where primordial attachments are impossible (see Robotham, 1998, p. 308). No less a cultural critic than Stuart Hall argued that it is this pervasive sense of "ruptures and discontinuities" that constitutes the "uniqueness of the Caribbean" (1994, p. 394). C.L.R. James emphasized that "these populations [of the Caribbean] are essentially Westernized and they have been Westernized for centuries" (quoted in Oxaal, 1968, p. 1). Other writers have reaffirmed this perspective, some writing very plainly that "the history of the Caribbean has been the history of imported peoples" (Lieber, 1981, p. 1). If some would argue that indigenous activists are "essentializing" their identities as consisting of a core of fixed traits (see Field, 1999), it's not like we have a superior alternative in these essentialisms of Caribbean people as "Western."

It is at this very point that the discussion could spiral out of control. We risk ending up in fruitless debates between essentialism and its not-so-different constructionist critics (see Friedman, 1996, pp. 129–130); between survival and invention (where those claiming to see invention clearly have fixed historical coordinates in mind for what they implicitly understand to be "non-invented" referents [see Sahlins, 1993]); between theories of primordiality versus instrumentality (casting indigenous peoples in a lose-lose situation: either they are too innocent and unthinking to engage in conscious political action, or they are cynical cultural manipulators who will make just about any claim to get a casino); or, in arguments between cultural change and cultural "loss"

—as Sahlins put it: "when *we* change it's called progress, but when they do...it's a kind of adulteration, a *loss* of their culture" (1999, p. iii). This volume, for its part, is not oriented toward directly revising and rebuilding analyses of creolization, essentialism, or invention, as much as it is about making certain histories, cases, and communities better known so that we can begin to rework our conceptual tools and to revise the materials on which theories of modern Caribbean cultural history have rested. If there is one theoretical tool that the contributors collectively offer, directly or by implication, it is that of reproduction and resurgence, which I will return to in greater detail below.

The arguments presented in this volume hinge on the belief that acknowledgment of the presence of the indigenous in Caribbean societies significantly challenges our understandings of the cultural complexity of the modern Caribbean. In addition, the contributions reveal how the same political and economic processes that have the effect of marginalizing contemporary Amerindians can sometimes provoke if not enable their reproduction as indigenous entities. We hope to fill a very critical gap in the literature of the modern Caribbean by focusing on *contemporary* indigenous peoples of the region, which does not mean forgetting history, indeed, most of the contributions offer significant historical foreground, without conflating indigeneity with archaeology.

Regrettably, no other volume has provided us with an overview of contemporary indigenous peoples of the Caribbean, not even ones with titles that might tempt us to think otherwise. For example, *Taíno Revival*, edited by Gabriel Haslip-Viera (1999), featuring contributions with derisive titles such as "Making Indians Out of Blacks" or the apparent mockery in "The Indians Are Coming! The Indians Are Coming!", focuses on Puerto Ricans, and does so in a manner that strongly suggests that contemporary Taínos are pathological, self-deluding holders of a false consciousness that blinds them to their true nature as Black. Hence, key terms such as "Taíno," "present day," and "traditional" rarely appear without the scare quotes. Far from offering "critical perspectives" on "cultural politics," as that volume's subtitle indicates, a number of the authors themselves intervene as hard-bitten cultural politicians, themselves reinvigorating racialized and essentialist notions of identity as they "critique" the "authenticity" of Taínos (see especially Jiménez Román, 1999). Indeed, the effort is to marginalize Taínos from writing their own history and sidelining scholars whose work advocates for those in the Taíno resurgence. That volume only provided room for one chapter by one Taíno leader, Roberto Mucaro Borrero of the United Confederation of Taíno People, who nevertheless did an admirable job of trying to counter some of the more litigious allegations of a volume that is perhaps an extreme manifestation of what Friedman has signaled as a disturbing anti-indigenous trend among contemporary anthropologists, for example (see Friedman, 1996, p. 127).

On the other hand, *The Indigenous People of the Caribbean*, edited by Samuel Wilson (1997a), makes a commendable contribution to knowledge in this field, with a carefully developed and detailed presentation of the archaeology, colonial history, and contemporary survival of indigenous peoples in the Circum-Caribbean region, while still incorporating at least one brief chapter by a contemporary indigenous representative, Garnette Joseph of the Dominica Carib Territory, who later became Chief of that Territory. However, even in this case, as two reviewers noted (Ferbel, 2000; McIntosh, 1999), the volume disappoints for not providing adequate space to the survival and revival of indigenous identities and communities in the region, one of the more striking features of the contemporary social and cultural landscape of the Caribbean. While that volume, with its emphasis on archaeological prehistory and early colonial history, risks reinforcing the notion that indigenous peoples of the Caribbean are to remain consigned to a frozen and distant past, reduced to material traces displayed in museums, clearly Wilson did not intend to grind that particular ax. As he encouragingly states in his introduction to that volume:

> What we find worthy of celebration is that, despite the ravages of five centuries of European conquest, the indigenous peoples of the Caribbean have survived. The role they have played in the formation of modern Caribbean culture is immense, and the voice of their descendants is growing ever stronger in the modern Caribbean. (Wilson, 1997b, p. 8)

In recent years, other volumes with broader purviews than indigenous peoples of the Caribbean alone, and some focusing only on the Caribbean archipelago, have provided some space for discussion of the presence and resurgence of indigenous communities in the region. For example, under the heading of *Ethnic Minorities in Caribbean Society*, Rhoda Reddock (1996) devotes half the volume to case studies on the Caribs of Dominica (Gregoire, Henderson, & Kanem, 1996), and Guyanese Amerindians (Fox, 1996). More ambitious, and certainly the earliest attempt to focus on contemporary Amerindians of the Caribbean island chain, was *Pueblos y políticas en el Caribe Amerindio* (1990), published by Mexico's Instituto Indigenista Interamericano, and only available in Spanish. It was a landmark effort in some respects; for example, the first article about the contemporary Caribs of Trinidad, and for a decade the only article, appeared in that volume (see Harris & Reyes, 1990). A year earlier, *Cultural Survival Quarterly* (Chapin, 1989) produced a collection of brief articles on Central America and the Caribbean that included Belize, Cuba, Dominica, and French Guiana. Since then, *Cultural Survival Quarterly* has featured individual articles on almost all of the communities in the present volume, apart from the Caribs of St. Vincent and Taínos in Puerto Rico and the Dominican Republic. One will of course also find single chapters and articles in larger works pertaining to the Caribbean (e.g., Eguchi, 1997; Layng,

1985). This preliminary overview of earlier attempts takes us to the scope of the present volume, its aims and its logic.

The Structure and Purposes of This Volume

The 14 contributors to this volume represent a diverse range of expertise. Four of the contributors are also Caribbean indigenous persons (Barreiro, Estevez, Palacio, and Bharath Hernandez), all of whom are active in their communities, with two of them, Barreiro and Palacio, being noted scholars in this field of interest. Contributors are affiliated with institutions across the Caribbean, Central America, South America, the United States, Canada, the Netherlands, the United Kingdom, and France, rendering this project, like so many cultural movements in the world today, a truly transnational effort.

The geographic coverage of the volume, while less than complete, presents cases spanning the Caribbean that was colonized by the Dutch, English, French, and Spanish. The chapters present us with insights concerning contemporary indigenous peoples in Belize, Cuba, the Dominican Republic, Dominica, St. Vincent, Trinidad and Tobago, Guyana, Suriname, and French Guiana, with parts of chapters also including the Puerto Rican Taíno diaspora in the United States. Regrettably, we were not able to present a chapter devoted entirely to Puerto Rico, certainly not because we concur with anti-Taíno assertions of extinction, but only because one contributor withdrew when it was too late to find an alternate author. In addition, while I have received numerous e-mail messages over the last seven years from individuals in territories such as Anguilla, Aruba, Barbados, Curaçao, Guadeloupe, Haiti, Jamaica, St. Kitts and Nevis, St. Lucia, and the US Virgin Islands, all of whom spoke of their indigenous ancestry, it was not possible to include these territories for a lack of authors available to contribute chapters. Clearly, much work remains to be done and we hope that a renewed effort at covering indigenous peoples of the Caribbean would appear some time in the future, especially if more students choose to pursue research projects in this field of study. What the current volume does provide, nonetheless, is the most comprehensive presentation to date on the contemporary indigenous peoples of the Circum-Caribbean, incorporating at least four mainland territories that have historically been associated with the island Caribbean both before and after Columbus.

Defining the Caribbean as a region is here, as in many other cases, problematic. This is true especially as soon as one moves beyond the archipelago, although even in that case there are many island possessions of mainland states such as Venezuela, Colombia, Nicaragua, Honduras, the US, and a number of European states. One could therefore broaden the definition of the

Caribbean zone to include all coastal areas that border on the Caribbean Sea, in which case this volume omits most of Central America, while including the Guyanas whose coastline faces the Atlantic Ocean more than the Caribbean Sea. Population movements within the region, cultural affinities, and historical ties make the matter even more complex. As is often the case, the decision to determine what is Caribbean for the purpose of this volume is a mixture of contingency and observation. All of the territories in this volume are either islands or have long-standing linkages with the societies and cultures of the archipelago. Precolonial indigenous population movements and trade networks, forced dislocations of the colonial era, and contemporary indigenous activism and cultural exchange unite these territories to varying degrees. Otherwise, there is no hard-and-fast definition of the region that will equally satisfy all interests and provide little more than a working template suited to a particular project.

The contributions have been organized according to the most prominent themes in both scholarly research on indigenous peoples of the region, as well as those themes arising from Caribbean indigenous activism itself. These themes are organized here under the headings of *presence* (i.e., survival and revival), *identities* (i.e., tradition and representation), *rights* (i.e., protecting access to resources), the politics of the *nation-state* (i.e., relations with the wider society), and *regional* networking (i.e., indigenous transnationalism). In terms of *presence*, chapters bring to light indigenous survival and revival in territories long assumed to be lacking any indigenous heritage (whether demographic or cultural). Nowhere have assertions of absence been as marked as they have been in the Greater Antilles, the first to bear the brunt of European conquest. How contemporary Amerindian communities maintain, rework, and articulate their *identities* is crucial to our understanding of the ways in which indigeneity in the Caribbean is reproduced and made present. Amerindian communities have also become active in asserting *rights* that have long been denied or that are currently facing renewed challenges. Their identities as indigenous peoples are critical in fashioning politico-economic strategies to resist attempts at undermining their presence. The *nation-state* in the Caribbean has proven to be a critical actor in either constraining or enabling the pursuit of indigenous rights, the recognition (or lack thereof) of the Amerindian presence, and the identities by which that presence is expressed. In confronting their local challenges, indigenous groups across the region have come to recognize that they share much in common and have begun to meet and organize either through various *regional* fora created by state sponsorship or by establishing their own conferences, gatherings, and regional bodies. The survival and revival of the indigenous presence, the articulation of indigenous identities, and the struggle for rights within the politics of the nation-state—all of these are increasingly worked out on a regional scale. It is this combination of themes that builds up into what we call *resurgence*.

Reproduction and Resurgence

"Salvage ethnography," the drive to document indigenous societies and their traditions before they disappeared, as they were assumed to be facing imminent cultural death, was a fundamental assumption of early American anthropology, one that has endured through many different theoretical projects. Cultural evolutionists of the late 1800s envisioned a world where all societies would evolve through the same set of stages, from savage to barbaric to civilized societies, with European societies of the present held to be the most advanced. The antievolutionist relativists and salvage ethnographers, such as Franz Boas, still assumed that indigenous societies would vanish, for different reasons. By the 1930s, "assimilation" was perceived by many anthropologists and policy makers to be the outcome of the indigenous encounter with an expansive West. From the late 1950s, with the advent of Modernization Theory, once again non-Western cultural traditions were held as backward and subject to disappearance with the spread of capitalist progress. Intellectual thrusts whose aim or effect is to de-indigenize the anthropological subject have been reproduced even in postmodern guises, with their stress on "unbounded" and "deterritorialized" cultures, seemingly never in place, never with a core of even relatively stable cultural contents (e.g. Appadurai, 1991, 1994; Marcus, 1986, 1994; Smith, 1994). The anthropological subject is thus rendered monstrous, an ever-shimmering, shape-shifting, boundary-transgressing creature of the likes one sees in Japanese horror films such as *The Ring* and *The Grudge*. Anthropology, in effect, has been a discipline with an ever-vanishing subject.

By the 1980s, a different discourse became apparent, as a number of social scientists started to recognize that indigenous peoples, far from vanishing, were making a "comeback." While there was little question that global capitalism had wrought changes in indigenous societies, new interpretations were offered that questioned the nature of those changes. Does change occur everywhere, in the same fashion? What causes those changes? Who directs the changes, and the pace of change? In this vein, Sahlins, perhaps the leading theorist of the reproduction of indigeneity, noted, "the very ways societies change have their own authenticity, so that global modernity is often reproduced as local diversity" (1993, p. 2). Others have argued that the emergence of global cultural processes accompanying the development of world capitalism have produced a world culture, "marked by an organization of diversity rather than a replication of uniformity" (Hannerz, 1990, p. 237). Indigenous peoples are often able to draw on material and symbolic resources from this broader world culture in reproducing their own indigeneity: "most peoples find critical means of their own reproduction in beings and powers existing beyond their normal borders and their customary controls" (Sahlins, 1999, p. 411). Indigenous identification therefore involves, "a *positioning* which draws upon historically sedimented practices, landscapes and repertoires of meaning, and emerges through particular patterns of engagement and struggle" (Li, 2000, p. 151). Reproduction, as Kelvin Smith argues in this volume is not invention; rather, the emphasis here shifts from reading identity against the validity of its references, to the contexts in which it is created and proclaimed. This is not "fake" indigeneity; this is the actual practice of indigeneity in real-world settings.

When we speak in this volume of survival and revival, we are aware of the limited utility of these received concepts. One can certainly speak of survival in the commonly accepted sense of the term, but *cultural* survival raises certain problems. Is culture to be likened to a biological organism, with a "life" and "death," and once "dead" can never be "resurrected"? This would not be the consensus in anthropology, especially where the ideational concept of culture is treated as a dynamic system of meanings, and meanings do not live natural "lives." Likewise, there is nothing to say that material practices, in their own dynamic relationship with cultural meanings, *necessarily* have an expiry date. When we speak of "identity," and specifically of identity as a process (i.e., identification) it is not at all fixed for eternity that an identity, a way of drawing boundaries in relation to others, must have a precise and finite set of contents around which the boundaries are drawn. Indigenous identities in the Caribbean are constantly being *reproduced*, not "invented," and how one is "Indian" in 2006 will not be the same as in 1492. As Lynne Guitar, Pedro Ferbel-Azcarate, and Jorge Estevez argue in this volume, "the idea that the Taínos of today must prove themselves to be comparable to the Taínos of 1492 ought to be as nonsensical as Spaniards today proving themselves to be comparable to Spaniards of 1492." Identity is relational, and the relationships constantly change.

The *reproduction* of indigeneity in the Caribbean also stands as a critique. In "A Bridge for the Journey," José Barreiro (this volume) notes, "in reviewing the many methods used by colonial apologists to attack the Native American world, the casual denial of identity and existence has been the most constant. Perhaps the majority of historians, anthropologists and archaeologists writing on the Caribbean region have accepted the fallacy of extinction." The fallacy, or myth of extinction, as Guitar et al. discuss in this volume, certainly served vital purposes to colonial administration, expansion, and even reform. First, the claim of impending extinction was used in antislavery campaigns focused on the tragic situations of Amerindians in Hispaniola and elsewhere. Second, the same argument was then recruited to argue in favor of importing African slaves. Third, as they argue, the extinction narrative could help to create a self-indulgent illusion of imperial control and power—a classic story, in fact, of "weaker" indigenous "species" thrown to the wall with the arrival of "civilization." (This is a story that is taken up in the guest commentary by Arthur Einhorn concluding this volume, which furthermore places Caribbean Amerindian history within a broader historical and comparative context.) Fourth, the myth of extinction served a variety of national and class interests, as all attempts at marginalizing the indigenous do in the other case studies in the volume. Indigenous peoples were, and to significant degree still are, targeted as "obstacles" to be removed from the path of "development" and the building of a "modern nation." Extinction, as I have argued elsewhere (Forte, 2005), has been a convenient trope for the expression of anti-indigeneity.

Reproduction, as a conceptualization, challenges notions of extinction and assimilation, notions that reflect what Sahlins refers to as the "anthropological demotion" of indigenous peoples (1993, p. 1). With reference to notions of culturally "extinct" groups "inventing" indigenous traditions for themselves, Sahlins' response frames these notions historically: "as an attack on the cultural integrity and historical agency of the peripheral peoples, they do in theory just what imperialism attempts in practice" (1993, p. 7), or, as Jorge Estevez puts it in this volume, proponents of extinction theses are guilty of "paper genocide." Both the chapters by José Barreiro ("Taíno Survivals," this volume) and Guitar et al., demonstrate the extent to which colonial records, previously neglected chronicles, and long-forgotten research can be mined precisely to throw the entire "factual" basis of the extinction myth into disarray. This is not a strategy peculiar to marginal island cases either, as Janette and Arif Bulkan note in the case of Guyana (this volume), where contemporary Amerindians, faced with losing oral histories, have turned to colonial records to validate their land claims and to recover their own sense of their own history.

The reproduction of indigeneity is not tantamount to a celebratory view of untrammeled indigenous cultures enjoying autonomy. One simply cannot dismiss the severe material, social, and political challenges that afflict indigenous communities across the Caribbean. What reproduction asks us to look at, however, is the fact that there are people *there* determined to meet these challenges head on, in the process affirming and renewing their self-definition as indigenous. As Kelvin Smith (this volume) explains with reference to the Caribs of Dominica, we must pay attention to "the role of socioeconomic contexts in shaping and defining possible cultural articulations," thereby inviting us to examine the material and social conditions involved in the reproduction of indigeneity. From this perspective, it is important to recall the ultimate political and material act that instituted "indigenous peoples" as a category: European colonial invasions (see Beckett, 1996, p. 5). In this regard, Paul

Twinn (this volume) narrates a land struggle in St. Vincent between Caribs and the Danish owners of Orange Hill Estates, where Caribs situated Danish acquisition within a genealogy of colonization, that is, "in a particular lineage from the genealogy of Carib history from the time of their autonomy until the present day. Within this lineage of Carib history the principal element in the creation of Caribs as Caribs, was the Carib/Land relationship." Smith seems to concur when he observes that in Dominica "the rise of Carib identity is tied to the relationship the community has to the land and space, as much as to its perception of history." The contributions by Smith and Twinn are emblematic of many of the approaches in this volume in that they ultimately intertwine identity politics and material politics, an approach with as much resonance for the mainland as for the islands. To the extent that the competition for resources is located in discourses of ancestry, Twinn shows us another facet of the reproduction of indigeneity in the contemporary Caribbean, one that is historically *oriented*, but not historically *derived* in any simple sense of direct continuity. Reproduction is not fossilization.

The international political economy of resource exploitation is central to the renewed defense of land that underpins the contemporary reproduction of indigeneity in many of the cases covered in this volume. Some of the socioeconomic transformations that appear in this volume, arising from indigenous engagements with world capitalism, include mining and logging; cash crop plantations; tourism; urbanization; and, international migration. Natural resource use, for its part, is a site of social action and contested cultural meanings that can act as a vehicle and catalyst for Amerindian resurgence in the Guyanas. The cases covered in this volume tend to reflect what Hodgson observed, in general terms, regarding indigenous rights struggles: "a key impetus for the emergence of indigenous activism on its current scale has been the sustained threats to indigenous land, territories, and resources by colonial and postcolonial state interventions, capitalist industry, and other incursions" (2002, p. 1041). This is painfully illustrated in the case of Suriname as outlined by Fergus MacKay in this volume, where the state has effectively produced a de jure extinction of the sizable native population by not admitting that indigenous peoples have any standing under the law, a fact that has allowed foreign corporations to plunder Suriname's interior. As Janette and Arif Bulkan explain in this volume, speaking of Guyana with specific reference to contestations surrounding forest resources, "[European] 'constructions' of the lands and the peoples they encountered beyond Europe continue to have the hegemonic force of law and custom into the postcolonial era." It is equally true that these European constructions continue to be met by indigenous opposition, a tension that is a key element in the Guyanese reproduction of indigeneity. Speaking of French Guiana, the one case in this volume of a territory that is still a colony, Gérard Collomb discusses the fact that struggles for land rights are tied to larger issues of indigenous cultural presence, noting that "the history of the Amerindian movement in French Guiana [has been] to validate a more fundamental claim, from which these land claims proceeded: that of the recognition of a specific cultural and political presence of the Amerindians." It is at least partly the case, then, that indigeneity in the Caribbean is constantly being reproduced in tandem with exogenous intrusions and usurpations. Indigenous political organization, as Collomb demonstrates in this volume, is in part a systemic and structural outcome of foreign conquest and continued expansions. The situation of indigenous peoples of the Guyanas, as Janette and Arif Bulkan argue, is thus "reminiscent of the colonial experience."

Yet, if many of the current struggles seem to echo or continue older colonial situations, then on what basis can we speak of *resurgence*, of something seemingly novel occurring in the last two or three decades? There are indeed some indigenous spokespersons who have taken me to task for speaking of resurgence, arguing that there is nothing new about the present except that academics such as myself are "suddenly paying attention," and in suddenly looking believe that what they are seeing there has only suddenly appeared. It is a valid objection, yet, there definitely is something that has been happening over the past 20 or more years that is not mere repetition of the past. First, one can point to the development of indigenous ideologies of renewal and autonomy, in some cases acquiring explicit labels as ideologies: "Caribism" in Dominica, or "Garifunaduo" in Belize, as discussed in this volume by Palacio in "Cultural Identity among Rural Garifuna Migrants in Belize City, Belize." In the case of Trinidad, while not explicitly formulated as a political and social manifesto, the Santa Rosa Carib Community has enunciated a sophisticated range of concepts and projects where traditions are concerned, including distinctly envisioned programs of "maintenance," "preservation," "retrieval," "interchange," "translation," and "reclamation" (see Bharath Hernandez & Forte in this volume). Second, and related to the first, we see the emergence of strong activist indigenous leaders across the region, whose names appear in most of the chapters of this volume.

Third, we see a spate of new organizations being formed over the last quarter century, or revamped versions of previously existing representative bodies. Just to briefly and randomly list a few, in Suriname there is the Association of Indigenous Village Leaders; in French Guiana, the *Association des Amérindiens de Guyane Française*; where Taínos are concerned, the Indigenous Association of Puerto Rico was formed, and several other organizations (some of which are discussed in Forte's chapter, "Searching for a Center in the Digital Ether," in this volume); in Guyana, the Amerindian Peoples Association and the Guyanese Organization of Indigenous Peoples are two of the more prominent bodies; in Central America, the National Garifuna Council and the World Garifuna Organization. Moreover, many of these bodies have joined larger, international, indigenous federations, such as the Caribbean Organization of Indigenous Peoples (see Palacio's "Looking at Ourselves in the Mirror," in this volume), the World Council of Indigenous Peoples, or the Coordinator of Indigenous Organizations of the Amazon Basin (COICA). Also, a number of these bodies have cooperated with indigenous bodies from outside of the region, such as the Assembly of First Nations of Canada. Indeed, the transnationalization of Caribbean indigenous organization and self-representation seems to be unheralded, especially as it now extends to the Caribbean diaspora in advanced capitalist countries. With greater access to the international media, the organization of their own regional gatherings (see Barreiro, this volume, on the Indigenous Legacies conferences in Cuba), their utilization of the Internet (Forte, chapter 13), Caribbean indigenous peoples have a voice and visibility that one could argue they have never had before.

Fourth, the growth of Caribbean nationalism, and projects of nation-building, which are especially recent in the Anglophone Caribbean, and are at best still emergent in the French Caribbean, have established a platform for new indigenous entanglements with the wider societies they inhabit. The economic transformations wrought by national development, and the increase in urbanization, is a situation that has challenged the maintenance of indigenous cultures while at the same time affording new bases for reproducing those cultural ties (see Palacio, chapter 9). Competition for resources in these new nation-states has also spurred the development of indigenous political organizations, as Collomb, MacKay, and the Bulkans show in their case studies. Expressions of local pride, and nationalist reinterpretations of the folk roots of the nation, have produced varied and often contradictory appropriations of indigeneity in places as varied as Puerto Rico, the Dominican Republic, St. Vincent, and Trinidad. Very simply then, to the extent that we could not speak of nationalism and state formation before the recent past, this is inevitably a new context for the reproduction of indigeneity addressed by the idea of resurgence.

Fifth, some would add that there has been a demographic resurgence as well, not just through increasing birth rates and decreasing death rates, but also through more individuals self-identifying as indigenous. Indeed, if there is one thing that this overview has deliberately shied away from is producing a more or less fixed number for the total indigenous population of the territories covered in this volume. This is either not known with any certainty, or is in a state of significant flux. Twinn notes in his chapter on St. Vincent that whereas less than 40 people in the 1981 census identified themselves as Carib, this figure rose to 1,500 by 1991. Similar results have been reported for St. Lucia (see Forte, 2002). Guyana reports one of the largest indigenous populations, exceeding 55,000. One estimate (Palacio, 1995) placed the total indigenous population of the mostly Anglophone Caribbean Community and Common Market (CARICOM) at roughly 150,000. If one consults linguistic databases, such as those of the Summer Institute of Linguistics, which span the entire region, both island and mainland, and takes into account all speakers of languages in the main Arawakan and Cariban language families, then we have a total that seems to change every time one consults the data, and depending on which territories one includes, the number can range from 347,000 to 738,380 persons (see www.ethnologue.com). On the other hand, the latter also reports that the indigenous populations of Dominica and St. Vincent are "extinct." Where extinction was widely assumed and asserted, Puerto Rico, the United States census for 2000 reported a population of 13,336 "Native American Indians" (see factfinder.census.gov). What is left unclear is whether these are "Native Americans" who moved from the mainland US to Puerto Rico (still a surprising number), or native Puerto Ricans who might have preferred to self-identify as Taíno, but checked the only box that came closest to their identity. In other words, the numerical map is simply all over the place, and statistics are not here, if anywhere else, a satisfactory route toward deeper understanding of the ongoing reproduction of Caribbean indigeneity.

Our collective ambition then is to help readers, especially students, those interested in the history and anthropology of the Caribbean or in indigenous studies on a global level, to admit the Caribbean into their appreciations of the indigenous cultures that are resurgent. For those of us who are anthropologists, the hope is that "resurgence ethnography" will become a distinct genre that replaces previous "salvage ethnography," helping to maintain the dynamism of a discipline that is as alive as the indigenous peoples who continue to teach us about the complexity of our world.

References

Appadurai, A. (1991). Global ethnoscapes: notes and queries for a transnational anthropology. In Richard G. Fox (Ed.), *Recapturing anthropology: working in the present* (pp. 191–210). Santa Fe, NM: School of American Research Press.

———. (1994). Disjuncture and difference in the global cultural economy. In Patrick Williams & Laura Chrisman (Eds.), *Colonial discourse and post-colonial theory* (pp. 324–339). New York: Columbia University Press.

Beckett, J. (1996). Contested images: perspectives on the indigenous terrain in the late 20th century. *Identities*, 3(1–2), 1–13.

Bruner, E. (1986). Ethnography as narrative. In Victor Turner & Edward Bruner (Eds.), *The anthropology of experience* (pp. 139–155). Urbana Champaign: University of Illinois Press.

Chapin, M. (Ed.). (1989). Central America and the Caribbean. *Cultural Survival Quarterly* 13(3).

DRLAS. (2000). Some important research contributions to the study of population history and anthropology in Puerto Rico: interview with Dr. Juan Carlos Martinez Cruzado. *Delaware*

Review of Latin American Studies, 1(2). Retrieved March 3, 2005, from http://www.udel.edu/LASP/Vol1-2MartinezC.html.

Eguchi, N. (1997). Ethnic tourism and reconstruction of the Caribs' ethnic identity. In Juan Manuel Carrión (Ed.), *Ethnicity, race and nationality in the Caribbean* (pp. 364–380). San Juan, Puerto Rico: Institute of Caribbean Studies, University of Puerto Rico.

Ferbel, P.J. (2000). The indigenous people of the Caribbean (review). *Ethnohistory*, 47(3–4), 816–818.

Field, L. (1994). Who are the Indians? *Latin American Research Review*, 29(3), 227–238.

———. (1999). Complicities and collaborations: anthropologists and the "unacknowledged tribes" of California. *Current Anthropology*, 40(2), 193–209.

Forte, M.C. (2002). Interview with Albert De Terville. *The CAC Review*, 3(2). Retrieved April 6, 2005, from http://www.centrelink.org/Feb2002.html.

———. (2005). Extinction: the historical trope of anti-indigeneity in the Caribbean. Paper presented at Atlantic History: Soundings, 10th Anniversary Conference of the Atlantic History Seminar. Cambridge, MA: Harvard University, August 10–13, 2005. (Available in *Issues in Caribbean Amerindian Studies* 6, Aug. 2004–Aug. 2005. Retrieved October 10, 2005, from http://www.centrelink.org/forteatlantic2004.pdf.)

Fox, D. (1996). Continuity and change among the Amerindians of Guyana. In Rhoda Reddock (Ed.), *Ethnic minorities in Caribbean society* (pp. 9–105). St. Augustine, Trinidad: ISER, University of the West Indies.

Friedman, J. (1996). The politics of de-authentification: escaping from identity, a response to "Beyond authenticity" by Mark Rogers. *Identities*, 3(1–2), 127–136.

Gregoire, C., Henderson, P., & Kanem, N. (1996). Karifuna: the Caribs of Dominica. In Rhoda Reddock (Ed.), *Ethnic minorities in Caribbean society* (pp. 107–172). St. Augustine, Trinidad: ISER, University of the West Indies.

Hall, S. (1994). Cultural identity and diaspora. In Patrick Williams & Laura Chrisman (Eds.), *Colonial discourse and post-colonial theory*, (pp. 392–403). New York: Columbia University Press.

Hannerz, U. (1990). Cosmopolitans and locals in world culture. In Mike Featherstone (Ed.), *Global culture: nationalism, globalization and modernity* (pp. 237–251). London: Sage.

Harris, P., & Reyes, E. (1990). Supervivencias amerindias en Trinidad and Tobago. In *Pueblos y políticas en el Caribe Amerindio* (pp. 55–64). Mexico City: Instituto Indigenista Interamericano.

Haslip-Viera, G. (Ed.). (1999). *Taíno revival: critical perspectives on Puerto Rican identity and cultural politics*. New York: Centro de Estudios Puertorriqueños, Hunter College, City University of New York.

Hodgson, D.L. (2002). Introduction: comparative perspectives on the indigenous rights movement in Africa and the Americas. *American Anthropologist*, 104(4), 1037–1049.

Hulme, P. (1992). *Colonial encounters: Europe and the Native Caribbean 1492–1797*. London: Routledge.

———. (1993). Making sense of the Native Caribbean. *New West Indian Guide*, 67(3–4),189–200.

Jiménez Román, M. (1999). The Indians are coming! The Indians are coming! The Taíno and Puerto Rican identity. In Gabriel Haslip-Viera (Ed.), *Taíno revival: critical perspectives on Puerto Rican identity and cultural politics* (pp. 75–109). New York: Centro de Estudios Puertorriqueños, Hunter College, City University of New York.

Kearns, R. (2003). Indigenous Puerto Rico: DNA evidence upsets established history. *Indian*

Country Today, October 6. Retrieved April 6, 2005, from http://www.indiancountry.com/content.cfm?id=1065462184.

Khan, A. (2001). Journey to the center of the Earth: the Caribbean as master symbol. *Cultural Anthropology*, 16(3), 271–302.

Layng, A. (1985). The Caribs of Dominica: prospects for structural assimilation of a territorial minority. *Ethnic Groups*, 6, 209–221.

Li, T.M. (2000). Articulating indigenous identity in Indonesia: resource politics and the tribal slot. *Comparative Studies in Society and History*, 42(1), 414–457.

Lieber, M. (1981). *Street life: Afro-American culture in urban Trinidad*. Cambridge, MA: Schenkman Publishing Co.

Marcus, G.E. (1986). Contemporary problems of ethnography in the modern world system. In James Clifford & George E. Marcus (Eds.), *Writing culture: the poetics and politics of ethnography* (pp. 165–193). Berkeley: University of California Press.

———. (1994). After the critique of ethnography: faith, hope, and charity, but the greatest of these is charity. In Robert Borofsky (Ed.), *Assessing cultural anthropology* (pp. 40–54). New York: McGraw-Hill, Inc.

Martinez Cruzado, J.C. (2002). The use of mitochondrial DNA to discover pre-Columbian migrations to the Caribbean: results for Puerto Rico and expectations for the Dominican Republic. *Kacike: The Journal of Caribbean Amerindian History and Anthropology*, December. Retrieved March 3, 2005, from http://www.kacike.org/MartinezEnglish.html.

Maybury-Lewis, D. (1997). Brave New World or more of the same? *Cultural Survival Quarterly*, 21(2). Retrieved April 6, 2005, from http://www.culturalsurvival.org/publications/csq/.

McIntosh, I. (1999). The indigenous people of the Caribbean (review). *Cultural Survival Quarterly*, 23(4). Retrieved April 6, 2005, from http://www.culturalsurvival.org/publications/csq/.

Oxaal, I. (1968). *Black intellectuals come to power: the rise of creole nationalism in Trinidad and Tobago*. Cambridge, MA: Schenkman Publishing Co.

Palacio, J.O. (1995). Aboriginal peoples: their struggle with cultural identity in the CARICOM region. *Bulletin of Eastern Caribbean Affairs*, 20(4), 25–40.

Pueblos y políticas en el Caribe amerindio. (1990). Mexico City: Instituto Indigenista Interamericano.

Reddock, R. (Ed.). (1996). *Ethnic minorities in Caribbean society*. St. Augustine, Trinidad: ISER, University of the West Indies.

Robotham, D. (1998). Transnationalism in the Caribbean: formal and informal. *American Ethnologist*, 25(2), p. 307–321.

Sahlins, M. (1993). Goodbye to *Tristes Tropes*: ethnography in the context of modern world history. *Journal of Modern History*, 65(1), 1–25.

———. (1999). Two or three things that I know about culture. *Journal of the Royal Anthropological Institute* 5(3), 399–421.

Smith, M.P. (1994). Can you imagine? Transnational migration and the globalization of grassroots politics. *Social Text*, 39, 15–33.

Wilson, S. (Ed.). (1997a). *The indigenous people of the Caribbean*. Gainesville: University Press of Florida.

———. (1997b). Introduction to the study of the indigenous people of the Caribbean. In Samuel Wilson (Ed.), *The indigenous people of the Caribbean* (pp. 1–8). Gainesville: University Press of Florida.

※ PRESENCE ※

Contemporary Paths of Survival after the Myth of Extinction

While the problem of establishing indigenous presence (understood in cultural, symbolic, demographic, and political terms) is one that confronts all of the indigenous societies in this volume, the Greater Antilles have been the *locus classicus* for the narrative of extinction. José Barreiro, himself of Cuban Amerindian descent, takes us to meet the *guajiro*-Taíno community of Caridad de los Indios, a peasant village of native extraction in eastern Cuba. There he introduces us to Panchito Ramirez, and to the diverse ways in which indigenous knowledge and everyday practices have been reproduced. As with the following chapter by Lynne Guitar, Pedro Ferbel-Azcarate, and Jorge Estevez, Barreiro unravels the dominant scholarship of extinction, expertly pointing out its many oversights and contradictions, and calling attention to accounts that have been passed by. The multivocal chapter by Guitar (historian), Ferbel-Azcarate (anthropologist), and Estevez (native Taíno of the Dominican Republic) is a seminal contribution that finally leaves the extinction narrative in ruins. Through a close textual reading of colonial records, added to analysis of documents that have been overlooked by many, as well as present-day ethnographic description of rural cultural practices, culminating in a personal testimony by a Taíno descendant, the three authors point our way to a history of the Caribbean that is *after* the myth of extinction.

※ CHAPTER TWO ※

Taíno Survivals: Cacique Panchito, Caridad de los Indios, Cuba

José Barreiro

In the deep Cuban mountains, *chin-chin* was present. Chin-chin is what the *guajiros* of eastern Cuba call a very special misty rain, light and lingering that suddenly descends in a cloud, touching the earth, as they say, with a gentle kiss. That morning, as the 50-some people of the Indigenous Legacies of the Caribbean tour group walked single-file down trails to the small cleared valley near the mountaintop, the *chin-chin* did indeed descend, enveloping all.

This was far up-country, in the eastern Cuban mountains beyond old Guantánamo, past a sugar mill town called Manuel Tames, then 35 more kilometers up a steep mountain road, with a brief stop at Caridad de los Indios to visit a clinic and a school, and then to La Ranchería, the home and small village of Don Francisco "Panchito" Ramírez Rojas, elder and cacique of the main enclave of Taíno descendants yet to be found in the eastern Cuban mountains. It was year five, or 2001, of the Indigenous Legacies of the Caribbean encounters—a conference process started in 1997 that would go two more years beyond this day.

I start with this day because it was a moment of great satisfaction, at last, after five years, to be allowed to take the Legacies group up to the cacique's home grounds. Many of the "Legacies regulars" had returned that year, along with many others from throughout Indian country and beyond. Our traveling group of nearly 50 people came from many cultures and several Native nations, including Mohawk, Onondaga, Kaw, Chumash, Navajo, Maya, Paiute, Apache, Jew, Palestinian, Anglo, Hispanic, and other Native and non-Native peoples. Among the well-known entities represented: the Smithsonian Institution, Cornell University, *Indian Country Today* (national newspaper), and several foundations. On other trips there have been Caribs, Garifuna and Mapuche, Ojibway, Menominee, and other tribes represented.

In a *batey* or small plaza of modest Cuban guajiro homes—the classical *bohío* of thatched roof with palm tree planks for walls—on this eastern Cuban mountain, several extended families gathered around Don Panchito. The elders, uncles and aunts and cousins, the grandchildren, grandnieces and grandnephews, and other relatives of Don Panchito are a core population of Amerindian descendants in the eastern mountains of Cuba. They have long roots that enjoy a substantial documentary record in a region inhabited by a substantial Taíno or insular Arawak population. This day they are gathered to greet us, serenading us with the old *changüi* music of the region on old three-string guitars, congas, maracas, *palito*, drum, and other instruments. They also brought out their communities' Indian drum, "tambor indio."

On the mountaintop, Panchito greets us in his home village. It is a great moment, realized after more than a decade of friendship and shared knowledge (see Fig. 1). Many obstacles have stood in the way of that moment, and that day, as always, beloved companions lost along the way would be remembered. Panchito's great uncle, Opublio, Doña Reina, and young community leaders like his daughter, Idalis, and his sons, Paquín and Vladis, flank closely around the *cacique*. Around them, other relatives, all dark-brown, on the short side and barrel chested, reflecting a variety of indigenous facial features.

Gently, hands held high, Panchito holds everyone back, arranging a core group of people into a circle. The extended clan of related families and then our large traveling group surrounds him. Then the Cuban officials, including army officers and local municipal leaders, several teachers, and others, also begin to press into the concentric circles. Panchito smiles widely, obviously very happy. "Brothers and sisters, Indian people from America," he says, slowly, breathing deeply. "Welcome to my humble mountain, our place on the land here, where our Indian people still live, where our culture is still in us."

He is a short, slight, brown man who trembles from deep inside. From deep inside too he speaks of beautiful and profound things, the kind of talk an Indian elder of large, extended families with many children to nurture tends to make.

"Before we eat and make our circle of friendship, our circle of families here," he says, "first let us smoke our tobacco, and let us welcome the day and your arrival with our oration to the Seven Powers of the Universe, which is our tobacco prayer. Let us talk to the Nature around us, to thank the Enchanted World of our mountain for your visit with us and to mention once again the spirits of the elements our grandparents said will always be with us."

Don Panchito is not only *cacique* at La Ranchería but also a well-respected *curandero*. He is sought after as a gifted "trembler," an ancient hummingbird healing tradition of these mountains. Panchito's healing ceremony invokes spiritual powers of various origins but his base, he says, is "the medicine power of nature," which is "our Indian culture, to be sincere with nature, to plant our seed into the Mother Earth." I focus on him here because he is the respected and recognized elder leader of his agricultural community of several large extended families. Panchito's orality offers a profoundly human and indigenous perspective. All direct quotes by Panchito Ramirez come from the book, *Panchito: cacique de montaña* (Barreiro, 2001).

Figure 1: Panchito Ramirez (left) and José Barreiro (right), in Guantánamo, Cuba, January 10, 2003. Photograph courtesy Millie Knapp.

Panchito's Mountain

I came to know about Panchito's community through the memories of my own elders from the nearby province of Camagüey. As a child, I had heard from my aunts and especially from my father, that the eastern Cuban mountains inland from Baracoa would reveal hamlets of Indian families of a deeply rooted Cuban Indian extraction. My father knew about it because during his own childhood, in 1906 at 10 years of age, he took part in a spiritual pilgrimage with his *guajiro* relatives to La Virgen del Cobre, the matron of Cuba. The *guajiro* or country people of Cuba, particularly in the eastern region, are primary inheritors of many customs from their Taíno ancestors, particularly in farming and in medicinal practices.

Panchito's people today mostly call themselves "indio" and/or "guajiro," or "un indio guajiro," or "indio de la montaña." Among the elders both Panchito and the elder woman, Reina Rojas, occasionally have used the term "Taíno." Both terms, Taíno and *guajiro*, are found in the early contact chronicles. By the term, Taíno, I mean those aboriginal people of the Greater Antilles islands, extended from present-day Puerto Rico to Hispaniola, Jamaica, and most of eastern Cuba, who spoke the insular variation of the Arawak language family. The term is first recorded by Dr. Diego Alvarez Chanca and by Christopher Columbus in 1493. Arrom (1999, p. xi) confirms that Taíno was used by "the native inhabitants of the Greater Antilles and some smaller islands [and] is based on the word that…the natives used in differentiating themselves from the Caribs."

About *guajiro*, Rouse (1948, p. 530) writes, "several [early contact] sources mention a term 'guajiro.' This may have applied to the common people. Las Casas, however, lists the *guajiros* before the nitaynos." Noeli Pocaterra, Arawak-speaking Wayuu Tiger clan mother (personal communication, 1996) reports that in her Wayuu language (Venezuela), "waxiri or waxeri," Hispanicized to *guajiro* in Venezuela (as in Cuba), means "a headman of his family line or man that heads a house." Arrom (1999, p. 12) reports "'guajiro'…from the Taíno…'our countryman,' 'our fellow-citizen'."

The *guajiro* pilgrims from Camagüey rode horseback east to El Cobre hill, near Santiago. There, at the chapel of the Virgen del Cobre, my father and his elders happened to meet two Indian families from the area of Yateras (Guantánamo). The Yateras Indians were in the chapel making good on a promise to pray at the beloved altar, apparently as spiritual payment for a young woman's successful labor and childbirth. My father never forgot it. As an old man, in 1978, he reminded me: "If you want to meet our most pure Indian people in Cuba, go up to Cobre, go up to the mountains between Guantánamo and Baracoa."

La Virgen del Cobre, a paramount Cuban spiritual deity, is a Catholic synthesis of the primary tricultural mythology of the Cuban nation. She is known as matron of women in labor. The popular legend depicts an Indian, an African, and a Spaniard in a Taíno canoe, picking up the Cuban Madonna from a turbulent sea. While the historical account reports two older Indian men and one African youth in the actual canoe, the Virgen del Cobre remains an essential Cuban reverence (Arrom, 1971).

In the late 1980s, news articles appeared in Cuban national papers, *Granma* (see Pérez Echevarría, 1987) and *Juventud Rebelde* (see Bendoyro, 1987), reporting on families from La Caridad de los Indios and nearby mountain areas. I would come across such articles at the Olin Library, Cornell University, when US Customs allowed them to enter the country. These articles brought me my first reports about the work of Dr. Rivero de la Calle in those mountains. Supported by photographs, they offered rare documentation of the continuous existence of the mountain population that my father told me about.

A mutual project during those days with Caribbeanist maestro, Don José Juán Arrom, enlivened my conviction. Arrom's work is a voluminous source on the Taíno presence in our culture and in our cosmo-vision. It was Arrom who deciphered the Taíno cosmology registered by Fray Ramon Pané in 1498, and intuited, after painstaking study, its relationship with various important Taíno archaeological pieces in museum collections. "Go to the eastern sierras, young man," Arrom said to me, "if I were younger I would go with you. You will find ethnographic treasures there. Those are our roots."

In Cuba finally in 1995, to take part in the conference, "Cuba: Nation and Emigration," I had the opportunity to rent a car in Havana, and at the end of the conference, to travel to Camagüey, Baracoa, and other points of the eastern mountains. Thus, piloted by Alejandro Hartman, town historian of Baracoa, and guided by Isabel "Chicha" Lautin, local researcher—both ardent students of Cuban history and culture—I took the trail for the first time from the sugar town of Manuel Tames to the mountain community of La Ranchería, where I could confirm for myself the reality of a community-based Indian population of the Cuban Oriente—the Ramirez, the Rojas, and other surnames, in the mountains of Guantánamo-Baracoa, a group in the hundreds, perhaps a thousand or more, who are people of substantial tribal tradition stemming from, among other sources, the indigenous Cuban root (Barreiro, 1996).

Consciousness of Indian Identity

Panchito's community is nestled in one of the most remote areas of Cuba. Caridad de los Indios, along with nearby towns such as La Escondida (the hidden one), sits within a mountain range that hid and nurtured generations of Taíno Indian people and their descendants. These mountain populations survived the conquest and most of the colony through long stretches of isolation and very slow intermarriage. The "Yateras Indians," from which Panchito's people descend, have a long and documented history in these Cuban mountains.

From the first day I met him, Panchito Ramirez and more than three dozen people around him—including all the elder women and men of their community—have asserted to me the survival of their families as Cuban Indians. "My folks are Indian," Panchito says comfortably. He explains further:

> They always were, here at La Ranchería, here at La Escondida, the hiding place of the Indians. Old people were always respected here, and I belong here, to my people, to the Ramirez-Rojas Ranchería and the other families with Indian roots around the mountains of Oriente. Although we have been here very long, few people know about us. Maybe that is why so many people say Cuban Indians do not exist, but the truth is that we do, here we are. But it is true that we are an Indo-Cuban generation. In Cuba, we are all equal, there's no discrimination, neither against blacks, nor whites or any race. But I say to whomever is listening, that the Indian exists. We exist, we are Cuban and we are Indian. We, the old folks, know that we are the descendants of Cuba's natural Indians. We are mountain Guajiros, and we are proud to be well entrenched, always ready to defend our homeland.

Taliman (2001, p. 17) a Navajo journalist who traveled to Cuba, writes in her Smithsonian article on Panchito Ramirez's community: "Panchito Ramirez somehow missed the news bulletin that his people had become extinct." "You ask me if there was extinction, I say, no," Panchito asserts.

> My parents said the same thing and I repeat it, many were killed, many have died, but the Indian is still rooted here. My grandfather told me, "Son, never let our culture fall." That is why since I was a child, I always tried to learn all that came from them, the things that come to us from long ago, about this, our natural life in the mountains, and about what we remember of the ancestors' teachings. I remember much about it, I think that's one of the reasons why the folks come to see me.

For over a century, most of Cuban academia has assumed that Taíno people became totally extinct, even as early as 1700. Nevertheless, for a country where the discourse on indigenous identity has been negligible, Cuban literature offers many references on the existence of an Amerindian Cuban population and descent, primarily from the Yateras area, but also from other parts of the Sierra Maestra mountains. A long train of parochial and municipal records, and a steady if somewhat unnoticed string of authors and researchers from the 1600s to the present, have documented this often-hidden reality. Cuban historian Pichardo Moya refers thus to this Cuban legacy: "What we call today our Indians from Yateras, Caujerí, Yara, Dos Brazos, Yaguaramas and other places, probably gave our guajiros that accented physical appearance, which we commonly call: 'Yucateques or Guachinangos,' as a way to deny our own Indians" (Pichardo Moya, 1945, p. 19). The contemporary Cuban historian Maria Nelsa Trincado is among those touching on this reality: "During nearly 200 years (16th and 17th centuries)...the aboriginal population was, to a great extent, in the majority and there is clear evidence that it imposed itself, in many aspects of the daily life, upon the Spaniards and the Cuban black people (African or Creole, enslaved or freed) in their precarious first moments in the island" (Trincado, 1999, p. 100). Pichardo Moya (1945, p. 28) refers us to the 18th century "Indian towns (pueblos de indios)...in Ovejas, Guanabacoa, Jiguaní, Caney, Tarraco, Yateras, Caujerí, Yara, Dos Brazos, Yaguaramas, and other places." Pichardo Moya cites a town official at a government house in the 1840s who writes that "in a few hours three and four hundred Indians [men] can gather...on Sundays they hear Mass, and they have their original dances" (1945, pp. 49–50). These "original dances" would be the famous *areitos* of the Taíno ancestors, recorded into the official logs 300 years after their supposed extinction. Cuban scholars Jose Antonio García Molina and Daisy Fariñas, in their book on Cuban indigenous survivals, make a strong case for how the form of these early *areitos* transformed into a contemporary Cuban spiritist cult, *Danza del Cordón* ("dance of the cord"), a ceremony still practiced in the eastern mountains and other parts of Cuba (García Molina, Fariñas Gutiérrez, & Garrido Mazorra, 1998).

Antonio Bachiller y Morales (1883, p. 244) mentions the "Indians of the river shore" in Camagüey, the small "enclaves" near Vertientes and on the north coast at Cubitas, in the mid-1800s. In 1846, according to court records, Indian families of El Caney (near Santiago) were driven from their lands while the Spanish "Audiencia" in Camagüey declared that the Indian community no longer existed, in order to clear title to the lands in question. Several documents detail cases of Indians claiming lands before the Audiencias.

A number of references to Indian family homesteads in remote areas can be found in the literature straddling the end of the 19th century to the early 20th century. Stewart Cullin (1902), followed by Mark Harrington (1921), both commented on substantial Indian survival among both "full-blood" and "mixed" families, also noting slight cultural practices during their time exploring the eastern mountains in Yateras and Baracoa. Harrington wrote: "the descendants of the original Indians...are not so rare, either, in the Baracoa district, for one will pass many persons of strongly Indian features in a day's journey in any direction" (Harrington, 1921, p. 166).

In the same region (La Guira and Dos Brazos), Irving Rouse also documented Indian population survivals (Rouse, 1948, p. 519). Two brothers with last name of Mosquera, local Indians, guided Harrington to the burial grounds and caves in these regions, where the American archaeologist found and removed 36 crates of Taíno artifacts—including the partial human remains of seven Taíno individuals, shipped to his employer to deposit in what was then collector George Gustav Heye's National Museum of the American Indian (NYC). Harrington mentioned his Indian contacts in the region and published photographs of Indian families and individuals (Harrington, 1921). These are but a few of the references tucked away in magazines and chapters of books rarely examined for this purpose through the 20th century.

In the 20th century, Cuban geographer Antonio Núñez Jiménez wrote of his encounters with Taíno descendant families in the eastern Sierras. He described his expedition along the Toa River in 1945: "for the 3,000 Indians from Yateras that survived, the refuge of these mountains is all they have left...it is a curious thing that they all have the same last names: Rojas and Ramírez" (Núñez, 1945, p. 197). Núñez related an interview with the *cacique*, Celestino Rojas, who had recently scared off from the mountains an engineer who tried to survey lands in his Indian territory. The noted speleologist also wrote about another region, the foothills that run along the coasts of the Turquino Peak, where he noted, "these are almost all inhabited by the descendants of Cuban Indians, from which they still keep part of their primitivism" (Núñez, 1945, p. 37).

In the 1960s and 1970s, several expeditions, most of them led by the dean of Cuban anthropology, Dr. Manuel Rivero de la Calle, visited the area. It is thanks to the work of Rivero that we continue to know who Panchito is and who were and are his relatives. In collaboration with Ramon Dacal Moure and other scientists, Rivero centered his attention on the Manuel Tames municipality, Guantánamo, where Caridad de los Indios and the Ramirez-Rojas Ranchería is located.

Using methods of physical anthropology, Rivero (1978) categorically concluded what was asserted by oral tradition and reported by Nuñez in the 1940s. Elders of the studied clan of extended families, according to Rivero, then as well as now, consistently claimed their Indian identity. Rivero's exhaustive research, which involved blood tests, dental measurements, size of head, lips, arms, and other traits and features, proved important, once again, in reasserting the obvious—Panchito 'and his folks exhibit all the physical characteristics associated with the indigenous peoples of South American and Caribbean origin: "short in height...scarce hair growth...straight, very black hair, kept into very old age...internal and external eye fold (epicanthus)...moderate obliqueness in the eyes, light brown skin with a reddish tendency, wide noses" (Rivero, 1978, p. 155). While indigenous communities these days often reject this type of physical anthropological study as intrusive, in this particular case the method was perhaps justified. In the Oriente region, the Cuban indigenous roots are not so hidden, but certainly there has been an intense resistance in the Cuban academy to accept Indo-Cuban survivals. Rivero's work is in that sense very appropriate. Most importantly, Panchito reports that his community collaborated voluntarily with the study, as they have wanted to give testimony of their existence for generations:

> I want my folks to recognize who they are, some more and some less but all native people from here. It's true we have marriages with different people, but the root remains here, so they can keep on loving the mountain, loving the forest, loving that wonderful nature we have, because the mountain is the real thing, everything comes from here. And we, the mountain *guajiro*, have our value. I have my community. It is not a developed one, but humble, yet we live as the fingers in a hand, together. We are not all the same, but we are all equal because of the blood that runs within us. Just here, in La Ranchería, there are still ten Indian houses and if someone butchers a pig, the ten houses eat from that pig. That way of being has been with us forever, it's the Indian way—that if *casaba* was made, everyone would eat from it, that if we hunted, fished, everyone would eat, and we would trade one thing for the other. When they say Taíno, to me it is that old Indian custom. The things I believe in, the *conuco* (raised mound garden), helping the family, that is Taíno. That's the way our ancestors said it: "there should not be disagreements among the Indians." And there are almost no disagreements among us here. If there's something between two neighbors, I try to settle things down. There cannot be violence here. I tell them, we all have to be equal. In La Ranchería, I tell them, let's plant, because the land wants to be planted, and that's what gives us life.

It will be interesting to many people that at the beginning of the 21st century, 400 hundred years after their supposed extinction, bases of this ancestral root are still found within the insular Cuban population. Núñez (1945) estimated the population of aboriginal roots in the Pico Turquino region (not Yateras) at about 3,000. Rivero de la Calle and Dacal Mouré (1978) estimated the total population of Indo-Cuban descent just in the area of Yateras/Caridad de los Indios at about 1,000 persons, over 100 families. Rivero de la Calle and Dacal Mouré (1978, pp. 158–159), writing about only Caridad de los Indios, estimated: "more than a thousand people from this area present such characteristics... known as 'Indians,' no one doubts who they are." They further reported other extended families of indigenous ancestry residing in various areas of La Sierra Maestra and throughout the eastern provinces, noting such places as Caujeri, Patana Abajo, Maisi, Rio Toa, Bartolome Maso, Yara, and Bayamo.

Historian Alejandro Hartmann, my collaborator and colleague in the field, describes a day's journey with Núñez Jiménez in 1995, along the Toa River, faraway from the Caridad de los Indios area, where they identified over 20 *bohíos* (homes) of Indo-Cuban families. In distant municipalities as Bartolomé Masó, Guama, in the environs of Turquino Peak, west to Manzanillo and Bayamo and into Camagüey through Najasa, it is not rare to meet farmers, fishermen, and people in varieties of trades, with predominant or at least recognizable Amerindian extraction. There continue to exist in these families old men and women with considerable transgenerational learning who carry oral tradition on naturalistic topics, medicinal plants, sowing methods, prayers and songs of invocation to natural elements requesting strength, as well as other cultural and spiritual expressions. Panchito is probably the most recognized among them (Moya León, 1996). Alejandro Hartmann is presently conducting a genealogical study through 2005 that has located extended families and small communities of Indian descendants throughout old Oriente, including in Jiguani and Manzanillo and Bayamo.

Indians under Maceo: The Hatuey Regiment of 1895

Among the Taíno descendants met by Rivero de la Calle in his 1964 expedition was the elder Ladislao Rojas, known by his Indian relatives in Caridad de los Indios as "Cacique Ladislao." Cacique Ladislao, photographed by Rivero de la Calle then at 92 years of age is a granduncle of the present *cacique*. Ladislao appears in Carlos Roloff Mialofsky's 1901 registry of veterans who participated in the Hatuey Regiment during the War of Independence. Roloff lists a total of 81 instances of the Rojas and Ramirez surnames in the annals of the registered Hatuey Regiment (Roloff, 1901, p. 74). Panchito, an excellent source of oral history, remembers his grandfather Ladislao's war stories. Some of them correspond quite well with findings of provincial historians about the War of Independence.

This piece of history, remembered by Panchito and recorded over 100 years ago by Roloff will shock many Cubans even today. The evidence is irrefutable that four centuries after the supposed "extinction" of Cuban Indians, in a regiment made up of people from the Yateras Valley of Guantánamo, in eastern Cuba, Cuban Indian descendants—from a Taíno, or insular Arawak region—fought the Spanish colonial government under the famous Cuban patriot, Major General Antonio Maceo.

At first, the Indian leaders, who had received recent land concessions from the Spanish government, were partial to the Spanish cause. The Indian community warriors fought for the Spanish and served as trackers. José Martí, as revolutionary leader, noted the sad reality of Indians scouting for the Spanish in his final campaign diary. Martí writes about being tracked by "the Indians of Garrido...the danger is felt. Since Palenque, they have been closely following our tracks" (Martí, 1982, p. 68).

In this area of the Sierra, at the end of the 19th century, at least two chroniclers of the insurrection besides Martí—Casasús and Miro Argenter—

make occasional references to the engagements of the Indian population. Writes Casasús: "In the hill of Palmarito, in an encounter with the Yateras Indians, Flor Crombet dies...his killer, a 17-year-old Indian named Rojas, who, in a short time, joins the Liberation Army" (Casasús, 1950, pp. 48–49). Miro Argenter confirms Casasús' facts: "Crombet was killed by the Indians of Yateras while he was defending José Maceo's encampment" (Miro Argenter, 1945, p. 23).

Among his final acts, Martí requests that General José Maceo work to win the Yateras Indians to the insurrectionist cause. Marti also writes about a night hosted by Domitila, an Indian woman, in her mountain *bohío*, two weeks before his death on May 19, 1895 (Marti, 1982, p. 54).

In his fascinating article, "La Capitana del Regimiento Hatuey," Sanchez Guerra (1998), official historian of Guantánamo, describes the genesis of the Hatuey Regiment. The Indian regiment was organized after a ceremony and spiritual trance of the midwife-medium, Cristina Pérez y Pérez, in May 1895. The midwife-medium, who later served honorably in the Army of Independence, was married to one of "the lesser *caciques*." During her trance the spirits of ancient Taíno *caciques* visited her and requested that the Indian fighters join Maceo and the cause of Cuba. Published in the heart of the region in question, this article is redolent with the sense of commonly accepted reality about the Indian identity of the fighters assembled for the Hatuey Regiment.

It was understandable that the Yateras combatants, upon joining the Cuban cause, would incorporate into a "Regimiento Hatuey," claiming the name of the first rebel Taíno cacique in Cuba, who was executed by the Spanish in 1513. Bartolomé de las Casas, in his *Brevísima Relación de la Destrucción de las Indias*, recounts the execution of the heroic Hatuey, who remains a revered figure in Cuban history and whose legend is sustained in a enduring spiritual tradition—the Light of Yara—in the southeastern region of Cuba (Barreiro, 2003, pp. 28–36).

The troops from Yateras Mountains, the Ramirez and Rojas bands, as well as other descendant families trained and marched at first with the Piñeda Regiment, later formalized as the Hatuey. The "Hatuey" was still "in process" as a regiment when under the command of the Dominican rebel officer, Dionicio Gil, and with the young part-Indian Lieutenant Silverio Guerra incorporated into its ranks, the Indian group fought in the important battle of Sao del Indio, August 31, 1895, early in the Cuban War of Independence.

Padrón Valdes described the battle action at Sao del Indio: "on the right flank they [the Spanish] are attacked by the Hatuey Regiment, led by the Dominican General Gil (Nomi), and which was mainly composed of Yateras guerillas that had joined our forces with their arms...these guerillas behaved heroically in their debut as patriots, they defeated the [Spanish] artillery and even seized their cannons" (Padrón Valdes, 1973, pp. 217–218).

Panchito Ramirez remembers from his granduncle Ladislao and other elders the oral history of his ancestors' participation in Marti's war for Cuban independence:

> One generation ago, the eldest here, my granduncle Ladislao, was called Ladislao Cacique. That grandfather of mine fought in the war against Spain; he was a Mambi [a Cuban term of respect for the independence fighters]. The folks respected his intelligence. He never studied his letters, but his farm gave him extra and he brought to the mountain a teacher for his children and grandchildren. He, as an old man, used to talk to me a lot and everybody knows it. Before and now, the old people pay attention to the qualities of children here. My grandfather, Cacique Ladislao, used to tell me: "Look, you are the one who can continue and defend the Indian culture." That is how he'd talk to me, when I was a child. My grandfather was one of those called "pensioners." Then, it was not like today when many people get retirement benefits. During my childhood, the "pensioned" were the veterans of the War of 1895. He wore one of those veteran's hats, a Mambi's hat. I asked him: "Abuelo, did the Indians fight for Cuba?" and he said, "Of course, they did. Why wouldn't they? Yes, they did fight." My granduncle Ladislao and my grandfather, Cancio fought under the orders of a chief called Rojitas. He was one of us, Rojas was his surname; he joined the Mambises in 1895 and he was the leader of the group of fighters who left from here to fight the Spaniards. My grandfather spoke of the Hatuey Regiment. He said: "Look, the Indians fought hard during the Independence War." I don't know very much about it, but I heard about Sao del Indio, and the battle that took place there. What my grandfather told me about it is that they were without food for so many days that they were about to collapse.

Spiritual Continuities

Panchito's folks' spiritual awareness and knowledge reflects an appreciation of "entities" in nature that resonates with indigenous peoples' cultures throughout the Western hemisphere. In the *cacique's* expression, one can notice millenary points of reference. If his beliefs are mixed, or a blend of cultures, many of his traditions converge with other known indigenous lifeways. This is evidenced in Panchito's extraordinary spiritual perception and his attention to the interchange of energy with nature; in his prayer recognizing the natural cycles of continuous creation; in his use of copal, cedar, and tobacco as sacraments; and, in the connection with the ancestors and with the Creator force in its cosmic dimension.

Panchito's prayer to the four directions, or celestial points (cardinal points), is common among many indigenous cultures of the Americas (see Fig. 2). The burning of tobacco and copal (*sahumerio*, prayer), the system of asking permission from the plant before taking it as medicine (reciprocity), the desire to keep the *conuco* (interplanting sowing system), the use of dreams as guides for spiritual healing—it is worth noting that these are knowledge bases with indigenous ecological value. Most revealing of indigenous connection among this Cuban mountain population is Panchito's expression of tender affection toward the widespread Amerindian complex of the Cosmic Family—Father Sun, Mother Earth, Grandmother Moon, the four "Uncles" or four winds, the faces of the ancestors reflected in the stars of the sky.

Figure 2: Panchito Ramirez conducts Four Directions tobacco prayer as Taíno remains returned by the Smithsonian are reburied. January 9, 2003. Photograph by Millie Knapp.

Some people will get easily mired by any effort to reconceptualize something as complex as the indigenous heritage of an American country. For Cuba and for the Caribbean area in general, indigenous heritage has been a remote and minimized theme. But those who study our histories and cultures most deeply will certainly discover that the persistence of indigenousness is valid in the Caribbean. The survival of general features and key pieces of indigenousness among Cuban people is evidenced in various regions of eastern Cuba. It is not starkly obvious, but interwoven and interlayered (transcultured) throughout history, geography, and culture; it ensured its own survival by persisting in quiet remembrance. Even in the cult of the Virgen del Cobre there is an indigenous base. The maximum Cuban spiritual deity is a Catholic synthesis of the primary tricultural mythology of the Cuban nation. It bears repeating: the foundational legend of Cuba's spiritual roots depicts an Indian, an African, and a Spaniard (Juan Blanco, Juan Moreno, Juan Indio) in a Taíno canoe, being saved by and retrieving the Cuban Madonna from a turbulent sea (Arrom, 1971).

Much of Cuban popular spiritualism is based on blends of Taíno (*cemi*) spirituality, African tribal deities (*orishas*), and Spanish Catholicism (Virgin cults, *santos*)—as well as "lesser" or unrecognized Catholic saints and other amalgamated nature entities. At many sites, particularly in caves and at rivers and lagoons, people make offerings and pray to natural forces. Garcia et al., mention the *güijes* or *jigües*, or little people of the Cuban natural springs and lakes. "Madre de aguas" or mother-of-waters cults persist and their possible connection to snake spirits suggests some indigenous background, even though it can be argued that it is a belief also found in Afro-Cuban religion.

Daisy Fariñas traces the associations of early Taíno *cemis*, Taíno spiritual entities often represented in tri-cornered sculptures, to present-day beliefs. Many *cemis* survived the conquest and colony. Over the centuries, their personalities and characteristics were layered into representations of popular "saints," such as San Lázaro/Babalu, a womanizer, irascible yet benevolent and peculiarly Cuban saint, not formally recognized by the Catholic Church. Fariñas relates San Lázaro in the popular memory to Yucahu Bagua Maorocoti, Taíno Great Spirit, and also to the *cemi* named Corocote, likewise known for womanizing (Fariñas Gutierres, 1995, pp. 125–128).

Panchito reveals some of these patterns in his own depictions of his spiritual beliefs and practices:

> My prayer is Indian, and when I say Mass, I don't mean a Catholic Mass but our own Mass, which is to pray, which is ceremony. In that prayer, there is a mix of everything and that is where the power comes from. It is difficult to explain, but the connection we have comes from heaven and from there I get my answers. They all come to me, together or separate: Mother of Earth, Spirits, and Saints like San Lázaro, Ceiba, Maja o Guaorao, Virgen del Cobre, and Mother of Waters. Our ancestors knew well that relation of powers. They might use a coconut, a *guira* or they might use some sand in a bottle, so that San Lázaro might join and help, or you could use a horn tied to a tree to stop the evil eye from working; you can also bury things, looking for peace, harmony and protection. It is still done that way; it's part of the beliefs in the

mountains, and among ourselves, we see results in those beliefs. There is nothing like the mountain. I see so much beauty in everything it gives. As I said before, I love her so much, sometimes I wouldn't plow her, or break her ground, but I have to live. We live from her. Unfortunately, some trees have to be cut down, but it hurts, because trees feel, just like human beings feel, and they have so much power, and give so much fruit to animals and human beings. I always try to communicate with them, because of their powers. In the spiritual world, I take shelter in everything. I don't ponder whether I take from the Catholic or from the African, because my foundation is the Mother Earth. I dream about something, and I do my ceremony to it. Nobody tells me to do it. I do it because I feel I have to do it.

Mountain Healing: Everyday Indigeneity

A seasoned small farmer and well-known herbalist and *curandero*, Panchito swears he will never leave the mountain. Along with the elder women of the community and his own uncle, Opublio, 92 years old, Panchito handles and prescribes a large variety of herbal medicines. Consider Panchito's thoughts on picking herbs for medicine:

> The world has powers. Our Cuban land is powerful. Everything has spirit; everything has its own energy. We know that and we carry that in our families; such is the respect, because that is essential. We work with herbs, and that should be respected. When I am going to pull off leaves from a plant, I must focus on those leaves. As I am going to snap off that branch, I ask the plant for permission, so that it can give me the power needed to cure whatever disease I need to cure. I approach the plant with a natural intention, so that it gives me the medicine to cure. I do the same if it is somebody else who comes to get the plant from me. If I take off a branch to perform a spiritual cleansing on somebody, I ask permission from the tree. I also cleanse people with baths of different plants.

Cuban tobacco, known for its odorous quality, is medicine for the mountain folk of Panchito. Again in this regard, the *cacique's* expression is laden with American indigenous concepts and sense of respect:

> Tobacco smoke is used by our healers. When you have to perform a protection ritual on someone, you take a handful of tobacco leaves, burn it and smoke with it. They take the seeds, toast it and get good medicine for flu. It is also good for inflammatory processes; you take a tobacco leaf, wither it and put it over the swollen area. It helps very much. When you use a plant for medicine, a piece of a cigar should be left there at the trunk, the same with Saint Lázaro, or the Saint or Spirit that you want to reach. You put that offering there, and it is the first offering that you make to a spirit: a cigar. For *nature* itself, the ceremony is of tobacco. The prayer to the Seven Potencies must use the tobacco. I say that certain trees have powers and the voices of the spirits, that has powers too. It is both the tree and the spirit that brings the message to you, sometimes in a dream. Some of those spirits are Indian, some are saints and some are African *abacuás*. But the main medicines that come for me, come from the mountain. That's why I take so much care of the mountain; I have taken so much medicine from

the trees and herbs that the earth gives that I have to love her. She is my mother; she is my everything.

Panchito and the Four Directions of Indigenous Peoples

While it is true that a great deal of indigenous tribal culture is particular to place, entwined with ecosystem and rooted in languages developed over millennia in specific geographic areas, nevertheless, for indigenous peoples, there are also elements that transcend—original principles and instructions.

This time, the circle formed around a recognized *cacique* of the surviving indigenous people of the Caribbean, the people who greeted Columbus. But at many, many such circles of native peoples across the Americas these past 30 years, the underlying elements that were present and invoked by Panchito that day would have been familiar.

When Panchito called to the Four Directions, using the words, "our center, how we stand planting our feet on the earth to make our supplication," his arms extended North and South, East to West, this was a reminder that the Four Directions are crux and crucible of most native ceremonies. Teachings on the Four Directions (sometimes six or seven directions, with acknowledgment to earth and sky and the praying person) come from nearly all the American Indian cultures.

Awareness of the four cosmic corners of origin, the four colors of corn, awareness of where one's belly-button and cord are buried, acknowledgment of the Four Directions and the Four Winds of the World—in myriad ways and in myriad perspectives, this is a prayer concept widely shared in Native cultures.

As the circle of people tightens, Panchito looks us, one by one, in the eyes. Among the large group, Ali El-Issa, president of the Flying Eagle Woman Fund, stands next to me; he has come a long way and the prayer Panchito is about to offer—Panchito asks me to translate—will include a good message for his late wife, Ingrid Washinawatok. Ingrid, a beloved Menominee woman leader who died tragically in 1999 while on a peace mission to Colombia, had pressed dearly in the years before her death to make this academic and cultural encounter in the Cuban mountains a reality (Barreiro, 1999, p. 2).

That way he began, remembering and thanking Ingrid and several other Indian people who had come to see their community. Then, he nodded to one of his sons, who went into the thatched-roof *bohío* and returned with several red-hot coals in the scoop of a small shovel that he placed at Panchito's feet. Panchito produced a large cigar. It was a home-rolled "macuyo," as he calls the cigar, a little rough but firm and made from dark leaf. He offered it to the sky in a circling motion, squatted down to the coals in the shovel and lit it, puffing on it long and deep, blowing into the earth a thick cloud of tobacco smoke. He stood, holding his arms out to his sides, first in North to South, then in East to West positions. Thus, starting with the Four Directions—the first of the Seven Potencies of his prayer—in the odorous smoke of tobacco, "nectar of the spirits," he blew out a greeting to each point of his prayer, "a los cuatro puntos cardinales."

The prayer, which he delivers in a conversational form, contains one of those fundamental traditional messages that percolates through a wide range of native cultures: the duty of human beings to express appreciation while remembering the elements of Creation, and, depending on the culture, to name the beings or being, who set Creation in motion.

Enveloped in *chin-chin*, that gentle rain that hangs like a veil, Panchito prayed. Watching the faces and postures of the people gathered, with essential elements being invoked, Panchito's mountain was that day an Indian "everywhere." Through the burning tobacco lighted from the coals of his own hearth fire, Panchito invoked the seven main elements that keep Creation in motion, and can receive thanks from us through the smoke of the tobacco: 1) Four Directions, four corners of the world; 2) Mother Earth, everything she gives, the medicines, the animals, the foods, the trees; 3) Father Sun, male ancestor, main power; 4) Water, the origin of life; 5) Wind, four winds, our constant breathing; 6) Moon, grandmother ancestor; 7) Stars of the Sky, spirit origins and eternal abode of all ancestors.

As Don Panchito intoned his Seven Potencies prayer, on that remote Cuban mountain, a widely representative group of Native people gathered to drink from that refreshing message still commonly and deeply felt throughout the Americas. Beyond politics and economic concerns—wisdom, knowledge, and spiritual connection can be shared in essential ways. Mutual recognition among indigenous peoples—particularly American Indians—based on a shared understanding of natural "indigenousness" is offered here as one of the serious ways of gauging Native peoples. This is no small matter, as beyond the academic knowledge base, i.e., by anthropologists, archaeologists, and other scientists, an equally or more cohesive interpretive mode has emerged from representations of indigenous communities themselves, at the United Nations, and in numerous and quite sophisticated national, regional, and international gatherings of Native peoples. Two full generations of Native peoples have now consciously moved across national boundaries to use every modern tool available to safeguard their cultural traditions. In this context, the survival quotient of Caribbean indigenous peoples becomes more easily understood.

Just in the circle of relatives and acquaintances that day on Panchito's mountain, a wide set of connections spun out, from Maya daykeepers to Onondaga herbalists, Chumash and Kaw curators, and Mohawk journalists and midwives, over a dozen Native people. I thought of many other Native representatives who had already met Panchito (Garifuna, Carib, Navajo, Cree, Northern Diné among them), as well as the many others who could have been there, for whom Panchito's prayer, based on a premise of communication with nature and invocations of the Four Directions and the "cosmic family," would also be completely acceptable as an indigenous tradition. In the voice of this gifted, traditional, community elder, whom his people call *cacique* and whom the pertinent Cuban anthropologists and historians no doubt can agree, is a genuine voice of the recognizable Cuban Indian cultural and tribal legacy, it was a prayer to encapsulate a hemisphere.

References

Arrom, J.J. (1971). *La Virgen del Cobre. Historia, leyenda y símbolo sincrético*. Madrid: Editorial Gredos, S.A.

———. (1999). *An account of the antiquities of the Indians: Fray Ramón Pané*. Durham, NC: Duke University Press.

Bachiller y Morales, A. (1883). *Cuba primitiva. Origen, lenguas, tradiciones e historia de los Indios de la Antillas Mayores y las Lucayas*. Havana: Librería de Miguel Villa.

Barreiro, J. (1996). The cacique's prayer. *Native Americas*, 13(1), 38–47.

———. (1999). A life counts. *Native Americas*, 16(2), 2.

———. (2001). *Panchito: cacique de montaña*. Santiago de Cuba: Ediciones Catedral.

———. (2003). Survival stories. In A. Chomski, B. Carr, & P. M. Smorkaloff (Eds.), *The Cuba reader: History, culture, politics* (pp. 28–36). Durham, NC: Duke University Press.

Bendoyro, R. (1987). An epitaph for the Amerindians of Cuba Juventud Rebelde. *Granma Weekly Review*, 22(3), 3.

Casasús, J.J.E. (1950). *La invasión: Estudio crítico-militar*. Havana: Academia de la Historia y Academia Militar de la República.

Cullin, S. (1902). The Indians of Cuba. *Bulletin of the Free Museum of Science and Art*, University of Pennsylvania, 3(4), 185–226.

Fariñas Gutierres, D. (1995). *Religión en las Antillas*. Havana: Editorial Academia.

García Molina, J., Fariñas Gutiérrez, D., & Garrido Mazorra, M. (1998). *Huellas vivas del Indocubano*. Toronto: Lugus Libros.

Harrington, M. (1921). *Cuba before Columbus*. Vols. 1 & 2. New York: Museum of the American Indian, Heye Foundation.

Martí, J. (1982). Diario de campaña. In R. Lubian y Arias (Ed.), *Martí en los campos de Cuba libre* (pp. 44–55). Havana: Grupo Cubano de Estudios Históricos.

Miro Argenter, J. (1945). *Crónicas de la guerra*. Havana: Instituto del Libro de la Habana.

Moya León, H. (1996). La Caridad de los Indios: a sui generis community. *Granma National Newspaper*, May 9, 5.

Núñez Jiménez, A. (1945). *El pico turquino, exploración y estudio*. Havana: Sociedad Espeleológica de Cuba

———. (1963). *Cuba con la mochila al hombro*. Havana: Ediciones Unión Reportaje.

Padrón Valdes, A. (1973). *El General José, apuntes biográficos*. Havana: Editorial de Arte y Literatura, Instituto Cubano del Libro.

Pérez Echevarría, A. (1987). The Tames Indians. *Granma Weekly Review*, 22(3), 3.

Pichardo Moya, F. (1945). *Los indios de Cuba en sus tiempos históricos*. Havana: Imprenta Editorial Siglo XX.

Rivero de la Calle, M. (1978). Supervivencia de descendientes de indoamericanos en la zona de Yateras, Oriente. In Modesto Martinez Castillo (Ed.), *Cuba Arqueológica* (pp. 149–176). Santiago de Cuba: Editorial Oriente.

Rivero de la Calle, M. & Dacal Moaré, R. (1978). *Archeología aborigen de Cuba*. Havana: Gente Nueva.

Roloff Mialofsky, C.R. (1901). *Indice alfabético y definiciones del ejército libertador de Cuba, datos compilados y ordenados por el inspector general del ejército libertador*. Havana: Imprenta de Rambla y Bouza.

Rouse, I. (1948). Circum-Caribbean tribes. *Handbook of North American Indians*, Bulletin 143, 4, 530.

Sánchez Guerra, J. (1998). La capitana del regimiento Hatuey. *Revista El Mar y la Montaña* (Guantánamo), October, 48–53.

Taliman, V. (2001). Defying the myth of extinction. *National Museum of the American Indian: Celebrating Native Traditions and Communities*, 2(2), 17–24.

Trincado. M.N. (1999). El Aborigen y la formación de la nacionalidad Cubana. *El Caribe Arqueológico*, 1, 100–103.

※ CHAPTER THREE ※

Ocama-Daca Taino (Hear Me, I Am Taíno): Taíno Survival on Hispaniola, Focusing on the Dominican Republic

Lynne Guitar, Pedro Ferbel-Azcarate, and Jorge Estevez

The island known as *Kiskeya* or *Quisqueya*, *Bohío*, and *Haiti*, which Columbus named "Hispaniola," shared today by the Dominican Republic and the Republic of Haiti, was the heart of the flourishing Taíno culture that, by the 1490s, encompassed most of the Greater Antilles. It was on Hispaniola that the myth of Taíno extinction began. The myth's most prevalent origin, as we shall explain, was the campaign of the Dominican friars, led by Bartolomé de las Casas, to abolish the *encomienda* system (in theory, mutually beneficial, whereby the Spanish Crown commended Taínos to an individual Spaniard who was to teach them to live like Christians—in return, they worked for him), and replace it with a mission system. Further, a myth of Taíno extinction provided the Spanish Crown with a perfect cover-up, concealing its inability to exert absolute control over the natives. Finally, alleging Taíno extinction provided a rationale for those colonists who benefited from importing African people as slaves. Over the centuries, the extinction myth was transformed in multiple ways to suit national and class interests, which helps explain its tenaciousness in the Dominican ethos. The reality is that over the years, a poor but landed peasantry developed from the original groups of Taíno, Africans, and Europeans, who blended both their genes and cultural traditions. Engaged in a struggle to live on the land, they used their repertoire of cultural knowledge to best survive. Naturally, they relied on their Taíno heritage, which represented many generations of knowledge, tradition, and oral history about the land. They further incorporated African and Spanish culture into this root Taíno heritage.

After centuries of unquestioning acceptance of Taíno extinction, scholars are beginning to challenge the assumption. Recent historical, ethnographic, ethno-archaeological, linguistic, and DNA studies are demonstrating multidisciplinary evidence for both Taíno cultural and biological survival.

This chapter examines the new evidence and takes an in-depth look at the paradoxical situation of today's Dominican Taínos, whose very existence continues to be denied. Complex questions about ethnicity aggravate the already-problematical areas of "race" and identity in this politically and economically challenged nation. Ironically, but understandably, the various Taíno revival movements began in Puerto Rico and the U.S.A. among Taínos of the diaspora, where there are sociopolitical and even economic benefits to being a member of a minority group, not in Cuba or the Dominican Republic, where there are no such benefits. With the weight of all the new evidence, the revival is approaching a critical mass, and Taíno survival is beginning to be recognized as a reality in the original Taíno homeland.

Beyond Columbus's Wake: Mounting Multidisciplinary Evidence for Taíno Survival

In this paper, "Taíno" is a simplified term to define the heritage or identity of Native American origin found principally in the Greater Antilles. "Survival" is both the qualitative and quantitative continuity of a cultural or biological feature shared by members of the same family, community, or region. The conclusions presented here on Taíno survival are the product of the authors' combined years of research in the Dominican Republic and the U.S.A.—more than 50 years among us. Historian Lynne Guitar's studies are grounded in critical ethnohistory, which was the basis for her dissertation research (Guitar, 1998), and are seasoned with her experience working in the Dominican Republic as a writer, teacher, historical guide, and administrator. Interdisciplinary archaeologist Pedro Ferbel-Azcarate's perspective is based in anthropology, the product of his dissertation research (Ferbel, 1995) and work as a teacher and field researcher in the Dominican Republic. As a self-identifying Taíno and museum professional, Jorge Estevez has been studying Taíno survival since he was a young man.

Initially we all began by assuming that what we read in the chronicles, textbooks, journals, and museums about the extinction of the Taíno was true. Romanticized representations of Taíno appeared in the histories and school textbooks, were used as decoration on buildings or to hawk products like mascots, always presented in ways that suggest they were "frozen" in a time before Columbus. We noted that there is little public discussion about history or cultural identity in the Dominican Republic, and the official channels that promote heritage and identity focus on celebrating the Hispanic past or a romanticized pre-Columbian Taíno past. For all intents and purposes, the Taíno of Hispaniola were extinct.

When we met in the mid-1990s, we began to share our evidence that the Taíno had, in fact, survived the "Encounter Era." We shared our knowledge of the many cultural forms of Taíno origin that are practiced in daily Dominican life, especially in the countryside. We found that many Taíno concepts are embedded in the modern-day Dominican worldview, even among those who live in the cities and abroad. We wondered how it is that Dominicans practice such strong indigenous cultural forms but that so few identify with them. Finding the answers to this and related questions has drawn us to work more closely together. The answers we are finding are complex.

In the colonized/globalized reality of the Dominican Republic, traditional cultural practices are seen as unprogressive and individuals are often ashamed by traditions that represent their "poverty" or "backwardness." For five centuries, the traditional components of Caribbean culture have existed in opposition to the economic realities of modernization or Hispano-Westernization. In such a way, development toward a Western economy has meant movement away from traditional Dominican culture, away from Taíno heritage.

In spite of this reality, it is still true, as Puerto Rican historian Jalil Sued Badillo suggests: "The Caribbean people are searching anxiously to extol symbols of identity as much as they are searching to prove the falsehood of colonial myths that have devaluated their human worth as well as that of their lands" (1992, p. 605). We believe it is important for scholars as well as the general public to understand the complexity of contemporary identity issues, including the role of racism, nationalism, and the politics of ethnicity, as well as to share our findings with the people who are proving to have Taíno ancestry and cultural heritage. Working together, we may assist in opening the door for all Caribbean people to understand their true history, identify with all their ancestors, celebrate their traditional culture, protect their natural and cultural resources, and use an informed perspective to find our path beyond Columbus's wake.

Reexamining the Historical Arguments and Colonial Documents: Perspective of Historian Lynne Guitar

Early Spanish colonization in the Caribbean has been well documented (see Deagan, 1988; Keegan, 1991; Parry & Keith, 1984; Sauer, 1966; Wilson, 1990). This is partly due to the nature of European-sponsored exploration into unknown lands, which demanded a legal description of "discovered" property. Accounts by Fray Ramón Pané, Bartolomé de las Casas, Peter Martyr D'Anghiera, Gonzalo Fernández de Oviedo y Valdez, and Christopher Columbus, among others, as well as the plethora of official reports and testamentary documents that passed back and forth between Spain and her colonies, represent a wealth of information concerning the land, people, and events of the colonial Caribbean; therefore, it is not surprising that textual evidence has driven interpretations about the Taíno in academic literature (see Keegan, 1991, pp. xii–xiii; Wilson, 1990, pp. 7–12). Even with the wealth of textual sources, however, interpreting Spanish historical accounts is difficult.

Beyond issues of intentional misrepresentation and selective accounting, Spanish texts are fraught with cultural biases that cloud the distinction between accuracy and invention. The biases are compounded during the processes of transcription and translation, especially of archaic documents. Finally, Spanish texts must be interpreted within their social context as part of a larger discourse of colonial policy, not merely as objective descriptions. When used as historical evidence, texts must be carefully evaluated against other documents and against archaeological, linguistic, geographical, and any other evidence available to provide consistency and veracity. Interpretation must also be situated according to the social and political positions of the authors and translators, as well as the intended audience of each document.

My first hint that histories about the Encounter Era on Hispaniola contained significant errors dealt with the topic of maize. In books by distinguished historians down the centuries, they repeated that the only bread the Taíno knew was *casabe*, made of yucca. Yet many original documents and chronicles clearly state that the Taíno ate bread made of both yucca and maize. It was a minor point, but the discrepancy bothered me, so I searched and discovered that Antonio de Herrera y Tordesillas began the error. King Philip II appointed him Master Chronicler of the Indies in 1596. Herrera was the first historian allowed to use royal documents that were closely guarded as crown secrets (these documents are available to scholars today in Seville's *Archivo General de las Indias*). They were the foundation for his *General history of the deeds of the Castilians in the islands and mainland of the Ocean Sea* in which Herrera wrote disparagingly that the Taíno "ate [bread made of] neither corn nor wheat," just *casabe* (pp. 23–24). He was so highly respected that subsequent scholars have repeated his error, despite contrary textual evidence and despite findings by archaeologists like Anna C. Roosevelt (1980) that the Taínos' forbearers in the Orinoco River valleys grew vast amounts of both yucca and maize.

The tendency of Hispanic historians to rely without question upon the voice of authority has often pitted me against "the establishment" in the Dominican Republic. Dominican historians have an admirable ability to quote from memory long lists of colonial-era officials, along with historic details. Most do not appear to understand, however, that those who made and wrote history in the past, as now, were human beings who could err and who had personal agendas that influenced their perceptions and what they chose to write in—or leave out of—the documents and histories. Ironically, I use many of the very same documents to prove Taíno survival that other historians have used to prove their extinction—for example, census records.

Compared to the number of Taíno on Hispaniola, very few Spaniards came, and those who did were overwhelmingly male (Boyd-Bowman, 1973, 1976). Although there has been extensive controversy about Taíno demographics, the general consensus today is that there were several million of them on Hispaniola in the 1490s (an excellent summary of the demographic arguments can be found in Verano & Ubelaker, 1992). Despite their relatively few numbers, the Spaniards, heady with the success of their *Reconquista* (the 1492 expulsion of the last Moors from Spain), implanted their own social, economic, and political order on Hispaniola, aided and abetted by their invisible allies—viruses and bacteria, against which the native peoples had no immunities. The impact of European colonization on the Taíno was devastating. It completely restructured the trajectory of their native lifeways, but did not eliminate them.

Confronted with deadly foreign diseases; unable to maintain their agricultural calendar; forced into Spanish systems of social, economic, and political domination; losing rights to land, free expression, and, in many cases, to life itself, the Taíno had to resort to radical ways to survive. Resistance took a wide variety of forms. Many Taíno fought against the intruders, who had the distinct advantage of coming from a place with a history of warfare, guns, steel swords, horses, and war dogs. Many Taíno ran away to other lands or hid in isolated *cimarrón* (runaway or Maroon) communities far from the Spanish towns and plantations, often accompanied by runaway African slaves. Others, from the very beginning of the Spanish colonization of the island, lived with or near Spaniards and their African slaves, starting a process of transculturation that gave rise to a new Creole culture (Guitar, 2000, 2003; García-Arévalo, 1992, pp. 245–262). The Taíno were forced into slave- or serf-like positions, although many Taíno females entered the Spanish system via marriage. Dominican historian Frank Moya Pons notes that intermarriage between Spaniards and Taíno women is clearly substantiated by the *Repartimiento* Census of 1514, which shows that 40% of Spanish men on the island had Indian wives or concubines (1992, p. 135).

Without doubt, many of those women were unwilling sexual partners, but there is documentary evidence that others voluntarily married Spaniards and bore *mestizo* children. The Spaniards' wives were baptized, took Spanish names, adopted Spanish dress styles, attended Spanish churches, lived in Spanish-style houses, learned to speak Castilian, and to all outward appearances "became Spanish." But that was the outward, public appearance. Inside their homes, where Spaniards had always jealously guarded their privacy, the lives of these mixed couples and their children remained quite indigenous, an idea first promulgated by American archaeologist Kathleen Deagan (1985, 2004). What the family ate; how food was stored and prepared; child-raising practices; home medicinal and religious practices; storytelling; the importance of song, music, dance, and naming patterns; even the concept of who is family, all have remained overwhelmingly Taíno in the Dominican Republic through the present day, with, of course, both Spanish and African influences. Sometimes indigenous patterns were hidden within Spanish ones, such as the way the Spanish custom of *compadrazgo* (godparenting), principally at baptism, was utilized by indigenous peoples across the Americas to replace their own systems of fictive kinship, significantly changing the Spanish system in the process (Foster, 1953). The Taíno, for example, had *guatiáo*, a system by which two adults could "exchange names" and become family, with the same reciprocal rights as family members by birth. In Spain, godparents have responsibility for the infant or child they sponsor when it is given a saint's name and baptized into the Catholic religion—but in the Dominican Republic, the strongest relationship is not between the adult godparent and the child, but between the adult godparent and the child's parents—like in *guatiáo*.

In Santo Domingo, the Spanish capital and administrative center, Spaniards reproduced their homeland's public infrastructures and cultural patterns as closely as they could. Nonetheless, Santo Domingo was a frontier city, so even in the public sphere the infrastructures and society that evolved were not perfect European replicas because of the island's unique geography and climate, its distance from Iberia, and the integration of Taíno and African beliefs and cultural traditions. The Spanish colonists were even less successful at replicating their European infrastructures and culture in the countryside.

Throughout the island's rural towns and villages, in the gold mining regions, and on the sugar-cane plantations, Spaniards were outnumbered by at least five to one by Amerindians, Africans, and mixed "others" long after the natives were supposed to have disappeared and long before most of the African slaves arrived (see Table 1). "Others" is a word used frequently in the island's early censuses. The terms "mestizo" and "mulatto" did not appear in colonial census records until the 1580s (Knight, 1990, pp. 44–45).

In fact, the Spaniards' domination of Hispaniola was illusory, for they actually controlled very little of the island's territory. Between 1492 and 1510, Spaniards founded only two cities—Santiago de los Caballeros and Santo Domingo de Guzmán—plus fewer than 20 small villages and a dozen fortresses. That left a lot of Hispaniola's territory with no Spaniards at all, except for occasional military patrols. Domination became even more difficult by the 1510s, when the Spanish population, never large to begin with, began to decrease. Despite repeated royal prohibitions, Spaniards left Hispaniola in massive numbers seeking gold, silver, pearls, and more native workers on Puerto

Rico, Cuba, the islands of the Lesser Antilles, the region known today as Panama, Venezuela, and Colombia, and later in Mexico and Peru (Archivo General de las Indias, Patronato Real 172, R35).

The Spaniards who remained on Hispaniola began to pull back to regions closer to the capital, which were better patrolled than the villages, had more European conveniences, and from which all shipping and commerce were conducted—that is, all the things that meant civilized life to Spaniards. As they pulled back toward Santo Domingo, Spain's enemies began to raid and then settle on the less protected northwestern shores of the island. In those and other peripheral parts of the island lived the *cimarrones*. More about them shortly, but first a brief summary of the encomienda system that the cimarrones were running away from.

The year 1510 is significant because that's when Antonio Montesino was chosen by the Dominican Order of Friars on the island to speak out against the encomienda system. The Order believed it was ineffective for conversion and that abusive *encomenderos* were killing off the Taíno. The friars wanted to eliminate the encomienda system and relocate the Taíno into missionary villages, believing that would improve conversion efforts and halt the death toll. Montesino's sermons convinced Bartolomé de las Casas to set his *indios* free and become a friar himself, the most outspoken of all the Dominicans. He spent the balance of his long life defending the natives through his actions and writing, wherein he encouraged the missionary system, raged at the injustice of the encomienda system, and exaggerated the encomenderos' abuses and exploitation in order to achieve his goals, which was accepted rhetoric in his day (see his *Short Account*, 1992). Las Casas' arguments finally succeeded in convincing the Spanish Crown to prohibit the encomienda system via the New Laws of 1542, but Spain's Protestant enemies picked up his stories and spread them throughout Europe, promulgating the Black Legend against the conquistadors. This legend is so embedded in the official Conquest history that even Spaniards today believe their ancestors were heartless monsters.

Most history books claim that "the last Taínos of Hispaniola" were those who rebelled with Cacique Enriquillo in 1519. (Enriquillo remained at large for 15 years, inspiring hundreds of other runaways.) The concept of Enriquillo's people as the last of the Taíno is very romantic and elevates Enriquillo to superhero status (see Galvan, 1989; Utrera, 1973). Perhaps this is why Dominicans today take an ironic pride in the supposed fact that it is only on their island that no natives survived the Conquest Era, but the factual evidence is quite contrary to the romantic concept.

Today we know that while some Taíno were killed by abuses endured under the *encomienda* system, others by the famines and sporadic wars of the 1490s, and still others by the systematic massacres ordered by Governor Nicolás de Ovando from 1502 to 1505, most of the Taíno died of illnesses like measles and influenza (and after 1519, of smallpox) because, unlike Europeans, Africans, and Asians, they had no immunities to them (Cook, 1993; Cook & Lovell 1992; García Arévalo, 1992, p. 229). Plagues created at least as much chaos within the Taíno agricultural system as forced labor had done, thus famine accelerated the decline. In tropical regions like Hispaniola, 80–90% of the natives died of plagues that often preceded the actual arrival of Spaniards to their villages, for the germs and viruses were carried by messengers bearing news from plague-ridden areas.

An 80–90% loss is a significant and horrifying loss. It is so horrifying that it obscures the fact that 10–20% of the Taíno survived. Clearly then, when the chroniclers wrote that "all of the Indians" of Hispaniola were gone, they were following the lead of de las Casas, who purposely exaggerated the Taíno decline. Simultaneously, other Spaniards on Hispaniola testified that growing numbers of *indios cimarrones* had the island "in the grip of such terror" that no one wanted to leave the Capital (Marté, 1981, pp. 359–360; see also Herrera Cabral, 1995, pp. 229–281). Letter after letter to the Spanish Court by encomenderos on Hispaniola repeated the same theme, exaggerating the number of deaths among their commended Taíno in order to gain sympathy and royal permission to import more African slaves, who were believed to be "stronger" than the Taíno because they did not fall prey to the diseases that decimated the natives (Sáez, 1994, p. 211; Klein, 1986, p. 25).

Historians and demographers generally use the censuses of the era, such as the census that accompanied the 1514 *Repartimiento* (redivision of the remaining 26,189 commended indios), to confirm that the Taíno were nearly extinct by then. They forget that Taíno had been fleeing from the Spaniards for more than two decades by then—since 1492. Governor Nicolás de Ovando himself wrote, as reflected in a 1503 royal report, that Taíno and Africans frequently ran away together, using the Indians' knowledge of the countryside to survive and to evade the Spanish patrols (CDIA, 1925–1937, Vol. 5, pp. 43–45). Juan Mosquera, in one of dozens of court testimonies that mention runaways, told the Jeronymite friars in 1517 that he had personally observed many Indians fleeing to the mountains "in order to consume spiders and tree roots and lizards" (the inference being that Indians needed Spanish guidance even to know what was good to eat). Jerónimo de Agüero testified that "indios want very much never to see Spaniards...so they frequently go to the mountains" (Rodríguez Demorizi, 1971, pp. 273–354). Martyr confirmed that "many of the indios, when their *caciques* call them...flee to the forests and mountains...hiding themselves so as not to suffer from that work" assigned to them by their Spanish encomenderos (1989, Fourth decade, Book 10).

There are hundreds more examples. Obviously the early Spanish censuses are not accurate for the island as a whole. How can you count people who are hiding from you? The censuses only account for those Taíno who stayed on the Spaniards' encomiendas. There is another problem with the early censuses. They are misinterpreted because people were categorized differently in the 16th century than they are today. Hispaniola's early residents were categorized as Spaniards, indios, or African slaves, but a lot of "others" also appeared on the censuses. Furthermore, categorization as Spaniard or indio apparently depended upon social factors and the personal judgment of the census taker, not on biological factors. If a Spaniard and a Taíno woman had a child who was raised in the city or a European-style town, spoke Castilian, was baptized Catholic, wore European clothes, received a European education, and "acted" Spanish, then the child was categorized as Spanish. If that same child lived in a *yucayeque* (Taíno village), spoke Taíno, practiced Taíno religious rituals, dressed as a Taíno, and acted Taíno, then he or she was placed in the indio category. The same held true for adults, such as Taíno women married to Spaniards—they were categorized as Spanish if they dressed and acted Spanish, as indio if they dressed and acted indio.

There are three extant censuses from the first half of the 16th century that illustrate the difficulties of categorizing those who lived and worked on Hispaniola's sugar-cane plantations. The first census was part of a lawsuit initiated July 19, 1533, between the civil and ecclesiastical councils in Santo Domingo. The headcount was actually taken in 1530 on 19 of Hispaniola's plantations, plus a scattering of small estates. The census enumerated 1,870 African workers, indicating that they were slaves, and 427 "Spaniards," most of whom, because they lived in the countryside, were probably mestizos. Although the legal papers pertaining to the case say there were "some" indios working on the plantations, the only actual numbers provided came from five plantations on the Río Nigua that, combined, had 200 indios. No numbers are provided for indios on the other 14 plantations, just question marks and a total of 700 unspecified "others" (Mira Caballos, 1997, p. 155). Probably no one wanted to release the actual numbers of indios connected to the estates, for the plantations' owners had previously written letters requesting royal permission to bring in African slaves, swearing that all of their commended indios were dead. Also, there was obvious confusion over how to categorize workers who were free Africans or people of mixed ethnic parentage. Remember, none of these censuses included categories for Africans other than slaves, or for anyone of mixed biological heritage.

Archbishop Alonso de Avila of Santo Domingo ordered a census taken in 1533 to determine the number of chapels and clergymen required to service the island's now 23 sugar-cane plantations. He reported that there were five plantations on the Río Nigua alone, plus several cattle ranches. Altogether, Avila wrote that there were "at least" 700 Africans, 200 indios, and 150 Spaniards who lived and worked in the region. Avila enumerated a total of 1,880

Africans, 412 Spaniards, and 200 indios (Archivo General de las Indias, Justicia 12, 149, ff10v-15).

The high ratio of Africans to Spaniards and Indians in Avila's census is the kind of ratio that other historians have cited, with Africans outnumbering Spaniards by almost five to one. The problem is that historians and demographers nearly always refer only to the quantities in the fixed categories and do not mention the "others" that the census takers made careful note of, nor the question marks or other indications that there were people outside the fixed categories who were not enumerated. On his census, Avila reported 1,525 "others"—820 more than in the 1530 census. In letters that accompanied his census, he wrote that these unspecified persons included "some Spaniards, Africans, and indios." He admitted that there were other persons, too, who were not included in the census—they "were mostly indios" (Archivo General de Indias, Justicia 12, 149, ff10v-15).

Twelve years after Avila's census, in a report from the island's Governor Alonso de Fuenmayor to Emperor Charles, there was only one more plantation listed on the Río Nigua, but the headcount there alone had risen from 700 Africans to 962, and from 200 indios to 1,212. Fuenmayor reported on a total of 29 plantations and *trapiches* (horse-powered mills). It is notable that Africans only outnumbered the indigenous workforce on 9 of the 29 plantations in his 1545 census. In total, Fuenmayor enumerated over 8,952 workers (he used the symbol "+" to indicate the additional numbers)—43% of them he identified as Africans and 57% as indios. Fuenmayor enumerated more than 5,000 indios.

The quantities listed in Fuenmayor's census are suspect because they reflect such a dramatic increase in indios over the 1530 and 1533 counts—the opposite of what would be expected due to population decline as other Spaniards were reporting. The 1520s and 1530s, however, were the peak years of *rescate*, a system whereby the Spanish Crown allowed the capture and enslavement of "cannibals" (see Otte, 1958, 1977), many of whom were sold on Hispaniola. There are other important differences between Fuenmayor's census and the previous two. He included among the plantation "slaves" all of the independent farmers whom the other censuses mentioned separately. Furthermore, Fuenmayor did not mention any "others," nor did he include question marks or workers of unspecified category—everybody was placed into the category of "African slaves" or "*esclavos indios*" (Peguero, 1975, pp. 217–221).[1] It could also be that Fuenmayor, who came to his office directly from Spain, counted everyone on Hispaniola who had the least bit of Native blood as "indio," without taking into account their education, appearance, behavior, and status, whereas locals would classify them as Spaniards. Alonzo López de Cerrato, president of Hispaniola's Royal Court and governor after Fuenmayor, wrote a letter to the emperor dated May 23, 1545. He reported the same "more than 5,000 *esclavos indios*" that Fuenmayor enumerated, insisting they were all "brought from elsewhere." Taíno, however, not "cannibals," were protected by the New Laws, which Cerrato was struggling unsuccessfully to enforce (Mira Caballos, 1997, p. 290).

Table 1. Comparison of Three Sugar-Cane Plantation Censuses

Year	Spaniards	Indians	Africans	Others	Total	Plantations
1530	427	200+	1,870	700+?	3,197+	14
1533	412	200+	1,880	1,525+?	4,017+	23
1545	—	5,125+	3,827+	—	8,952+	29

The majority of the indigenous peoples on Hispaniola who lived and worked with Spaniards, and their progeny, eventually "passed" for Spaniards, or at least as "others," in part to avoid paying tribute (Susan R. Parker found the same thing in St. Augustine, Florida, 1993, pp. 2 & 5). Many indios, however, didn't even work for or live near the Spaniards. The cimarrones fled to peripheral regions of Hispaniola, or sometimes to other islands or the mainland. Cimarrones hid out in Hispaniola's mountains and deserts, preferring to leave behind their fertile river valleys and remain free in less hospitable terrain than live under Spanish domination.

A royal advisory dated July 31, 1556, reported that in 1555 a Spanish patrol discovered four entire towns "full of indios about which no one previously knew." One was near Puerto Plata; another, very near it, on the Atlantic Coast; one on the Samaná Peninsula; and another in the northwest at Cape St. Nicholas (CDIU, 1885–1932, p. 10). Apparently, after 50 years, some cimarrones had decided they could move back to the fertile coasts and valleys of the north that the Spaniards had abandoned.

By the middle of the 16th century, the Spanish population and Spanish control of Hispaniola had dwindled considerably as the crown's focus turned to Mexico and Peru and the official port shifted from Santo Domingo to Havana. (Other Caribbean islands, such as Jamaica and Trinidad, experienced the same marginalization within the Spanish Empire.) Most Spaniards who remained on Hispaniola pulled back to Santo Domingo and its nearby towns for protection from encroaching European enemies. Thus cimarrones, as well as Spain's European enemies, could settle outside the Spanish holdings.

Many of the inhabitants of those four towns "full of indios," were probably not of Taíno parentage alone. Doubtlessly some had Spanish fathers or grandfathers, and others were the offspring of Africans or other indigenous peoples brought to the island as slaves—and their culture was a tripartite mixture as well. These *Criollo* (Creole) peoples in what became the Dominican Republic eventually were perceived as "Spaniards," partly because of the myth that the Taíno had died out, but also due to the prevalent belief that anything Spanish was better than anything African or Indian.

Discrimination against other peoples and their cultures was deeply imbedded in the Spanish conquest. Those who came to Hispaniola to "civilize" it were Europeans who considered both the African and indigenous peoples to be "backward," at best. Unfortunately, the stigma against indios still exists in the Dominican Republic. While Taíno of the pre-Columbian past are elevated to a heroic pedestal, it is for nationalistic and commercial reasons, not because they are really admired. History books, text books, magazines, museum exhibits, tourist attractions, souvenir shops, all extol the indigenous glory—500 years ago. But to *be* an Indian is a shameful thing. "Me, an indio?" responded Vinicio, a Dominican friend, when asked if I could take his picture to document his strong indigenous features. Shaking his head in denial, he ironically added, "My mother was a full-blooded india, but *I'm* not indio." (Note that Dominicans still use the color schematic that includes *indio claro*, *indio oscuro*, and other variations that avoid using the color "black," a schematic mandated by President Trujillo for 30 years in order to set them apart from Haitians, but this does not mean that Dominicans accept indigenous survival.)

It is time to help change the negative Hispanic attitude against anything Indian by reevaluating the documents and histories of the colonial past and passing the new interpretations and new evidence from a wide variety of academic fields on to Dominicans and other peoples of the Greater Antilles, both on the island and abroad. The public exhibitions, textbooks, and popular histories used throughout the Dominican Republic's educational system, in particular, need to be updated, for they are among the most powerful tools of the past, present, and future.

Taíno Survival Identified within the Politics of Race and Ethnicity, National Identity, and Biological and Cultural Heritage: Perspective of Interdisciplinary Archaeologist Pedro Ferbel-Azcarate

Physical anthropology teaches us that the word "race" is synonymous with species. As humans belong to only one species, *Homo sapiens sapiens*, we must interpret racial differences as mere sociopolitical constructs that arose with the particular conditions of European colonization in the Americas and the importation of peoples from Africa as slaves. The color-based hierarchical system of racism is found today in the rigid categories and prejudices that divide people who may actually share ancestries and cultural heritages. Definitions of "race" often confuse the more flexible concepts of ethnicity and identity, which are self-ascribed and based on shared ideas of community identity.

Like other populations of people in the Americas with mixes of Native American, African, and European ancestry, Dominicans have phenotypic appearances that are not easy to put into a "box" or racial category. Just because Dominicans have multiple ancestries, however, does not mean they cannot legitimately celebrate their Native American heritage. Just because they speak Spanish does not mean that their strongest cultural root comes from Spain. And just because a person with multiple ancestries wants to celebrate their Taíno roots does not necessarily mean they want to negate their African, European, or other heritages.

For anthropologists, ethnic identity is proving to be a dynamic entity, influenced by national, class, and other sociopolitical boundaries that are constantly changing through time (Anderson, 1983; Brow, 1990; Clifford, 1988). There are fierce debates among anthropologists and sociologists as to what defines Native American ethnicity (Blu, 1980; Forbes, 1993). The definition of an ethnic group often is not so much about measures of blood quanta or a catalogue of cultural traits, but involves the intimate interrelations of the members of a group's thoughts, feelings, and shared experiences, which are constantly changing through time. The question of ethnic authenticity can become political if such privileges as self-government and rights to land are at stake. Governments often discourage marginal ethnic groups from strengthening their group identities so that they do not become political threats. In other words, ethnic "authenticity" has little to do with the ways people feel bound together as a group, but how larger political bodies view them.

Miller (2003) provides multiple examples from around the world for how indigenous groups have defined themselves in particular ways distinct to their community. Miller cites Native American tribes like the Snohomish who chose to avoid a relationship with the state as a strategy for their survival. Ironically, the Bureau of Indian Affairs (BIA) uses historical documentation and treaties as contemporary evidence for tribal recognition. Many Native American tribes, as well as amalgamations of Native peoples with runaway African slaves, and others, chose a path of avoidance with the state as their form of resistance and cultural survival. Further, Miller documents how bloodlines have rarely been used as a means to define tribal inclusion in the Americas. Yet, bloodlines are one of the most important of the BIA's recognition criteria.

In anthropologist James Clifford's (1988) analysis of the Mashpee Indian petition for federal recognition, he finds that the community's abstract experiential knowledge about ethnic cohesion threatened stereotypic ways of defining a people with static cultural traits. Clifford points out that defining ethnic identity is not as simple as the presence or absence of feather headdresses or shovel-shaped incisors. Brow (1990) suggests that the dynamism of ethnic communities should be the focus of study, whereby the arenas for such concepts as "the past" and "tradition" are not solid old buildings but structures perpetually being rebuilt and reused by people in the socio-historical present. In such a way, the ethnicity of people with multiple ancestries in the Americas and the Caribbean would be understood in their own terms. We should be informed to understand the racist implications of why one drop of African blood makes a person "Black" while a higher standard is used to determine whether a person is an "Indian."

The authors of the recent volume *Taíno Revival* (Haslip-Viera, 2002) have suggested that those who identify as Taíno are simply denying the fact they are Black. While the authors focus on nationalistic identity politics in Puerto Rico, they take the myth of Taíno extinction at face value. While there is no doubt that national identity agendas in the Spanish-speaking Caribbean have romanticized the Taíno and downplayed the contributions of Africans, the authors chose to substitute one mythology for another by not considering the evidence for Taíno survival and by promoting a more racialized and Afrocentric version of Puerto Rican identity. This is not to say that people of the Spanish-speaking Caribbean may not identify as "Black" or "African," but that they have the right to consider their identities outside the boxes of "race."

The national identity of the Dominican Republic is based on an idealized story of three cultural roots—Spanish, African, and Taíno—with a selective amnesia of the tragedies and struggles inherent to the processes of colonial domination and resistance. Further, African, Taíno, and mixed Afro-Mestizo culture have been marginalized in favor of nationalist ideologies of progress and civilization found in the embrace of Hispanidad and Catholicism. In such a way, Dominicans have been disconnected from their African, indigenous, and their mixed Afro-Mestizo or Criollo ancestry and cultural heritage, even though these ancestries and heritages mark Dominicans with the significant emblems of their contemporary identity.

Like many Native American communities, Caribbean people often base their identification with their Taíno roots on family experiences and cultural traditions. There are some individuals and families who are fully aware of their Taíno ancestry, many tied to particular regions like the Cibao. Their identity may include kin ties to ancestors, oral traditions passed on through time, a bond with a fixed geographic homeland, and/or the collection of cultural traits that symbolize their Taíno history. While many facets of contemporary native Caribbean culture are also tied to an identification with their nation's particular history and with their heritage from African and European culture, many salient themes from their shared indigenous past can be said to constitute a distinctive Taíno identity.

While Taíno heritage is seen in many daily lifeways in the Dominican Republic, its strength as an element of Dominican identity has not been encouraged via governmental channels in the arenas of education and cultural heritage programs. Museums and monuments of Taíno heritage, pre-Columbian archaeology, education, and heritage tourism have a relatively minimal role in the composition and promotion of Taíno identity (Ferbel-Azcarate, 1995). Since these official channels have had such a relatively small influence, the persistence of Taíno-derived cultural forms can be seen as a testament to their underlying strength. Perceptions about the Taíno past, however, are often framed around a Hispanic nationalism that marginalizes or romanticizes the native component of Dominican identity. Ultimately, concepts of ethnicity and national identity are flexible and shift according to sociopolitical factors in the present.

An emphasis on biological versus cultural survival is often overdone. For most native peoples of the Americas, there are few cases where blood quanta determines acceptance into a tribal community (Blu, 1980; Clifford, 1988). Even though the BIA uses such definitions, determining identity based only on a particular percentage of biological ancestry is, by its nature, racist. Just as racist miscegenation laws in the United States took rights away from people with just "one drop" of African blood, so too, laws that define inclusion in a Native American category by bloodlines alone take rights away from people with indigenous ancestry. With all multi-biological populations, the concept of race is challenged by the offspring of parents who come from two or more different "racial" groups. What race are the children? Many colonizing groups, including the Spaniards, created complex systems to define the various mixes of African, European, and Native American people. Not only could these terms not be adequately standardized, they were not even reliably identifiable. Further, the phenotypic expression of an individual does not always reflect his or her genotype. The fact that the definitions of group inclusion change according to contemporary politics ought to suggest that we discard the concept of race entirely.

Unfortunately, race, class, and power have been intricately interwoven through the venture of European colonial expansion in the Americas and still remain firmly in place. So it may be that a majority of people who identify as Taíno in fact have a variety of biological ancestries, including African and European. Where is the arbitrary line drawn to determine how much "indigenous blood" is needed to be considered Taíno? Anthropologists struggle with the question. So, too, should other scholars. In fact, physical anthropologists suggest that most populations around the world are mixes of ancestries and cultures, so the idea that the Taínos of today must prove themselves to be comparable to the Taínos of 1492 ought to be as nonsensical as Spaniards today proving themselves to be comparable to Spaniards of 1492.

While "race" is a complex social construct, biological and DNA studies are providing provocative new scientific evidence of indigenous continuity among Caribbean populations, contrary to popular belief and the writings of early Spanish chroniclers. Recent DNA work by Puerto Rican biologist Juan Carlos Martínez Cruzado (2002), and Dominican physical anthropologist Fernando Luna Calderón[2] (2002) while aimed at tracing human migration patterns, suggest that both Puerto Rican and Dominican populations have retained high percentages of indigenous genetic markers. Genetic and biological studies don't answer questions, however; they engender more. Any Native American with shovel-shaped incisors will be quick to tell you that if their brother or their son did not inherit the gene for shovel-shaped incisors, it does not mean they are no longer relatives or no longer Native American. Further critical thinking of anthropological convention on shovel-shaped incisors was pointed out to me by Jorge Estevez: "At first I felt like I had finally gotten the proof I had been waiting for regarding my Native American identity when I found out I had shovel-shaped incisors...but then I wondered, according to that criterion, will I still be considered a Taíno when I get old and my teeth fall out?" Common sense tells us that biology is just one part of the complex human equation.

Cultural heritage may be defined as the legacy of customs, beliefs, and social practices that contemporary people have carried on from their ancestral past to create their communal identity in the present. Taíno heritage can be found in the Dominican Republic in an extraordinary number of categories, including linguistic features; agricultural practices; use of yucca and casaba (see Figs. 3 & 4); indigenous fruits, vegetables, and tobacco; medicinal knowledge; fishing techniques; architecture; crafts, tools, and technologies; folklore and religion; arts, poetry, and literature (see Fig. 5); popular identity; and popular culture (Ferbel-Azcarate, 1995; Garcia Arévalo, 1988, 1990; Vega, 1981). This Taíno heritage has been passed on for generations, originating with the indigenous peoples who migrated into the Caribbean beginning around 6000–4000 B.C. Archaeologists believe a distinct Taíno culture had developed in the Caribbean by the year 600 A.D., thus flourishing for 900 years before Columbus (Rouse, 1992; Weeks & Ferbel, 1994). Given this time frame, it should come as no surprise that the Taíno rooted their culture with a profound understanding of the Caribbean landscape.

Figure 3: Peeling bitter yucca for the production of *casaba* bread, outside of Los Indios, Dajabón Province, Dominican Republic. Photograph by Pedro Ferbel-Azcarate.

Figure 4: María De Los Santos preparing the "second face" of a *casaba* bread on her *buren* (griddle) at her outside kitchen in GuaGuï, La Vega Province, Dominican Republic. Photograph by Pedro Ferbel-Azcarate.

Figure 5: Dominican artist Gina Rodriguez showing a mixed media work inspired by her Taíno heritage. Barrio El Ensueño, Santiago Province, Dominican Republic. Photograph by Pedro Ferbel-Azcarate.

The survival of Taíno culture has been documented in the work of two important studies addressing Taíno heritage in the Dominican Republic—Bernardo Vega's (1981) "La herencia indígena en la cultura dominicana de hoy" and Garcia Arévalo's (1988) *Indigenismo, arqueología, e identidad nacional*. Recent work in this area (Ferbel-Azcarate, 2002) has expanded on these earlier studies. Proceedings from a conference on Taíno survival that was presented at the Museo del Hombre Dominicano in 2002 have been published in the journal *Kacike* (Guitar et al., 2002).

The practice of Taíno cultural forms reveals a deep knowledge and shared oral tradition, and implies a strong continuity from past to present. The obvious conclusion is that there is significant cultural heritage of Taíno origin that has persisted in the Dominican Republic and the other islands of the Greater Antilles to this day. Bernardo Vega (1981, p. 12) conservatively suggests that "the Indigenous must not be exaggerated in [Dominican] culture.... What is fair to point out, however, is the surprising persistence of certain indigenous cultural legacies, given the very brief period of contact" (translated in García Arévalo, 1990, p. 273). But, we may ask ourselves, why is the persistence of these Taíno cultural traits necessarily surprising? As Reid (1992) points out, Dominicans living in traditional rural settings seem to have more in common with the Taíno who were conquered by the Spaniards than with the Spaniards themselves. Perhaps the period of Spanish Indian contact was not so brief after all. Certainly any discussion of the persistence of Taíno culture would come as a surprise to those who have accepted the traditional explanations of the historical extinction of the Taíno.

Ocama-Daca Taíno (Hear Me, I am Taíno): Perspective of Jorge Estevez, a Taíno from the Dominican Republic

Ocama-Daca Taíno. I am Dominican and I am Taíno. Kiskeya was once the heartland of the Taíno people. Yet the denial of our culture and heritage has been ingrained in all Dominicans with just about every book or magazine article we read on the subject. Historians, teachers, and scholars in all fields, as well as other well-meaning people and institutions, have perpetuated the myth that our indigenous ancestors perished within approximately 30 years of contact with the Spaniards, leaving hardly any trace of our complex culture. We are told that the union between the Spaniards and the African slaves they imported to the islands of the Greater Antilles is what gave rise to the modern-day peoples and culture on these islands. While it does appear true that wars, the encomienda system, slavery, and disease killed off great numbers of my ancestors, the social discrimination practiced by the Spaniards throughout the colonial era, and "paper genocide" practiced by historians ever since, have been just as cruel on my people. With the stroke of their pens, the legacy of my ancestors was wiped out.

I find the notion disturbing that the Taíno are not my ancestors, but rather my "precursors" because they are "extinct." This notion disconnects me, and others like me, from our islands, rendering us, in a sense, immigrants in our own homelands. It also disturbs me when the prehistory of the Caribbean is romanticized so that the Taíno are elevated onto a pedestal so high that no one can reach them—they are placed in the realm of things legendary rather than real, which again, I interpret as an attempt to disconnect indigenous people like me from our ancestors.

So why, despite all these problems, do I and others who are involved in Taíno movements feel such a strong connection to our indigenous ancestors? For me, it is because, since I was a child, my mother and grandmother told me stories of the *campo* (countryside) and our hometown in Jaibón, Kiskeya. They spoke of farming methods, myths and legends, casabe bread, and basket weaving, which are important to life in Jaibón. At the time, I thought these were unique to us in Kiskeya. I later realized that we share these stories and practices with the campo people of Puerto Rico and Cuba. Distinctive words such as *chin-chin, caimito, burén, ciguato, cacata, naiboa,* and *güiro,* among hundreds of others, are unrecognizable to people in other Spanish-speaking countries, yet familiar to us in the Spanish Antilles. Tobacco ceremonies, our aversion to owls, the belief that *cocuyos* (fireflies) are the eyes of the dead, are just a few of the many spiritual beliefs that we share. (Fundamental indigenous beliefs and practices also survive in Haiti—see the appendix in Deren (1991)—but the indigenous culture there appears to have been submerged more deeply under the African than it was in the Dominican Republic, no doubt due to the many centuries of French and Haitian dependence upon sugar and slavery.)

Many of us who, today, identify with the indigenous part of our multiethnic heritage, heard stories about a grandmother or other family member who was "a real Indian." Some of us—like me—were told outright that we descend from indios. I became curious and began to look deeper into my history. Much to my dismay, I found notable contradictions between my family's oral histories and the "official" history taught in schools and national museums. Most scholars claim that indios in the Spanish Antilles have long been extinct. I and the others with whom I began to compare notes discovered, however, that there were crucial inconsistencies in the extinction stories, so we began to investigate them. Among the inconsistencies we found in a multitude of books were the claims that the Taíno burned their crops and ran off into the mountains in their desperate effort to escape Spanish domination. Supposedly the ploy backfired on them, because they were said to have starved to death in those mountains they had called home for thousands of years. Yet the African slaves who escaped into those very same mountains, terrain that was totally unfamiliar to them, survived in the thousands (see, for example, Moya Pons, 1995, p. 41).

The above is just one example of the senseless contradictions we have found. The more we research our history and the more we question our elders, the more perceptive we become. We know that the true story of our ancestors has not yet been told, but some scholars are finally beginning to ask the same questions that we have been asking, have finally begun to revise the inconsistencies and errors of the past. Many historians and anthropologists, such as Samuel Wilson and Fernando Luna Calderón, who previously wrote about the plight of the peaceful and gentle Taíno who were wiped out as a result of warfare and disease, are now beginning to realize that they may have perpetuated the myth of Taíno extinction without having weighed all of the facts. They accepted history at face value. Besides, it is much more romantic to write about a vanished race of "noble savages" than it is to contemplate that human interactions in the Greater Antilles were much more complicated than historians described them.

Taíno, who once populated all the islands of the Greater Antilles, died in great numbers, yes, but African and Spanish men were intermarrying with Taíno women in great numbers, too, and producing children who were more disease-resistant than their mothers. It should come as no surprise, then, that so many people of Taíno descent and so many aspects of Taíno culture remain to this day on Hispaniola and the other islands of the Greater Antilles.

Some people, however, including many academics with whom I have communicated, view the current Taíno revival efforts with contempt. They and others accuse us of being "romantics." My associates and I hear this and variants of "fanatics wanting to be Indian" coming frequently from their circles, or the battering ram: they are denying their negritude (i.e., Haslip-Viera, 2002). When we compare the interpretations of those who would deny us our Taíno heritage to our families' oral histories, and when we point out the historical oddities and inaccuracies, they counter with a series of arguments to blot out the critical facts, using what I can only call circular logic. Recent DNA studies, however, are now providing a line of evidence that cannot be denied.

Recent mitochondrial DNA sequencing studies have revealed that not only are there indigenous genetic markers in the current population of the Greater Antilles, but the quantity is so staggeringly high it directly challenges the "facts" of Taíno extinction (Martínez Cruzado, 2002). Genetic evidence is not brushed off the way the revisionist historians, anthropologists, and their evidence often are, for it is "scientific." Recent DNA studies, however, are now providing a line of evidence that cannot be denied as easily as shared experiences, beliefs, and traditions.

Recently I took a BGA (Bio-Geographical) nuclear test through DNA Print Genomics. This test, according to the company's specialists, provides individuals with the percentages of their genetic background within five generations. My test results showed that I have a significantly high quantity of indigenous genetic markers. In fact, it was explained to me that, just four generations ago, my ancestors were what used to be called "full-blooded" natives. Four generations are roughly 80 to 100 years. That's 400 years after natives supposedly "disappeared" from Kiskeya.

While recognizing the importance of genetic studies, I feel that we Taíno, as a people, validate the DNA evidence, not the other way around. This journey of self-discovery that I and so many others are undertaking is about culture, not genes, for genes say little about us as a people. In fact, at the beginning of the Taíno restoration movements (through which we mean to restore the Taíno to their proper place in the histories and societies from which their supposed extinction has erased them), we did not have DNA to back up any claims to native ancestry that were made. All we had were oral traditions and staunch native assertions. The movements took off from this, not from a laboratory.

The Taíno restoration movements began in the late 1980s, when individuals of Puerto Rican descent began gathering at cultural events to discuss family oral histories and historical inaccuracies about our ancestors. Among the popular events we attended were the Native American pow-wows (festivals), where some of us found like-minded people who were seeking to learn more about their Taíno heritage. It became evident that an organization needed to be created to pull together all the resources that became available once we started to pool our resources. Some of us began researching and disseminating information, and the numbers grew. This is how the Asociación Indígena de Puerto Rico (Indigenous Association of Puerto Rico), or AIPR, was born.

The AIPR started out well, but almost as soon as it was created it became obvious that its focus varied from individual to individual. Some members were more interested in spiritual aspects, others with academic, and still others with the politics of asserting native identity. The group splintered and became two separate entities: the Maisiti Yucayeque Taíno (MYT) and the Taíno Nation. Within the MYT there were family units or subgroups focusing on culture, such as the Arawak Mountain Singers, a group that performed pow-wow-style music at Native American festivals. The Taíno Nation would, in time, encompass the entire Spanish-speaking Caribbean in scope, evolving more into a "tribal government" in that its leaders make decisions on behalf of all Taíno people and represent Taíno peoples internationally. Soon after the formation of the Taíno Nation and its splinter groups, people of Cuban and Dominican extraction in the US also began joining, bringing with them aspects of Taíno culture that had almost disappeared from Puerto Rico due to American assimilation. As of this writing, there are at least 25 Taíno organizations with thousands of members from New York to California and from Florida to Puerto Rico, and the numbers are still growing.

For those of us who identify with our Taíno roots, these are exciting times. For more than two decades, Taínos like me, who live in the US, have been working vigorously to reclaim our Taíno culture and identity. New evidence is mounting to prove that we are who we say we are—and not only are our numbers growing; the movement is also spreading back to our home islands.

We celebrate the fact that we are Taíno, for our common Taíno roots are what make us uniquely Dominican, Puerto Rican, and Cuban. We respect and acknowledge our African and Spanish ancestors as well. Understanding that we have tripartite biological, cultural, and linguistic influences does not subtract from, but rather adds to, our human experience. Our Taíno heritage, however, is what makes us a Native Caribbean people.

Taíno heritage stretches across time, since long before the arrival of the European invaders and the African people they enslaved and brought to our ancestors' islands. In such a way, the European and the African became a part of the native Caribbean. We are Caribbean peoples, and our roots will always be indigenous.

Conclusion: Taíno Survival

Manuel García Arévalo notes that "the persistence of a Taíno genetic component in contemporary Dominican life, along with the survival of certain undeniably indigenous beliefs and traditions (kept alive in rural areas and passed along through oral tradition) requires the recognition of a native substratum in our midst today" (1990, p. 275). Indeed, we believe the tenacity of Taíno cultural expression and biological continuity suggests that a reexamination and reclamation of the Taíno past has finally arrived and that it is spreading in the Dominican Republic.

Most Dominicans who reflect on the Taíno past that they were taught in school and see around them in national heritage programs realize that it is only a partial story of their identity. Taíno cultural forms are basic and integral parts of many Dominicans' everyday lives, so the contradictions taught in schools and in popular culture cause a dissonance. Since it is notoriously difficult to contend with an established nationalistic ideology, this dissonance is relieved through the perpetuation of a distant, romanticized native past.

In the 21st century, even though most former Caribbean colonies are independent nations, an economic dependence on the West has given them "Third World" status. For poor countries, history and archaeology are simply not high priorities, and the job of studying the past often falls to foreigners. Puerto Rican historian Jalil Sued Badillo suggests: "Caribbean historiography is just as poor, neglected, dependent, ideologized, and irrelevant, in other words, colonial, as it manifested itself centuries ago." He continues:

> Academic historiography (archaeology included), as practiced by both natives and non-natives, remains at the margins of the [Caribbean's] cultural debates, and with the exception of Cuba, the dominant historiography is based on archaic textbooks, irrelevant news coverage, and official promotion of ideologized historical festivities, all of which, nonetheless represent a formidable instrument of domination. (1992, pp. 600–601)

North American Indians are now making their political voices heard. Nancy Shoemaker writes: "With European diseases and dispossession of their lands and way of life, Indians came close to not surviving as a people. But they have survived and...are no longer at risk of being remembered in history as the 'vanished' Indians" (1999, p. 103). Dominican educator Antonio de Moya assesses the need for critical thinking in Dominican history, too. He courageously writes in an official educational publication, "the [Taíno] genocide is the big lie of our history...the Dominican Taínos continue to live, 500 years after European contact" (1993, p. 10).

Figure 6: Banner unfolded as part of the "March for Human Dignity" protest, December 5, 1992, commemorating the 500th anniversary of the landing of Columbus on the island of Hispaniola. A referent to the popular Dominican/Catholic St. Michael icon, the image depicts a Taíno figure as the saint, slaying a Columbus figure in place of the devil. Photograph by Pedro Ferbel-Azcarate.

In essence, an admission of Taíno survival is a critique of the state control of history and identity. It is also a critique of colonialism, socioeconomic dependency, and globalization (see Fig. 6). We may conclude that Taíno survival and revival is a reflection of a growing dissatisfaction with the status quo of the state of dependency borne from colonial history in the Caribbean and passed on to the present. We may also conclude it is the movement of a dispossessed people, struggling to reclaim the history and culture that is rightfully theirs. Finally, we may conclude that it is part of a shift in time and consciousness, returning the spirit of a people who were violently encountered by others, forced to a state of restless sleep, and who are now reawakening to a new time where they may be properly grieved, honored, celebrated, and listened to carefully for the wisdom they bring us through their victory in a 500-year-old battle against "extinction."

Notes

1 Peguero claims to have had access to Fuenmayor's documents, perhaps in a private collection, for I (L. Guitar) have not been able to locate a copy of this census in the U.S.A., Spain, or the Dominican Republic.
2 Dr. Luna Calderón passed away in December of 2005.

References

Anderson, B. (1983). *Imagined communities: reflections on the origins and spread of nationalism*. London: Verso.

Blu, K. (1980). *The Lumbee problem*. Cambridge, UK: Cambridge University Press.

Boyd-Bowman, P. (1973). *Patterns of Spanish immigration to the New World (1493–1580)*. Buffalo: State University of New York.

———. (1976). Patterns of Spanish emigration to the Indies until 1600. *Hispanic American Historical Review*, 56(4), 580–604.

Brow, J. (1990). Notes on community, hegemony, and the uses of the past. *Anthropological quarterly*, 63(1), 1–6.

Casas, B. de las. (1992). *A short account of the destruction of the Indies*. London: Penguin.

Clifford, J. (1988). *The predicament of culture: twentieth century ethnography, literature, and art*. Cambridge, MA: Harvard University Press.

Colección de documentos inéditos para la historia de Ibero-América/Hispano-América (CDIA), 15 vols (1925–1937). Madrid: Compañía Ibero-Americana de Publicaciones.

Colección de documentos inéditos relativos al descubrimiento, conquista y organización de las antiguas posesiones españoles en Ultramar (CDIU), Vol. 18 (1885–1932). Madrid: Real Academia de la Historia.

Cook, N.D. (1993). Disease and the depopulation of Hispaniola, 1492–1518. *Colonial Latin American review*, 2(1), 213–245.

Cook, N.D., & Lovell, W.G. (Eds.). (1992). *"Secret judgments of God": Old World diseases in colonial Spanish America*. Norman: University of Oklahoma Press.

Deagan, K. (1985). Spanish-Indian interaction in sixteenth-century Florida and Hispaniola. In *Cultures in contact: the impact of European contacts on Native American cultural institutions*. Washington, DC: Smithsonian Institution Press.

———. (1988). The archaeology of the Spanish contact period in the Caribbean. *Journal of world prehistory*, 2(2), 187–233.

———. (2004). Reconsidering Taíno social dynamics after Spanish conquest: gender and class in culture contact studies. *American antiquity*, 69(4), 597–626.

Deren, M. (1991). *Divine horsemen: the living gods of Haiti*. New York: McPherson.

Ferbel-Azcarate, P.J. (1995). When a canoe means more than a water trough: Taíno Indian heritage in the post-quincentennial Dominican Republic. Unpublished doctoral dissertation, University of Minnesota, Minneapolis.

———. (2002). Not everyone who speaks Spanish is from Spain: Taíno survival in the 21st-century Dominican Republic. *Kacike: Journal of Caribbean Amerindian History and Anthropology*. Retrieved July 10, 2002, from http://www.kacike.org/FerbelEnglish.html.

Forbes, J.D (1993). *Africans and Native Americans: the language of race and the evolution of red-black peoples*. Urbana: University of Illinois Press.

Foster, G.M. (1953). Cofradía and compradrazgo in Spain and Spanish America. *Southwestern journal of anthropology*, 9(1), 1–28.

Galván, M. de J. (1882 [1989]). *Enriquillo*. Santo Domingo: Ediciones de Taller.

García Arévalo, M. (1988). *Indigenismo, arqueología e identidad nacional*. Santo Domingo: Museo del Hombre Dominicano & Fundación García-Arévalo.

———. (1990). Transculturation in contact period and contemporary Hispaniola. In D. H. Thomas (Ed.), *Columbian consequences, Vol. 2* (pp. 269–280). Washington DC: Smithsonian Institution Press.

———. (1992). *Santo Domingo en la ocasión del quinto centenario*. Santo Domingo: Colección del Quinto Centenario.

Guitar, L. (1998). Cultural genesis: telationships among Indians, Africans, and Spaniards in rural Hispaniola, first half of the sixteenth century. Unpublished dissertation for Vanderbilt University, Nashville, TN. Available in microfiche from UMI Dissertation Service, Ann Arbor, MI, No. 9915091.

———. (2000). Criollos: the birth of a dynamic new Indo-Afro-European people and culture on Hispaniola. *Kacike: Journal of Caribbean Amerindian history and anthropology*. Retrieved July 10, 2002, from http://www.kacike.org/LynneGuitar.html.

———. (2002). Documenting the myth of Taíno extinction. *Kacike: Journal of Caribbean Amerindian history and anthropology*. Retrieved July 10, 2002, from www.kacike.org.

———. (2003). Criollos: el nacimiento de la identidad Americana y de la cultura Americana en la Hispaniola. *Boletín del Museo del Hombre Dominicano*, 34, 111–129.

Haslip-Viera, G. (Ed.). (2002). *Taíno revival: critical perspectives on Puerto Rican identity and cultural politics*. Princeton, NJ: Markus Wiener Publications.

Herrera Cabral, C. (1995). *Colección César Herrera, Junta de Procuradores, 1518–1545, Vol. I*. Santo Domingo: Patronato de la Ciudad de Santo Domingo.

Herrera y Tordesillas, A. de (1934; originally 1601). *Historia general de los hechos de los castellanos en las islas y Tierra Firme del Mar Océano*. Madrid: La Academia de la Historia.

Keegan, W.F. (1991). *Earliest Hispanic/Native American interactions in the Caribbean*. New York: Garland Publishing.

Klein, H.S. (1986). *African slavery in Latin America and the Caribbean*. New York: Oxford University Press.

Knight, F.W. (1990). *The Caribbean: the genesis of a fragmented nationalism*. New York: Oxford University Press.

Luna Calderón, F. (2002). Mitochondrial DNA in the Dominican Republic. *Kacike: Journal of Caribbean Amerindian history and anthropology*. Retrieved July 10, 2002, from www.kacike.org.

Marté, R. (1981). *Santo Domingo en los manuscritos de Juan Bautista Muñoz*. Santo Domingo: Ediciones Fundación García-Arévalo.

Martinez Cruzado, J.C. (2002). The use of mitochondrial DNA to discover pre-Columbian migrations to the Caribbean: results from Puerto Rico and expectations from the Dominican Republic. *Kacike: Journal of Caribbean Amerindian History and Anthropology*. Retrieved July 10, 2002, from www.kacike.org.

Martyr D'Anghiera, P. (1989). *Pedro Martir de Angleria, Primer cronista de Indias: décadas del Nuevo Mundo*. Santo Domingo: Sociedad Dominicana de Bibliofilos.

Miller, B.G. (2003) *Invisible indigenes: the politics of nonrecognition*. Lincoln: University of Nebraska Press.

Mira Caballos, E. (1997). *El indio Antillano: repartimiento, encomienda y esclavitud (1492–1542)*. Seville: Ediciones ALFIL.

Moya, E.A. de (1993). Animación sociocultural y polisíntesis en la transformación del sistema educativo dominicano. *La revista de educación*, 1(2), 6–10.

Moya Pons, F. (1992). The politics of forced Indian labor in La Hispaniola, 1493–1520. *Antiquity*, 66, 130–139.

———. (1995). *The Dominican Republic: a national history*. New Rochelle, NY: Hispaniola Books.

Oviedo y Valdez, G. F. de (1959; originally 1535). *Historia general y natural de las Indias, 5 vols. Biblioteca de Autores Españoles, vols. 117–121*. Madrid: Gráficas Orbe.

Pané, Fray R. (1988). *Relación acerca de las antigüedades de los indios*. Santo Domingo: Ediciones de la Fundación Corripio.

Parry, J.H., & Keith, R.J. (1984). *New Iberian world: a documentary history of the discovery and settlement of Latin America to the early seventeenth century, 3 vols*. New York: Times Books.

Peguero, L. J. (1975; originally 1763). *Historia de la conquista de la Isla Española de Santo Domingo trasumptada el año de 1762*. Santo Domingo: Publicaciones del Museo de Las Casas Reales.

Reid, A. (1992). Waiting for Columbus. *The New Yorker*, Feb. 24, n.p.

Rodríguez Demorizi, E. (1971). *Los dominicos y las encomiendas de indios de la Isla Española*. Santo Domingo: Editora del Caribe.

Roosevelt, A.C. (1980). *Parmana: prehistoric maize and manioc subsistence along the Amazon and Orinoco*. New York: Academic Press.

Rouse, I. (1992). *The Taínos: rise and decline of the people who greeted Columbus*. New Haven, CT: Yale University Press.

Sáez, J.L. (1994). *La iglesia y el esclavo negro en Santo Domingo*. Santo Domingo: Patronato de la Ciudad Colonial de Santo Domingo, Colección Quinto Centenario.

Sauer, C.O. (1966). *The early Spanish Main*. Berkeley: University of California Press.

Shoemaker, N. (1999). *American Indian population recovery in the twentieth century*. Albuquerque: University of New Mexico Press.

Sued Badillo, J. (1992). Facing up to Caribbean history. *American antiquity*, 57(4), 599–607.

Utrera, Fray C. de (1973). *Polémica de Enriquillo*. Santo Domingo: Editora del Caribe.

Vega, B. (1981). La herencia indígena en la cultura Dominicana de hoy. In *Ensayos Sobre Cultura Dominicana* (pp. 9–53). Santo Domingo: Museo del Hombre Dominicano.

Verano, J.W., & Ubelaker, D.H. (Eds.). (1992). *Disease and demography in the Americas*. Washington, DC: Smithsonian Institution Press.

Weeks, J.M., & Ferbel, P. (1994). *The ancient Caribbean: research guides to ancient civilizations, vol. 4*. New York: Garland Press.

Wilson, S.M. (1990). *Hispaniola: Caribbean chiefdoms in the age of Columbus*. Tuscaloosa: University of Alabama Press.

※ IDENTITIES ※

Articulating Indigenous Identities and Spaces in the Contemporary Caribbean

Establishing points of reference by which contemporary Carib communities of the Lesser Antilles re-create places to which their identities are tied is one of the main themes that is present in these case studies of Dominica, St. Vincent, and Trinidad. Kelvin Smith explains how the establishment of a tourist-oriented "model village" in Dominica's Carib Territory, a project wrested from Carib hands, has both challenged and enabled the reproduction of Carib identity. The conflicting tendencies between tourist visitation and indigenous self-expression have caused the project to founder. The case is an instructive one for both St. Vincent and Trinidad, which have planned variations of this same model village idea. Paul Twinn tells us of another conflict over space, when a property was sold to a group of Danes, leading to an island-wide debate that encompassed issues not only of Carib identity and identification with the land but also of national integrity. The issues raised by the land sale became entwined within wider discourses of indigenous rights, slavery, and conquest. It also served to refocus national attention on a group of people who had hitherto been marginalized within the nation state. Ricardo Bharath Hernandez, chief of the Santa Rosa Carib Community of Arima, Trinidad, and Maximilian Forte outline the ways that Carib reinterpretations of the history of the former Mission of Arima, coupled with diverse programs for maintaining and reviving traditions, have served to reproduce Carib identity with Arima as its home.

✳ CHAPTER FOUR ✳

Placing the Carib Model Village: The Carib Territory and Dominican Tourism

Kelvin Smith

The Caribbean has been a place of production and consumption for the past five centuries. In a series of industries, coffee, sugar and fruit have been exported across the Atlantic, whilst the imagery of nature, exoticism and luxury have become standardized motifs and icons of literature and Western discourse (Sheller, 2003). In recent years, however, a reemphasis has taken place, redefining it from a region of production and trade into a space of leisure (Pattullo, 1996, pp. 4–8). This has been manifest in the European and global trade agreements of the 1990s that have undermined the banana industry of the Lesser Antilles. Like neighboring islands, having been brought to the point of economic collapse,[1] Dominica has had to look to tourism as an answer to the island's difficulties, a move supported and encouraged by international aid agencies (International Monetary Fund, 2003). With tourism, however, the consumer has been brought into the region—guided around the islands to directly purchase, experience and take in the scenery and people. This consumption is more immediate, heightening in some cases the evident disparities of wealth and power (Pattullo, 1996), but also suggesting the opportunity for a possible dialogue between producers and consumers. For communities who wish to express particular ideas of their past, the heritage center or cultural museum, whilst remaining an economic transaction, has also contained the hope of communicating local understandings of history and identity. As part of the proclamation of their indigeneity, therefore, heritage sites have been built or proposed by communities on St. Vincent (see Twinn, this volume), Trinidad (see Bharath & Forte, this volume) and the Carib Territory of Dominica.

Macdonald argues that such sites give a text written by the community. Through analysis of the construction and selection of what is displayed, she suggests, an insight into the framing of local identity and its performance can be gained (Macdonald, 1997, p. 155). In the case of the Carib Model Village, situated on Dominica, however, it is its silence that must be read. Despite having its own history of proposals and draft documents going back to the early 1970s, following its completion in 2002, the site has never been used. The presentation of an indigenous cultural identity has continued at other sites, through performances by the Territory's two cultural groups[2] and individually run cassava and canoe building workshops.[3] In the meantime, craft vendors, in a bid to grab the attention of passing tourists, have built small *mouina*, traditional Carib huts, or "trash houses" made from wooden poles and leaves. It is apparent that the community is not opposed to the tourist industry or to the presence of its cultural identity within that economy, yet all these practices and economic exchanges circumnavigate the resource that was purportedly built to assist the community in these goals.

To understand the text of the Model Village it is necessary to look beyond, at the histories, identities and economic developments that locate the site, both physically and socially. To use an idea from Appadurai (1996), we can see the Village lying on various "scapes": ethnic, financial or technological. Rather than a single expression of the community, the Village is understood as seen from varied perspectives and within differing contexts. This is not a call, however, to move beyond the bounded place of the Model Village to an analysis of global interconnectedness (see Gupta & Ferguson, 1997). The theoretical descriptions of global flows, mobilities and networks have a tendency to adopt such a high vantage point that they overlook that people live their lives and grow their crops and construct their social relations in limited, tangible places. It is the lives and day-to-day economic realities of the Carib community that concern this chapter, but with the understanding of how national and global, political and economic factors can structure, shape and frame their way of life.

The discussion in this chapter moves down to the Model Village through a series of spaces. From looking at Dominica as a tourist destination, we turn to creation of the Carib Territory as a Carib area and the development of the Carib identity, before engaging with the Carib Model Village as both a tourist site and possible place for the articulation of a community identity. In this way, the Model Village provides a vantage point from which to appreciate, in part, the world in which the Caribs live.[4]

Image, Space and Place

As cheap flights and low-cost airlines have made travel available for much of the Western world, so tourism has grown. The outcome is a market in which cities, regions and nations must now advertise themselves as destinations (MacCannell, 1999, pp. 194–195). Dominica, as such a destination, has had to reengage with the world, therefore, through the medium of image and advertising. Seeking to turn its underdevelopment to its advantage, the tourist literature tag line is that Dominica is the "Nature Island of the Caribbean":

> Beautiful, dramatic angles are everywhere. Energetic rivers run vigorously. Dynamic forests remain untouched. When you first ride through the countryside, the uncompromising beauty of the island-rolling hills, secluded coastlines, virgin woods, will make you feel as if you're at the end of the world. Dominica is without doubt, "The Nature Island of the Caribbean." So come and explore or simply bask in nature's simple pleasures. (Dominica Division of Tourism, 2004)

The motifs of purity, nature and the untouched landscape, coastline and waters echo the words found in Jefferys' promotional atlas of 1775:

> Its appearance is rugged and mountainous, especially towards the sea: but the ascents are commonly easy... and the inner part contains very rich vallies with several fine plains.... The island [is] watered by a great number of rivers full of fish and...the climate is remarkably hot even for this part of the world, though the air is pure and very thin, which circumstance has given the country the reputation of being healthy.... There are besides several springs of mineral waters, whose virtues are extolled for several disorders. (Jefferys, 1775, p. 21)

In both passages, Dominica is a land of health, beauty and nature; the otherworldly paradise that has been a feature of European writing on the Caribbean since Columbus (Sheller, 2003). The scene Jefferys depicts, however, is meant to promote the island as a scene for colonization and development. This is the beginning of history, he suggests, for the island. In contrast, the Dominican Division of Tourism seeks to present an island that has never seen development, one that is separate from the history that developed, deforested and "civilized" the rest of the Caribbean. Not only, as Wiley reports (1998), does this gloss over the infrastructure, such as hydropower plants, that make the island available for tourists, but in the presentation of a virgin land of the past, the history that has created that wilderness of today is ignored. The Carib resistance to the French and British colonization; the slave resistance during the Maroon wars; the postemancipation resistance to estate labor and the political resistance to Crown rule by the Colored Ascendancy are all aspects of Dominica's past that have influenced and impacted upon the development of the island (Honychurch, 1995). None of this, however, is acknowledged. As MacCannell argues, having denied the grand narratives of modernity, and thereby its history of exploitation and genocide, "the central drive of postmodernity is to stop history in its tracks, and the central drive of postmodern tourism is to discover places that seem to exist outside of history: unspoiled nature and savagery" (MacCannell, 1992, p. 26). Dominica, in its reincarnation as the Nature Island, therefore, is also an island that places itself outside history.

The emphasis upon nondevelopment has meant that the island's tourism has developed along two paths. The stay-over visitors are "ecotourists," interested in hiking to the waterfalls, hot springs and mountain views throughout the island and visiting its noted diving sites. The majority of the island's visitors, however, are cruise ship passengers, for whom Dominica is one island on an itinerary of stops down the Caribbean chain. The luxury of the ship compensates for the lack of facilities onshore. Once on the island, the overwhelming practice, for both cruise and ecotourists, is to tour the island in daylong excursions. Despite the image of nondevelopment, modern technologies of movement are integral to Dominican tourism as minibuses or hired four-by-fours circle the island from either hotel or berth. The landscape is to be toured through in journeys that connect places where nature can be further experienced: waterfalls and springs to bathe in, vistas to contemplate or reefs to be dived. Each site is consumable within a few hours, thus allowing the movement on to the next site and for the journey to be completed within the timeframe of a day. Not only, therefore, is Dominica clearly defined as a conceived space, to use Lefebvre's phrase, as "The Nature Island," but it is also a perceived space of spatial practice (Lefebvre, 1991, pp. 38–39). Time and space on Dominica are dominated by the movement and flow of tourists through a suggested pristine landscape.

Heritage, Community and the Territory

The *Lonely Planet* guide for Dominica (Anglin, Bedford, Ingmanson, McKinnon, & Schechter, 2001) presents, as it journeys around the island, the Carib Territory as a "Place to See." It is, we are told, an area on the less populated eastern coast of roughly 3,700 acres and "home to most of Dominica's 3,000 Carib Indians." Bold type emphasizes the Salybia church and L'Escalier Tête Chien rock formation at Sineku as sights to be visited. A paragraph explains that basket making and canoe building occur in the Territory and a price range of US$5–US$30 for a basket is suggested. The Territory, however, is not a "Place to Stay" or a "Place to Eat" and so, having seen and bought, we are guided on and eventually back round to the hotels on the west coast.

As the guide's qualifier, "most of," highlights, there are various communities along Dominica's eastern coast that can claim, in part, an indigenous past. Following British colonization in 1763, however, the cartographic label *Caribs* and the region designation *Carib Quarter* was only applied to the area surrounding Salybia Bay. Still in use a hundred years later, it was this label, rather than known cultural practices, that guided the first anthropologists to the region (Ober, 1880; Bell, 1902). To their dismay, they found that much of the indigenous way of life, recorded in precolonization accounts, had disappeared. Even greater consternation was leveled, however, at the marriages and liaisons with the surrounding Black communities that had occurred over the previous hundred years. In 1903, therefore, the Carib Reserve, the official title of the Territory, was created for the express purpose of maintaining the Carib community as distinct, both culturally and racially.

Although there is evidence of its use prior to the establishment of the Reserve,[5] the self-identification of the community as "Carib" has grown in strength over the hundred years that the Reserve has now been in existence. Initially the defining of the region and giving official recognition to the Chief, gave the community a manner and means by which to articulate its concerns and grievances to the national authorities. In 1930, this came to a head in a violent altercation known as the Carib War,[6] following which the post of Chief was removed from the Reserve until 1953. By the early 1970s, however, Owen argued that a social and political Carib identity had developed, drawing upon the distinct institutions of the Carib Reserve and the Chief to define a difference for the community within Dominican society (Owen, 1974). This continued into the 1980s with a renewed interest in the region's indigenous and Carib past. Traditional crafts, as mentioned by the *Lonely Planet*, were re-adopted and relearned within a rediscovery of a Carib "heritage" (Frederick, 1983; Gregoire, Henderson, & Kanem, 1996), whilst a sense of the community's permanence and right to the land, as indigenous people, was highlighted in the informal name change from Carib "Reserve" to "Territory."

Carib culture, a Territory activist explained to me, is like a Ford car: always appearing as a new model, but remaining in essence a Ford. This view confronts the idea that the Carib culture can be lost through the disappearance of certain practices or racial features, but maintains its objective and historical continuance. Attempts to present such linear and essentialist connections to practices, beliefs and communities of the past, have been viewed by some, as the "invention" of culture (Hobsbawm & Ranger, 1983; Linnekin, 1983). Certainly, the literary and historic analysis of the region's indigeneity shows the "Carib Indian" to have been a colonial construct, feeding into European discourses of a monstrous Other and legitimating the actions taken against a supposed uncivilized savage (Hulme, 1986; Sued Badillo, 1995). As Hulme notes, however, with reference to Baker's application of this invention critique to the Caribs (Baker, 1988), the error has been to recognize the invention process as only the preserve of indigenous groups (Hulme, 2000, pp. 288–290). The creation and articulation of an identity is a universal process, in which all communities are involved in the dynamic understanding and utilization of the past in a way that is meaningful and relevant to its present situation. The emphasis shifts from reading the identity against the validity of its references, to the contexts in which it is created and proclaimed (Friedman, 1992, p. 856). The Carib identity is seen, therefore, against the backdrop of the indigenous rights movement, in particular North American Indian activism and the parallel regional articulations of Black, and more recently Creole, heritages (Honychurch, 1997, p. 215; Hulme, 2000, pp. 261–262).

In a much more grounded way, however, identity is also a product of the economic and day-to-day situation of the community. The rise of Carib identity is tied to the relationship the community has to the land and space, as much as to its perception of history. The land in the Territory is held in common, being available to all residents. Clearing, cultivating and maintaining a garden establishes a particular and sole right to use of that land, which remains unless *grand bwa* (tall wood) returns. Labor is generally supplied by the immediate family, although a *koudmen* (work party), involving extended family members and other individuals, is used for major tasks.[7] By planting fruit trees, or coconuts, a land claim can be maintained, as any tree that an individual has planted, and the fruit that it produces, remains that individual's property. There are, therefore, areas of land held by extended families that have been handed down for generations, as well as complex interrelations of land being worked by one individual, but with the tree crop going to another. The garden provides, therefore, a focal point for family and community relationships, as well as holding practical and symbolic meanings of independent livelihood.

For Lefebvre, this sense of community is the lived space of the area:

> space as directly lived through its associated images and symbols, and hence the space of "inhabitants" and "users," but also of some artists and perhaps of those, such as a few writers and philosophers, who describe and aspire to do no more than describe. (Lefebvre, 1991, p. 39)

As he then notes, this space forms a triad, with the perceived and conceived spaces dominating. Not only is the lived space defined and represented from outside the community, but the community can only articulate itself through the overarching motifs of the perceived and conceived spaces (Lefebvre, 1991, pp. 38–39). The Carib Reserve, therefore, was an imposed conception of the Salybia region that defined the community as Caribs, but in doing so, also provided a means for the community to express itself. The Reserve itself fitted into a conceived idea of Dominica as divided into large stretches of estate or Crown land.

From the 1950s, however, the emphasis shifted to the managed collection of produce, predominantly bananas, grown by individual growers, which was then exported or, to a limited extent, processed on the island. This agricultural industry was marked, therefore, by an independence and autonomy it gave to each community and grower. In many ways, this profited the companies, by ensuring that the costs and difficulties of production were shouldered by the grower (Grossman, 1998). Trouillot, however, notes that the ready access to marginal land, outside the viability of the estate economy, had already enabled a valued independence within Dominican socioeconomic life. The banana, and similar industries, he suggests, thrived because of the support they gave to the growers' valued independence (Trouillot, 1988). The defining space and practice on Dominica under agricultural production has therefore been of networked, independent communities moving produce out from their gardens to central sites, be they the regional banana boxing plant or the Roseau market. The agricultural spatial framework therefore took the Carib Reserve and incorporated it into its own need for community run areas of production. The timing of the authorities' reinstatement of the Chief in 1953 coincides with the shift of economic policy away from the estates, whilst the integration was consolidated by the construction of a new road through the region in the late 1960s. The community's willingness to be part of this exercise is highlighted by the request made early on for "economic plants" (Administrator's visit, 1953, p. 51). By the 1980s, large forest clearances had taken place, the environmental effects of which are only now being realized.

The industry, however, through this greater use of the land, also encouraged a greater cohesion of the community. Not only was more land brought into and kept in production, but by doing so the interactions and structures of community and kinship were extended and strengthened. The agricultural industry also brought the Territory into the network of producing communities, against which it could define itself. Crucially for the Caribs, however, this dominant conception of the island did not contain an ascription of ethnicity and thereby did not replace the spatial idea of the Carib Reserve. In line with this nonascription, attempts were made in the 1960s to eradicate the aberration of the Carib Reserve (Owen, 1974, pp. 99–106). The authorities' lack of success in this policy can be seen, however, as derived from the lack of an alternative ethnic description of space. The conceived economic space merely had no purpose for Carib indigeneity, rather than a direct challenge to it. The agricultural space of the island in the postwar years has therefore provided the ground from which the Carib identity could grow. It strengthened and extended the social structures of the community, whilst giving it a relative independence. Most importantly, it did not attempt to reconceive the Salybia region, thus enabling the Carib sociopolitical identity already developing from the Carib Reserve's supposed cultural and racial demarcation of space, to further establish itself.

The development of tourism means more than just a change in the economy. It redefines the space of the island and thereby the manner in which the Caribs, as a community, can be understood and can express themselves. The tourist literature has shifted to a representation of the Caribs' indigeneity as one that can inhabit the natural, ahistoric landscape. The promise is of an exotic Other, a mainstay of the tourist experience (Craik, 1997, p. 114). Furthermore, as we have seen, the tourist spatial framework shifts away from a regional and network framing of space, within which the Carib Territory has been able to find a place, to one based on sites and locations within linear movement around the island. The challenge is for the Caribs to maintain a viable and useful identity as the economic framing of space is reconfigured. The Carib Model Village is therefore a manifestation of this time of economic change and the reworking of the notion of "Carib."

Performance, Politics and the Carib Model Village

In the same manner that the Carib Territory was incorporated into the agricultural spatial framework, so the Carib Model Village is a previous concept that has been co-opted for the tourism industry. The idea for a "Carib Indian Village," as a site for the Caribs to demonstrate and sell their crafts as well as display their heritage, first appeared in 1972. Based on his own experience of North American Indian tourist villages, Arthur Einhorn, then a visiting anthropologist, drew up a proposal for a similar venture in the Carib Territory (Einhorn, 1972). Einhorn claims, however that the concept was already envisaged by various individuals in the Territory, both collectively and separately (personal communication, July 2, 2004). Indeed, the year prior to Einhorn's proposal Chief Faustulus Frederick had published *In Our Carib Indian Village*; a child's description of the traditional practices of the Territory (Frederick & Shepherd, 1971). Developed out of this book, Frederick's own 1976 proposal for a "Carib Cultural Village," was taken up by the International Labor Organization in 1982, whose professional consultancy team prepared a report outlining recommendations for the project's further development (International Labor Organization, 1982). Although it made its way through various report stages, the project stagnated in the late 1980s due to lack of funds. In 1994, however, the Model Village was revived as part of the Upgrading of Ecotourism Sites Project (UESP), a Caribbean Development Bank initiative, which sought to provide loans for improvements to five tourist sites around the country. Work began in 1998 for an eventual cost of EC$860,000, with an extra EC$721,000 needed for the access road (Honychurch, 1997, pp. 213–214; Cowater International Inc., 1998).[8] The original community project, envisaged as a means to give an understanding of the surrounding region, was thereby reconceived into a distinct site within the tourist's experience of the island. This consolidated the craft shops, demonstration workshops, cultural performances and places of interest spread across the Territory that required the tour buses to make several stops. Instead, the model Village provided a single accessible site that allowed for the continued movement around the island.

Furthermore, as Eguchi has pointed out, Carib tourism has been, in the past, a problematic concept for the government. Historically, the island's authorities have been resistant to the Caribs' increasingly vocal demands for social and political recognition, seeing it as conflicting with the need to build a unified nation (Owen, 1974; Gregoire et al., 1996). Given this antagonism to the Carib identity, the necessary promotion of a distinct, culturally different Carib community within tourist advertising has created a dilemma for government policy. On the one hand there is the wish to enable tourism in the Carib Territory and on the other the desire to curb any basis for Carib separatism (Eguchi, 1997, pp. 374–376). The Carib Model Village, however, provided the opportunity for a separation of these elements into the Carib Territory as the setting of Carib identity and the Carib Model Village as the place of Carib imagery and tourism. This distinction between the space of the Carib community and the Carib site of tourism is apparent in the construction of the Village and its access road.

The Village was built around the Crayfish River Falls within a band of disused land created in the 1960s when the construction of the new road, approximately 500 meters above the previous dirt road, caused the gardens and houses to shift up the ridge. At present, apart from a single home next to the car park, there are no houses visible from the Village and it is the bush of long overgrown gardens that encroach onto the site. Whilst a tourist consultant that I spoke to expressed delight at the "lovely situation," others have noted that the site is secluded away from the community and the public road. For the stall holders presently set out beside the road at Point to relocate would require daily transport for their goods, whilst losing the passing trade on which they rely. Inhabitants in Sineku, Mahaut River and the Concord valley, all situated at far ends of the Territory, are especially cynical about the relevance of the Model Village for their livelihoods.

The access road to the Village only serves to reemphasize the distance between the community and the site. It is a steep climb of a mile and a half up the access road, built along the path of the old road, until it reaches the new road at Point. Used to only building access roads to gardens, the contractors did not recognize the different demands of tourist use. The access road, therefore, is only wide enough for one vehicle or light four-by-four traffic, as would be needed for access to a hillside garden. The road cannot accommodate the two-way flow of buses and hired jeeps of the tourists. The twists and turns, in fact, make the road impassable for the larger 'coaster' buses. The attempt to apply the infrastructure from the agricultural space onto the Model Village has only served to demonstrate the different practices and movement that the site demands. The long-term solution to this problem, however, as expressed by those involved in the project, is the extension of the access road further along the old road to Bataka. At present, this is no more than a barely visible path. This route would allow, it was explained to me, the tourist buses to complete a circuit from Bataka, to the Model Village, up the present access road to Point and back round to Bataka via the Horse Back Ridge. The flow and constant movement of this plan contrasts with the static nature previously assumed within the road's construction. This route, however, would further bypass to a large extent the Carib community. Although there are houses along the path of the proposed road, the main areas of habitation would still be hidden behind trees and further up the ridge. Rather than increasing the connection to the community, the planned road would maintain the reality of Territory life at a distance in order to promote the movement of the tourists through an image of nature, nondevelopment and seclusion.

Finally, as a government-run development project, the construction of the Carib Model Village was put out for competitive tendering. As no Carib had the financial resources to make a bid, this effectively excluded all Caribs from the building of their own project. Not only did this curtail any financial return or sense of involvement for the community, but it also severed the means by which the site, as a geographical place, could be established as a social part of the Territory. It is through the social and communal work needed to construct or maintain any garden or building that a place is brought into the social life of the Territory and given a place within the networks of the community. By using outside contractors this necessary inclusion process did not take place. Furthermore, many Caribs, when discussing the Village, raise the complaint that the contractors failed to cut the timber at dark moon. Local knowledge dictates that timber, unless it is cut at this period, will quickly rot. For the Caribs, the current disrepair of the Village, therefore, is directly attributed to this error. Not only is Carib labor missing from the project, the complaint suggests, but also the socially understood methods of construction have been excluded, making it a construction that could never have been built by Caribs.

The Model Village does not build, therefore, upon the existing structures of the Territory, but is instead deliberately located away from them. It has demanded construction methods and an infrastructure at odds with the agriculture-based practices currently employed in the Territory. It lies beyond the practical limits of the community, screening off the inhabitants' houses. Even the means by which the Model Village could be perceived as within the community have been severed. Instead, it sits within the tourist space of imagery and movement that is being laid over the island. It appropriates the image, not the lived spatial practices, of the community and thus creates a greater distance and domination over the lives of the community.

With the community marginalized, the government has been able to ensure a degree of control over the Model Village. Although a Carib Project Manager was appointed in 2002, ultimate authority for the Carib Model Village has remained with the Minister for Tourism. The government has been further strengthened by the heightened role, as a central enabling and coordinating body, which the tourist industry confers on it. Not only is there a need to construct and present a unified image of the island, but the economy depends upon an interdependence between sites and communities. If tourists travel to the Carib site, then visitor numbers at other sites along the journey may also be increased. Unlike previous industries, tourism demands the island's economy to be conceptualized and managed as a national project, a point underlined when the Minister of Tourism is reported as wishing that the Carib Model Village would "engender and foster a sense of pride, hope and a sense of nationalism among the Carib people" (Auguiste, 2000, n.p.).

The picture painted of Carib tourism by Lennox Honychurch, however, appears to acknowledge and embrace such a disconnection of community and image. Discussing the Caribs' production of tourist imagery, he questions the assumed reference by many writers of imagery and displays of indigeneity to any "truth" or reality. The Caribs, he argues, are not bound by the need to present statements of themselves or their community that can be externally validated, but instead are self-consciously able to create cultural narratives that have a use in their present economic situation.

> The Caribs...are rejecting the premising and privileging of visual truth, preferring to use the poetics of image and object, metaphor and quotation drawn from the past and set in the present, to achieve some economic advantage from those whose preconceived ideas of Caribness "buy into" the fantasies of popular consumption. (Honychurch, 1997, p. 65)

The recognition that indigenous people need to work within and through dominant discourses is important (see Lattas, 1993). Performance and the display of indigeneity have been, and remain, a major element in the development of the Carib heritage. Cultural activism remains focused around the Karifuna and the Karina Cultural Groups, both of which have dance troupes that perform songs and dances, based on perceived indigenous practices, for the tourists and at community events. The gearing of the performances to their audience is undeniable, with English lyrics adopted, for instance, for American coach parties.

It is equally important to realize that, as Friedman has pointed out, mutable, polyphonic concepts of identity are generally held only by academics. Identity for most people is real and nonnegotiable (Friedman, 1992). Honychurch's suggested self-conscious packaging of the Carib heritage appears to forget that, for the Caribs, there is an authenticity, or "Carib essence," that they believe exists. The recognition, as some Caribs acknowledged to me, that adopting particular forms of dress, or language, is profitable is not a basis for empowerment. Instead it highlights the conflict, as noted by Hulme, between the desire of the Carib community to represent itself, against the economic pressure to conform to preconceived ideas of "Carib" and "Indian" (Hulme, 2001, pp. 296–297). The question becomes how far the Caribs, as with anyone, would be willing to compromise the notion of themselves purely for economic advantage.

The further suggestion that it is possible to usurp or "exploit" (Honychurch, 1997, p. 65) Western discourses must also be treated with caution. Honychurch's claim that the Caribs have a control over the production and marketing of their imagery repeats the argument presented for video making by the Kayapo in Amazonia (Turner, 1992). As Faris counterargued at the time, the reception, distribution and definition of imagery and concepts surrounding indigeneity are ultimately accomplished by Western audiences and actors. The adoption of identities or imagery that appeals to these audiences thereby also imposes the limits on actions and practices understood by those audiences. As predicted, when their modern lifestyles and economic practices became apparent, the supposedly exotic Amazonian groups fell from political favor (Faris, 1993; Conklin & Graham, 1995). In the same manner, adopting or conforming to tourists' ideas of the Caribs can only bring a comparison with the reality of life in the Territory. Whilst the community now understands and expresses itself as a distinct indigenous group, for the passing traveler, more than ever before, the community appears to be, like the rest of the country, a community of French Creole-speaking, church-going, peasant farmers. By holding up, and even promoting, a mythic image of a pristine Carib way of life located at the tourist site, the space of the Carib Territory can only be read as a loss of culture, or an inauthenticity. The Territory is therefore made into a diminished Carib space, undermining the proclaimed sociopolitical Carib difference. In the meantime, the Carib site, under government stewardship, becomes the focal point of Caribness on the island.

The creation of a Carib tourist product cannot move away, therefore, from the concept of authenticity. Both the tourists and Caribs look for their interactions to be based upon some "truth" of the indigenous history and life in the Territory. The reference for that truth and authenticity, however, shifts under the influence of the tourist industry. The Caribs' claims of indigeneity were previously made to express a strengthened notion of community in terms derived from a colonial ascription of the local region. The "vestige" (Taylor, 1938, p. 109) of indigeneity found in practices, beliefs and myths by prewar anthropologists was reconceptualized as the "Carib essence" of the Carib activists. The reference point was therefore a personal understanding that individuals in the region had of themselves. Unlike the agricultural industry, however, tourism has ascribed an ethnicity to the Salybia region, setting up an image of Carib indigeneity to which the community must relate. Rather than expressing the internally held belief in their Carib indigeneity, the community is now expected to demonstrate their relationship to this external image.

The satisfying of this image, however, creates a particular role for the Carib community, as outlined by the Minister for Tourism:

> This project is to foster a significant increase in the number of visitors... to the Carib Territory, who will need food, guides, accommodation, souvenirs, transportation and other services. (cited in Auguiste, 2000)

The community is seen as performers, service providers, guides and workers for the producing and fulfillment of the tourist experience that is centered upon the Carib Model Village project. The division of site and community is, therefore, a separation of labor and the place of production. Rather than the Model Village providing economic opportunities for the community, the Village uses the community.

In many ways, there is a resemblance in the spatial practice of peripheral village and a central site, with the estate economy envisaged in the mid-19th century postemancipation period. In both situations the community is seen as sustaining itself through limited agriculture whilst providing a labor force for the exporting site of production. In this case, the production of the tourist experience is undertaken at the Model Village. Trouillot has detailed, however, how the estate system was undermined by the refusal of the labor force to lose their independence to the constraints of wage labor. With marginal land available across the island, many simply founded self-sufficient livelihoods away from the estates. Those that remained, over a period of time, were able to negotiate the adoption of various sharecropping systems that maintained an independence and autonomy from direct estate control (Trouillot, 1988, pp. 69–97). The dominating space of the estate economy was, therefore, circumnavigated, challenged and subverted.

This, we can argue, is the fate of the Carib Model Village. The community has refused to lose control of their production and labor. The Territory has provided the space in which the Caribs can attempt to maintain control of their tourist production, manifest in the various workshops, stalls and performance areas of the Territory. Others, however, have moved further into the industry, taking jobs as tour guides for the minibus parties. In this nonprescribed role, as one guide explained, there is the opportunity to give a greater picture of Carib and Dominican life. As with the sharecroppers, they seek to enter into the economy on their own terms. As has occurred in the past, the Caribs are challenging and subverting the structures of the dominating industry, both by creating new locations away from the logic of the tourist space and by taking up empowering roles within the industry. Whether the future is to continue with this contest between community and site, or whether some reconciliation is possible, remains to be seen.

Conclusion

For Bourdieu, collective identities and expressions are becoming increasingly difficult within the global neoliberal project. The development of global institutions, such as the International Monetary Fund, he contends, has promoted the realization of economic theory over the recognition of social reality. When combined with the rise in the mobility of people and capital, the result has been an ethos of high marketplace flexibility and competition, antagonistic to any barriers or constraints. Bourdieu's discussion centers upon the industrialized West, and therefore points to the rise in individual contracts and work responsibility as part of the undermining of the working collectivities that have in past sort to safeguard workplace conditions (Bourdieu, 1998). It is the same process, however, in the Carib Territory. The demand is for a flexible transition to a new economy that can attract and divert the flows of people and money. Whilst previous industries constructed, in various ways, the idea of a Carib collectivity, tourism fragments it; identity is divided from image and the community from production. Finally, the Model Village, not only denigrates the collectivity of the Caribs, but also, in its need for select displays of Carib craft, brings an emphasis upon individual artisans and performers.

What is apparent is that to discuss cultural identity as "articulations" and "texts" can suggest a level of agency that does not exist. Such metaphors give an author and an audience, but by abstracting the world into language and communication, can neglect the social, economic and political structuring of the world. The language of identity and the expression of communities are constrained, limited and determined by the dominating structures of the world in which those communities exist. Each industry in the Caribbean has reshaped the islands, defining the means in which locations, histories and identities can be imagined. The debate over the constructed nature of identity and culture turns, therefore, not to the politics employed by indigenous activists, or to imagined communities, but rather to the role of socioeconomic contexts in shaping and defining possible cultural articulations.

Notes

1   The establishment of the European Union and the World Trade Organization in the early 1990s brought an end to the preferential trade agreements upon which the Eastern Caribbean banana industry was based. Attempts have been made to concentrate on the organic and fair-trade markets, but this has required, on Dominica, a focusing of efforts onto a limited number of large producers (Sandiford, 2000).

2   The Karifuna Cultural Group was established in the late 1970s, whilst the Karina Cultural Group formed in the early 1990s. Both incorporate dance and song performances into their promotion of Carib indigeneity, the Karina performing in their purpose-built "Karina Cultural Village" in Bataka, whilst the Karifuna use the Resource Centre recently built in

Sineku. Both groups have toured abroad with their shows. *Karifuna* and *Karina* are self-identifiers of Caribbean indigeneity drawn from 17th century French missionary ethnography. Along with *Kalinago*, these are terms used by activists when presenting an indigenous identity. The term *Carib* is used in this paper as it remains the identification given and understood within general day-to-day life in the Territory.

3   During my fieldwork, Napoleon Sanford erected a traditional-style demonstration hut for his canoe building, whilst Daniel Frederick maintained a cassava-processing hut nearby. Another cassava hut was being constructed opposite the Sineku Resource Centre as I left.

4   A further vantage point is provided my fieldwork in the Carib Territory, from February to August 2003, as part of an ESRC-funded Ph.D. program. I wish to thank all those who gave their time, thoughts and energy in assisting my research and express appreciation at the generosity and hospitality I experienced.

5   The period between the late 18th century and the turn of the 19th century is notable for a lack of references to the Caribs. A handful of letters written by Catholic priests working in the Salybia region in the mid-19th century give a few details of interest. In 1892, two rival chiefs sent letters to a Royal Commission based in Dominica, requesting services and support for the community. All these, and other documents are collected in Hulme & Whitehead (1992).

6   On September 19, 1930, a group of policemen, in an unprecedented move, raided two houses in the Reserve, seizing tobacco, rum and other unlicensed goods, and arresting both James Lessainte and Madame Titwa (Ester Frederick). In the commotion that ensued, the police opened fire, killing two men and wounding three others. The crowd in response forcefully chased the police out of the Reserve. The island's Administrator responded by deploying the warship *HMS Delhi* and a contingent of marines to the Reserve. Seven Carib were arrested, as well as Chief Thomas John, but all were acquitted at trial. Thomas John was however removed from office, leaving the Territory without an officially recognized chief (Hulme & Whitehead, 1992, pp. 281–298; Honychurch, 1997, pp. 183–187; Hulme, 2000, pp. 155–192).

7   A *koudmen* involves gathering a group of workers, who are then provided with rum, cigarettes and food during the day. Cash payment, however, is now also used. The Caribs have problems securing development loans as the communal land system means they do not own land that can be put up as collateral. Furthermore, I was told that banks, having requested receipts, refuse to countenance the purchase of rum, as needed for a *koudmen*, with the money they have loaned.

8   The East Caribbean dollar is presently fixed at an exchange rate of EC$1.00 = US$2.69. The cost of the Model Village was therefore around US$320,000 or UK£210,000.

References

The administrator's visit to the Carib Reserve. (1953, March). *Dominica Welfare News*, 50–51.

Anglin, K., Bedford, N., Ingmanson, M., McKinnon, R., & Schechter, D. (2001). *Lonely planet: Eastern Caribbean*. 3rd ed. Melbourne, Australia: Lonely Planet Publications.

Appadurai, A. (1996). *Modernity at large: cultural dimensions of globalization*. Minneapolis: University of Minnesota Press.

Auguiste, M. (2000, June 30). $M model village for Carib people. *The Chronicle*. N.p.

Baker, P.L. (1988). Ethnogenesis: the case of the Dominica Caribs. *América Indígena*, 48(2), 377–401.

Bell, H. (1902). *Report on the Caribs of Dominica*. (Report No. 21 Dominica). London: His Majesty's Stationery Office.

Bourdieu, P. (1998, December). The essence of neoliberalism: utopia of endless exploitation. *Le Monde diplomatique*. N.p.

Conklin, B.A., & Graham, L.R. (1995). The shifting middle ground: Amazonian Indians and eco-politics. *American Anthropologist*, 97(4), 695–710.

Cowater International Inc. (1998). *Community development programme for the Carib Territory, Dominica*. Bridgetown, Barbados: Caribbean Development Bank.

Craik, J. (1997). The culture of tourism. In C. Rojek & J. Urry (Eds.), *Touring cultures: transformations of travel and theory* (pp. 113–136). London: Routledge.

Dominica Division of Tourism. (2004). *Official website of Dominica*. Retrieved July 29, 2004, from http://www.dominica.dm.

Eguchi, N. (1997). Ethnic tourism and reconstruction of the Caribs' ethnic identity. In J.M. Carrión (Ed.), *Ethnicity, race and nationality in the Caribbean* (pp. 364–380). San Juan, Puerto Rico: Institute of Caribbean Studies, University of Puerto Rico.

Einhorn, A.C. (1972). *Proposal for development of a Carib 'Indian Village' and the economic development of the Carib Indian Reserve on the island of Dominica, British West Indies*. Held by the Tunubuku reference library, Carib Reserve, Dominica.

Faris, J. (1993). A response to Terence Turner. *Anthropology Today*, 9(1), 12–13.

Frederick, F., & Shepherd, E. (1971). *In our Carib village*. New York: Lothrop, Lee & Shepard.

Frederick, H. (1983). *The Caribs and their colonizers: the problem of land*. London: EAFORD.

Friedman, J. (1992). The past in the future: history and the politics of identity. *American Anthropologist*, 94(4), 837–859.

Gregoire, C., Henderson, P., & Kanem, N. (1996). Karifuna: the Caribs of Dominica. In R. Reddock (Ed.), *Ethnic minorities in Caribbean society* (pp. 107–365). St. Augustine: University of West Indies.

Grossman, L.S. (1998). *The political ecology of bananas: contract farming, peasants, and agrarian change in the Eastern Caribbean*. Chapel Hill: University of North Carolina Press.

Gupta, A., & Ferguson, J. (Eds.). (1997). *Culture, power, place: explorations in critical anthropology*. Durham, NC: Duke University Press.

Hobsbawm, E.J., & Ranger, T. (Eds.). (1983). *The invention of tradition*. Cambridge, UK: Cambridge University Press.

Honychurch, L. (1995). *The Dominica story: a history of the island*. London: Macmillan.

———. (1997). *Carib to Creole: a history of contact and culture exchange*. Unpublished doctoral dissertation: University of Oxford.

Hulme, P. (1986). *Colonial encounters: Europe and the native Caribbean, 1492–1797*. London: Methuen.

———. (2000). *Remnants of conquest: the Island Caribs and their visitors, 1877–1998*. Oxford: Oxford University Press.

———. (2001). Survival and invention: indigeneity in the Caribbean. In G. Castle (Ed.), *Postcolonial discourses: an anthology* (pp. 294–308). Oxford: Blackwell.

Hulme, P., & Whitehead, N.L. (Eds.). (1992). *Wild majesty: encounters with Caribs from Columbus to the present day: an anthology*. Oxford: Oxford University Press.

International Labor Organization. (1982). *Report on proposals for the creation of a Carib Cultural Village*. Roseau, Dominica: Ministry of Community Development.

International Monetary Fund. (2003). *Dominica: first review under the stand-by arrangement and* requests for extension of the arrangement and for waiver of performance criteria. (Country Report No. 03/293). Washington, DC: International Monetary Fund.

Jefferys, T. (1775). *The West Indian atlas or, general description of the West Indies: taken from actual surveys and observations by Thomas Jefferys, Geographer to the King*. London: Robert Sayer & John Bennet.

Lattas, A. (1993). Essentialism, memory and resistance: aboriginality and the politics of authenticity. *Oceania*, 63, 240–267.

Lefebvre, H. (1991). *The production of space*. London: Basil Blackwell.

Linnekin, J. (1983). Defining tradition: variations on the Hawaiian identity. *American Ethnologist*, 2, 241–252.

MacCannell, D. (1992). *Empty meeting grounds: the tourist papers*. London: Routledge.

———. (1999). *The tourist: a new theory of the leisure class*. Berkeley: University of California Press.

Macdonald, S. (1997). A people's story: heritage, identity and authenticity. In C. Rojek & J. Urry (Eds.), *Touring cultures: transformations of travel and theory* (pp. 155–175). London: Routledge.

Ober, F.A. (1880). *Camps in the Caribbees: the adventures of a naturalist in the Lesser Antilles*. Edinburgh, UK: David Douglas.

Owen, N.H. (1974). *Land and politics in a Carib Indian community: a study of ethnicity*. Unpublished doctoral dissertation, University of Massachusetts.

Pattullo, P. (1996). *Last resorts: the cost of tourism in the Caribbean*. London: Cassell / LAB.

Sandiford, W. (2000). *On the brink of decline: bananas in the Windward Islands*. St. Georges, Grenada: Fedon Books.

Sheller, M. (2003). *Consuming the Caribbean*. London: Routledge.

Sued Badillo, J. (1995). New approaches to the question of ethnicity in the early colonial Caribbean. In N.L. Whitehead (Ed.), *Wolves from the sea: readings in the anthropology of the native Caribbean* (pp. 61–89). Leiden, The Netherlands: KITLV Press.

Taylor, D.M. (1938). The Caribs of Dominica. *Smithsonian Institute: Bureau of American Ethnology Bulletin*, 119, 103–159.

Trouillot, M-R. (1988). *Peasants and capital: Dominica in the world economy*. Baltimore, MD: Johns Hopkins University Press.

Turner, T. (1992). Defiant images: the Kayapo appropriation of video. *Anthropology Today*, 8(6), 5–16.

Wiley, J. (1998). Dominica's economic diversification: microstates in a neoliberal era? In T. Klak (Ed.), *Globalization and neoliberalism: the Caribbean context* (pp. 155–177). Lanham, MD: Rowman and Littlefield.

※ CHAPTER FIVE ※

Land Ownership and the Construction of Carib Identity in St. Vincent

Paul Twinn

To state that land is an ideological construct for Caribs in St. Vincent is, of course, a truism, insofar as what such a statement means is that land is always discursively constructed as part of a social reality. That is not to assert that this is necessarily a distorted perception of land, a false consciousness, but rather that it is the ideological perception that informs the actions of individuals in relation to land. As such their ideological perception of land is part of a social discourse distinct from a strictly juridical or geological discourse. It is this particular configuration of associated ideas and sentiments that differentiates the Carib *notion* of land from that of other Vincentians. I use the term *notion* advisedly, since it conveys the nebulous quality of the term insofar as ideas associated with land are not fully conceptualized discursively but rather emerge in praxis. It is in the everyday doing and being of life and the discourse of those doings that a sense of the uniqueness of the Carib notion of land, in a Vincentian context, is made manifest. There is, though, no specifically Carib discourse of land as a thing in itself, but the idea that "this is our Land," articulates with other norms and behavior in a different way to that prevalent within wider Vincentian society. Whereas for most Vincentians a notion of land is predicated on the articulation of familial relations and property rights (Besson, 1987; Rubinstein, 1987), for the Caribs discourses relating to land have an extra, historical dimension. It is this dimension which will be the main theme of this chapter.

The North Windward Carib Community

The land that most Vincentians mean when they refer to the Carib country extends north on the Windward side of the island from the Rabacca (Dry) River through the villages of Waterloo, Orange Hill, Overland and Magum, London, Sandy Bay, Point, Owia and finally Fancy. There are other parts of St. Vincent associated with Caribs, the North Leeward area, for instance, and the village of Greggs in the Central Windward is home to some of the descendants of the small group of Black Caribs who escaped the mass deportation at the end of the 18th century. Most Vincentians are aware of these groups and their location but when speaking of the Carib country their reference will invariably be to the North Windward. At Fancy the coastal road ends and there are no further settlements before Richmond on the Leeward side of the island. The whole landscape is dominated by La Soufrière, the volcano that rises to over 4,000 feet above sea level and that has had such a dramatic effect on life in the north of the island. The eruption of this volcano precipitated the sale and subsequent breakup of the last large plantation on St. Vincent, the 3,500 acre Orange Hill Estate, by its owners, the Barnard family. A similar eruption, though on a larger scale, had, ironically, caused the previous owner, Alex Porter, to sell up to the Barnards in the first instance. Colonialist mythology credits William Young with being the first European to scale the summit of the volcano and name it. In fact La Soufrière was already shown by that name on earlier French maps of the island. Given the relationship between England and France in the 18th century and their desire to validate their imperialist claims, it is almost inconceivable that William Young would have used a French name were it not already well established. But nomenclature here, as elsewhere, in St. Vincent manifests the long struggle for dominion over the land by Caribs and Europeans as well as Anglo-French rivalry. With the exception of Owia, all the settlements in the Carib lands bear British, or at least anglicized names, often deriving from the estate with which they were associated. Rivers and other physical features, on the other hand, tend to retain their original Carib names; although the term *Morne* from the French "mons" is usually coupled with a Carib name to designate a hill. A notable exception to this is "God Save the Queen River," which Caribs and other Vincentians tended to assume derived from an action in the Carib Wars but which nobody I spoke to was able to identify.

Some Caribs, especially politically active ones, were aware of the social dynamics involved in this naming, although they tended to accept it as a fait accompli and there was no discernible desire to reinstate previous names and indeed little evidence that enough of a tradition had survived to enable this to occur should such a desire exist. It is also clear that the preponderance of English place names in the far north of the island militates against this area being considered central to Carib settlements in the historical period of Carib autonomy. Indeed, south of the Rabacca River there are far more settlements which have retained their Carib names such as Byera, Biabou (reputedly named after a clan of Caribs who settled there from Martinique following the French occupation of that island) and Iambou, although, again, settlement names associated with estates predominate here too.

Of the settlements within what is known as the Carib Community there is a variation in size from small hamlets such as Orange Hill with no more than a dozen or so families, to Sandy Bay with a population of possibly upward of 6,000 and rising. That is not to say that all persons living within this area will identify themselves as a Carib or even of mixed Afro/Carib ancestry. Indeed the total number of Caribs is difficult to ascertain especially when one considers that in the 1981 census fewer than 40 people described themselves as Carib for the whole state and these were located in the Grenadines. This figure rose to some 1,500 by 1991, possibly due to the manner in which the census questions were framed but also because of what appears to have been a changing self-perception by the inhabitants of the north of the island. Here, even more so than on other parts of the windward coast, the narrow coastal plain restricts settlement. In the case of Sandy Bay, this close proximity to the Atlantic Ocean has not been without difficulties. Sporadic hurricanes have destroyed a swathe of houses immediately adjacent to the shore and caused the inhabitants to relocate along the coast at London and Magum, a new village adjacent to Overland. The establishment of New Sandy Bay itself was the result of a natural disaster. Shortly after the Second World War, according to informants, there was a flood from one of the many small rivers that flow down from the mountains, which destroyed the village of Old Sandy Bay, which is situated about a mile to the north of the present settlement, beyond Sion Hill. Old Sandy Bay was abandoned save for a few inhabitants who remained and the new village was built on its present site. Little remains of the original village but ancient wells that have been preserved as archaeological sites and the area around them adorned with designs similar to those found on the petroglyphs that occur throughout the island.

Within Sandy Bay itself, there is a wide variation in the style and structure of housing, from small wooden shacks with no amenities such as running water or electricity, to substantial concrete bungalows and two-story houses in the style typical of the island as a whole. The center of the village is built in four tiers that extend up the side of the hills that surround the small bay and comprises a mixture of houses interspersed with a few general stores and bars. Immediately to the north of this area are the old primary school, post office and medical center as well as the two telephone kiosks that serve the community. An electrification scheme reached Sandy Bay in the mid-1990s and this has had a dramatic impact on the social life of the village. Prior to this, people had relied on kerosene lamps or, in the case of the proprietors of a few shops and bars, generators to provide light. Reminiscing on these times it was often remarked how people had made their own amusement without the trappings of the 20th century. One favorite pastime on nights of the full moon would consist of groups of people carouseling, strolling around the village and along the beach singing. In more recent times the focus of entertainment has become localized. At the northern end of the village the construction of a dance hall, known as the "Hog Hole," has rapidly transformed the nightlife of the village at weekends. With bright festoons of lights illuminating it and situated at relatively high level, it is a visible symbol of the changes that have taken place in the village.

To the south the village has extended on to an area known as "Big Level," an adjacent bay with a relatively broad coastal strip some six meters above the beach. The beach itself has been marked up as a soccer pitch and children can always be seen there playing. Big Level itself consists of a few new, concrete houses and a Seventh Day Adventist church. The land was acquired by the present occupiers from the Barnard family after the volcanic eruption of 1979.

One informant related how he had bought a couple of acres for his family so that his children would be able to build houses of their own there, but such was the general antipathy by financial institutions at the time to Caribs, who were not generally deemed credit worthy, that his attempt was viewed with suspicion. It was assumed that he would not be able to find the deposit, or that if he did, it could only come from some illegal activity. In fact he sold some livestock, a couple of cows, and used the proceeds. In an interview with this elderly man, he could not hide the pride that he felt in having proved the doubters wrong and that he, a Carib, had been able to provide for his family's future. This attitude of denial of perceived stereotypical assimilation could be found throughout the village. The image of the Carib as being unable to progress beyond the most menial of occupations and hence condemned to remain at the bottom of the social pile, whilst still in evidence in some quarters of the wider society, was refuted in areas such as Sandy Bay by people such as my informant who had developed a clear sense of not only self-worth but a worth inextricably linked to being Carib. Here the focus was clearly on Carib inclusion within the broader society. There were, though, a few exceptions, as in the case of another resident of this area, who claimed descent from the Carib chiefs of the Windward, who had purchased a house plot and had constructed the huge copper bowl used in the preparation of cassava bread, one of the few foods which the Caribs could claim as their own. Glinting in the evening sunlight, this bowl proclaimed the distinct heritage claimed by the occupant of the house.

Continuing some 200 meters along the road one encounters the Garifoona Bakery, one of the few institutions that proclaim a Carib heritage. This bakery, along with a couple of bread vans, serves the needs of this and adjacent villages and a constant trickle of people can be seen going to and from it throughout the day and into early evening. But despite its nomenclature that proclaims an indigenous ancestry the bakery does not represent anything other than a place where bread can be purchased; it is substantively no different from any other bakery on the island. If it is a Garifoona bakery this is merely because of its location rather than because it does anything different from any other, it certainly does not provide any products that are distinctively Carib. Nonetheless, these two constructions are the only visible material evidence of the existence of the Caribs as an identifiable group, or at least a category, of people in Sandy Bay.

This paucity of concrete manifestations of the existence of a Carib community mirrors the lack that is frequently expressed by Caribs regarding their culture. There are sites around the island associated with pre-Columbian populations, the petroglyphs, but these are scattered and not associated with existing Carib settlements. Archaeological evidence also suggests that they were in fact pre-Carib. They symbolically belong therefore not specifically to the Caribs themselves but are part of the general patrimony bequeathed to Vincentians by their collective forebears. This is so because they do not belong to the landscape as experienced by Caribs. Located in fields, scattered about the island they are alienated from the Caribs in their everyday existence. Indeed for tourists and other interested travelers, access to these cultural artifacts is indeed mediated by locals who are non-Carib. In a sense therefore the very closeness of the Caribs of the North Windward with their land precludes the establishment of claims to artifacts in other parts of the island. It is therefore not that the Caribs of the North Windward do not identify with the petroglyphs as part of a wider Amerindian patrimony, but rather that they are constrained physically from asserting it. That is not to say that there is no archaeological interest on the part of the Caribs. On the contrary, local Caribs were actively involved in the extensive archaeological excavations made by Earl Kirby, the curator of the museum located in the botanical gardens in Kingstown. Rather it is that they feel alienated from these artifacts, which, as soon as they are discovered are removed into the safe keeping of the state. Many Caribs expressed a feeling of alienation to these remnants of their Amerindian culture, an alienation which was represented as resulting from their appropriation by the state. This sense of alienation was heightened by a sense of exclusion from the material benefits that accrue from tourism.

Despite containing two of the major natural excursion sites on the island, La Soufrière and the Falls of Balleine, the Carib community has no institutionalized cultural center. This scenario is exacerbated by the existence of precisely these types of amenities on other adjacent islands. A further irony is that present-day Caribs rely entirely upon European accounts and wood cuts to describe traditional Carib buildings. Nonetheless, several members of the Carib community expressed the desire to see an example of a "traditional Indian dwelling" erected. One of these mentioned several locations that might prove suitable and interestingly stressed that what mattered most was that the building should visually represent Carib culture but could equally be constructed using a modern concrete frame. Throughout discussions with various members of the community there was a pragmatic approach to the reintroduction of Carib architecture into Sandy Bay. The aim was never to simply recreate a building as a museum piece but to integrate it into a wide-ranging program of development aimed at attracting tourist dollars. Culture was clearly a resource that could be commoditized and utilized to regenerate the village and surrounding hinterland. That is not to say that there is no sense of *art for art's sake* amongst the inhabitants of Sandy Bay; on the contrary the construction of an edifice, identifiably Carib, was widely viewed as the concrete manifestation of their newfound confidence. The pragmatic approach adopted in respect to projects such as this was rather the recognition of the constraints imposed by government which itself was strapped for cash and forced to operate within limits imposed externally. What was clearly evident from the conversations that took place during my period of fieldwork was the difficulty in organizing among such a factious group. The whole village appeared to be split down the middle regarding political affiliations, and upon this political axis there were further divisions based on religious denomination.

The New Democrat Party (NDP) and the Unity Labor Party (ULP) both had considerable support in the North Windward constituency, although in recent years the ULP appears to be becoming more dominant in its support base here as elsewhere in the island. In addition there is a significant number of Christian denominations active in the area ranging from the long-established Catholic and Anglicans, Methodists, Seventh Day Adventists and other Pentecostal groups to the Spiritual Baptists or Shakers as they are sometimes called. Nonetheless the one episode during which the community was able to demonstrate a united front to the rest of the island was precisely when its relationship to the land was brought into question.

Before turning to this question in detail it is also necessary to consider how the position of relative isolation has modified Carib and non-Carib attitudes regarding the category of people who are either identified as Carib by Vincentians in general or who self-identify as Carib. Public transport consisted of small buses that carried 17 passengers huddled tightly in and carried, usually at high speed, along the twisting roads. The majority of these buses run a shuttle service to and from Georgetown, the main town in the north of the island, whilst a few make the long run to Kingstown in the south of the island. Although only just over 20 miles as the crow flies, the tortuous roads and their general state of disrepair means that this journey takes around one and a half hours. There also remain a few converted flatbed trucks which run from Kingstown all the way to Fancy and which double up as supply vehicles carrying hardware, building materials and bulk provisions. Since the vast majority of buses from Kingstown stop at Georgetown there is a general perception, especially in the south of the island, of the North Windward being a remote and isolated area. The main factors in this are twofold: first, the coastal road to the Carib country has to cross the Rabacca Dry River (which in fact is never completely dry) and lacking a bridge it degenerates into a rock-strewn dirt track. Drivers are obliged to cross via a shifting ford that can rapidly be transformed into a dangerous torrent, following storms in the highlands. At one time, certainly in the early part of the 20th century there had been a footbridge over the river and the failure of the government to build a new bridge capable of carrying traffic is seen as another instance of the Caribs being treated as second-class citizens. The second factor is that historically, prior to the construction of a new paved road beyond the Dry River, access into the Carib country was difficult with anything other than a four-wheel-drive vehicle. Even today, passing beyond Owia in a normal sedan is difficult and many car-hire companies based in the south of the island prohibit use of their vehicles beyond the Dry River.

The improvements to transport and the advent of electricity have combined to allow Sandy Bay (nobody calls it New Sandy Bay but rather designate the original site as Old Sandy Bay) and other parts of the Carib community to emerge as a location for recreation at weekends. Below Owia village there are a series of salt ponds that have been incorporated into a small park. This park has developed into a picnic and bathing area that attracts many visitors from outside the "Carib country," as both Caribs and non-Caribs usually term it. It has become something of an institution on Easter Monday for large numbers of people to gather there and have a "cook" by the sea, and large convoys of cars, vans and even trucks heavily laden with all the accoutrements of picnicking can be seen traveling there. The economic decline of Georgetown following the collapse of the sugar industry in 1985 coincided with the growth of Sandy Bay, and whereas people would have traveled to Georgetown from Sandy Bay to sample what nightlife was on offer, now the flow has been reversed. At night during the weekend the center of Sandy Bay is full of cars that have come "over the river." This in turn has generated secondary economic activity in the form of roadside vendors selling food and drink. There is a sense in which Sandy Bay has retained connotations of the exotic for the people below the Dry River; to go beyond the river at night at least was to experience "otherness." The distinction between day and night is important. During the day, the amount of people going up to the farms of the old Orange Hill Estate to work, and the nature of the work, growing bananas, makes it an everyday experience. People will visit their plots on a daily basis or go up to work as agricultural laborers from beyond the Dry River much as they might travel to Biabou or Colonerie to work. To go by day is to work; to go at night is to mingle with the Caribs and since the Caribs are perceived as wild, a trope that has endured for some five centuries (although that wildness is seen in very different terms today) the whole experience has the implication of "a walk on the wild side."

Plantation Ownership and Political Action

The vast majority of the population of Sandy Bay derives what income they have from the land. Many have formerly been workers on the Orange Hill Estate growing a wide variety of crops from citrus fruit and pineapples to the ubiquitous banana and coconuts and a substantial proportion of these had leased plots under the government's Land Redistribution Scheme. This scheme has been one of the central planks of the NDP policy, being the culmination of a series of estate takeovers and redistributions commencing in the 1970s. The aim of this, according to one high-ranking party official, was to create a "property-owning democracy" such as Margaret Thatcher had purportedly done in Britain through the "right-to-buy scheme." But the scheme itself does not receive the support that one might expect from many Caribs, who feel that they have somehow been deceived. The land is theirs by right and the government is doing no more than selling them what they already should own. Whilst the Barnards still occupied the land these sentiments could only be expressed in terms of a general anticolonialist discourse. The eruption and subsequent departure of the Barnards redefined the relationship of the Caribs to the land away from this discourse and, it will be argued here, made possible the emergence of a new discourse of indigenous rights. Thus whilst the present dispute over land has its immediate causes in the changes that took place following the eruption of 1979, the sentiments that are invoked have a "genealogy"[1] that extends back to the original annexation of St. Vincent by the British in the 18th century. It is this historical dimension that differentiates the Carib community from the rest of the population with respect to land.

The news that the Barnard family had sold Orange Hill Estate was the catalyst that sparked a response from the Carib community and created the conditions under which various competing groups could coalesce to form a unified interest group. This is not say that prior to this there had been no emergent Carib consciousness or that Carib identity was caused, in some way, by this incident. On the contrary, it was the existence of an unarticulated Carib consciousness (at the level of political action) and self-identification as "other" within the Vincentian state that allowed the sale of lands to become the means by which a hitherto unarticulated consciousness was able to articulate through apparently spontaneous political action. The perceived alienation of the "ancestral Carib lands," for such was the ideological status of Orange

Hill, enabled those Caribs who were politically active to mobilize enough public support to reach a critical mass within the community. Despite the fact that land redistribution had been a central part of NDP policy there is evidence to doubt that, without the impetus of widespread social unrest within the Carib community, the government would have embarked on what was its most ambitious scheme to date.

The circumstances of the initial sale of Orange Hill Estates led to widespread coverage in the local press of the day. The first indications of the impending sale of Orange Hill were made in the newspaper *Unity* (the organ of the Movement for National Unity) in January of 1985. Rumors abounded that the Barnard family was moving out and that the estate had been sold to an unnamed group of foreigners. Then, as now, the "Aliens Land-Holding Act" covers sales of land to foreigners. The question immediately arose, given that the Government knew nothing of an application under the terms of the Act, as to how its provisions had been circumvented and by whom. It transpired that on February 18, 1985, the office of a prominent Vincentian barrister incorporated three companies. These were Rose Cottage Ltd., Denver Portland Ltd., and ZBF Ltd. The following day another company Blue Ridge Ltd. was also incorporated. These four companies, whose directors were comprised of four Vincentians and four Danes, then formed Windward Properties Ltd., which purchased Orange Hill Estates Ltd. from the Barnard family for some $2.1million, approximately $5.6 million Eastern Caribbean (EC) and the deed of conveyance was registered on March 22, 1985. It further transpired that the Vincentians involved were employees of the local law firm that had arranged the transaction. These events occurred after the Government had written to Orange Hill Estates Ltd. in January and again on March 14, 1985, expressing an interest in the public purchase of the lands.

The position of the Government was compromised to some extent insofar as the law firm involved, that of Othneil Sylvester, was closely associated with the NDP and has acted as legal advisor to the party on numerous occasions. The opposition parties were naturally not slow in advertising this fact, which was doubly embarrassing given that land reform had been one of the central planks of NDP policy and, in particular, had been associated with Prime Minister James Mitchell. Mitchell had in fact instituted the first estate takeover in 1974 with the purchase of the Lauders Estate. Therefore the Orange Hill Estates, by far the largest at some 3,440 acres and the most productive agricultural enterprise on the island, could be construed as symbolic of the government's commitment to creating a property-owning democracy. Its sale to foreigners could not be reconciled with this, especially as many Vincentians of various political persuasions saw it as crucial to the future prosperity of the island.

It would seem that, coming so soon after Independence, the acquisition by a foreign company was something that the general population was unwilling to countenance. But there is some evidence that the changes which the Danes made to production techniques and most importantly the rise in basic wages which followed were welcomed by at least some of the workers on the estate. Certainly some informants described how they had rapidly gone from earning a pittance under the Barnards to the prospect of sustaining themselves and their families at something other than subsistence level. However, the present context in which many of the recipients of land, under the government's leasing scheme, feel betrayed may lend something of a golden glow to this episode when viewed in hindsight. The plans which Windward Property advertised were certainly aimed at winning over the local workers: there was to be widespread mechanization with the latest technology; a model farm set up in which workers would be trained in modern intensive techniques and some workers would have the opportunity to travel to Denmark and study techniques there; and there was to be an option to purchase or lease small plots of land from the company to work privately and the establishment of food processing plants such as canneries to maximize the salable product. The lack of the latter establishments has been and continues to be the basis of widespread complaint on the island, as so much food is perceived to rot on the ground for want of a market. There was even a plan to utilize the waters of the Rabacca River to generate electricity. From a purely economic point of view, therefore, the advent of the Danish acquisition of the Orange Hill Estates might have been welcomed within the Carib community, but it rapidly became apparent that what was at stake was far more than the ownership of a major agricultural business.

The first signs of popular protest immediately appeared as some 30 people, pointedly described as Caribs in the local press, picketed Orange Hill Estates with banners and placards demanding the handing over of the land to its rightful ancestral owners. This initial demonstration appeared to be the catalyst that galvanized the Carib community into action. In fact catalysis may be the wrong metaphor to use in this instance, for what was occurring was equally the result of a long process of social exclusion, deprivation and cultural subordination under both the old colonial administration and in the immediate aftermath of Independence in 1978. A more appropriate metaphor might rather be one of crystallization, although this is only possible post hoc and itself is the result of the new awareness of Carib issues created at that time. The issue is, though, precisely how were the Caribs able to overcome both their own internal divisions, the prejudices of wider Vincentian society and, specifically, the petite bourgeoisie who formed a large and vocal element within the NDP, to make the land at Orange Hill a national rather than purely Carib issue.

The most obvious answer to the first part of this question is that the issue of the land transcended the political and religious differences within the community. As long as cooperation was defined by this single issue, dissension could be contained. One could say, therefore, that there was a material underpinning in the need for families and individuals to safeguard their livelihoods at a time of considerable uncertainty, but this safeguarding always has within it a supramaterial dimension, since what is being safeguarded is not in itself purely material but is culturally specific. What was being safeguarded was not family or individuals as an abstract concept but Carib families and Caribs. The context in which the purchase of Orange Hill Estates occurred was such that it could not be a purely economic act within the consciousness of the Caribs and this context consisted in a particular lineage from the genealogy of Carib history from the time of their autonomy until the present day.

Within this lineage of Carib history the principal element in the creation of Caribs as Caribs, was the Carib/Land relationship. It is not that Caribs simply define themselves in relation to the land in the sense of territorial occupation, although such occupation was integral to the relationship. It was rather that both the land and the people that occupied it were mutually constructed within this relationship: the land consisted in being the land it was by being Carib as much as its occupiers were Caribs though their integral connection to it in the praxis of their daily lives. Within this dyadic relationship work on the land was the process through which the dual construction of land as Carib land and people as Caribs operated and any perceived disturbance in this could only result in a reaction by the actors involved, which itself invoked the historical lineage for its defense. How this particular historical lineage was discursively articulated can be illustrated by a brief article that appeared in the newspaper *Unity* (March 27, 1985). Under the heading, "Chatoyer's Community Farm: No Guarantee of Safety," an anonymous author specifically alluded to the purchase Orange Hill Estates in terms of the annexation by the British of the Carib lands following the Second Carib War:

> This is the area where every blade of grass was covered with the blood of wounded Caribs as they fought valiantly in primitive style to defend the inalienable rights of their community. This is the place where children were killed in the arms of mothers by Foreign savages and robbers of our land.

The connection with the past is constantly alluded to and both Chatoyer and Duvalier are invoked as the guiding spirits that will lead the insurrection against this new wave of foreign usurpers. The effects of that original expropriation are, according to the letter, also visible in the suffering that the Caribs have subsequently endured:

> We have been dispossessed and distressed. We are still forgotten, neglected and mocked at but the end of our silent suffering is over in this year of remembrance of Chatoyer's final stand against the invasion of covetous Foreign land sharks at Grand Sable which later provided fertile soil for the germination of the seeds of serfdom and

the consequential destitution and dehumanization of our people....We are treated as fifth class citizens or as a national after thought.

The responsibility for dealing with this "neocolonialism," as it might be termed, is placed squarely at the doors of the Government, widely seen to have connived in the land deal, hence the writer finishes on a call for action and a veiled reminder of an old jibe:[2] "The ambiguous question as to who is really prime minister of *Hairoun* [St. Vincent] must be clarified and settled at once. *Aloa Hatu Grat* [Caribs Never Fear Death]."

This piece manifestly exemplifies the way in which the past is invoked by the writer to contextualize the present. But it is not any past: it is not the past of Vincentian schoolbooks, not the past of academic discourse, nor yet the past of stories that happened once upon a time. It is not a fictitious past but a genealogical past, a past based on assumed affinity, of relations that are fictive rather then fictitious, for although fictive, this history is not the product of imagination but of praxis, it is not simply thought but lived, and lived in thought. The genealogical relationships of this historicity of the present enable and empower that present but only if that historicity itself is authenticated in praxis. The figure of Chatoyer is central to this genealogy; he stands as the true spirit of Carib resistance that cannot be vanquished. But the Chatoyer of the history bequeathed by the white planters and promulgated in the literature of the colonial administration will not serve this purpose. Within this tradition Chatoyer is leader of the Black Caribs, a Maroon leader, and an ersatz indigene. But if Chatoyer is (re)assimilated within the Carib tradition, as the hero of Vincentian Caribs then what of the exiles? They too need their ancestor and this is provided by Duvalier as genealogy demands. The Caribs of St. Vincent are thus rendered the children of Chatoyer and their kinsmen will come to their aid in time of peril. The author thus announces the apocalyptic nature of the events that have come to pass. The world truly will be turned upside down: the private plantation estates of the foreigner will become the community farm of the aboriginal eponym; the diaspora will return and the Europeans retreat to from whence they came.

Within this discourse the Danes are no more than simulacra. Having the appearance but lacking the imperialist attributes of the old European colonists, they exist merely as the outward manifestation of a concept of European colonialist power whose embodiment allows its symbolic as well as physical expulsion. By divesting the Danes of the land and returning it to the Caribs it would appear that the cycle is closed, but there is more. Though the Europeans bear the brunt of this assault the rest of Vincentian society does not go unscathed. Dispossessed and distressed may refer to the former, but forgotten, neglected and mocked clearly alludes to this latter. Lost in the shadow of La Soufrière, deprived of light and power, ridiculed as too foolish to discern rum from aviation fuel, the grievances of the Caribs boiled to the surface. It was to the non-Carib majority of the Vincentian population that this diatribe was directed. Hence the need to rebut the typical stereotypes may have had their origin in the colonial plantation system but the claim is that they have been internalized and perpetuated within the broader community. Carib women, aesthetically approximating the exotic images of a Gauguin painting, were widely sought after by resident Europeans whilst never attaining anything more than the status of casual concubines. They remain objects of desire in a society where a chromatic hierarchy dominates sexual aesthetics and where the blackness of a woman's skin may cause her to be called "Congo-arse." But the pride felt by many Caribs regarding this aesthetic appeal is tempered by a deep fear of a total miscegenation that might render them invisible. One old Carib woman remarked to me that in her day, "Carib married Carib," but now that all that had changed she feared that hers would be the last generation that maintained a separate identity. It must also be remembered that at the time of this piece in 1985 access to the Carib land was far more difficult and there seems to have been active discouragement of Carib girls mixing with non-Carib Vincentians. Non-Caribs from Georgetown remarked as to how Caribs were jealous of their women and attempting to talk to them led to fights.

There are also clear indications that the author (who is not named) was focusing very clearly on the attitudes of the majority population as much as to the elite who held power on the island. The term used for St.Vincent is Hairoun, which although it has a Carib etymology is not the usual term used by Caribs themselves to designate the island. But *Hairoun* has become the term that non-Carib Vincentians often use to refer to the island and translates as, "Home of the Blessed," while *Iouloumain*, the original Carib term, has only recently reemerged. The references to being treated as fifth-class citizens reiterates the sense of isolation imposed upon them by the rest of the population. But there is also a sense that this marked a realization that their fate was in their own hands and that they could not depend on the rest of the society for anything. This sense was recounted on several occasions by informants who participated in the protests of the sales in the estate.

The most important practical result of this tide of sentiment of which the piece in *Unity* was both provocative and evocative was the eventual formation of the Campaign for the Development of the Carib Community, or CDCC as it became known. A series of ad hoc local action groups emerged in the aftermath of the sale of lands to the Danes which became formalized as the CDCC. This was the first truly Carib organization to emerge on the island. Hitherto various national political parties had courted the Caribs for support, but beyond the run-up to pollingday their needs were largely ignored. The CDCC was to provide both a forum for an emerging historical and social consciousness and the means by which leverage could be exerted on the national government. Although consisting mainly of local Caribs from the north of the island one of its early organizers was Nelcia Robinson who, though not a Carib herself according to the definitional perspectives of some informants, actively championed the rights of the Carib minority on the island.[3]

For the Caribs to achieve anything in respect of the land north of the Rabacca River, they needed to mobilize wider support, and polarizing their community with respect to the non-Carib majority could not attain this. What was necessary was for the demands of the Caribs to resonate with the fears and aspirations of the wider community. The remarkable success that they ultimately enjoyed in this endeavor is demonstrated by the government's rapid action to nationalize the land of Orange Hill Estates that was announced at the beginning of May 1984. A precise description of the factors which allowed the Caribs to gain support for their demands from the wider community would require a study in its own right, but it's clear that the timing of the events, coming so soon after Independence, was crucial. The rhetoric of politicians of all persuasions emphasized what were perceived as the "neocolonialist" ambitions of the Danes as representative of the old imperial powers. The old colonialists were Europeans who appropriated the ancestral land of the Caribs; likewise, the Danes too were Europeans who by legal maneuver sought to appropriate the land, ergo the Danes were colonialists. The Danes had also received very unfavorable publicity in setting up a reform school on the island, the Richmond Vale academy, and this had sharpened the public response to the acquisition of Orange Hill Estates. It was this confluence of the deep structural discourse of Carib identity with the immediate configuration of national political struggle that allowed the mobilization of support against the Danish acquisition of the land in the North Windward district.

An indication of how widely the takeover of Orange Hill Estates was felt by the Vincentian community as a whole can be seen from a letter on behalf of the "SVG Support Committee UK," which appeared in *The Vincentian* (March 12, 1985). Here the Danes who had purchased Orange Hill are compared to the Vikings who raided Europe in the early Middle Ages. Citing Michael Bradbury as a source, the author claims "that the Ice man—the Caucasian male—is oppressive, exploitive, sexist, racist and violent because of the conditions under which they lived during the Ice Age. Thus when the people of the ice meet the people of the sun there is a clash in cultures—and our sun culture is opposite to that of Ice Men." The private property of the Ice Men is contrasted with the communalism of the Africans and Caribs who share a common heritage and make up as people of the sun. The letter exhorts the Government to re-establish ownership of the land on a communal basis for the benefit of the Caribs with annual surpluses going toward the cost of repaying for its purchase. It concludes, "we say kick the Danes out. Send the Ice men home! Give the land to the Caribs. They deserve it in recompense for all the injuries they have suffered in the past."

Not surprisingly, given its predilection for Thatcherism as a model of government, the NDP showed no inclination to set up a cooperative north of the Rabacca River. But this letter clearly demonstrates how what was essentially a Carib grievance could be exemplified as an instance of neocolonialism at best and imperialism at worst. The Danes became typified as the slave-owning plantocracy reincarnated. The symbolism of ice and sun effected the disappearance of the antagonism, which at times existed, between the Caribs and the population at large in St. Vincent. It was this expansion of debate from within the confines of the Carib community into wider Vincentian society both at home and in the diaspora that made political action vital.

The immediate result of the public takeover was the creation of Rabacca Farms, a new state-owned company that ran the estate whilst the Government sought to resolve the question of compensation. There were numerous calls for the Government to confiscate the land under the terms of the "forfeiture provisions" of the Alien Land-Holdings Act, but given the ambiguity that surrounded the legal status, this would have been a hazardous course and one that may have had very damaging international repercussions. The case was not resolved for some seven years, during which time Rabacca Farms slowly ran down its production. But having been mobilized in respect to the land sale, the Carib community had at least found an effective voice.

The CDCC became formalized and began to actively campaign for better conditions beyond the Rabacca River and worked to raise the consciousness of the Carib community both of its historical legacy and the links with other Carib groups, most notably the Garifuna of Belize and the Caribs of Dominica. This was given an impetus by the arrival of two staff members of the Saskatchewan Indian Federated College, which offered training and advice to indigenous groups in the Caribbean. As a consequence, a formal conference was held in Kingstown in August 1987. The objectives of this conference were fourfold:

1. To give national and international recognition to the importance of indigenous people in the Caribbean community and internationally.
2. To make critical analysis of the social, economic and political context of the countries and communities.
3. To share opinions and strategies on how Indigenous people can effectively advocate and address their needs, and to lay down guidelines for addressing the development needs of Indigenous peoples.
4. To establish a basis for greater collaboration and communication between and among the Indigenous people regionally and internationally.

The conference included field trips by the delegates to the Black Carib community at Greggs and the area north of the Dry River and the opening ceremony was held at Sandy Bay with over 1,000 people attending. It highlighted the problems that had arisen out of the state takeover of Orange Hill Estates. It was noted that whilst under the control of the Barnards there had been daily work for the local population (albeit with wages at a very low level) and that following the takeover and creation of Rabacca farms work had been reduced to just three days per fortnight at a rate of $10 EC for men and $7.80 for women (Mondesire & Robinson, 1987). The situation for the population north of the Rabacca River, far from being ameliorated by the government takeover, was pushed further into destitution. The situation was further complicated by the legal wrangle over compensation on the part of the Danes that was to last until November 1991 when a settlement of some US$4.7 million was agreed.

According to newspaper reports, by 1992 the number of employees had decreased to just 7 compared to the 120 permanent laborers and 6 managers whom it previously employed (*The Vincentian*, April 16, 1992). There had been some reform, but only a fraction of land available had been redistributed. By 1991 some 229 farms had been established but these were all of a small size ranging from two to seven acres and were held on a 10-year lease at a rate of $720 EC after the first year and $1,523 EC subsequently. This proved totally unacceptable to the ex-workers on the Estate who deemed that the years of toil by themselves and their ancestors entitled them to a more equitable settlement. The quincentenary celebrations of the voyage of Columbus in that year only heightened the sense of outrage felt by the Caribs along with many other indigenous groups in the New World.

In July some 400 people, mostly assumed in the local newspapers to be Caribs, marched through the streets of Kingstown and held a meeting in Union Square. Many more would-be protesters were unable to make the trip to town due to the lack of adequate transport and still others were dissuaded from attending by the local NDP representative who wished to save the government from embarrassment. At the meeting, Patricia Fraser, a Carib activist from Sandy Bay, catalogued the grievances of the Caribs and other residents north of the Rabacca River. These included no electricity, no telephone, no proper health facilities such as a resident doctor and "to make matters worse, there is now this wicked land reform to deal with" (*The Vincentian*, July 3, 1992). In particular it seemed that the Carib farmers were dismayed at the high price of the lease and some claimed that they had not been fully aware of the details and had been coerced into signing with threats that if they did not they would forfeit their claim to any land. In many ways this demonstration was the high point of Carib social cohesion as the Caribs were forced to accept the Government's conditions or else face the prospect of the land being bought up by outside interests, that is to say farmers from "over the river." In many ways the very form that the land reform took and the way it was financed has aggravated the sense of grievance within the Carib community.

It is clear from the foregoing that throughout the debates which surrounded the emergence of Carib claims to the land at Orange Hill, and indeed to their relationship to their land in general, there is always a historical dimension. That is not to say that history is of no importance to the non-Carib Vincentians—quite the contrary—but that the notion of land is produced using a specifically Carib genealogy of historical relations. Thus the discourse of land amongst the inhabitants of the North Windward is constructed with reference to assumptions about the past, which though changing from time to time, is construed as permanent. It is thus to specific genealogy that one needs to turn to elaborate more fully how land, and in particular a particular area of land, became so important for Carib social identity.

Notes

1   The concept of genealogy that is employed here derives from the work of Michael Foucault (1977). Its use is based on a requirement to understand actors use of the past not within a theorized discourse of history but rather as part of an ongoing linkage with the past in praxis.
2   For a full discussion on the antipathy that could be roused by notions of slavery and freedom and how they articulate between Carib and non-Carib in a Vincentian context, see Gullick (1985). According to the author, Caribs laid great emphasis on the fact that they preferred to die rather than be enslaved unlike the majority of the population.
3   Nelcia Robinson is from Greggs, a village in the central Windward, which became home to a small group of Black Caribs who were granted amnesty in 1805 and were not exiled. As such she is part of another indigenous group who are generally considered to be distinct from the Caribs of Sandy Bay, themselves descendants of "Yellow" Caribs, as they were termed by the colonial administration of the day. She therefore could at times be construed as an outsider or non-Carib coming from over the river and at others as being part of a wider indigenous resurgence, depending on informant and context. Since this article is concerned primarily with Carib consciousness evoked by the sale of land in the north of the island, the term Carib is used for those who live in that area, whilst it is fully recognized that in different contexts other persons will be deemed Carib and the distinction Black Carib will not be necessary.

References

Besson, J. (1987). A paradox in Caribbean attitudes to land. In Jean Besson & Janet Momsen (Eds.), *Land and development in the Caribbean* (pp. 13–45). London: Macmillan Press.

Foucault, M. (1977). Nietzche, genealogy, history. In Donald F. Bouchard (Ed.), *Language, counter-memory, practice: selected essays and interviews by Michel Foucault* (pp. 139–164). Ithaca, NY: Cornell University Press.

Gullick, C.J.M.R. (1985). *Myths of a Minority*. Assen, The Netherlands: Van Gorcum.

Mondesire, A., & Robinson, N. (Eds.). (1987). *Report on conference of indigenous peoples: Caribbean indigenous revival.* Kingstown, St. Vincent: n.p.

Rubinstein, H. (1987). Folk and mainstream systems of land tenure and use in St. Vincent. In Jean Besson & Janet Momsen (Eds.), *Land and development in the Caribbean* (pp. 70–87). London: Macmillan Press.

※ CHAPTER SIX ※

"In This Place Where I Was Chief": History and Ritual in the Maintenance and Retrieval of Traditions in the Carib Community of Arima, Trinidad

Ricardo Bharath Hernandez
Maximilian C. Forte

> One shall gather what remains of all my people
> Under his protecting arms here in
> This place where I was the Chief, and through
> His love and pity and by favors shown
> Shall...assuage the pain of being conquered.
> [And] shall rescue all my people from a dark oblivion.
> And he...shall then create
> An interest in my unhappy people
> A people who were always here.
> —Words spoken by the character of Chief Hyarima in a Trinidadian passion play
> (Hosein, 1976, pp. 26–27)

Expectations surrounding the presence or absence of indigenous descendants in Trinidad are often loaded with presumptions that need to be understood from at least two different angles. On the one hand are the products of colonial and nationalist historiographies, with an abundance of contestation over the identity of Trinidad's aboriginals (e.g., Espinosa, 1968; Oviedo y Valdés, 1959; Vespucci, 1500 [1963]); disputes surrounding their "true nature" as "wild" or "civilized"; conflicting accounts of the degree to which they were assimilated into a dominant Hispanic and then Creole[1] culture as Trinidad passed from Spanish to British rule in 1797; or arguments surrounding their purported virtual extinction, the facts of their continued existence and the degree of indigenous cultural "survival" (e.g., Borde, 1876, 1883). All of these debates and doubts have been voiced by competing interests: early slave traders, imperial chroniclers, missionaries, landed oligarchs, colonial governors, and later some of the early intellectual nationalists of the new nation-state of Trinidad and Tobago (see Burnley, 1842; Coleridge, 1826; Cothonay, 1893; Williams, 1962). Almost entirely absent from the colonial historical record for Trinidad is an Amerindian perspective on the question of indigeneity in Trinidad.

If there has been anything approaching even the semblance of a consensus in the writings of early amateur historians (Bullbrook, 1940, 1960; De Verteuil, 1858; Joseph, 1838 [1970]), subsequent anthropologists and then professional historians (Brereton, 1979), it is a perspective that speaks of a near total dearth of indigeneity in Trinidad (i.e., Lieber, 1981). This presumption often extended to asserting the "virtual extinction" of Amerindians (e.g. De Verteuil, 1858, p. 172; Kingsley, 1877, p. 74). Virtually no analyst, therefore, would ever entertain the extent to which Amerindian societies may have contributed to the making of postconquest Trinidad's society and culture, except perhaps for considering the Amerindian as a symbolic artifact in a folkloric repertoire housed in the nation's imagined museum of cultural history. What such approaches cannot account for is the current existence of a Carib community in Trinidad, that is, without resorting to implausibly extreme notions of invention based on a theory of unfettered agency whereby a small group can somehow convince the rest of the society of its legitimacy.

On the other hand, there is another source of history, a living one pertaining to the contemporary Santa Rosa Carib Community in the Borough of Arima. After all, the onus lies on those arguing the extinction thesis to put forth evidence, other than the anecdotal hearsay of travel writings circulated amongst elites. The Santa Rosa Carib Community (SRCC) is formally recognized by the Trinidadian state, from which it has received various packages of financial support for the past 14 years. A national Amerindian Heritage Day, occurring each year on October 14, was approved by parliament for inclusion in the national calendar of commemorative days (*Hansard*, 2000, July 18). Former Prime Minister Basdeo Panday committed government to allocating lands to the Carib Community (Panday, 2000), which has since begun to take shape under a new government (*The CAC Review*, 2002). In the meantime, regional and international recognition of the SRCC grew considerably throughout the 1990s, as the SRCC became a member of the Caribbean Organization of Indigenous Peoples (COIP), received visiting delegations of chiefs from various Canadian First Nations, took part in regional and hemispheric indigenous gatherings, and had at least one member schooled in a First Nations program at a Canadian university. Members of the SRCC have represented the community on trips to Belize, Canada, Cuba, Dominica, Florida, Guyana, St. Kitts and Nevis, St. Vincent, Suriname, and as far away as India. Media coverage of the Arima Caribs has increased rapidly in recent years, but stretches back to the early 1800s. To the extent that identity is relational, SRCC relationships with a wide array of institutions and agents serve to confirm their identity in contemporary Trinidad.

It is also true that even some of the dominant social science texts on the Caribbean and Trinidad have made an "exception" in granting a continued Carib presence in Arima, speaking of the Carib Queen, the Caribs' Santa Rosa Festival, and other surviving Carib traditions (see Lewis, 1968, p. 393; Ottley, 1955, p. 4; Wood, 1968, pp. 43–44). The SRCC continues to maintain several public rituals that help the community to stay together, such as the annual Santa Rosa Festival, and has developed projects of cultural retrieval. Finally, numerous Trinidadians, in numbers even larger than the core membership of the SRCC, are publicly and proudly proclaiming their indigenous ancestry, as can be glimpsed by the many entries in online message boards and guest books utilized by Trinidadians.[2] Those who wish to argue extinction now face significant challenges on numerous fronts. Equally problematic are interpretations that stress the "dilution" of Carib identity, their "racial impurity," and their "untrue nature" as Caribs, arguments that derive from colonial ideologies and racial theories that were used to expropriate Amerindian lands (see Forte, 2003, 2004).

We thus have a tension between different renditions of history, between absence and presence, between textual authority and oral sources, between views from afar and actual practice on the ground. To what extent do the Arima Caribs speak of survival? What do they mean by revival? How do they go about defining and reproducing themselves as Caribs? What is the Carib perspective on tradition and history?

The Carib leadership does *not* speak in terms of uninterrupted cultural continuity and some Carib spokespersons are troubled by the expectations of visitors who imagine them living in the forests, "in loincloths, beads and feathers," in an unchanging cultural state since time immemorial. Carib self-representations acknowledge the sometimes significant cultural changes that have occurred, stressing repeatedly that little of the original Amerindian religion has survived, much of the language has been lost (apart from nouns referring to an array of household, agricultural and culinary items), and that they have intermarried with members of other ethnic groups. What they do challenge are some of our external and imposed definitions of indigeneity. The SRCC is largely a modern, creolized, urban aboriginal body that has experienced many of the same social and cultural transformations found among aboriginal communities across North America, for example. What we challenge is the notion that transformation is to be equated with loss, rather than serving as a vehicle for cultural diffusion via new creolized forms. If there is one discourse that has become conventional to the point of being canonical, it is that the Caribs have been ever-vanishing people, always predicted to fade into oblivion and extinction, for almost five centuries. The romance of extinction has been an enduring narrative in modern Caribbean cultural history, mirroring dominant liberal capitalist ideologies of modernity and progress at the global level which have been wrongly predicting the demise and disappearance of the traditions of the non-Western Other for quite some time.

Positing Presence

Few would argue that self-identified Amerindians in Trinidad exercise an overwhelming presence in an overt, publicly held, or socially distributed consciousness of the makeup of the nation, or that they are recognized as one of the major ethnic groups of the country—at least for the time being, though there are indications that this may be changing.[3] While the Arima Caribs do make front-page headlines, especially during the Santa Rosa Festival, and Cabinet meetings and parliamentary reports have discussed their situation, one cannot say they are a primary focus of daily public attention. Recognition of an Amerindian presence on the margins of Trinidadian society, and specifically within Arima, has been the case. Elsewhere, Forte has described at length the degree to which the national media, political parties, organs of the state, commercial entities, the Roman Catholic church, fictional novels and poetry, and schools, to name a few, have widely disseminated images of the Caribs of Trinidad as a contemporary presence (e.g., Forte, 2001, 2005). Here we wish to focus attention on the extent and nature of representations of Carib cultural survival in some of the most consulted texts on Trinidadian history to have been published in the last five decades,[4] the height of the modernist project of development in Trinidad and Tobago.

Carlton Ottley's *An Account of Life in Spanish Trinidad* (1955) has been one of these dominant texts, especially as it was once taught in secondary schools. Ottley was perhaps the first writer to refer, in nationalistic terms, to Amerindians as the "First Trinidadians," crediting them with launching the struggle for freedom, "as dear to those early West Indians as it is to us today" (1995, p. 3). Ottley was also one of the first writers to argue mutual assimilation between Amerindians and Spaniards during the period before British occupation in 1797. Spaniards were as "Amerindianized" as Amerindians had been "Hispanized": "In order to ensure survival, the white man was forced to adopt the way of life of the Indians. They paid no attention to manufactures, except for some raw sugar and cassava flour" (Ottley, 1955, p. 50). He states that Port of Spain in the late 1700s was populated by "Indianized half-breed Spaniards" living in "mud huts," the town being a collection of "seventy-eight mud huts covered with thatch" (Ottley, 1955, pp. 51, 53). The people of Port of Spain were, "for the most part, the offspring of the many unions, some of them faithful and lasting, between the early Spanish settlers and the native Indian women whom they had taken for wives" (Ottley, 1955, p. 54). Indeed, Ottley locates the beginnings of Trinidadian creolization, later to become "the normal social pattern," within this period of interaction between Amerindians and Spaniards (1955, p. 54). In the case of Arima itself, the last surviving mission town, evidence of the Amerindian influence on everyday ways of living is even stronger. One researcher found that as late as 1931, "out of a total of 1,909 dwellings...1,528 were made with Tapia walls and thatched roofs, the typical Amerindian practice" (Garcia, 1991, p. iii).[5] In addition, Garcia argues that "in many Arima homes" one can find household items for food preparation, such as corn and cassava graters, river stones for crushing spices, as "still standard equipment" with many persons reporting that "food prepared with the Carib implements have a much better flavor" (1991, pp. 50–51).

Indeed, one of the themes uniting the works of Ottley (1955), Wood (1968) and Brereton (1979, 1981) is that Amerindians influenced the daily material reproduction of the rural working class throughout the 1800s and part of the 1900s. This, some Trinidadians know intuitively; for example, most know that hammocks did not originate in India, and yet most hammocks manufactured today in Trinidad are produced by people of East Indian descent with past rural roots. What is commonly referred to as "bush medicine" involves a great deal of knowledge about plants indigenous to Trinidad, so that knowledge of the medicinal properties of these plants could not simply have been imported from Africa or India. Ottley, though arguing that most Amerindians had simply vanished from Trinidad, concedes that Trinidadians inherited from the Amerindians "certain skills which today still serve us in as good stead as they did those from whom they originated," such as "the technique of making Carib baskets, of manufacturing fish pots of bamboo, the preparation of cassava bread on hot stones, are all of them cultural remains" (1995, p. 4). The crucible of Trinidadian creolization has a rural locus as much as an urban one, if not more so.

Donald Wood, whose *Trinidad in Transition* (1968) is perhaps one of the foundational texts of the modern academic historiography of Trinidad, made arguments similar to Ottley's. Wood noted that with the cocoa boom in Trinidad from the 1870s through the 1920s, there was a major influx of so-called "peons" from the Venezuelan mainland, people referred to in derogatory terms as "Cocoa Panyols," who were primarily of Spanish and Amerindian descent, as well as African and Amerindian descent, or mixtures of all three. Wood notes that "from the Spaniards they had inherited their language and their religion; from the Amerindians they had derived the art of weaving baskets and cassava-strainers, they ate cassava, unlike other Trinidadians, and slept in bark hammocks like the Indians of the Orinoco" (1968, p. 34). While Wood generally speaks in terms of the decline and disappearance of Trinidad's Amerindians, making a partial exception for those of Arima, he was one of the first writers to speak of the amalgamation of Trinidad's Spanish-Amerindian descendants with those of Venezuela (1968, p. 43)—Wood thereby adds a second layer of amalgamation, the Trinidad-Venezuelan one added to the Spanish-Amerindian amalgamation noted by Ottley. This renewed bridge would then have reinforced and revitalized Trinidad's Spanish-Amerindian culture, not diminished it—an observation that unfortunately escaped Wood. In fact, by the 1860s, as many as 2,000 Venezuelans were arriving every year (Moodie-Kublalsingh, 1994, p. 7), renewing Trinidad's former long-standing cultural integration with the mainland.

Bridget Brereton, a Trinidadian historian, began by extending Wood's work and making similar arguments, sometimes overstated, as to the disappearance of Amerindians, often implicitly defined in terms of "blood" and racial purity. Like Wood, she drew attention to the influx of mixed Spanish-Amerindian-African "peons" from Venezuela, referring to them as "a group of partly Amerindian descent which made an important contribution to the opening up of the island to cultivation and settlement" (1979, p. 131), thereby suggesting a prominent presence of these people in the rural, agricultural labor force. These people, she says, had the effect of "reinforcing the dwindling numbers of indigenous Hispanized Amerindians" (Brereton, 1979, p. 8).[6] What Brereton does in her 1979 text is to assume that Spanish cultural elements were paramount in linking Venezuelan "Panyols" with Trinidad's Amerindians. However, by 1981, Brereton placed the accent on the sharing of Amerindian cultural elements and their general impact on rural people as a whole: "In general, the Arawaks and Caribs influenced the life-style of rural Trinidadians in the nineteenth and twentieth centuries, particularly the people of the Spanish-speaking community of Venezuelan origin" (Brereton, 1981, p. 22). She then expands on this theme:

> Techniques of preparing food were also influenced by the Amerindians. Rural folk of diverse racial origins in Trinidad adopted Amerindian foods and cooking methods.... From the Indians, later Trinidadians learned the techniques of making bark hammocks and weaving baskets; log mortars and wooden pestles for pounding maize, cocoa or coffee, until recently still found in rural kitchens, were probably Amerindian survivals. The Indian *corial*, or canoe, made from a single tree trunk, continued to be used. (Brereton, 1981, p. 22)

Unsurprisingly then, to this day, there is a convention in parts of Trinidad, such as the northeast, of using the labels "Spanish" and "Carib" as synonyms.[7]

In terms of the Amerindian cultural influence in Trinidad, the three historians cited are not generally enthusiastic proponents of Amerindian survival, and yet they nonetheless indicate that rather than going extinct, Amerindian culture was diffused. As for Amerindians themselves, rather than simply disappearing in basic biological and demographic terms, they intermarried with others and were reinforced by the arrival of Venezuelan counterparts, more or less close kin. To the extent that the reader accepts these arguments, Trinidadian cultural history, especially with reference to creolization, thus needs to be seriously revised.

Unfortunately, where Amerindians are concerned, the British colonial legacy of producing depictions of peoplehood based on racialized conventions has exercised a firm grip on both popular and academic discourse. The only "real Caribs" are the "pure Caribs"...but the only "pure Caribs" today are "dead Caribs." Given that the Caribbean has become for anthropologists a virtual *locus classicus* for the process called "creolization" (see Khan, 1998), it is somewhat ironic that conceptions of creolization should in practice reduce to simple racial formulae (e.g., De Verteuil, 1858, p. 172) and treat cultures as substances, where mixture is tantamount to fakery, that is, an impure result. In this simplistic alchemy, today's "living Caribs" are "not real Caribs" because they are "mixed Caribs." Likewise, survival and tradition are both equated with stasis and immobility in such discourses, assumptions that we do not share. Indeed, as noted repeatedly by today's Carib leadership, it is owing to the efforts of those who are "mixed" that more of the Amerindian culture has been carried forward to present times. In many cases, those who might be deemed "pure" Amerindians have done everything possible to negate their Amerindian ancestry, possibly given the social stigma and shame assigned to the "cannibalistic" and "primitive" Carib identity. It is worth remembering that some of the strongest survivals of Amerindian culture in the Caribbean are to be found amongst populations such as the Garifuna in Belize, whose ostensible ancestry and outward appearance is primarily African.

The Historical Emergence of the Santa Rosa Carib Community

History is a vital resource to contemporary Caribs' interpretations of their own identity and position as a community. It is rare for one of the leading spokespersons of the SRCC to speak of times before the Indian Mission of Arima, which lasted from approximately 1786 until its apparently illegal dissolution circa 1849 (on the latter point, see Forte, 2003). The history of this mission is paramount, indeed, shaping the way the community has named itself officially since the early 1970s. While Carib leaders obviously see their historical roots as preceding those of the Mission, the spirituality of those closest to present times, the ex-Mission Amerindians, provided contemporary Caribs with a source of "strength" in communal terms.

The mission was formally devoted to St. Rose of Lima, patron saint of the New World and the Philippines, and was thus titled the Mission of Santa Rosa de Arima. The historical details of the period from the late 1780s to the early 1900s are quite complex and elaborated at length elsewhere (Forte, 2002, 2005). What we present here is more of a condensed and selective synopsis.

The Mission of Santa Rosa de Arima was instituted as a result of several momentous changes that made it expedient to displace Amerindians gathered in the missions of San Agustin de Arauca, San Pablo de Tacarigua and the Partido de Quare, away from areas destined to service the new sugar economy that was to be built by incoming planters and slaves from the French Caribbean (De Verteuil, 1858, pp. 299–300; Wise, 1938, p. 40). The majority of the Amerindians on those three missions have been identified as Nepuyos, whose language belonged to the mainland Carib language family (Boomert, 1986, p. 12; Espinosa, 1968, p. 37; Figueredo & Glazier, 1991, p. 238; Noel, 1972, pp. 36–37; Ottley, 1955, p. 2; Wise, 1938, p. 87). While still a Spanish colony, Trinidad sought capital investment to transform the country into a sugar exporter, alongside other Caribbean territories that were producing what was then a lucrative cash crop. The law allowing French Caribbean planters and slaves to enter Trinidad en masse was the 1783 *Cédula de Población*. Lands surrounding Arima are hilly and unsuited to sugar cultivation.

The mission operated in effect as a reservation, the Amerindians officially segregated from the rest of the population, purportedly "for their own good" (Leahy, 1980, p. 102), with lands held in common and as compensation for the loss of the lands they held in the prior missions from which they were displaced (De Verteuil, 1858, pp. 299–300). Identity and the possession of land thereby became tightly linked under the law. Within the colony as a whole, different identities were rewarded differentially—those identified in a particular manner might be subjected to coerced labor, or attached to particular crops, or awarded land. This is a critical observation: when we speak of the "disappearance" or "decline" of those marked with a particular identity, in such a context, we are dealing with a fact of political economy, not something immanent to ethnicity as such. In the baptismal registers of the Mission of Santa Rosa de Arima, all children born of Amerindian parents—thus with legal right to access common lands—were formally marked as "Indio" or "India" in the margins by the priest. Once their lands had been expropriated, these designations suddenly vanished (see Forte, 2003, 2005). Put bluntly: no land, therefore, no Indians.

The "extinction" of the Amerindians was a fact of political economy, directing the act of writing them out of Arima, using the arbitrary ascriptions of the time—but it should not be understood as a faithful and accurate documentation of cultural reality. Indeed, as has been shown elsewhere (Forte, 2003), by the 1880s the governor's office was acutely conscious of the need to *not* recognize Arima's *surviving* Amerindian families, as this would have entailed thorny issues of restituting lands that had been put up for sale illegally, as well as admitting that Britain had violated the terms of the 1802 Treaty of Amiens, the condition for Spanish cession of the island. Just as much as "the Indian," as a category, was the invention of colonizers, so was the category of the "non-Indian," or the extinct Indian more precisely. To continue to write that Trinidad was a deserted island until the British seized it, that the 19th century is Trinidad's foundational century, and that the Amerindians disappeared or wilted under the sway of new arrivals, is to take part in what is fundamentally a colonial discourse of dispossession.

The history of the Mission of Arima is not, however, solely one of marginalization and dispossession in the eyes of the Carib community in Arima. The annual Santa Rosa Festival, practiced since the early years of the mission, has proven to be an enduring vehicle for ensuring community cohesion. The Caribs have reinterpreted the figure of St. Rose as their very own patron saint: a legend surrounding the appearance of St. Rose to three Carib hunters emphasizes the role of this saint in reconciling the Caribs to Christianity. The labor that the community invests in preparing for this festival, the selection of the King and Queen of the Festival, work overseen traditionally by the Queen of the Caribs, all serve to provide a structure that reinforces the community as a unit whilst making it publicly visible. The collective work tasks in the forest and at the SRCC Centre, the drinks and jokes passed around, the meals shared in common, create an ambience of communality. During the Festival, many ex-Arimians, some with familial ties to members of the Carib community, return and renew relationships with relatives and friends who remained behind, which serves to cement social relationships over the long-term, both within the confines of the Carib community and in the circles surrounding it. There is also some evidence to suggest that the Santa Rosa Festival has grown in terms of the elaborate nature of the preparations and the public pageantry that is displayed, not to say that this growth has been linear and continuous (Harricharan, 1983, p. 31; De Verteuil, 1858, pp. 300–301). To say that the Santa Rosa Festival is continuously reproduced is not to say that it is falsified or rendered somehow "inauthentic," as it is to say that new life is constantly breathed into this ongoing cultural production. What is critical to note is that although the festival is obviously the product of Catholic inculcation, it is celebrated most distinctly by members of the Carib community alone, in ways different from even their most immediate neighbors.

There is also some question as to the nature and degree of Amerindian assimilation into European culture that took place within the mission context.

Despite evangelization, Amerindian shamans continued to practice within some missions (De Verteuil, 1995, p. 79). Both the village headmen (*caciques*) and the shamans were exempt from labor, ascribed a higher status by the missionaries, and assigned the role of civic leaders within mission settlements. Some Amerindians occupied important positions of authority within the mission, assigned titles such as "Don," or given high military rank (Captain and General being some of those recorded) (De Verteuil, 1995, pp. 67–69). Some have discerned the possibility that while separate communal structures may have been dissolved and reoriented toward the church—such as the decline of the communal meeting house (the *carbet*)—the Amerindian household may have acquired greater significance in helping to perpetuate aspects of Amerindian social and cultural life (Whitehead, 1988, p. 66). While the nuclear family seems to have become a dominant form for organizing the household, accompanied by the adoption of European kinship terminology, "the domestic household seems to have proved to be one of the most durable of all Carib institutions, surviving to the greatest degree, the irreconcilable patterns of European and Amerindian ways of life" (Whitehead, 1988, p. 67). In a sense, Amerindian cultural practice receded from the exterior and public sphere, to a more private sphere, inevitably changing as a result, yet providing alternate platforms for the maintenance of certain traditions—many of these constituting the core around which contemporary Caribs draw the lines defining their identity as modern Caribs. Finally, missions served to preserve or perpetuate elements of indigenous society in Trinidad, to some extent, possibly well beyond what might have been the case otherwise.

Likewise, the "decline" of the Mission of Arima presented acute challenges to Amerindians and their descendants in that locality. In contravention of a number of laws, recognized by previous Governors such as Sir Ralph Woodford (1813–1828), and an international treaty, British Governors from 1834 onward put measures in place to effectively undermine the Mission (see Forte, 2003). In 1834, Amerindians were brought under common law; in 1849, a new territorial ordinance was passed that put up for sale lands that were held by the Mission Amerindians (De Verteuil, 1858, p. 300). Up until then, 1,320 acres belonged to the Amerindians; they were free from coerced labor; they were provided with free medical care; and they were exempt from taxation (Burnley, 1842, p. 109). In 1812, Wood (1968, pp. 43–44) found that 229 Amerindians lived in the Mission of Arima. In 1824, Coleridge (1826) indicates that the population of the Arima Mission was 278 people (60 men, 77 women, 81 boys, 60 girls). Coleridge cites the *Trinidad Almanac* for 1824 in stating that the total Amerindian population in Trinidad was 893—presumably counting only those who could be counted, i.e., those in missions. According to the last *corregidor* of the Mission, Martin Sorzano, the number of Amerindians in the Mission never exceeded 600 and by the time the government had made first steps to alienate Mission lands in the late 1830s, they had "now fallen off to less than half that number" (Burnley, 1842, p. 109).[8] Wood claims that by 1846, only nine Amerindian families remained in Arima (1968, p. 44). How "family" is defined in this case (nuclear, extended or expanded), and the nature of the kinship ties, is left unstated.

The problem with "numbers"—especially as demographic statistics can be used to show the rapid decline if not disappearance of the Amerindians from Arima—is that they were purely informed by racial categorizations imposed by colonial administrators. By "Indians" they meant "racially pure Indian types." Responding to a question from the Burnley Commission on what accounted for the "decline" of the Amerindian population, Martin Sorzano explained that this was due "Chiefly to the gradual *mixture* of the races. As *pure Indians* they were compelled to remain at the mission, and conform to the regulations; but the children born of Spanish and Creole fathers *could not be so classed*, and would not submit to the restraint of remaining there" (Burnley, 1842, p. 109; emphasis added). What this system of classification decidedly does not do is obviate the fact that Amerindian descendants continued to live in Trinidad. If one accepts the argument that cultural survival can take place through creolization (see, for example, "Interview with Joseph Palacio," 2002, on the Garifuna), then Sorzano's statement can just as easily be used to support the thesis that Amerindian culture in Trinidad did not simply vanish. Biology and culture are two separate phenomena.

The cocoa boom of the 1870s–1920s was as much bane as boon for the Amerindian descendants in Arima. It was baleful in that intense pressures were exerted by elites seeking to grab their lands, reducing many of them to squatters on the outer edges of Arima (Moodie-Kublalsingh, 1994, p. 5). It was also propitious in that the need for additional laborers ushered in the Venezuelan Panyols, often of Amerindian descent themselves with a very similar cultural background as the Arima Mission Amerindians. The large numbers of these Panyols, their independent hold on lands as peasant cultivators, and their relative economic power amongst the island's working class, made them a presence of especial influence, both demographically and culturally. Forte (2005) outlines the nature of the transformations and the partial cultural re-Indianization of Arima and environs as the second Amerindian resurgence of the 1800s (the first, he argues, was Sir Ralph Woodford's legal entrenchment and territorial expansion of the Mission in the early 1800s). The Panyols certainly added some new influences as well, some arguing that they initiated the tradition of Amerindian masqueraders in the annual Carnival celebrations (see Bellour & Kinser, 1998, p. 2). They also introduced and/or revived dances and songs based on Amerindian themes (see Moodie-Kublalsingh, 1994, p. 95; Forte, 2005). In addition, their presence helped to revitalize the Santa Rosa Festival, which had undergone a certain degree of secularization.

The Santa Rosa Festival, Forte (2005) argues, is in structural terms a public rendition of the household religious rituals particular to the Panyols, known as the *velorio de la cruz* (cross wake). The details of this ritual and the ethnohistoric evidence are quite complex and beyond the immediate scope of this chapter—however, suffice it to say that the chief organizer of the *velorio* was always the female head of the household, the so-called keeper of the cross, or *ama de la cruz*. In many ways the special prominence of the Queens of the Caribs, from the late 1800s onward, seems to derive symbolic, spiritual and ritual legitimacy from her household counterpart, being the *ama de la cruz*. The argument here is not that the Panyols "invented" the Santa Rosa Festival—as De Verteuil (1858) was an eye witness to festivals that preceded the largest influx of Panyols—but that they helped to revitalize and reinvent it, giving the Queen a far more prominent position in the festival than had ever been recorded in previous accounts.

It is without doubt that some degree of resurgence *must* have occurred between the 1840s and the early 1900s. By the middle of the 19th century, writers were speaking of the decline or disappearance of the Arima Amerindians. Yet, a century later, there was already firm recognition of the publicly acknowledged Queen of the Caribs in Arima (see Bullbrook, 1960, p. 57). Public references to the Caribs of Arima in fact appeared in the press, and in Hosein's play, as early as the 1930s (see Forte, 2005).

The Carib Queen occupied a paramount position until at least the 1970s. She had no power of governance over the Caribs—her position only really became active in leading preparations for the annual Santa Rosa Festival, in maintaining traditional techniques of basket weaving, the preparation of herbal remedies, and the processing of cassava. These were some of the core Amerindian cultural traditions that had apparently been maintained by being located within the confines of the domestic household. In addition, it seems that the position of Queen was usually hereditary. The 1970s introduced some critical transformations.

By 1973, Ricardo Bharath Hernandez, then living in Detroit, returned to Trinidad, with an especially keen plan of maintaining and revitalizing the traditions of the Arima Caribs that he knew as a child and which he saw as entering a period of decline. The community he grew up in was itself increasingly scattered. He sought to reorganize the community and seek a communal residential land base. In the process of seeking a land grant, the Carib community was fundamentally altered. Both the state and the Roman Catholic Church had been approached for land, but both required that the Carib community be formally registered as a corporate entity in order to receive land. In 1976, the community became registered as a limited liability company, with formal officers, articles of incorporation, and so forth (Companies Registry, 1976a, 1976b). The result was a restructuring of internal positions of authority in the community, state surveillance, demands for tax returns even when no revenues had been earned, and a series of other bureaucratic impositions that had no relevance to the actual structure, internal relations and aims of the Caribs. Bharath became the President and the Queen became more of a titular figurehead. Lands from the state were not forthcoming; as for the church, lands were donated, but the deed to the lands was not signed over to the SRCC. While the bureaucratic transformation of the SRCC was largely unnecessary, the degree of formalization and "modernization" of its structure seemed to be advantageous. The SRCC was now a formally recognized body, with a structure that permitted it to receive state recognition and support in the future.

One of the SRCC's long-standing aims since the 1970s has been the acquisition of a significant land base for the reconstruction of an Amerindian village. The function of this recreated village is, in the view of leaders such as Bharath, to provide a common residential space, combined with a jointly held economic base, for a continuous period of time, in order "to truly live as a community," and to better facilitate the maintenance of traditions.

As Bharath explains, concepts of "tradition" and "culture" are intertwined in contemporary Carib thinking on these subjects. "Culture" is defined as the sum of the practices of a people developed and maintained over time, as a way of life, defined in terms of everyday practices and special rituals, as well as the meanings assigned to them. "Tradition" is something that is practiced over a period of time, carrying important shared meanings, and upheld either consciously or unself-consciously.

Ethnic Survival or Revival?
Tradition and Ritual amongst the Arima Caribs

Increased attention has been paid to colonial authorities' expedient manner in deploying ethnic labels to designate Caribbean aboriginals, with Trinidad possibly representing an extreme case of rapid situational variation (Hulme, 1992; Forte, 2004, 2005). "Carib," as a label in the historical literature, refers to a caricature—a fierce cannibal given to eternal war—and is almost utterly devoid of any ethnographic substance. Deployed expediently by colonial powers, to one moment mark one locality as inhabited by "Caribs" when it was convenient to target them as enemies and as potential slaves, only to declare them the opposite, "Arawak," in the next moment, the historical literature consists not just of outsiders' accounts, but often outsiders with axes to grind against the Amerindians. If the Carib label has been maintained by today's SRCC, it is not because it is meant to have a specific set of referents for defining traits of "Caribness"—if that is even possible given what was explained above—but as a generic, socially accepted label, also rendered conventional by the works of social scientists (see Forte, 2005).

Contemporary Caribs are not museum pieces. Instead, the historical framework of their self-presentation as Carib tends to focus on practices, customs and objects that found their way into the creolization process and that may have been perpetuated as a result. Even this is a relatively novel approach, since little of the extant literature on Trinidad speaks of the Amerindian dimension of the creolization process.

Contemporary Carib representatives do not speak in terms of seamless cultural continuity. Bharath, for one, has often repeated to visitors and the media that much has been lost in terms of the sorts of cultural practices that outsiders often associate with Amerindians. The core cultural contents of contemporary self-definitions as Carib tend to consist of kinship and genealogy, household and horticultural practices, botanical knowledge, and independent involvement as a community in overtly Catholic religious rituals—not that this list is meant to be exhaustive or wielded inflexibly. The outer representations of "Caribness," whether these be a stereotyped notion of racial appearance, daily usage of an Amerindian language, or a style of dress that some might perceive as being Amerindian, tend to be minimal or nonexistent. The primary thrust of self-identification as Carib is not simply reference to a bundle of traits, rather it is a stance on the cultural history and ethnopolitics of Trinidad: that Amerindians are a part of the nation's history and that pride in one's Amerindian heritage means finding solace, comfort and a sense of home on *this* land, rather than harking back to distant shores of Africa, India or Europe. Yet, while we would agree that there is no one way of "being" inherently Carib (Hulme, 1992, p. 65), SRCC leaders have enunciated certain positions where the practice of tradition is concerned.

A "tradition," in the view of SRCC representatives, is a custom, ritual or body of knowledge that has been (or was) practiced over a period of long temporal duration. This does not mean that there have been no changes to these traditions, that the meanings assigned to an object or ritual have remained static, or that there has not been a necessary degree of reinvention and reinterpretation in order to sustain the practice of a tradition. What it does mean is that, by and large, the ostensible contours of a practice remain familiar and recognizable to its practitioners through time.

Given the degree of formalization of the SRCC as an organization since 1976 and the fact that it regularly represents itself to a wider public, leaders such as Bharath have articulated a distinct set of orientations toward tradition that make allowance for both continuity and change. Amongst the goals of the SRCC, where traditions are concerned, "maintenance" and "retrieval" are the two most important. One of the primary themes in this self-described "ethnic revival" is to make a contribution to the body of knowledge about national history, rather than proposing some vision of ethnic segregation.

The primary retained traditions that SRCC leaders seek to maintain consist of the following. Household culinary practices are one, including cassava cultivation and processing, using the woven implements historically associated with this processing, such as the *matapi* or *sebucán* used to strain the grated cassava, and the *manare* used to sift the strained and grated cassava (see Fig. 7). The cassava is then processed into either crispy, flat round bread, or into a roasted cereal known as *farine*. The liquid residue derived by straining the cassava is used as a condiment and for making Amerindian delicacies such as "pepper pot," while the starchy sediment can be used to thicken sauces, make sweets or types of porridge. The construction of Amerindian dwellings, known alternately by names such as *ajoupa* or *benab*, is also a specialized practice of a number of SRCC members, requiring knowledge of which palms are to be used for thatching roofs, such as *carat*, *timite* or other palms. According to the late John Newel Lewis, an architect renowned in Trinidad not just for his designs but also for his exhaustive architectural history (Lewis, 1983), the *ajoupa* underwent cultural diffusion to become the vernacular architectural form of much of Trinidadian housing over the past two centuries. Weaving skills using vines and reeds not generally used by other Trinidadians (such as the *terite* reed, known as *quaroman* in Dominica, and the *moriche* palm also used by Amerindians in Guyana and the Warao in Venezuela), and the application of these skills in creating Amerindian implements such as those already mentioned, are one of the SRCC's hallmark traditions. Such knowledge is gradually diffusing to the wider society through the instructional classes offered by SRCC members such as Bharath Hernandez. Various individuals in the SRCC and the wider Arima Carib community possess knowledge of herbal medicines, and it is difficult to generalize if their knowledge has either diminished or increased over time.

Among the retained traditions that they seek to maintain are those that are the product of cultural contact—not usually Amerindian in origin, but practiced with especial vigor by the Arima Caribs. These range from the simple production of *warap*, a fermented cane juice, to the annual preparations for the Santa Rosa Festival (see Fig. 8). It should be noted that no other group in the parish of Arima, the largest Roman Catholic parish in a country where Roman Catholicism draws the largest number of adherents, is involved in the month-long preparations for what is one of the oldest festivals in Trinidad. While the festival is ostensibly Catholic, these preparations remain in the exclusive hold of the SRCC, shrouding the festivities in symbols that have meaning more for SRCC members than for many of their co-residents in Arima. Only the Caribs carry the statue of St. Rose through the streets of Arima and, when entering the church for the High Mass of the festival, they enter last, as a separate group, and are seated in pews reserved for the SRCC alone at the front of the congregation. Another of their more prominent creolized traditions that they have retained—though by no means exclusively—is the music of *parranda* (see Moodie-Kublalsingh, 1994), called "parang" in contemporary Trinidadian parlance. Two parang bands have emerged from, or been tied to, the SRCC in the last 20 years.

Figure 7: Maintained traditions: Julie Calderón sifts cassava that has been grated and strained, in preparation for baking. She is shown here using a *manare*, an item woven from the *terite* reed. Weaving and cassava processing are two of the Arima Caribs' maintained traditions. Photograph by Maximilian Forte.

Figure 8: Retained traditions: a section of the Carib Community is shown here in their procession to the church for the Santa Rosa Festival in August 1998. Photograph by Maximilian Forte.

With respect to the foregoing, some Carib representatives alter the definitional emphasis on "maintained" versus "retained" traditions, though the two terms would appear to be synonymous. Maintained traditions, as some use the concept, involve those traditions that are of precolonial origins (such as the making of cassava bread). Retained traditions are those cultural practices they acquired through the colonial period—traditions not originally stemming from Amerindians, but increasingly falling within their domain of practice.

The fact that SRCC leaders such as Bharath speak of "revival," more often using the phrase "cultural retrieval," is an explicit recognition of historical discontinuity, while speaking to the desire to conduct a personal "archaeology" of one's ancestors. Given the tremendous conceptual and practical labor necessary for the restitution of traditions that, with time, have become alien to many of the current SRCC members, "retrieval" is proceeding at a very slow and uncertain pace. Retrieval involves acquiring traditions by essentially learning and adapting them from other indigenous communities in the proximity of Trinidad that practice these traditions. These include knowledge and use of Amerindian languages such as Lokono (a surviving mainland language that was the basis for the Island Carib language)—with workshops conducted in recent years by visiting delegations of Guyanese Amerindians. As a result, "cultural interchange" is another term used by SRCC leaders in conjunction with retrieval, suggesting the interchangeability of traditions across proximate Amerindian spaces, and implying a formal network of contemporary contact with several indigenous communities in the region (most notably those of Dominica, Guyana and Suriname). In addition, some members have opted to unofficially acquire indigenous middle names and to dress in the *guaiuco* (loincloth), feathered headdresses and other body adornments for the public practice of the smoke ceremony.

The "smoke ceremony"[9] is itself a complex ritual with many layers of meaning and diverse origins, rendering it difficult to characterize as a "retrieved" or a "translated" tradition (see below). Though the ceremony defies the summarized description permissible within the limits of this chapter, it usually involves making offerings of cassava, corn and tobacco, burned in a clay receptacle containing resinous incense, with prayers and offerings made in the four cardinal directions. Virtually every element described here reflects the process of retrieval, but in some measure, we can also speak of this ritual in terms of "translation."

By "translated traditions," SRCC spokespersons usually mean those rituals, or components of rituals, that have no known Amerindian cultural provenance, but unlike "retained" traditions, have a more contemporary origin in the wider society, or, involve a ritualized amplification of ethnically unmarked household traditions that are not unique to contemporary Caribs. Many Caribs, like their Panyol kin, maintained religious practices separate and apart from the corpus of ritual played out in the Catholic Church. Burning incense in the home, either alone or as part of a *velorio* is nothing unusual. Burning incense in a public ritual, with the added dimension of offerings to the four guardians of the universe, is an expansion and elaboration that gives the smoke ceremony, for example, a translated quality. Another example of a translated tradition involves the blasting of the cannon atop Calvary Hill to mark the start of preparations for the Santa Rosa Festival, and to punctuate key moments during the Festival day itself in late August. Members of the SRCC have "translated" the cannon blast as standing in for previous rituals, such as the firing of rockets, and before that, the blowing of a conch shell. Taking these translations back a step further, they see all of these as standing in for the "voice of Chief Hyarima" calling his people together, referring to the famed historical Nepuyo *cacique* who dominated northeastern Trinidad in the early 1600s (knowledge of which has come to them from allied historical researchers). Another of the translations concerns the annual celebration of the Maypole, accompanied by what elder SRCC members refer to as the "*Sebucán* Dance" along with parang music. The Maypole itself is undoubtedly of European origin, though the form the actual Maypole takes differs across Europe. In this case, a group of 12 to 16 children dance around the pole, with colored ribbons fastened to top of the pole held by each child, and as they dance the steps they take end up in weaving the ribbons along the length of the pole. The final product is woven in the same way as a *sebucán*, thus participants see it as resembling the cassava strainer, in what is a rather simple if not unusually transparent case of translation.

Finally, some SRCC members, most notably past researchers within the group such as the late Elma Reyes, raise the issue of cultural "reclamation." This process essentially involves the creation of documentation arguing that certain ethnically unmarked practices, in the wider Trinidadian society, are in fact of Amerindian origin and ought to be recognized as such. One of these reclamations, predating the work of Bellour and Kinser (1998), was to assert that the presence of "Wild Indian" figures in Carnival were of Trinidadian Amerindian origin, stylized and reinterpreted by other Trinidadians and perpetuated to the present. Another reclamation involves claiming that certain hunting practices, such as bathing a hunting dog in a river using special herbs, is of Amerindian origin. Certain tales of forest-dwelling creatures (such as *duennes* and *Papa Bois*), or an owl calling out as it flies over a home (interpreted as a sign that an occupant of the house will soon die, hence, the statement "dead bird calling"), can also be attributed to a distant and subsequently creolized Amerindian cultural input.[10]

Not all of these stances equally preoccupy members of the SRCC. Overall, the maintained/retained traditions are the ones to which most adhere. Retrievals are of recent origin and it is difficult to estimate the long-term impact of these processes of interchange. Translations involve symbolic constructs that reside in the minds of members and may or may not be shared within the group or taught to youths. Reclamations are performed mostly in the written work of SRCC researchers. Taken together, however, this is a robust body of practices and discourses whose formal articulation is itself indicative of a process of resurgence. What it also means is that the SRCC, like many other indigenous communities, speaks with no one "voice" on tradition.

State Support and International Recognition

A striking dimension of the Carib resurgence in Trinidad over the past 30 years has been the degree of official state recognition and government support that the SRCC has received, well beyond any group of comparable size in the country. The fact that Bharath has himself been elected to four consecutive terms in the Arima Borough Council as a candidate for the People's National Movement (PNM)—and at the time of writing is the Deputy Mayor—has not prejudiced the views of other parties when in power. As he indicates, every political party in office has provided some support to the SRCC, suggesting that this recognition transcends partisan divisions (which can be quite pronounced) and speaks more to a national need to broaden awareness of the country's cultural heritage. From this point of view, the SRCC has been remarkably successful in realizing one of its primary goals: obtaining wider recognition in the society and from the state.

Soon after its formalization in 1976, the SRCC received the assistance of the Community Development Division under the Office of the Prime Minister, then Eric Williams of the PNM. Williams' successor, Prime Minister George Chambers awarded a grant of $20,000 to build the SRCC's first headquarters in 1982. Both Chambers and the President of the Republic, Sir Ellis Clarke, attended celebrations of the Santa Rosa Festival. Formal recognition of the SRCC came under the government of the National Alliance for Reconstruction led by Prime Minister A.N.R. Robinson. In a Cabinet directive of May 8, 1990, it was stated: "Cabinet has decided that the Santa Rosa Carib Community be recognized as representative of the indigenous Amerindians of Trinidad and Tobago, and that an annual subvention of $30,000 TT be granted to them from 1990" (Information Division, 1990).[11] In 1991, a further $5,000 TT was granted to the SRCC for Amerindian Heritage Week. Under the PNM government led by Prime Minister Patrick Manning (1991–1995), in 1992 as Trinidad played host to Carifesta V, the Manning government allocated $250,000 TT to the Arima Borough Council and the SRCC, as the center for Amerindian delegations from across the Caribbean (since referred to as "The First Gathering" of Caribbean Amerindians). In 1993, the SRCC received the National Award of the Chaconia Medal (Silver) for Culture and Community Service, from the President of the Republic, Noor Hassanali.

In 1995 the state again aided the SRCC in hosting Caribbean Amerindian delegations for Carifesta VI, on a much smaller scale. Under the PNM, the SRCC's current Community Centre was finally completed. In March 2000,the government of the United National Congress led by Prime Minister Basdeo Panday met with members of the SRCC and agreed "in principle" with allocating lands to the SRCC, as well as agreeing to fund the hosting of a "Third International Gathering of Indigenous Peoples" at the SRCC Centre in August of 2000, with $150,000 TT allotted, and agreed with the proposal to establish an annual "Day of Recognition" for Trinidad's Amerindians. For its part, the Arima Borough Council has provided an annual subvention of $5,000 TT since 1996.

Of the more critical acts of state support, in addition to various awards of recognition and funding over the past 14 years, has been the grant of an annual national day of recognition and the grant of 300 acres in a forest reserve north of Arima, which is to be the basis for the SRCC's own version of Dominica's Amerindian model village. This process has officially begun and the SRCC stands on the cusp of altogether new possibilities for growth.

At the international level, the SRCC has acquired an extensive array of working relationships with indigenous communities across the Caribbean and further afield. These include membership in the Caribbean Organization of Indigenous Peoples (see Palacio, this volume), participation in a hemispheric gathering sponsored by the Assembly of First Nations of Canada in 1991, and a landmark visit from the Assembly of Manitoba Chiefs in 1999. Members of the SRCC, as mentioned before, have traveled to almost all of the neighboring territories that have indigenous communities. Multiple workshops designed to advance traditional skills—part of the process of cultural interchange mentioned before—have been conducted at the SRCC Center in Arima from the late 1980s to the present. The SRCC has itself hosted three large regional gatherings at its Center. In addition, delegations of Amerindians from Dominica, Guyana and Suriname have traveled to Arima to participate in the Santa Rosa Festival. All of these connections and exchanges have served not only to maximize media attention paid to the SRCC in Trinidad, but they have also served to galvanize internal cohesion and pride. In addition, given that problems of youth disinterest in traditions, the loss of elders with traditional knowledge, and the diminution of select elements of their cultural heritage (such as the language) are common to most if not all of the SRCC's indigenous partners abroad, these contacts have had the paradoxical effect of reassuring the SRCC of its own indigeneity in a modern context.

Prospects for the Carib Resurgence

Perhaps then, one of the defining features of the Carib resurgence in Trinidad is the active and conscious cultivation of tradition in an international context, in conjunction with other indigenous organizations, in participation with national institutions, and guided by an anxiety surrounding the perceived threat of continued "cultural loss." It is a considerable challenge, to those interpreting (Forte), and those representing (Bharath), the complex mix of continuity and discontinuity in Carib traditions and the ways these are currently practiced, to define the "essence" of Carib identity especially as it is largely an identity in motion. What we may both agree on, to paraphrase Steven Webster (1993, p. 228) who writes of the contemporary Maori, is that a resurgent Carib identification process renders the ongoing *quest* for a Carib identity the same as the identity itself: Carib culture is not something that has been "lost," it is the "loss," that is, the attempt to stall further loss, and the project to retrieve history. *Being* a Carib, to adapt Webster, is *struggling* to be a Carib.

Notes

1 "Creole" can have many meanings in Trinidad. In most cases, the term is used for the largely Christian, English-speaking, urban, African-descended population along with those most closely intertwined with them through marriage, language and a variety of customary practices. More broadly, however, it refers to that which appears to be a "mix" of all peoples and cultures, combining to form something approximating a "national culture."

2 See, for example, the guestbooks for the Santa Rosa Carib Community website at http://www.kacike.org/srcc/ and the First Nations of Trinidad and Tobago site at http://www.centrelink.org/fntt/.

3 Trinidad and Tobago, according to varying estimates based on census data over the years, is primarily composed of people of African, East Indian, Chinese, Middle Eastern and European descent, the two largest groups being African and East Indian, each of these accounting for over 40% of the population, respectively. If my own surveys of members of the SRCC are anything to go by, most self-identified Amerindian descendants tend to opt for the "Other" and "Mixed" categories when these are available. According to data gathered by Price (1987, p. 1), the ethnic composition of Arima, out of a total population of 24,112 (in 1980) was as follows: African: 8,305; White: 74; Indian: 5,030; Chinese: 231; Mixed: 10,320; Syrian-Lebanese: 46; Not Stated: 106—meaning that "Mixed" and "Not Stated" accounted for 43% of Arima's population. What one can find increasingly in individuals' letters to newspaper editors, newspaper columns, tourist brochures, museum displays and other sources is the insertion of "Amerindian" into continually reproduced inventories of the multiethnic makeup of the national population.

4 Coverage of texts published over the past two centuries is available in Forte (2004, 2005).

5 The nature of the creolization process sometimes makes it difficult to single out a particular item as being of this or that cultural provenance. Tapia—walls made of mud, grass and pebbles layered onto a wooden framework and left to dry—has come to be associated with a rural Hispano-Indian peasantry in Trinidad, without much distinction as to whether the practice was originally Spanish or Amerindian.

6 Forte (2004) has argued that whether Trinidad's Amerindians are seen as "Hispanized" or as "indigenizing" Hispanic cultural elements, involves interpretations that are subtly shaped by the dominant political economic context of the period in question. Groups once said to have "Caribized" European cultural influences are later said to have been "Hispanized"—the primary difference being power rooted in political economy, perceptions of the "strength" or "weakness" of indigenous societies, rather than cultural process as such. Not all socioeconomically "weak" groups simply abandon their culture in toto in order to better resemble the powerful, and while power and culture are certainly intertwined, we are not dealing with a formula derived from physics.

7 It is true that to a great extent the designation "Spanish" in Trinidad is notoriously fluid and ambiguous (see Khan, 1993). In northeastern Trinidad, however, where the term has been grounded in a social concentration of people of Iberian, Venezuelan and Hispano-Amerindian descent, there are certain important qualifications that limit the flexible ascription of the label. Simple markers, such as a Spanish surname, a Roman Catholic background, certain culinary practices, participation in select rituals, are routinely called upon in classing someone as Spanish. A person of African descent, with wavy hair and a light brown skin tone, would not generally pass as "Spanish" in Arima, contra the examples referred to by Khan (1993) in her study of Trinidadians of East Indian descent, those who are known for engaging in the most flexible appropriations of the term. In summary, in northeastern Trinidad, "Spanish" seems to function as a substitute for an older term that

fell out of use as speakers of French patois and then Anglophones became numerically dominant by the mid-19th century, that term being "mestizo." Overlooking these important regional differences in Trinidad has been one of the shortcomings of the anthropology of Trinidad.

8   The documented number of "Amerindians," according to the definitional conventions used by colonial authorities, at the time the Mission of Arima was founded was 632 (Moodie-Kublalsingh, 1994, p. 13).

9   For further details on this ritual, see Forte (2005) as well as First Nations of Trinidad and Tobago website at http://www.centrelink.org/fntt/.

10 Arthur Einhorn (personal communication) notes that the belief in the power of the owl to herald death, as in the "owl calling one's name," is also a belief present in native North American cultures. For information on duennes and Papa Bois, see the website of the National Library of Trinidad and Tobago at http://www.nalis.gov.tt/Folklore/TRINIDAD-AND-TOBAGO-FOLKLORE.htm.

11 The figure is in Trinidad and Tobago dollars. Estimating the value in US dollars will vary—at the time of the first subvention, one US dollar was worth just over three TT dollars. Now, one US dollar purchases just over six TT dollars.

References

Bellour, H., & Kinser, S. (1998). Amerindian masking in Trinidad's Carnival: the House of Black Elk in San Fernando. *The Drama Review*, 42(2), 1–23.

Borde, P.G.L. (1876). *The history of the island of Trinidad under the Spanish government, first part (1498–1622)*. Paris: Maisonneuve et Cie, Libraires-Editeurs.

———. (1883). *The history of the island of Trinidad under the Spanish government, second part (1622–1797)*. Paris: Maisonneuve et Cie, Libraires-Editeurs.

Boomert, A. (1986). The Cayo complex of St. Vincent: ethnohistorical and archaeological aspects of the Island Carib problem. *Antropologica*, 66, 3–68.

Brereton, B. (1979). *Race relations in colonial Trinidad, 1870–1900*. Cambridge, UK: Cambridge University Press.

———. (1981). *A history of modern Trinidad 1783–1962*. London: Heinemann.

Burnley, W.H. (1842). *Observations on the present condition of the island of Trinidad, and the actual state of the experiment of Negro emancipation*. London: Longman, Brown, Green, and Longmans.

Bullbrook, J.A. (1940). *The Ierian race*. Port of Spain, Trinidad: Historical Society of Trinidad and Tobago.

———. (1960). *The aborigines of Trinidad*. Port of Spain, Trinidad: Royal Victoria Institute Museum.

The CAC Review. (2002). "Lands for the Arima Caribs." Retrieved July 28, 2004, from http://www.centrelink.org/Dec2002.html.

Coleridge, H.N. (1826). *Six months in the West Indies*. London: John Murray.

Companies Registry, Registrar General's Office, Ministry of Legal Affairs. (1976a). Draft copy of declaration of compliance of the Santa Rosa Carib Company Limited, Form 41, T-544, September 22.

———. (1976b). Draft copy of memorandum and articles of association of the Santa Rosa Carib Company Limited, T-544, September 22.

Cothonay, R.P. M-B, O.P. (1893). *Trinidad: journal d'un missionaire Dominicain des Antilles anglaises*. Paris: Victor Retaux et Fils, Libraires-Editeurs.

De Verteuil, A. (1995). *Martyrs and murderers: Trinidad, 1699*. Port of Spain, Trinidad: St. Mary's College.

De Verteuil, L.A.A. (1858). *Trinidad: its geography, natural resources, administration, present condition, and prospects*. London: Ward & Lock.

Espinosa, A.V. de. (1968). *Description of the Indies (c. 1620)*. Washington, DC: Smithsonian Institution Press.

Figueredo, A.E., & Glazier, S. D. (1991). A revised aboriginal ethnohistory of Trinidad (1978). In W. F. Keegan (ed.), *Earliest Hispanic/Native American interactions in the Caribbean* (pp. 237–240). New York: Garland Publishing.

Forte, M.C. (1999). Reviving Caribs: recognition, patronage and ceremonial indigeneity in Trinidad and Tobago. *Cultural Survival Quarterly*, 23(4), 35–41.

———. (2001). 'Our Amerindian ancestors': the state, the nation, and the revaluing of indigeneity in Trinidad and Tobago. *Issues in Caribbean Amerindian Studies*, 3. Retrieved July 28, 2004, from http://www.centrelink.org/Forte.html.

———. (2002). Re-engineering indigeneity: cultural brokerage, the political economy of tradition, and the Santa Rosa Carib Community of Arima, Trinidad and Tobago. Ph.D. Diss., University of Adelaide.

———. (2003). *How the Amerindians of Arima lost their lands: notes from primary and other historical sources, 1802–1880*. Arima, Trinidad: Santa Rosa Carib Community. Retrieved July 28, 2004, from http://www.kacike.org/srcc/landreport.html.

———. (2004). Writing the Caribs out: the construction and demystification of the 'deserted island' thesis for Trinidad. Paper presented at *Indigenous Cultures, 1500–1825: Adaptation, Annihilation, or Persistence?* International Seminar for the History of the Atlantic World. Cambridge, MA: Harvard University, August 02–10.

———. (2005). *Ruins of absence, presence of Caribs: (post) colonial representations of aboriginality in Trinidad and Tobago*. Gainesville: University Press of Florida.

Garcia, B.P. (1991). The Borough of Arima: the war years and beyond, 1938–1988. M.A. thesis, University of the West Indies, St. Augustine, Trinidad.

Hansard. (2000, July 18). Port of Spain: Parliament of the Republic of Trinidad and Tobago. Retrieved January 10, 2001, from http://www.ttparliament.org/hansard/senate/2000/hs20000718.pdf.

Harricharan, Fr. J.T. (1983). *The Catholic Church in Trinidad, 1498–1852. Vol. 1*. Port of Spain, Trinidad: Inprint Caribbean Ltd.

Hosein, F.E.M. (1976). *Hyarima and the Saints: a miracle play and pageant of Santa Rosa*. Marabella, Trinidad: John S. Mowlah-Baksh.

Hulme, P. (1992). *Colonial encounters: Europe and the Native Caribbean 1492–1797*. London: Routledge.

Information Division, Office of the Prime Minister. (1990). News Release No. 360: Recognition of Santa Rosa Carib Community, May 8.

"Interview with Joseph Palacio." (2002, April–May). *The CAC Review*. Retrieved August 02, 2004, from http://www.centrelink.org/AprMay2002.html#first.

Joseph, E.L. (1838 [1970]). *History of Trinidad*. London: Frank Cass & Co.

Khan, A. (1993). What is 'a Spanish'?: ambiguity and 'mixed' ethnicity in Trinidad. In K.A. Yelvington (ed.), *Trinidad Ethnicity* (pp. 180–207). Knoxville: University of Tennessee Press.

———. (1998). Constructing identities in Trinidad. *American Ethnologist*, 25(3), 499–500.

Kingsley, C. (1877). *At last: a Christmas in the West Indies*. New ed. London: Macmillan and Co.
Leahy, V. 1980. *Catholic Church in Trinidad, 1797–1820*. Arima, Trinidad: St. Dominic Press.
Lewis, G.K. (1968). *The growth of the modern West Indies*. New York: Monthly Review Press.
Lewis, J.N. (1983). *Ajoupa*. Port of Spain, Trinidad: J. Newel Lewis.
Lieber, M. (1981). *Street life: Afro-American culture in urban Trinidad*. Cambridge, MA: Schenkman.
Moodie-Kublalsingh, S. (1994). *The Cocoa Panyols of Trinidad: an oral record*. London: British Academic Press.
Newson, L. (1976). *Aboriginal and Spanish colonial Trinidad: a study in culture contact*. London: British Academic Press.
Noel, J.A. (1972). *Trinidad, Provincia de Venezuela: historia de la administración española de Trinidad*. Caracas, Venezuela: Biblioteca de la Academia Nacional de la Historia.
Ottley, C.R. (1955). *An account of life in Spanish Trinidad, from 1498–1797*. Diego Martin, Trinidad: C.R. Ottley.
Oviedo y Valdés, G.F. de. (1959). *Historia general y natural de las Indias, ii*. Madrid: Real Academia Española.
Panday, B. (2000). Remarks at the launching of the International Indigenous Gathering, Santa Rosa Carib Community Centre. June 29. Port of Spain, Trinidad: The Official Website of the Government of the Republic of Trinidad and Tobago. Retrieved September 10, 2000, from http://www.gov.tt/speeches/speeches/indigenous_gather.html.
Price, C.M. (1987). The Arima Borough Council: its organization and operation (1962–1982). M.A. thesis, University of the West Indies, St. Augustine, Trinidad.
Vespucci, A. (1500 [1963]). Por el Mar Caribe. In L.N. D'Olwer (ed.), *Cronistas de las culturas precolombinas* (pp. 43–47). Mexico City: Fondo de Cultura Económica.
Webster, S. (1993). Postmodernist theory and the sublimation of Maori culture. *Oceania*, 63, 222–239.
Whitehead, N.L. (1988). *Lords of the tiger spirit: a history of the Caribs in colonial Venezuela and Guyana, 1498–1820*. Dordrecht, The Netherlands: Foris Publications.
Williams, E.E. (1962). *History of the people of Trinidad and Tobago*. London: André Deutsch.
Wise, K.S. (1938). *Historical sketches of Trinidad and Tobago, Vol. III*. Port of Spain, Trinidad: Historical Society of Trinidad and Tobago.
Wood, D. (1968). *Trinidad in transition: the years after slavery*. London: Oxford University Press.

※ RIGHTS ※

Indigenous Rights, International Conventions, and Current Legal Frameworks within the Circum-Caribbean

Contestations surrounding access to natural resources have served as a platform for the political and cultural resurgence of Amerindian communities in Guyana and neighboring Suriname. Janette and Arif Bulkan take us through the difficult history of laws and policies for administering and marginalizing Amerindians. Their chapter presents the responses (including resistance) of Amerindians, the wider national society, and international indigenous rights organizations to the new tools, methodologies and forest classificatory systems that have been established. The chapter also includes a discussion of international standards regarding indigenous rights over forests, and traces the ways in which indigenous (self-)identification have been strategic, instrumental and positional in the same periods. Few will come away from Fergus MacKay's case study of Suriname without a deep sense of alarm over the renewed attack on indigenous peoples from the state and foreign corporations. Indigenous and tribal peoples, whose rights to their territories and resources are not recognized in Surinamese law, have vigorously condemned the invasion of their lands and territories. They have demanded that all existing concessions be suspended and that no more be issued until their rights are recognized in accordance with international human rights standards and enforceable guarantees are in place in Surinamese law. They have also begun to organize and proactively seek recognition and protection of their rights in various domestic and international fora. Indeed, both chapters reveal the extent to which national laws and international treaties provide tools taken up by new Amerindian political bodies, organizing themselves locally, nationally, and in connection with international indigenous and nongovernmental bodies, in a process of resurgence where survival itself is at stake.

✴ CHAPTER SEVEN ✴

"These Forests Have Always Been Ours": Official and Amerindian Discourses on Guyana's Forest Estate

Janette Bulkan
Arif Bulkan

The forests of Guyana have an undeniable reality, as anyone flying into or above the country can readily attest. Four hundred plus years after the first Dutch outposts were established in the early 1600s, the United Nations' Food and Agricultural Organization estimates that 78.5% of a country the size of Britain retains its original forest cover, and deforestation rates are low.[1] Locally, and most importantly, however, the forests themselves are the homelands of the majority of Guyana's 60,000 indigenous people who live in or close to them, and in developmental terminology, have "managed" them sustainably for millennia. The converse also holds, namely that Amerindians[2] comprise the majority population living in or close to the forested regions of Guyana, and depend on them for both subsistence and as a source of tradable commodities like timber, nontimber forest products and minerals, generally supplementary to a subsistence way of life. Under Dutch, later English, colonialism, most of the forested interior—that is, Amerindian homelands—was codified as Crown Forests and Crown Lands. This chapter will present a snapshot of the distinct conceptions of land ownership held by local forest peoples on the one hand, and by the colonial and postcolonial state, on the other, that explains in part the fractured nature of inter-ethnic relations in Guyana today.

The seeds of Amerindian dispossession from their forest homelands favored by outside economic interests were liberally sown in the colonial period. This is a reality that is often ignored, particularly by First World activists, who reserve their opprobrium for current government policies. Quite apart from the skewed perspective that such a position embodies, to hold on to it even now is also to overlook the tremendous gains achieved by Amerindians in

Guyana in the generation since Independence in 1966 regarding land rights, and to a lesser extent, self-determination.

Amerindian relationships to the country around them, rooted in distinct historical and cultural understandings and interdependence for nurture and well-being, increasingly in the present come up against a variety of external interests in forests. The competing external pressures have intensified since the 1980s, ranging from conservationists seeking total exclusion of all humans from a putative pristine Nature to resource extractive business interests, increasingly adept at forming alliances with international conservation nongovernmental organizations (NGOs).[3]

Guyana is located in the center of the Guiana Shield, described as being one of the three remaining "frontier forests" in the world, and therefore critical to international conservation interests. However, within the prevailing neoliberal economic model, which promotes incorporation into the global market, frontier forests represent new commodity sources. Predatory capitalist interests are attracted to such areas, which tend to be populated by forest-dependent peoples, often with limited recognition of their tenure rights, and distant from regulatory or legal protection. The frontier forests of the Guiana Shield provide a textbook illustration of this pattern.

As a result of global trends, forests and forest-dependent communities have been confronted with intensifying levels of outsider intervention or intrusion over the past generation, each with widely different designs on the same forests. A number of grand narratives provide justifications: recast from "bush" to "rainforest" to Guiana Shield forests of high floristic endemism in stories with a conservation bias (Funk, Zermoglio, & Nasir, 1999); in the sustainable forest management trope, site of sustainable forestry with a potential to make an appreciable contribution to national economic life, if linked to international capital investment (Seymour & Dubash, 2000); repository of legendary gold and diamond and other mineral deposits; possessing comparative advantages for Nature tourism; provider of global biodiversity services; potential source of new plant and animal-based medicines and so on. Each narrative possesses its own backers who then jostle for the attention of the small cadre of coastal-based power brokers with control over access to these lands (McAfee, 2000). Most schemes are devised from the outside, with local people learning about them only after commercial, conservation or research agreements have been signed, and outsiders show up in their homelands.

The colonial dispensation of indigenous lands, then, has continued to underpin the relationship between the Guyanese state and forest peoples, a dispensation that is now to some extent being dismantled in Guyana. Legal and anthropological studies carried out in many places discount colonial claims that these lands were unclaimed or unused. Amerindians in precolonial times had clearly defined territories and traded in forest and other products over an extensive region (Butt Colson, 1973; Dreyfus 1983–4). However precolonial trade neither affected social property relations nor was it embedded in an unequal system of social relationships, defining features of the colonial and post-colonial periods. Since then, interaction with the larger society has resulted in varying degrees of dependence on the market for livelihood. Aside from the moral compunction to redress historic wrongs, legal guarantees of land rights shield indigenous people from the compulsions of that market. It is not fortuitous that those indigenous communities that are heavily dependent on wage labor outside their homelands, or on the income garnered from resource extractive activities within it, are also the location of the most significant ecosystem degradation and social dislocations.

The larger struggle for land rights, then, is inextricably intertwined with issues of livelihood which in the present involve some commercial link with outside interests. Overall, the pattern of these encounters has followed the colonial model in which indigenous people supply labor or access to the resources on their lands on terms set by the powerful outsider. While some Amerindian leaders have more experience in negotiating contracts relating to communal resources, nevertheless it remains true that equitable contracts remain the exception at the individual and community levels. In consequence, indigenous leaders and their communities tend toward distrust of outsiders, expecting to be cheated. In the Guyana context, however, Amerindians have for centuries conformed to an acceptance of a larger nation-state, viewed as a neutral arbiter. Increasingly, Amerindian communities have come to rely on the Ministry of Amerindian Affairs or the Amerindian Peoples Association, the most important of the indigenous NGOs, to represent them in the twin struggles for land rights and dealings with outside business interests. A common sentiment expressed is that relations should be marked by equity and mutual respect, to break with the colonial inheritance of legal dispossession and social marginalization.

Threads of Continuity

Land is not a commodity in indigenous societies. Western property laws changed under capitalism, leading to the gradual erosion of common property systems and the conversion of land into a freely tradable commodity. In contrast, indigenous lands that have remained under indigenous control continue to be held communally, thereby guaranteeing access to the means of subsistence. In the indigenous philosophical system, the natural world is intimately linked to origin myths, the social order, and the regulation of daily life. Sacralized spaces are still recognized and protected by many communities, some known as the site of primordial beginnings of their ancestors, others the homes of spirit masters of various animal species (Forte, 2001). At the same time, it remains true that from the time of "first contact," communities have guardedly welcomed outsiders interested in trading in forest products (Benjamin, 1988). Indigenous peoples simultaneously assert their primal claims over their homelands while embracing opportunities to collaborate with the outside world.

The record of recent collaboration with multinational and national interests has been exploitative in the main. In addition to economies of scale, that can leverage capital and technology, many resource extractive companies are now forming alliances not only with weak governments but, in some cases, with international environmental interests, in what has been termed the "NGO-industrial complex" (Gereffi, Garcia-Johnson & Sasser, 2001). The reasons for the increasing involvement of international and national front companies in forested countries include stricter forestry controls in Asia (the provenance of the forestry companies dominant in Guyana and Suriname), including logging bans in natural forests in many nations, fewer remaining unallocated forests in weak nation-states, and the insatiable demand for pulp and other wood products in Asia and the global North (Durst, Waggener, Enters & Cheng, 2001; Sizer & Plouvier, 2000). Indigenous and other forest-dependent communities in Guyana are no match for the Asian forestry companies that have dominated the interior landscape and the forestry industry from the mid-1990s. However, when the commercial resources have been mined out, the environmental and social costs will be borne locally, by present and future generations.

Indigenous Responses

The historical record of indigenous resistance to the takeover of their lands is uneven. By the late 20th century, however, as the global human rights movement rose to prominence, indigenous peoples were increasingly able to get a public hearing and also started to form strategic alliances of their own, both nationally and internationally. However, it can hardly be surprising that a 350-year-old colonial legal system that underpinned and justified the appropriation of their lands would remain largely intact in the postcolonial world, particularly as global power structures have remained unchanged. Nevertheless, Amerindians have consistently resisted that dispensation.

On the eve of formal Independence in 1966, the visionary Amerindian leader, Stephen Campbell, successfully led the struggle for recognition of indigenous land rights (Pierre, 1993). The drawback was that land rights, when finally awarded a decade later, were limited and circumscribed. These limitations were compounded by the absence of any sustained developmental policy so that titled Amerindian villages did not gain access to forest management, technical or marketing skills or the funding necessary for them to be transformed into forest managers and/or running sustainable business enterprises, as successive official reports during the 20th century had recommended (Knapp, 1965; Peberdy, 1948). Minimally supervised by the Interior Department, and from 1980 by the Regional System of Government, accessible Amerindian communities were beset by predatory forestry enterprises intent on acquiring their commercial timbers. That system of "backing,"[4] now coupled with insatiable capitalist expansion into the last remaining frontier regions of the world, continues to pit the indigenous peoples of the Guiana Shield in an unequal struggle, reminiscent of the colonial experience.

Colonial Appropriations

European accounts of the fateful contacts in the New World, including those that took place on the Guiana coastlands, corroborate later anthropological findings that indigenous peoples had recognized homelands, manifested among other ways by their oral histories, intimate knowledge of the country around them, and, in the precolonial world, formal processes for trading and allowing safe passage to other peoples passing through their territory. Their property rights systems, in which a linguistic- or geographically based unit of people collectively were recognized as ancestrally linked to a particular area, to which they had management rights are now described by such terms as "common property," "customary rights" and "ancestral lands," the antithesis of postenclosure European norms of "freehold," and private property rights (Ostrom, Burger, Field, Norgaard & Policansky, 1999). The Dutch and other European adventurers encountered intact Amerindian political and social entities—many more Amerindian nations or tribes 500 years ago than there are today. Entire nations died out in the century after contact—from new diseases to which they had no immunity, the trade in Amerindian slaves during the Dutch period, and dislocations in the traditional social order (Forte, 1988). These processes resulted in some depopulated areas, including coastal areas, inadvertently contributing to the European conceit of *terra nullius* or empty lands, available for appropriation (Reynolds, 1996). However, the continuing presence of indigenous people on their lands did not deter the Dutch, or later the English, from also laying claim to those lands, described as left unproductive under indigenous control.

Dutch seamen/traders began to establish a permanent presence on Guyana's shores from the 1680s, looking to gain a toehold on the continent granted by papal decree to the Spanish and Portuguese kingdoms. The Amerindians they met tolerated, even welcomed them, on account of the high value and desirability of European trade goods. The Dutch exchanged salt (obtained from the Caribbean) and European-manufactured goods like cutlasses, knives and beads for local food (cassava bread, fish, forest fruits and garden produce), and forest products, particularly letter wood, and annatto dye (*Bixa orellana*) preserved in crabwood oil (*Carapa guianensis*). Over time, the Dutch built forts, and encouraged colonists to settle and begin plantation agriculture, using African and Amerindian slaves, the latter to plant gardens, hunt and fish. With Amerindian support, the Dutch repelled their enemies, primarily the Spanish, but also fellow interlopers—English, French and Portuguese. Gradually, the Dutch transformed themselves from tolerated guests in Amerindian lands into rulers who claimed the territory for Holland (Benjamin, 1993).

Over time, the Dutch imposed their laws and regulations on all—their citizens, slaves and previously sovereign Amerindian peoples, whose homelands they incorporated unilaterally in the colonies they laid claim to. Dutch laws, indigenous slave trafficking, co-optation of Amerindians in their bush police force that hunted down escaped African slaves, and Dutch dispensation of land grants to Europeans even before the end of the 17th century would all prove profoundly disruptive to the Amerindian host nations who had welcomed them to the Guyana shores (Thompson, 1987). Yet, the hegemonic view then—unilateral appropriation set out in official legal documents—has had lasting power. In his 1966 magnum opus on land law in British Guiana, Fenton Ramsahoye considered in one sentence the possibility that the Amerindians might have had a system of customary law relating to land, before devoting his entire work to the legal system relating to land instituted by the Dutch and British (Ramsahoye, 1966).

Whenever the opportunity presented itself, however, Amerindians reminded these overlords that they had never been conquered. There are recorded instances of their expulsion of early European settlements from the Guiana Coast, but in the end they supported the Dutch and English as being preferable to the Spanish based on the Orinoco River. As the historian Menezes noted: "The Indians themselves were not unaware of their rights. Evidence given by them in the 1890s regarding the Guyana-Venezuela boundary issue illustrated the fact...[of their claims to] their country. At the same time they acknowledged the earlier jurisdiction of the Dutch and later the British, some of them describing themselves as 'English Caribs' and 'English Subjects'" (Menezes, 1988, n.p.).

Further justification for claiming territory in the name of a European sovereign was put forward in the view that the Amerindians had not transformed the untamed landscape that came to be known as "the Wild Coast." Here, as elsewhere, the putative European superiority was baseless: the exquisite Saladoid pottery of the mainland and islands is sui generis, and the evidence from shell mounds, middens, raised agricultural fields, and surviving ethnohistorical accounts provide glimpses of what were complex and unique polities (Rivière, 1984; Williams, 1985).

While the Dutch maintained a trade in forest products, their outposts, and later settlements, were located along the coasts and riverbanks.[5] Few in number, they made good their claims to the interior landscape by pointing to the allegiance of indigenous peoples. As noted above, the indigenous peoples they encountered never conceded sovereignty over their homelands. Their understanding of the arrangement was generally one of acceptance of Dutch, French or British trading posts on what had become a depopulated coast, in opposition to Spanish claims to sovereignty.

Europeans, for their part, were able to impose their notions of state sovereignty and private ownership on other lands and peoples by their possession of superior force, and voluminous documentation of the divine and pragmatic justifications for their actions. Their "constructions" of the lands and the peoples they encountered beyond Europe continue to have the hegemonic force of law and custom into the postcolonial era. Set down in stable narratives in weighty law books and textbooks, these discourses tend to attain the status of "truth claims." The constructions have changed over time, as new institutional communities—foresters, ecologists, multinational and national bureaucrats—have formulated novel prescriptions relating to forests. Nevertheless, it remains true that most of the "framings" of the forests and forest peoples through time have been those of the outside world. Indigenous understandings have a place in these tableaux but are generally not center stage, reflecting the continuing repositories of power on the outside.

Not surprisingly, the contestations of these claims by the people who were transformed into subjects of empire have never enjoyed the same currency. In the case of forest peoples everywhere many even now have only a vague notion of the superstructure that underpins the claims of others to their lands or its allocation. Some nations have also lost their languages and oral histories, and with them origin myths. Ironically, many indigenous peoples have recourse only to colonial records to vindicate their rights or recover their history. Writing about India, the historian Bernard Cohn has argued that the British project of "converting Indian forms of knowledge into European objects," to aid their understanding of alien peoples in the end unwittingly served the subaltern cause also. As Cohn put it, "the vast social world that was India had to be classified, categorized, and bounded before it could be ordered. As with many discursive formations and their discourses, many of its major effects were unintended, as those who were to be the objects produced by the formation often turned it to their own ends" (Cohn, 1996, n.p.). In Guyana also, both colonial texts and oral histories are deployed to corroborate land claims.

Amerindians and State Lands/State Forests

Dutch proprietary dealings with land reflected the unapologetic European stance that ownership of overseas territory was vested in the sovereign in whose name it was taken. Indeed, so enduring was this philosophy that on the eve of Independence, Ramsahoye, Guyana's preeminent legal historian, could write: "the ownership of all land in British Guiana can be traced to the prerogative by virtue of which ownership of land vested in the Crown at cession, or to grants from the Dutch West India Company and later from the Crown in favour of the Colonial Government, private individuals and in some cases, corporations" (Ramsahoye, 1966, n.p.). However presumptuous such a view may seem given contemporary values—not to mention how inaccurate it is, given evolving legal doctrines regarding indigenous title—at the time it found expression in the virtual carte blanche enjoyed by the Dutch (followed later by the English) regarding disposition of the land. Conveniently for them however, land rights conflicts and issues did not assume major significance during the early colonial period.

In 1803 the territory changed hands from the Dutch to the English, but with no corresponding changes in the systems of production and social relations, nor in the legal system. Over time, English colonial rule was even more disastrous for Amerindians, as penetration of the interior for natural resources extraction quickened in the final decades of the 19th century. Like the Dutch, the English viewed all land in the territory as belonging to the Crown, and as Ramsahoye sweepingly propounded, "at the time of cession that portion of Guiana...vested in the Crown subject to the rights which were acquired by previous alienations those rights having been specifically preserved by the Articles of Capitulation of 1803, and subject to alienations during the intervening period, this continued to be the position until 1954 when the land vested in the Crown was made to include the continental shelf" (Ramsahoye, 1966, n.p.). There is no mention made here of the original owners of the land who merit only a cursory reference in Ramsahoye's treatise. As to what claims of ownership they might have, on this view they amount to naught, for as Ramsahoye propounds "there can be no doubt that the same principle [that is, the Crown as absolute owner of all the land from the first settlement] applied to British Guiana at cession and it would be properly assumed that where land in the territory is not claimed by an owner it is to be deemed the property of the Crown" (Ramsahoye, 1966, p. 114).

Consistent with these views, Amerindian rights over lands and forests were systematically contracted throughout the 19th century as the interior was opened up to mining and forestry. Under the early enactments, such as Ordinance N° 6 of 1838, rights of residence and cultivation on any land were conceded to Amerindians, and this included even private lands in the interior

(Benjamin, 1993). Such largesse, however, was not destined for longevity. While subsequent Ordinances in 1861 and 1871 did not interfere with these usufructuary rights, an enabling provision in Ordinance N° 12 of 1871 set the stage for future action by empowering the governor to "define" Amerindian rights and privileges on state lands. Initial regulations made pursuant to this Ordinance generously allowed Amerindians to cut timber of a specified size and troolie (*Manilkara bidentata*) on ungranted Crown lands, as well as to make shingles, but they were superseded in 1887 by new regulations, which, far from "defining" Amerindian privileges on Crown lands, vastly contracted them. Significantly, whereas Amerindian rights to reside and cultivate on ungranted Crown lands had been expressly recognized since the 1838 Ordinance, by the 1887 Ordinance only rights of residence were recognized on Crown lands. Henceforth, Amerindians could only cultivate lands that had previously been cleared and worked out—a provision seemingly designed to ensure that the valuable timber and other resources on these lands would be kept in their pristine state to be given out as the state saw fit. These regulations remain part of the law today.[6] Current regulations also govern Amerindian rights to remove products of the land, and they are expressly forbidden from cutting certain types of trees, bleeding balata and digging for subsurface minerals (State Lands [Amerindian] Regulations, 7–9).

A complicating factor is that these regulations currently apply only to state lands, not state forests (Forests Act, 67:01, s. 4). This is a distinction of considerable importance to Amerindians since 135,800 km^2 of Guyana's total forested area of approximately 163,377 km^2 constitute state forests (ibid., section 3). While section 37 of the Forests Act saves pre-existing Amerindian rights and empowers the minister to make regulations defining the privileges and rights to be enjoyed by Amerindians in state forests, the trouble is that no such regulations have ever been made pursuant to this section. Given this lacuna, compounded by the fact that these issues have never engaged the attention of the courts, the precise extent of Amerindian rights on untitled lands in state forests is a somewhat arcane matter.

Ultimately, as land continues to be parceled out to investors, both local and foreign, the issue of usufructuary rights is increasingly secondary and that of Amerindians' entitlement to land is assuming increasing significance. However, one measure of the success achieved since Independence in 1966 is that Amerindians today hold title to some 11.2% of national territory, in contrast to 0% in the colonial period. As mentioned already, for most of the 20th century Amerindian land rights were completely neglected by the colonial administration.

The earliest laws that dealt with Amerindians specifically were two ordinances enacted in 1902 and 1910, but neither addressed land rights directly. By the Aboriginal Indians Protection Ordinance passed in 1902 a reservation system was put in place, under which the governor could declare unoccupied Crown lands to be an Indian reservation. Under this law 10 such reservations were declared, but the actual ownership of these areas was not entrusted to the Amerindian residents. Instead a "Protector of Indians" was appointed, who was empowered to draw up rules and regulations to govern those living on the reserves but neither addressed issues of land ownership or self-government.

The 1902 Ordinance was replaced by the Aboriginal Protection Ordinance in 1910, which retained the system of reservations. Consistent with the tone set by its predecessor, this Ordinance empowered the Governor-in-Council unilaterally to vary the boundaries of a reservation by proclamation—a startling feature when one considers that the whole idea behind the reservation system was to secure the integrity of an area occupied by indigenous people. Presumably, however, this power was meant to function as an escape clause, so to speak, whereby if access to the land was needed for its timber or mineral resources this could be obtained with the minimum bother and notwithstanding the presence of Amerindian communities thereon—as actually happened in 1959 when one-third of the Upper Mazaruni Amerindian Reservation was dereserved and gazetted as a mining district.

Finally in 1951 the Amerindian Ordinance was enacted, which is still in force today. The concept of "reservation" was now abandoned, and in its place were substituted "Districts," "Areas" and "Villages." Regulations passed thereunder established several such districts, areas and villages but even then the colonial administration did not transfer legal ownership of these lands to the Amerindian residents. Somewhat sanctimoniously perhaps—and certainly hypocritically when one considers that the British had had more than 150 years to do this—settling the question of Amerindian land rights, including issues relating to legal ownership, rights of occupancy and other traditional and customary rights, was included as a condition of independence by Britain in 1966. As happened elsewhere, it ensured the continuation of the colonial project of sowing and maintaining distrust among subject peoples, with benevolence reserved for the departing European power.

In the year following Independence, an Amerindian Lands Commission was set up and, pursuant to their report, the 1951 Amerindian Act was amended in 1976 to confer titles to 64 communities. According to the Amerindian Act, these titles are subject to revocation or modification by the minister in certain specified situations—in the public interest, upon any attempt by the Amerindian community to part with its land or an interest in the land, where the minister is satisfied that members of the community are disloyal or disaffected to the state. In addition the minister may revoke or modify the titles of those villages that lie within 10 miles of any international boundary if it is necessary for the state to occupy such land in the interests of defence, public safety and order. The minister may also suspend titles indefinitely.

These powers conflict with Article 142 of the Constitution which protects property rights against expropriation and Article 149 which prohibits discrimination on grounds related to race and ethnicity. Additionally, the powers are vague and overbroad and would not be saved under any exceptions to the constitutional guarantees. However, it is important to note that they have never been used, except that in 1977, two districts were created under the Amerindian Act but titles were not transferred. (Both of these districts—Kanashen and Baramita—were granted absolute title in 2004.)

In 1991 titles were issued to 10 additional communities. Simultaneously, the previous 64 titled communities were issued with documents of title under section 3 of the States Lands Act (Cap 62:01). These titles, which were made by a presidential grant, are absolute and forever and recognize the occupation by Amerindian communities since time immemorial. The minister's powers under the Amerindian Act do not apply to the 1991 titles. Additionally, since 2004 approval was given for the issuance of title to four communities in Region 10. Titles have not yet been issued as the government is awaiting the outcome of the titling process in other regions so that all titles may be issued at the same time. In 2004 titles were issued to the Wai Wai in Region 9 over an area comprising 2,378 square miles and to the community at Baramita in Region 1 to 568 square miles. Both of these titles were made by presidential grant under the authority of the State Lands Act. These two additional titles bring the land ownership by Guyanese Amerindians to 11.2% of the total area of the country.

Amerindian lands held by title under the State Lands Act are freehold in nature and therefore have all the usual incidents of ownership of property, such as the right to exclude people from entering on the land. In relation to natural resource use, Amerindians are free to cut timber, hunt, fish, farm, etc., whether on a commercial or traditional basis. However if any nontraditional resource use is likely to have a significant impact on the environment, then Amerindians must comply with the procedures set out in the Environmental Protection Act 1996, which apply to all Guyanese. Title to property in Guyana does not include subsurface rights. However, pursuant to the Government's current administrative policy, mining concessions are not granted over titled areas. In any event, unlike other Guyanese, Amerindians have traditional rights to mine that are recognized in the Mining Act 1989.

A number of social actors impelled the sequence of legislative acts outlined above. Principally, as noted already, indigenous leaders did not cease to agitate for recognition of their land rights. In the post-Independence era, they were able to amplify their voices in national indigenous and human rights NGOs, often supported by international NGOs and Western civil society movements. These alliances were able to deploy the changing policies of international organizations like the World Bank and the International Labour Organization to force change in land rights policies on the Guyanese state.

Amerindians in Guyana, as in many other places, were not well prepared to manage their lands after they finally secured legal title. As the following sections outline the change from reserves of the state to full citizens, with a guarantee of land title for many communities, this was not accompanied by the commensurate technical and managerial training necessary to deal with new waves of outsiders, first national, more recently Asian, intent on securing minerals and timber from Amerindian lands at the lowest price possible, and secure in the knowledge that there is little oversight of titled Amerindian lands from state regulatory agencies.

Indigenous Knowledge and Labor in the Colonial Scheme

From the mid-18thcentury to the present, the economy of Guyana has been focused on primary agricultural production on the coastal plain. First the Dutch (from the 1640s to 1803) and then the British (1803–1917) had sequentially imported first African slaves, and after the abolition of slavery in 1833, East Indian indentured servants until 1917, to provide the requisite labor power for plantation agriculture. The colony's settlement and economic pattern—the majority of the population settled on the narrow coastal plain and engaged in production of primary export commodities—have persisted into the present, and continue to shape both economic life and inter-ethnic relations.

Amerindians did not provide direct labor power to the plantation economy. Their chief use to the colonizers during the era of slavery was as a standing army, to serve as a deterrent to any contemplation of escape by the Black slaves, capture runaway slaves and put down insurrections if and when the need arose. The antipathy that has endured into the present between Amerindians on the one hand and Africans (and East Indians later) on the other is encoded in the pejorative language used on both sides, for example, and can be traced back to this origin (Williams, 1991).[7]

After the abolition of slavery in 1833, the British Government discontinued the practice of giving annual and triennial presents to the Amerindians who had formed a *cordon sanitaire* behind the coastal estates. Those Amerindians who had resettled near to coastal plantations drifted back to the vast interior. Amerindians were thus both the original and new forest peoples, with some groups consigned to that ascription by the colonial system of social relations and production (Menezes, 1973, 1977).

In the second half of the 19th century, Amerindians in the interior began to encounter more free African men, drawn to the gold and timber industry. However, only a minority of coastlanders settled permanently in the interior, and those tended to intermarry with indigenous Amerindians, with their progeny termed "Bovianders" or over time becoming indistinguishable from the indigenous majority. As an aside, while Amerindians continue to be essentialized as the primordial Guyanese, and thereby consigned to the timeless slot, by the majority coastlander society, both African and East Indian, increasing contacts often lead to a shared sense of a common history of oppression, buttressed by first colonial, then nation-state monopoly on productive forces, and beyond that, by a global capitalist system of production and social relations (Drummond, 1977).

Other interior industries included a half century's boom, then bust, in the nontimber forest product, balata latex, (from the 1860s to the end of World War I), and, during the 1920–80 period, bauxite mining and alumina production. Gold and diamond mining, ranching, forestry and balata bleeding—each fostered contact between coastal peoples and Amerindians. All were carried out on Amerindian lands, all were dependent on Amerindian labor and local knowledge in these new industries, but in the racialized colonial (and postcolonial) world, Amerindian knowledge and labor were treated as undifferentiated and remunerated at the lowest levels (Forte, 1998, 1999). As Amerindian Development Officer Peberdy noted, "All credit is due to the Amerindian people for having provided, and continuing to provide, three major hinterland industries, namely cattle, timber and balata, with a unique and competent labour force" (1948, n.p.). His recommendation to the British Government to provide technical and other assistance to Amerindians so that they might control and manage these industries, rather than be consigned as the reserve army of labor, was never taken up. His negative assessments of the dubious benefits of colonial society on Amerindians were echoed by most observers in the colonial period (Giglioli, 1943; Henfrey, 1964; Myers, 1993).

Amerindians and the Timber Industry

The timber industry was developed in the second half of the 19th century by British Guianese coastal business interests, all either ethnically English or Portuguese. From the beginning, the familiar colonial pattern of racialization extended to the timber industry, with policies that favored English and Portuguese Creoles in the award of timber grants, setting in train a pattern of inequitable access to Crown forests. Amerindians secured employment as wage workers in this industry, supplying key local knowledge of tree species and familiarity with the terrain. African men, in particular, acquired annual licences to extract products from unassigned Crown forests or worked under contract on timber grants—bleeding balata, and making shingles, staves and posts from walaba (*Eperua falcata*) for the local and Caribbean market.

Colonial foresters admitted their reliance on Amerindian classification of forests, system of nomenclature of trees and identification of the over 1,000 species of trees. This was not surprising since the teeming biodiversity of tropical rainforests was unknown to Europeans. Writing in the early decades of the 20th century, the forester Wilgress Anderson noted, "the names of the trees as given in this report are with few exceptions those by which they are known to the Arawak Indians, and which have been adopted generally in the Colony" (1912, n.p.). At that time, however, as is still often the case today, knowledgeable Amerindians were informants, rarely collaborators. Anderson admitted that his publications were based on local indigenous knowledge, even though he solely was credited with authorship. In the 1940s and 1950s, the noted colonial forester D.B. Fanshawe similarly noted his reliance on the local knowledge of his Arawak collaborator, Jonah Boyan, and on forest experts in other tribes (Fanshawe, 1949, 1954). However, then as now, this knowledge is relegated to the "traditional" nonscientific slot, and consigned to recognition in the footnotes of technical publications.

The Forest Department to which Fanshawe was attached was delinked from the Mines Department and set up as a separate entity in 1925. Fundamentally it supported the coastal-based timber industry, colonial natural history expeditions and tropical forestry research. Then as now, there were no institutionalized links with local forest peoples, even those who also earned a living from forest-based activities. However, small grant holders, and Amerindians, were always willing to learn forestry techniques from, and supply logs to, the Forest Department (British Guiana, 1935). Yet, as Peberdy and others noted, the aspirations of interior peoples to share equally in the benefits enjoyed by coastal society remained largely unmet.

In the decades following the ending of East Indian indenture in 1917, East Indian entrepreneurs were drawn to the timber industry and by the 1970s came to dominate it, following the exodus of the Portuguese from Guyana after Independence. For most of the 20th century, sawmills were predominantly Portuguese and East Indian family businesses, with logging concessions of their own and informal agreements with "sprinters" (contracted loggers) to supply specific quantities of timber as orders came in. Many Amerindian men in the coastal districts worked as sprinters, preferring the independence it allowed them over salaried labor. The sawmilling enterprises themselves benefited from the monopoly they enjoyed over the forest estate, with access to traditional markets in Europe and the US and generous direct and indirect subsidies in the post-Independence era from international governments and agencies like the Food and Agricultural Organization and the Canadian International Development Agency (FAO, 1971).

The globalization of the world economy that intensified in the late 20th century led to the dismantling of domestic tariff barriers and local institutions like the Guyana Timber Export Board, and the opening up of domestic economies to the free movement of capital. The frontier forests of Guyana and

Suriname also were swept up in this tidal wave of neoliberal economic prescriptions, and foreign investment in the sector was touted as a key component for economic development, including downstream processing (starting with plywood production), and job creation. This time round, however, globalization's sweep and reach, and the pace of its penetration, were a quantum leap removed from its manifestations in previous centuries.

The Government's adoption of an International Monetary Fund (IMF)-dictated Structural Adjustment Program (SAP) from 1986 also inaugurated a number of policy changes that would bring significant changes to the timber industry. Among these changes were the opening of the forests to foreign investment, and the ending of import controls, including on chainsaws. The state owns 83% of all national forests, of which 44% have been zoned as production forests. As a result of this monopoly, this policy shift had far-reaching results on forests and forest peoples after 1992. The first agreement signed with an international company was with a subsidiary of the Samling Group of Malaysia in 1991 to 1.6 million acres of forests. This agreement with a large foreign company was followed by others, ending the monopoly on timber production and conversion by the national timber sector. The practical results of this policy include a perpetuation of the historical inequities in the allocation of state forests. By 2003, 18 large forestry concessions (between 60,000 and over 1 million acres), of which seven are foreign-owned, managed two-thirds of all production forests, in comparison with the remaining 257 small and medium concessions, each with a concession smaller than 20,000 acres.

Forestry exploitation in Guyana is even more of an enclave sector today than it was in 1991.[8] Most of the traditional sawmilling operations have shifted from producing sawn timber for local consumers or for export to the role of subcontractors of hardwood logs for two or three Asian companies. Ten years of globalization have reversed the small gains in secondary processing of timber (sawn lumber) for export. In its place, the de facto foreign control of the sector is manifest in the intensified extraction of prime hardwood species for export to Asia in log form, the attenuation of in-country downstream processing of timber and, ironically in a country of high unemployment, the unregulated importation of tribal and other peoples from East Asia to labor in the forests of Guyana.

As a result, the small- and medium-scale sector, called "chainsaw loggers," supply much of the local demand for timber. Amerindians and others were able to gain entry into the chainsaw logging sector on account of the availability of hire purchase terms for chainsaws. In the same period, the historical inequities in the allocation of production forests have been reversed to some extent by the state's allocation of annual leases to small operators. The small- and medium-scale sectors have never received the kind of subsidy or support from the state and international institutions like that given to large forestry enterprises. However, operating in the interstices of the system, their contribution to local livelihoods and the national wood-processing sector surpasses that of the favored large companies.

Forestry on Titled Amerindian Lands

The demand for timber has brought increasing pressure on timber resources on titled communal lands also. Under the Amerindian Act, the Village Council holds land title on behalf of the entire community. The Village Council is therefore also a corporate body, with the authority and power to operate like a business. However, many Village Councils have been duped by predatory forestry operators, and have signed legally binding contracts without first seeking legal advice through the Ministry of Amerindian Affairs or an indigenous NGO. As mentioned before, the awards of land title in 1976 and 1991 were followed by no official policy or program to help Amerindian communities access forest management or marketing or any of the other skills needed to manage forest lands and resources sustainably.

What happened in many areas was that community-owned forests that were/are accessible to roads and navigable waterways were then treated as "open access areas," facilitated by corrupt community members. Most logging operations in Amerindian areas function under the system of "backing" outlined earlier. Few contracts are signed or honored (if a contract exists). The familiar pattern is that Amerindians are routinely out-maneuvered and logs are sold at cutthroat prices. Many of the Amerindian loggers never get out of debt to the outsiders, leading to a form of debt peonage. Few members of the community benefit from these unequal exchanges, which have also resulted in the localized extinction of commercial timber and nontimber forest products, in most of the accessible Amerindian communities.

From the 1990s, incoming Asian companies or their agents perpetrated other swindles in Amerindian areas. One is subcontracting for raw materials, or issuing contracts (often verbal) for softwood logs for the plywood mill and hardwood species for export. Many communities have only bitter experiences to relate of these transactions—boats never arriving; logs left to rot on the landing; the contract to purchase not honored, or the buyer only paying for logs they deem usable, even though the deterioration in the condition of logs was caused by the delay in collection; fruitless, expensive trips to the offices of these Asian companies, the Forestry Commission, and the Ministry of Amerindian Affairs, in an effort to recoup even some of the financial outlays. Beyond the immediate financial losses lies the permanent loss from the unsustainable harvesting of commercial timbers.

Another Asian swindle involves duping Amerindian communities into signing contracts that hand over the exclusive rights to a front company to extract logs from Amerindian concessions in exchange for minimal payments. Among other egregious clauses, these contracts further exempt the outside operators from payments of taxes and fees, with clauses guaranteeing automatic renewal for the outside company but with sole rights to them to terminate, and wide confidentiality clauses.

Traditional Amerindian leadership has come under stress as some villagers (including elected leaders in some instances) flaunt the village rules when they sign contracts like these or extract and sell those resources themselves, disregarding the need for environmental management or payment of royalties to the Village Council. Increasingly Amerindian communities are revisiting traditional management systems and collaborating with national regulatory institutions and NGOs. At a recent meeting to discuss the draft National Standard for Forest Certification held at the Bina Hill Institute in Annai District, an Amerindian leader related that representatives of another Amerindian community had been boasting of the 180 chainsaws owned and operated in their titled area. He said that he and other Amerindians present pointed out to the shortsighted chainsaw-rich community the dangers of yet another "boom and bust" cycle, but this one with far-reaching undesirable consequences for the children yet unborn.

Amerindians readily admit that the environmental challenges of today are different from those of long ago. There is greater pressure on natural resources from outsiders and by the growing Amerindian population. First World technology is widely available. There are more roads and bridges. These transformations underline the urgent appeals heard within Amerindian communities to recover and pass on traditional environmental knowledge encoded in old peoples' stories, and to devise ways of combining that knowledge with modern environmental management systems.

Prescient Amerindian leaders articulate a vision that is rooted in the pragmatism born of a long history of oppression and disempowerment. They recognize that many of the inequities of the colonial period persist so promote the need to work with NGOs and state institutions to balance livelihood needs with sustainable forestry. However, landscapes are shaped by those who have power over them and now, as in the colonial period, that power reposes in economic forces that are dependent on ever-increasing extraction of natural resources. In this familiar scenario, Amerindians largely remain in the powerless slot.

Notes

1   Statistics like these obscure the alarming rates of forest degradation that are the result of intensified selective logging practices since the 1980s when a Structural Adjustment Program was imposed on Guyana by multilateral financial agencies. Since then, stagnation

in the coastal, agricultural-based, export-oriented economy has been in lockstep with the expansion of natural resource extractive industries, (forestry and gold and diamond mining), most located in interior forested areas (Colchester, 1997).

2 The terms "Amerindian" and "indigenous people" are used interchangeably in this chapter.

3 See the article by anthropologist Mac Chapin, in *World Watch*, 2004, for a summary of the issues.

4 "Backing" is the local term used to describe the transaction in which an outside business interest makes advances of fuel and rations, generally, to a local person with access to communal resources, in return for a specified quantity of timber or nontimber forest products. In practice, many of these transactions have been less than honorable, with Amerindians being routinely cheated through dishonest practices or unequal terms of trade set solely by the outside interest.

5 "Europeans in the early modern period were waterborne parasites: quick to command trade or settle at the coast, or along rivers, but slow to penetrate inland. In Asia, Africa, and in much of the Americas, their real influence was limited by their dependence on local allies. It was only during the next century, when technologies such as steam engines, applied to shipping, railways, migration, and war, changed the balance, that Europeans became able to impose relations of "collaboration" on their own terms" (Drayton, 2000, p. 92).

6 In the State Lands (Amerindian) Regulations, made pursuant to the State Lands Act, Chapter 62:01.

7 The list of epithets is endless, the majority painfully derogatory. The pejorative use of the word "Buck" to refer to Amerindians has continued down the centuries. Persons who are mixtures of Amerindian and African are called "Buck and people." There is no shortage of equivalents on the Amerindian side. Makushi speakers, for example, refer to African Guyanese, and to a lesser extent, East Indian Guyanese, as *omakon*, which translates as "fearsome beasts," subhuman at best.

8 An enclave economy has been defined as one where linkages are lacking between the export sector and the internal economy.

References

Anderson, C.W. (1912). *Forests of British Guiana. General report on the forests of the easily accessible districts of the colony*. Georgetown, Guyana: Department of Lands and Mines.

Benjamin, A.J. McR. (1988). The Guyana Arawaks in the 16th and 17th centuries. *Proceedings of the conference on the Arawaks of Guyana*, 5–21. Georgetown: University of Guyana.

———. (1993). A preliminary look at the free Amerindians and the Dutch plantation system in Guyana during the 17th and 18th centuries. *Guyana Historical Journal*, IV and V. Georgetown: The Free Press.

British Guiana. Forest Department (1935). Forestry in British Guiana. Supplementary statement prepared by the Forest Department for presentation to the Fourth British Empire Forestry Conference (South Africa), No. 8/1935. C.S.O. No. 3421/32. Georgetown, Guyana: Legislative Council.

Butt Colson, A. (1973). Inter-tribal trade in the Guiana Highlands. *Antropológica*, 34, 5–70.

Chapin, M. (2004). A challenge to conservationists. *World Watch*, November/December, 17–31.

Cohn, B. (1996). The command of language and the language of command. *Colonialism and its forms of knowledge*. Princeton, N.J.: Princeton University Press.

Colchester, M. (1997). *Guyana, fragile frontier: loggers, miners and forest peoples*. London: Latin American Bureau.

Drayton, R. (2000). *Nature's government: science, Imperial Britain and the "improvement" of the world*. New Haven, CT: Yale University Press.

Dreyfus, S. (1983–4). Historical and political anthropological inter-connections: the multilinguistic indigenous polity of the "Carib" Islands and Mainland Coast from the 16th to the 18th century. *Antropologica*, 59–62, 39–57.

Drummond, L. (1977). The outskirts of the Earth: a study of Amerindian ethnicity on the Pomeroon River, Guyana. Ph.D. diss. University of Chicago.

Durst, P. B., Waggener, T.R., Enters, T. & Cheng, T.L. (2001). *Forests out of bounds: impacts and effectiveness of logging bans in natural forests in Asia-Pacific*. Bangkok: FAO.

Fanshawe, D.B. (1949). Glossary of Arawak names in natural history. *International Journal of American Linguistics*, 15(1), 57–74.

———. (1954). Forest types of British Guiana. *The Caribbean Forester*, 15(3 & 4), 73–111.

Food and Agricultural Organization (FAO), based on the work of G.H. Grayum. (1971). *Logging and forest management*. Guyana: Forest Industries Development Survey. Rome: FAO.

Forte, J. (1988). Los pueblos indígenas de Guyana. *América Indígena*, 67(2), 323–352.

———. (1998). Impact of the gold industry on the indigenous peoples of Guyana. *Transition*, 27–8, 71–96.

———. (1999). Karikuri: the evolving relationship of the Karinya people of Guyana to gold mining. *New West Indian Guide/Nieuwe West-Indische Gids*, 73(1 & 2), 59–82.

———. (2001). *Iwokrami pantoni. Stories about Iwokrama*. Georgetown, Guyana: North Rupununi District Development Board and Iwokrama International Centre for Rain Forest Conservation and Development.

Funk, V., Zermoglio, M.F., & Nasir, N. (1999). Testing the use of specimen collection data and GIS technology in establishing protected areas in Guyana. *Biodiversity and Conservation*, 8, 727–751.

Gereffi, G., Garcia-Johnson, R. & Sasser, E. (2001). The NGO-industrial complex. *Foreign Policy*, 125, July–August, 56–65.

Giglioli, G. (1943). Malariological survey of the northern Rupununi savannah. Legislative Council Paper No. 3/1944. Georgetown, Guyana: Legislative Council.

Henfrey, C. (1964). *The gentle people*. London: Hutchinson.

Knapp, S.C. (1965). Report of the Amerindians of British Guiana and suggested development programmes. MS. Georgetown, Guyana.

McAfee, K. (2000). Green conditionalities: conceptual problems and lessons from practice. Paper commissioned for the MacArthur Workshop on Globalization, Governance, and the Environment. April 14–15. The Institute of International Studies, University of California at Berkeley.

Menezes, M.N. (1973). The Dutch and British Policy of Indian subsidy: a system of annual and triennial presents. *Caribbean Studies*, 13(3), 64–88.

———. (1977). *British policy towards the Amerindians in British Guiana, 1803–1873*. Oxford: Clarendon Press.

———. (1988). The Amerindians of Guyana: original lords of the soil. *América Indígena*, XLVIII(2), 353–376.

Myers, I. (1993). The Makushi of the Guiana–Brazilian frontier in 1944: a study of culture contact. *Antropológica*, 80, 3–99.

Ostrom, E., Burger J., Field, C.B., Norgaard, R.B., & Policansky, D. (1999). Revisiting the commons: local lessons, global challenges. *Science*, 284, 278–282.

Peberdy, P.S. (1948). *British Guiana: report of a survey on Amerindian affairs in the remote interior*. Georgetown, Guyana: Colonial Development and Welfare, Scheme No. D. 246.

Pierre, L.A. (1993). Stephen Campbell, first Amerindian national politician of British Guiana, 1957–1966. M.A. thesis, University of Guyana, Georgetown.

Ramsahoye, F.H.W. (1966). *The development of land law in British Guiana*. Dobbs Ferry, N. Y.: Oceana Publications.

Reynolds, H. (1996). *Aboriginal sovereignty: reflections on race, state and nation*. St. Leonards, Australia: Allen & Unwin.

Rivière, P.G. (1984). *Individual and society in Guiana: a comparative study of Amerindian social organization*. Cambridge, UK: Cambridge University Press.

Seymour, F.J., & Dubash, N.K. (2000). *The right conditions. The World Bank, structural adjustment, and forest policy reform*. Washington, D.C.: World Resources Institute.

Sizer, N. & Plouvier, D. (2000). *Increased investment and trade by transnational logging companies in Africa, the Caribbean and the Pacific: implications for the sustainable management and conservation of tropical forests*. Brussels: WWF-Belgium, World Resources Institute's Forest Frontiers Initiative.

Thompson, A.O. (1987). *Colonialism and underdevelopment in Guyana 1580–1803*. Bridgetown, Barbados: Carib Research and Publications Inc.

Williams, B. (1991). *Stains on my name, war in my veins: Guyana and the politics of cultural struggle*. Durham, NC: Duke University Press.

Williams, D. (1985). *Ancient Guyana*. Georgetown, Guyana: Department of Culture, Ministry of Education, Social Development and Culture.

※ CHAPTER EIGHT ※

Indigenous and Tribal Peoples in Suriname: A Human Rights Perspective

Fergus MacKay

Suriname is a small former Dutch colony on the northeast coast of South America. It became independent in 1975 after attaining formal autonomy within the Kingdom of the Netherlands in 1954. The Independence Agreement with the Netherlands guaranteed a substantial amount of development assistance leading many to conclude that Suriname was in for a rosy future in which aid money and abundant natural resources could ably support its small population of around 400,000. However, falling prices for bauxite caused revenues to drop and a brutal military dictatorship (1980–87, 1990–91) characterized by economic mismanagement and gross violations of human rights led the Dutch to suspend all aid in 1982. A few years later in 1986, armed conflict erupted pitting Maroon insurgents against the dictatorship, further damaging the economy and destroying much of the country's infrastructure. The cumulative effect was macro-economic crisis.

In 1991, democracy and Dutch aid were restored and the new government formed by a coalition of political parties calling itself the New Front sought to revive the economy, in part by agreeing to an International Monetary Fund structural adjustment program and by seeking foreign investment, especially in the timber and gold sectors. In 1996, the New Front lost the election and was replaced by the National Democratic Party (NDP), headed by former military dictator, Desi Bouterse. The NDP presided over a second economic meltdown causing inflation and foreign exchange rates to spiral out of control. Dutch aid was suspended again in 1998 citing corruption, gross mismanagement and bad relations in part due to the trial in absentia of Bouterse for drug trafficking. The situation has only marginally improved since the New Front was restored to power in 2000. Today, Suriname is one of the three poorest countries in the western hemisphere.

The preceding has had severe consequences for indigenous and tribal peoples. In an attempt to reduce dependency on bauxite revenues and aid, Suriname has now turned to their traditional territories to generate income and has issued numerous logging and mining concessions, both to large- and small-scale foreign and domestic enterprises. Analyses of contracts for both logging and mining operations have revealed, however, that the Surinamese treasury will receive few if any benefits and that the environment and indigenous and tribal peoples will suffer irreparable damage (WRI, 1995).

Indigenous peoples comprise approximately 3–4% of the Surinamese population. They self-identify as four distinct peoples: Kalinya (Carib), Lokono (Arawak), Trio (and associated peoples, i.e., Wai Wai and Akuriyo) and Wayana. Suriname's rainforests, savannahs and coastal forests have sustained them since time immemorial and for the most part remain their most important source of subsistence resources.

Suriname is also home to six nonindigenous tribal peoples known as Maroons—Saramaka, N'djuka (or Aucaner), Matawai, Kwinti, Aluku and Paramaka—comprising approximately 15% of the total population. Maroons are the descendants of escaped African slaves who fought themselves free from slavery, established viable autonomous communities along the major rivers of Suriname's rainforest interior in the 17th and 18th centuries and have maintained distinct cultures comprising an amalgamation of African and Amerindian traditions. Their freedom from slavery and rights to lands and territory and the autonomous administration thereof were recognized in treaties concluded with the Dutch colonial government in the 1760s and reaffirmed in further treaties in the 1830s (Kambel & MacKay, 1999, pp. 55–80). Maroons qualify as tribal peoples according to international definitional criteria and for the most part enjoy the same rights as indigenous peoples under international law. In practice, Suriname treats indigenous peoples and Maroons as similarly situated and equivalent in terms of rights and status.

Indigenous and tribal peoples' rights to own and control their lands and resources are neither recognized nor guaranteed in Surinamese law and are routinely violated in practice. This is especially the case in connection with resource exploitation operations, but also pertains to, among others, nature conservation activities, agriculture, and infrastructure development. Indigenous and tribal peoples have mobilized to oppose further degradation of their lands and to defend their rights. In doing so, they have established a number of increasingly influential organizations such as the Association of Indigenous Village Leaders in Suriname, undertaken a variety of projects, such as mapping traditional occupation and use of their territories, attempted to initiate dialogue with the state and made use of available domestic and international legal remedies. Their ultimate aim is to secure recognition of, and respect for, their political, territorial, cultural and other rights in the laws of Suriname and in practice. Territorial rights are considered to be of paramount importance as respect for these rights is directly related to cultural integrity and survival; as indigenous peoples and Maroons jointly declared in 1996: "Our lands are of fundamental importance for our survival as Indigenous and Tribal peoples. Without the land, forests and rivers there are no trees, birds, animals and fish and we as Indigenous and Maroon Peoples will not be able to survive" (Gran Krutu, 1996, Res. 3).

During the colonial era, with a few exceptions, indigenous peoples and Maroons were largely left to their own devices and, despite postcolonial assimilationist policies and systematic discrimination, their cultures and societies remain vibrant and intact. Their focus at present is largely directed toward safeguarding their contemporary cultures and possession of lands and resources, both of which have been increasingly under threat in the past 15–20 years. While cultural resuscitation, at least for now, is not seen as urgent, their struggle at its core is one that seeks restoration of and respect for their historical autonomy/sovereignty, expressed in contemporary terms as the right to self-determination. They understand self-determination, within the framework of the Surinamese state, to be: "the right to maintain our own traditional authorities, the use of our own legal systems and the free determination of the development of our communities within our territories. The exclusive disposition, control and administration of our territories and natural resources is a fundamental condition for the effective exercise of our right to self-determination as well as for the development of our present communities and those who will come after us" (Gran Krutu, 1996, Res. 2).

This chapter provides an overview of the human rights situation of indigenous and tribal peoples in Suriname with a focus on rights to lands, territories and resources. I will also discuss indigenous and tribal peoples' attempts to seek protection for their rights and the decisions and conclusions of international human rights bodies in response to these efforts. Finally, I will discuss the case of the Saramaka Maroon people, which is pending before the Inter-American Commission on Human Rights, as well as the implications that this case may have for all indigenous and tribal peoples in Suriname. This is the first formal, international legal case against Suriname that deals directly with land and resource rights and may set a precedent that all other indigenous and tribal peoples can benefit from.

General Human Rights Situation

Discrimination with Regard to Health and Education

Indigenous and tribal peoples, especially women and children, fall at the bottom of all economic indices and are the most disadvantaged and impoverished sectors of Surinamese society. Indigenous and tribal peoples receive fewer services than other sectors of society, both quantitatively and qualitatively. Discrimination is systematic and pervasive, particularly with regard to basic services, such as health and education, and recognition of their traditional rights and autonomy. According to UNICEF, only 50–60% of indigenous and tribal communities have access to primary schooling compared to 98% of the nonindigenous/tribal population, and the schools are understaffed and lacking basic supplies (2002). Bilingual and inter-cultural education is also not provided in schools in the interior.

The same applies to the provision of health services. Immunization rates, for instance, are 50% lower than on the coast (UNICEF, 2002). Many communities do not have functioning health care facilities; those that do have such facilities have few, or in some cases no, supplies and are rarely visited by a qualified doctor. While the situation on the coast is far from ideal, the level of health services enjoyed there is far higher than in the interior. Moreover, little has been done to ameliorate the substantial impact on health caused by mining and logging activities in the interior (see below). In the case of both health and education, the state has abdicated all responsibility for provision of these services to (underfunded) missionary organizations.

Resource Exploitation

> "We are in danger of losing our very way of life. The government is giving logging companies concessions in our area, and they are destroying the forest, polluting the water, and taking our land." ("Maroon Tribe in Suriname," 2002)

In the past 15 years, Suriname has authorized numerous resource exploitation operations in indigenous and tribal territories that have had and continue to have a substantially negative impact on indigenous and tribal peoples' human rights, environment, health, dignity, resource base, standard of living and quality of life. Indigenous and tribal women and children disproportionately suffer the negative effects of these activities (Kambel, 2002; Sanomaro Esa, 1999).

Surinamese law provides no mechanism for, nor recognizes any right of, indigenous and tribal peoples to be consulted about and participate in decisions that affect them. Suriname has no comprehensive environmental laws that regulate or control the environmental impact of mining, logging or other resource exploitation activities. Logging concessions presently encompass around 40% of the country and include some 60% of indigenous and tribal communities; mining concessions encompass approximately 30% of the country and affect anywhere up to 40% of the communities. This only accounts for authorized, lawful activities and does not take into account a multitude of illegal operations.

There are between 15,000–30,000 Brazilian small-scale miners operating with state-issued permits in Suriname and many thousands of local small-scale miners and it is estimated that 20–30 tonnes of mercury are released into the environment every year (WWF, 2000; Mol et al., 2001). A report by the United States Army Corps of Engineers on water quality in Suriname states: "Due to... mercury contamination in the surface water, the water is in danger of becoming unusable in areas" (2001, p. i; PAHO/WHO, 1999). These same rivers are heavily populated by indigenous and tribal peoples and are one of their primary sources of drinking water and fish. Additionally, diarrhea, skin diseases and vomiting are all attributed to turbidity caused by mining. Sexually transmitted diseases including HIV/AIDS, partly as a result of prostitution in mining camps, are also reaching alarming proportions (Medische Zending, 1995, p. 60).

Malaria, which is greatly exacerbated by mining activities, has reached "epidemic" proportions in many parts of the interior (CEC, 1999). According to the Pan American Health Organization, Suriname has the highest incidence of malaria infection in the Americas (2000) and some 25% of the 10,000 diagnosed cases of malaria identified in the interior in 1999 were in indigenous and tribal children under the age of five (1999). Malaria has a debilitating effect on the agricultural cycle, leaving many without adequate food. This also makes them more susceptible to further infections and lengthens recovery periods. Malnutrition among once self-sufficient communities is now common. The children, especially the very young, suffer the most and it is highly probable that in some areas their normal physical, intellectual and emotional development is affected. According to UNICEF, "in some Amerindian villages, the levels of acute malnutrition were found at 22% and chronic malnutrition was 35% for children under 2 years" (2002).

The effects of these activities and the failure of the government to recognize and respect indigenous and tribal land and resource rights are substantially negative. Subsistence activities are seriously threatened in some areas, in others they are no longer possible (Struiken, 2003, p. 13). Agricultural areas in particular are damaged and destroyed by small-scale and multinational operators alike with impunity.

Rights to Territories and Resources

As noted above, Surinamese law presently neither recognizes nor guarantees the rights of indigenous and tribal peoples to own and control their traditional lands and resources. This is the case despite archaeological evidence that demonstrates that indigenous peoples have occupied and used many of the same lands they occupy today for thousands of years (Versteeg, 1998) and despite recognition of their rights in treaties and laws promulgated during the colonial era (Kambel & MacKay, 1999).

Under Surinamese law, almost all land in the interior of Suriname is presently classified as privately-owned state land (*domainland*) (Quintus Bosz, 1980, 1993; Kanhai & Nelson, 1993; Kambel & MacKay, 1999). As the state is considered in law to be the private, rather than public, owner of land, all rights to land in Suriname must derive from a valid grant issued by the state (Quintus Bosz, 1993, pp. 329, 337; FAO, 1996, sec. 3.3.8; Kambel & MacKay, 1999, pp. 22–43, 82–99). Indigenous and tribal peoples, who cannot show title issued by the state, are therefore regarded as merely permissive occupiers of state land, without effective rights or title thereto (FAO, 1996, sec. 3.3; Kambel & MacKay, 1999, pp. 22–43).

The primary legislation in Suriname concerning *domainland*, known as the L-Decrees, provides that indigenous and tribal customary entitlements (as opposed to rights) to their villages and agricultural plots shall be respected as much as possible, unless there is a conflict with the general interest.[1] General interest is understood to include the execution of any project or activity conducted pursuant to an approved development plan.[2] These provisions substantially limit the rights of indigenous and tribal peoples to the point that they become essentially meaningless (FAO, 1996, sec. 4.6.2).

Under this law, indigenous and tribal peoples are the only Surinamese citizens whose land or other rights are only to be "taken into account as much as possible," and as the explanatory note reveals, only during the period that they are not yet assimilated into Surinamese society: "[o]f course, this principle will have to be applied during a—possibly long—transitional period in which the forest population will be gradually incorporated into the total socioeconomic life."[3] Moreover, indigenous and tribal entitlements only apply to their villages and current agricultural plots and do not account for their larger territory and other lands occupied and used for hunting, fishing and other subsistence activities. This excludes a priori large areas from the purview of the illusory protections provided by legislation.

Finally, the only form of title that presently can be obtained in Suriname is land lease (*grondhuur* in Dutch). Land lease is a revocable,[4] 15–40-year lease of state land,[5] which "is issued unilaterally by the state."[6] Land lease titles can be held only by recognized legal persons.[7] Indigenous and tribal peoples, their communities and traditional land holding entities are not recognized as legal persons for the purposes of holding title, and, in the words of the UN Food and Agriculture Organization, "are effectively invisible to the legal system and incapable of holding rights" (FAO, 1996, sec. 4.6.2).

The preceding stands in stark contrast to Suriname's obligations under international law to recognize, guarantee and respect indigenous and tribal peoples' rights. Inter-American human rights jurisprudence, for example, guarantees indigenous peoples' rights to own, manage and control their lands, territories and resources traditionally owned or otherwise occupied and used (IACHR, 2002, 2003a; IACtHR, 2001). The Inter-American Commission on Human Rights (IACHR) has held that special measures are required to ensure the recognition of indigenous peoples' collective rights to their traditional lands and resources and "their right not to be deprived of this interest except with fully informed consent" (IACHR, 2002, para.131). Most recently, the IACHR "acknowledged that the property rights of indigenous peoples are not defined exclusively by entitlements within a state's formal legal regime, but also include that indigenous communal property that arises from and is grounded in indigenous custom and tradition" (2003, para. 116).

Concerning the precise nature of state obligations, the IACHR and the Inter-American Court of Human Rights have held that states are required to effectively delimit, demarcate and title indigenous peoples' territories, "an obligation that must be fulfilled by the state in full collaboration with the [indigenous] people and in accordance with their customary land use practices" (IACHR, 2003, para. 129; IACHR, 2001, para. 149). Concerning mineral and timber concessions on indigenous lands, the IACHR has stated that these may only be granted "based upon a process of fully informed consent on the part of the indigenous community as a whole" (IACHR, 2003, para. 141). The same conclusions have been reached by United Nations human rights bodies (HRC, 1990, p. 1; HRC, 1994; CERD, 1997; CESCR, 2000; CRC, 2003, para. 4).

Lack of secure land tenure coupled with a massive expansion of resource extraction operations and nature conservation activities in the past 15 years have all caused immense problems for many indigenous and tribal communities. The N'djuka village of Nieuw Koffiekamp, for example, presently faces forcible relocation for the second time in 40 years (MacKay, 2002; OAS/UPD, 1997). Another N'djuka village, Adjoemakondre, is surrounded by three active bauxite concessions. In September 1998, the community petitioned the president, without result, stating that "our agricultural plots and houses have been destroyed; our river has been polluted so badly that we can no longer use it; health problems have occurred from villagers using the river water; and use of dynamite by the company causes noise pollution and has contributed to the loss of game animals we use for food" (Adjoemakondre, 1998).

In late 2003, Suriname granted bauxite concessions to Suralco/Alcoa and BHP/Billiton in west Suriname. These concessions will affect at least three indigenous communities and will mostly likely be accompanied by one or more dams to provide hydroelectric power, a deep-water harbor and other infrastructure. The Wayana indigenous community of Kawemhakan is presently surrounded by mining concessions issued to local and multinational mining companies and has reported extensive pollution and deprivation of its subsistence resources.

Indigenous and tribal peoples' rights are not only violated in connection with resource exploitation, but also in connection with ostensibly benign activities such as nature conservation areas. Protected areas in Suriname now cover approximately 12% of the national territory. Most of the existing and proposed areas (15 of the 22), are located within or near indigenous and Maroon peoples' traditional territories (Kambel & MacKay, 1999, p. 111) and their rights are not adequately guaranteed in associated laws. The 1954 Nature Protection Act, which governs 10 protected areas, contains no guarantees at all. Article 2 of the Nature Protection Resolution of 1998 that established the Central Suriname Nature Reserve (CSNR), an area of approximately 1.5 million hectares, provides that the "villages and settlements of tribal bushland inhabitants will be respected, unless (a) the general interest or the national goal of the established nature reserve is harmed; or (b) it is provided otherwise." No protection is provided for agricultural, hunting, fishing and gathering areas or for sites of religious and cultural significance and, pursuant to subsection (b), protection of rights to villages and settlements is entirely dependent on the goodwill of the state.

Initiated by Conservation International, a US-based conservation organization, the CSNR was officially announced in New York attracting substantial international media attention and praise for Suriname. Discussing the CSNR a Kwinti Maroon leader later observed, "the reserve comprises about three-quarters of lands we consider to be our lands. It was established and proclaimed without any notice to us. We were not informed officially; we heard the news from the press" (Emanuel, 2001, p. 4). Similarly, indigenous peoples living on the Lower Marowijne River often state that "turtles have land rights, Indians don't," in reference to the Galibi Turtle Reserve (MacKay & Pané, 2004). The latest nature reserve to be proposed, and opposed by the affected communities, is a sacred site for the indigenous peoples of west Suriname.

Indigenous and Tribal Peoples' Attempts to Gain Recognition of Their Rights

Indigenous and tribal peoples have been actively seeking a solution to their land and resource rights concerns for decades (Kambel, 2002, pp. 42–55; Struiken, 2003, p. 13). They have made numerous good-faith efforts to enter into constructive dialogue with the state about rights to lands and resources, all of which have produced no concrete results. Two agreements have been concluded with the state (Peace Accord of Lelydorp, 1992, and the Buskondre Dey Protocol, 2000); neither has been honored nor implemented, and two government commissions on land rights have come and gone without even producing a final report. Domestic remedies, both judicial and administrative, have proved ineffective and indigenous and tribal peoples remain subject to pervasive discrimination in law and fact. As a consequence, their internationally guaranteed rights are presently violated with impunity. A report on Suriname by the OAS Unit for Promotion of Democracy confirms this conclusion:

> This lack of legal recognition was always a concern to the traditional rulers in the interior of Suriname. The recent encroachment, however, of determined multinationals seeking to fix legal claims on vast lumber and mineral concessions—cutting right through what for over two hundred years or more Maroons and Amerindians considered their subsistence resources—has turned this concern into panic. Cries for help and for recognition of some sort of rights, have spurred an abundance of reflection and discussion, but yielded no concrete results to date. (2001, p. 102)

Peace Accord of Lelydorp

The Interior War, which pitted mostly Maroons against the military dictatorship, and later Maroons against some indigenous people, began in 1985 with a series of armed attacks on military posts carried out by Maroons under the leadership of Ronnie Brunswijk, an ex-bodyguard of military dictator Desi Bouterse. The military launched a counteroffensive, indiscriminately targeting Maroon noncombatants in the process and initiating a period of systematic human rights violations. The war was officially concluded in 1992 with the signing of the Peace Accord of Lelydorp.

The Peace Accord, which has no official legal status (Kambel & MacKay, 1999, pp. 120–129), provides in article 10 that "the government shall endeavor that legal mechanisms be created, by which citizens [individuals] who live and reside in a tribal setting will be able to secure a real title...in their areas of residence," and around these areas, "the Government will establish an economic zone where the communities and citizens living in tribes can perform economic activities, including forestry, small-scale mining, hunting and fishing." Over 12 years after the Peace Accord was concluded, article 10 has not been implemented. Moreover, the Peace Accord merely requires that the state "shall endeavor" to recognize and protect indigenous and tribal peoples' rights to lands and resources.

The Redan and State Lands Commissions

Two commissions on land rights were established by Suriname, both of which became defunct without result. The first, the 1995 Redan Commission, ceased to function after two meetings without any report. The second, the 1996 State Lands Commission, was mandated to "make an inventory of the problems of the Indigenous peoples and Maroons regarding subjective rights to *domainland* in the interior and to provide the Government with concrete proposals and recommendations in order to come to a fundamental solution of this issue" (GOS, 1997, p.1). Its three-page interim (and only) report concluded that "the government must come up with a proposal for the creation of development poles (concentrations of villages) along roads, that the lack of funds and appropriate legislation were major obstacles to overcome and that three months were not enough to carry out its task" (GOS, 1997, p. 1).

The Gran Krutus

> We, Indigenous Peoples and Maroons, reaffirm in particular our definite intention to work together and support each other as brothers and sisters in our collective struggle for a better future for our children and children's children. (Gran Krutu, 1996, Res. 1)

Despite residual animosity from the Interior War, in 1995, Maroon and indigenous leaders began a process of attempting to minimize and resolve their differences and to speak with a unified voice. In 1995 and 1996, two *Gran Krutus* (Great Gatherings) were held to develop a common position in light of the threats to their ancestral homelands posed by extractive industries and the refusal of the government to recognize their rights. Although the leaders expressed a multitude of concerns, their paramount concern was land and resource rights. In particular, they called for a freeze on additional concessions and suspension of existing concessions until their rights were fully recognized in the Constitution and laws of Suriname (IWGIA, 1996).

The government's response was justly characterized as "hysterical" and "threatening" (Kambel, 2002, p. 93). In a radio interview held immediately after the conclusion of the 1995 Gran Krutu, the Minister of Natural Resources stated that "powers have been active [at the Gran Krutu] which have tried to stir up an atmosphere of incitement and resistance to the city. These powers must be suppressed quickly and forcibly because they constitute a threat to national integrity" ("First Reaction to the Gran Krutu," 1995). Similar sentiments were also expressed by the president and in the national press.

The Buskondre Dey (Interior or Bushland Day) Protocol of 2000

Confronted by incessant calls for recognition of land rights during the election campaign of 1999–2000, then-president Wijdenbosch decided to call a meeting of some indigenous and tribal leaders to discuss the issue. The result was the April 2000 *Buskondre Dey Protocol*. Termed a Framework Orientation Agreement, the protocol provides that the "collective rights" of the people of the interior are now recognized subject to the power of the state to exploit or authorize others to exploit natural resources without indigenous and tribal peoples' consent. The Protocol was given legal status in July 2000, when it was issued as Presidential Decree 28/2000. However, the Decree is valid only to the extent that it does not conflict with legislation, which it does and as a consequence is largely inapplicable. The Decree also reformulated the language recognizing indigenous and tribal collective rights in general so as to narrow and limit it to collective rights to lands only.

Domestic Courts

Indigenous and tribal peoples' attempts to utilize the courts to safeguard their rights have also not yielded any concrete results. The first of these attempts dates back to 1975–76, when the (now-defunct) Association of Indigenous People filed three cases asserting ownership rights to various areas of Suriname.[8] These cases were all summarily dismissed by the courts as lacking legal merit. Twelve years later, a number of indigenous village chiefs filed a counter-claim in *Tjang A Sjin v. Zaalman and Others*.[9] The judge rejected their demands on the grounds that any rights they may claim were void because the non-indigenous party held real title to the land. In so holding, the judge rejected the captain's defence that the land was traditionally and immemorially owned by the Lokono indigenous people of Wanshishia and that it also fell within the economic zone contemplated in the 1992 Peace Accord.

Most recently, in July 2003, in *Celientje Martina Joeroeja-Koewie et al. v. Suriname & Suriname Stone & Industries N.V.*, the members of the indigenous community of Pierre Kondre challenged the grant and exploitation of a sand mining concession and asserted communal land rights based on traditional occupation and use. This sand mining concession was located less than 50 meters from one of the residents' houses and in the area legally set aside for community-based timber harvesting. The court, however, rejected the community's claims as lacking "any support in law" and appeared to say that the community and its members lacked legal personality to seek protection of their rights.[10]

International Scrutiny of the Situation in Suriname

Given the preceding, it should come as no surprise that indigenous and tribal peoples have begun to look outside of Suriname for redress. Concluding that domestic legal and political options are largely futile, in the past few years they have filed a series of formal complaints and reports with international human rights bodies. While concrete changes have yet to be realized in Surinamese law and practice, international pressure is mounting on the government to finally address indigenous and tribal peoples' rights in processes and substance that are consistent with Suriname's international legal obligations.

Indigenous and tribal peoples' efforts to focus attention on the situation in Suriname have resulted in positive language in the reports and decisions of various human rights bodies. The first was the UN Committee on the Rights of the Child in 2000, which expressed serious concern about discrimination against indigenous and tribal children and the lack of bilingual education in interior schools (CRC, 2000). The UN Human Rights Committee (HRC) also began a dialogue with Suriname in October 2002 based on two reports submitted by the Forest Peoples Program (FPP, 2002a, 2002b).

A few months later, in December 2002, the IACHR decided to submit a case concerning the 1986 massacre of 40 women, children and elderly persons at Maroon village of Moiwana to the Inter-American Court of Human Rights. Importantly, the complaint filed with the Court seeks an order requiring Suriname to adopt measures necessary to demarcate and title the village's communal lands as part of the reparations. An order of the Court is legally binding on Suriname and may be enforced in domestic courts. Should Moiwana obtain collective title to land, this will provide substantial support to all indigenous and tribal communities in Suriname. A hearing was held on this case at the Court on September 9, 2004, and a decision was expected in 2005.

In March 2003, two highly important statements were issued in large part due to formal complaints submitted by a coalition of indigenous and tribal organizations (AIVL et al. 2002a, 2002b). First, the UN Commission on Human Rights' Special Rapporteur on the situation of human rights and fundamental freedoms of indigenous people reported on a series of rights violations (Stavenhagen, 2003, para. 21). Second, the UN Committee on the Elimination of Racial Discrimination (CERD) adopted Decision 3(62) under its Early Warning and Urgent Action mandate which states that the problems faced by indigenous and tribal peoples in Suriname call for "immediate attention," and that "serious violations of the rights of indigenous communities, particularly the Maroons and the Amerindians, are being committed in Suriname" (CERD 2003, para. 3–4).

CERD and the HRC issued statements on Suriname in March and May 2004, respectively. Concerning rights to lands, territories and resources,

CERD recommended: "legal acknowledgment" of indigenous and tribal peoples' rights to own, develop, control and use their communal lands and resources (CERD, 2004a, para. 11); "urgent action by the state party in cooperation with the indigenous and tribal peoples concerned to identify the lands which those peoples have traditionally occupied and used" (CERD, 2004a, para. 12); and it invited Suriname to make use of technical assistance from the Office of the UN High Commissioner for Human Rights "for the purpose of drafting a framework law on the rights of indigenous and tribal peoples" (CERD, 2004a, para. 30).

CERD also acknowledged the validity of numerous "complaints by indigenous and tribal peoples about the deleterious effects of natural-resource exploitation on their environment, health and culture" (2004a, para. 15). The associated recommendation states:

> development objectives are no justification for encroachments on human rights, and that along with the right to exploit natural resources there are specific, concomitant obligations towards the local population; it recommends adoption by the State party of a legislative framework which clearly sets forth the broad principles governing the exploitation of the land, including the obligation to abide by strict environmental standards. (CERD, 2004a, para. 15)

The HRC reached many of the same conclusions when it examined Suriname's report two weeks later, expressing concern "at the lack of legal recognition and guarantees for the protection of indigenous and tribal rights to land, and other resources" (HRC, 2004, para. 21).

The Case of the Saramaka People

Suriname is presently defending a case before the IACHR that squarely addresses the rights of indigenous and tribal peoples to own and control their traditional lands, territories and resources and to consent to concessions issued by the state. This case was filed by the Upper Suriname River Saramaka Maroon people, who number around 20,000 persons living in 61 villages, and represents the first occasion that either indigenous peoples or Maroons have formally challenged Suriname's failure to recognize and respect their land rights by submitting a formal case to an international human rights body.

Beginning in 1996, a series of logging and mining concessions were issued in Saramaka territory, the former encompassing most of the 61 villages. The Saramaka only became aware of the concessions when the employees of a Chinese logging company calling itself NV Tacoba arrived in the area in 1996/7. Other concessions, particularly gold and stone concessions, were subsequently discovered when the Saramaka obtained a map of concessions via an

NGO. Another Chinese company calling itself Ji Sheng surfaced in the area in 2000.

Tacoba and Ji Sheng's operations have included substantial damage to the forest and water quality, a reduction in game animals, destruction of subsistence farms, restrictions on community access to hunting, fishing and farming areas and intimidation by company employees. In addition to destroying subsistence farms and polluting water sources, Ji Sheng obtained the services of the Surinamese National Army to guard its concession. A military post was established in the concession and military forces actively prevented Saramaka from accessing hunting, fishing and farming areas.

The concessions held by Tacoba, Ji Sheng and others were all granted without informing the Saramaka people, without consulting with them and without their agreement. The rights of the Saramaka people to their ancestral territory and resources were not considered or respected and they have received no compensation for the timber extracted from their lands or for the damages to their lands, waters and crops caused by these companies. Moreover, Suriname failed to respond to or address in any way a series of petitions and formal complaints filed by the Saramaka people in connection with the operations of these companies.

In light of the preceding, the Saramaka sought the protection of the IACHR and filed a petition there in October 2000. Submitted by the Association of Saramaka Authorities, an organization composed of the traditional leaders of the Upper Suriname River Saramaka communities, and 12 village leaders representing each of the Saramaka land-owning matrilineal clans, the petition cited Suriname's failure to recognize Saramaka rights to land, territory and resources as defined by the American Convention on Human Rights and active violation of those rights due to the logging and mining concessions granted in Saramaka territory.

In March 2002, the Saramaka were informed that the Commission had formally opened *Case 12.338 Twelve Saramaka Clans (Suriname)*. Following further submissions by the Saramaka, in August 2002, the IACHR issued precautionary measures—interim measures designed to avoid threats of grave and irreparable harm. The precautionary measures requested that Suriname "take the appropriate measures to suspend all concessions, including permits and licenses for logging and mine exploration and other natural resource development activity on lands used and occupied by these clans" (IACHR, 2003b, III, 3(c), para. 75). To date and despite repeated requests by the Saramaka, there has been no action to implement the precautionary measures. Not only has Suriname not honored the precautionary measures, it has also issued a number of additional concessions, most recently in August 2003.

The Saramaka have attempted, to no avail, to resolve the case through mediation. Because of Suriname's refusal to negotiate about ownership of lands, in August 2004, they requested that the case be submitted to the IACHR for a binding judgment. Based on recent developments, it is expected that the case will be submitted to the Court in 2005. Should the Saramaka prevail, all indigenous and tribal peoples may benefit from the ruling as it most likely will require that the government adopt legislation recognizing and securing collective ownership of traditional lands and resources in general and providing mechanisms by which these lands can be identified and demarcated.

Conclusion

Indigenous and tribal peoples in Suriname have maintained most of their traditional governance systems and customary laws and, despite postcolonial assimilationist policies and dispossession of lands and resources, have been largely able to maintain their cultural integrity and autonomy within their traditional territories. In the past 20 years, however, they are increasingly threatened by an onslaught of resource exploitation operations that are causing serious social, health, environmental and other problems, institutionalized discrimination, pressure to migrate to urban areas in order to secure education, employment and basic services, and the intransigence of the state with regard to recognition of and respect for their rights. In some areas, their traditional ways of life and means of subsistence are now seriously compromised and their autonomy is being eroded as the state seeks to derive profit from their lands and resources.

Indigenous and tribal peoples are actively seeking to address this situation and are making use of all available remedies, including at the international level. As the editor of the national newspaper, *De Ware Tijd*, observed a few years ago, they are no longer willing to "be brushed off with vague resolutions and promises" ("The Land Rights Issue," 2002). Suriname has thus far failed to take any constructive steps towards meeting indigenous and tribal demands. On the contrary, it continues to characterize indigenous and tribal peoples' demands and internationally guaranteed rights as illegitimate, divisive and discriminatory vis-à-vis other sectors of society, and in some cases as a threat to national security and territorial integrity. In the near future, however, Suriname will most likely be faced with legally binding international judicial decisions requiring that it recognize and guarantee indigenous and tribal rights. It will then have to decide if it wishes to remain, in defiance of international law, the only state in the Americas that has failed in any way to recognize indigenous and tribal peoples' rights to their territories and resources.

Notes

1. Decree L-1, 1982, Basic Principles on Land Policy, art. 4.1.
2. Decree L-1, 1982, art. 4.2.
3. Ibid.
4. Decree of 15 June 1982, containing general principles concerning Land Policy (Decree Principles Land Policy), SB 1982, no. 10, art. 9(2).
5. Decree Allocation Domain Land, art. 14(3).
6. Decree Principles Land Policy, art. 14(1).
7. Decree Allocation Domain Land, art. 2.
8. *Case No. 165 Association of Indigenous People v. Suriname 1975*; A.R. No. 753160, 13 Jan. 1976 and A.R. No. 754180, 26 Sept. 1975
9. *Tjang A Sjin v. Zaalman and Others*, Cantonal Court, First Canton, Paramaribo, 21 May 1998.
10. *Celientje Martina Joeroeja-Koewie et al. v. Suriname & Suriname Stone & Industries N.V.*, A.R. no. 025350, Cantonal Court, First Canton, Paramaribo, 24 July 2003, at 3.

References

Adjoemakondre. (1998, September). *Petition to the Suriname Government concerning the situation in Adjoemakondre.*

Association of Indigenous Village Leaders (AIVL) in Suriname et al. (2002a). *Persistent and pervasive racial discrimination against indigenous and tribal peoples in the Republic of Suriname. Formal request to initiate an urgent procedure to avoid immediate and irreparable harm*, December 15.

———. (2002b). *Formal communication made pursuant to Commission on Human Rights Resolution 2001/57: Failure of the Republic of Suriname to recognize, guarantee and respect the rights of indigenous and tribal peoples to lands, territories and resources, to cultural integrity and to be free from racial discrimination*, June 12.

Caribbean Epidemiology Center (CEC). (1999). *Communicable diseases feedback report 1999.* Retrieved September 18, 2002, from http://www.carec.org/data/comm-dis/99wks39-52.

Committee on Economic, Social and Cultural Rights (CESC). (2000). *General Comment 14, The right to the highest attainable standard of health: 11/08/2000.* UN Doc. E/C.12/2000/4, August 11.

Committee on the Elimination of Racial Discrimination (CERD). (1997). General Recommendation XXIII (51) concerning indigenous peoples. Adopted at the Committee's 1235th meeting, August 18, 1997. UN Doc. CERD/C/51/Misc.13/Rev.4.

———. (2003). Prevention of racial discrimination, including early warning measures and urgent action procedures, Decision 3(62), Suriname. UN Doc. CERD/C/62/CO/Dec.3, March 21.

———. (2004a). Concluding observations of the Committee on the Elimination of Racial Discrimination: Suriname. UN Doc. CERD/C/64/CO/9/Rev.2, March 12.

———. (2004b). Summary record of the 1614th Meeting, 64th session. UN Doc. CERD/C/SR. 1614, February 27.

Committee on the Rights of the Child. (2000). *Concluding observations of the Committee on the*

Rights of the Child: Suriname. 28/06/2000. UN Doc. CRC/C/15/Add.130.

———. (2003). *Day of General Discussion on the Rights of Indigenous Children, Recommendations.* 34th Session, Sep 15–Oct 3.

Emanuel, O. (2001). *Presentation of the Kwinti at the conference on Indigenous Peoples and Protected Areas in the Three Guyanas,* April 2001.

First Reaction to the Gran Krutu by Minister Romeo van Russel. (1995, August 17). Radio Paramaribo.

Food and Agriculture Organization (FAO). (1996). *Strengthening national capacity for sustainable development of forests on public lands; Report of the Legal Consultant, Cormac Cullinan,* FAO Project TCP/SUR/4551.

Forest Peoples Program (FPP). (2002a). *Submission of the forest peoples programme concerning the Republic of Suriname and its compliance with the International Covenant on Civil and Political Rights s. Articles 1, 26 and 27: The Rights of Indigenous Peoples and Maroons in Suriname,* January 30.

———. (2002b). *Second submission of the forest peoples programme concerning the Republic of Suriname and its compliance with the International Covenant on Civil and Political Rights. Articles 1, 26 and 27: The Rights of Indigenous Peoples and Maroons in Suriname,* August 20.

Government of Suriname (GOS). (1987). *Commissie domeinland inheemsen en marrons* [State Lands Commission], Paramaribo.

Gran Krutu. (1996). *Resolutions of the third Gran Krutu of indigenous and tribal peoples.* Galibi, 20–22 November 1996.

Human Rights Committee (HRC). (1990). Bernard Ominayak, Chief of the Lubicon Lake Band vs. Canada, *Report of the Human Rights Committee,* 45 UN GAOR Supp. (No.43), UN Doc. A/45/40, vol. 2.

———. (1994). General Comment No. 23 (50) (art. 27), adopted by the Human Rights Committee at its 1314th meeting (50th session), April 6, 1994. UN Doc. CCPR/C/21/Rev.1/Add.5.

———. (2004). Concluding observations of the Human Rights Committee: Suriname. UN Doc. CCPR/CO/80/SUR, March 30.

Inter-American Commission on Human Rights (IACHR). (2002). *Report N° 75/02,* Mary and Carrie Dann (Case N° 11.140 [United States]), Dec. 27. OEA/Ser.L/V/II.116, Doc. 46.

———. (2003a). *Report No. 96/03,* Maya indigenous communities and their members (Case 12.053 [Belize]), October 24.

———. (2003b). *Annual report of the Inter-American Commission on Human Rights 2002.* OEA/Ser.L/V/II.117, Doc. 1 rev. 1, March 7, 2003.

Inter-American Court of Human Rights (IACtHR). (2001). *The Mayagna (Sumo) indigenous community of Awas Tingni v. The republic of Nicaragua,* Judgment of August 31, 2001.

International Work Group for Indigenous Affairs (IWGIA). (1996). *Indigenous Affairs,* No. 1, Jan./Feb./March 1996.

Kambel, E.R. (2002). *Resource conflicts, gender and indigenous rights in Suriname: local, national and global perspectives.* PhD Diss., University of Leiden.

Kambel, E-R., & MacKay, F. (1999). *The rights of indigenous peoples and Maroons in Suriname.* Doc. No. 96. Copenhagen: International Work Group for Indigenous Affairs. Updated, Dutch translation: Kambel, E.R., & MacKay, F. (2003). *De Rechten van Inheemse Volken en Marrons in Suriname.* Leiden, The Netherlands: Koninklijk Instituut voor Taal-, Land- en Volkenkunde, KITLV Uitgeverij.

Kanhai, I., & Nelson, J. (Eds.). (1993). *Strijd om grond in Suriname: verkenning van het probleem van* de grondenrechten van Indianen en Bosnegers [The struggle for land in Suriname: the land rights problem of Indians and Maroons]. Paramaribo, Suriname: Mimeograph.

"The Land Rights issue is not so easy to resolve [Editorial]." (2002, April 1). De Ware Tijd, p. 3.

MacKay, F. (2002). Mining in Suriname: multinationals, the state and the Maroon community of Nieuw Koffiekamp. In L. Zarsky (Ed.), Human Rights and the Environment (pp. 57–78). London: EarthScan.

MacKay, F., & Pané, R. (2004). Protected areas in Suriname: fifty years of disrespect. Cultural Survival Quarterly, 28(1), 43–7.

Maroon tribe in Suriname produces map to claim land rights, halt logging. (2002, October 16). Associated Press.

Medische Zending. (1995). Jaarverslag [Annual Report of the Medical Mission], Paramaribo, Suriname.

Mol, J.H., Ramlal, J.S., Lietar, C., & Verloo, M. (2001). Mercury contamination in freshwater, estuarine, and marine fishes in relation to small-scale gold mining in Suriname, South America. Environmental Research, 86, 183–197.

Organization of American States/Unit for the Promotion of Democracy (OAS/UPD). (1997). Natural resources, foreign concessions and land rights: a report on the village of Nieuw Koffiekamp. Washington, DC: Unit for Promotion of Democracy, General Secretariat, Organization of American States.

———. (2001). Peace and democracy in Suriname. Final report of the Special Mission to Suriname (1992-2000). Unit for Promotion of Democracy, Organization of American States (OEA/Ser.D/XX SG/UPD/III.2).

Pan-American Health Organization (PAHO). (1999). Country health profile for Suriname 1999. Retrieved May 30, 2002, from http://165.158.1.110/english/sha/prflsur.html.

———. (2000). Situation of malaria programs in the Americas. Retrieved May 27, 2002, from http://www.paho.org/English/SHA/be_v22n1-malaria.htm.

Pan-American Health Organization/World Health Organization (PAHO/WHO). (1999). Sectoral analysis of drinking water supply and sanitation in Suriname, Paramaribo. Plan Regional de Inversiones en Ambiente y Salud. Serie Análisis N° 1, Pt. 9, Pan American Center for Sanitary Engineering and Environmental Services/Pan American Health Organization/World Health Organization.

Quintus Bosz, A.J.A. (1980). Drie eeuwen grondpolitiek in Suriname [Three Centuries of Land Policies in Suriname]. Paramaribo, Suriname: Vaco Publishing.

———. (1993). Verzamelde werken van Prof. Mr. A.J.A. Quintus Bosz [Collective Works of Prof. Mr. A.J.A. Quintus Bosz]. Paramaribo, Suriname: Vaco Publishing.

Sanomaro Esa. (1999). Indigenous rights, women and empowerment in Suriname. Tilburg, The Netherlands: Global Law Association.

Stavenhagen, R. (2003). Report of the Special Rapporteur on the situation of human rights and fundamental freedoms of indigenous people, Rodolfo Stavenhagen, submitted in accordance with Commission resolution 2001/65. UN Doc. E/CN.4/2003/90, January 21.

Struiken, H. (2003). Land policy, administration and management: the Suriname experience. Paper presented for the Workshop on Land Policy, Administration and Management, Port of Spain, Trinidad, March 19–21 (IDB, USAID, DfID, GoTT). Retrieved June 19, 2004, from http://www.mhtc.net/~terra/carib_workshop/pdf/surinameces.pdf.

UNICEF. (2001). Suriname multiple indicator cluster survey. Funded by UNICEF, March. Retrieved August 27, 2002, from http://www.childinfo.org/ MICS2/ newreports/ surinam/ surinamreport.PDF.

UNICEF-Caribbean. (2002). *Suriname*, 21 May 2002. Retrieved March 1, 2003, from http://www.unicef-cao.org/ publications/ Reports/ PromiseToCaribbeanChildren/ Suriname2.html.

US Army Corps of Engineers. (2001). *Water resources assessment of Suriname*, December. Retrieved May 27, 2002, from http://www.sam.usace.army.mil/en/wra/Suriname/ Suriname%20 Water%20 Resources%20 Assessment.pdf.

Versteeg, A.H. (1998). The history of prehistoric archaeological research in Suriname. In Wong, Th.E. de Vletter, D.R. Krook, L. Zonneveld, J.I.S. & A.J. van Loon (Eds.), *The History of Earth Sciences in Suriname*. Kon. Ned. Akad. Wet. & Ned. Inst. Toegep. Geowet. TNO, p. 203–234.

World Resources Institute (WRI). (1995). *Backs to the wall in Suriname: forest policy in a country in crisis*. Washington, DC: WRI.

World Wildlife Fund (WWF). (2000). Summary of the proceedings of a conference on mercury and artisinal gold mining, March 30, Paramaribo. Retrieved June 11, 2002, from http://www.wwfguianas.org/gfecp05.htm.

✳ NATION-STATE ✳

Modern Incorporations and Challenges to Articulating and Organizing Aboriginality

Joseph Palacio, who is both a Garifuna and an anthropologist, is uniquely positioned for providing an account of the ways the Garifuna have encountered, engaged, and experienced the wider national society. Palacio focuses on recent urbanization among the Garifuna of Belize, demonstrating the continuation of bonds and practices that they brought from the village as well as changes in their cultural identity that have been induced by the urban social setting. There is an analysis of the significance for Garifuna identity in the rural-to-urban transition, and the ways in which Garifuna culture is reproduced in and through new settings. As one of the Caribbean's most traveled populations, exiled first from St. Vincent, spread across the Caribbean coast of Central America, and relocated to Los Angeles and New York, amongst other metropolitan centers, Palacio's study helps us to better understand how modernity has been adapted to Garifuna ends. In French Guiana, the French state expects Amerindians in its colony to assimilate. Indeed, as Gérard Collomb reveals, there can be no indigeneity where the assumption is that all subjects are not ethnics, but rather nationals. The Amerindian political movement in French Guiana originated in the 1980s among the Kali'na (Caribs) on the bases of a territorial claim as well as a call for the recognition of their culture and indigenous language. These claims were addressed to the French state, thus reproducing a long-established relationship between France and the indigenous peoples during the colonial era. However, in the last decade the Amerindians have developed different political strategies in that they initiated a move onto the transnational stage, where potential new international laws concerning indigenous peoples are being discussed. Through these processes, the Amerindians of French Guiana have succeeded in breaking their exclusive link with the state, established during the colonial era.

※ CHAPTER NINE ※

Cultural Identity among Rural Garifuna Migrants in Belize City, Belize

Joseph O. Palacio

In discussing the lack of focus on indigenous peoples in the history of creolization within the West Indies, Honychurch (2000, p.18) added, "in this the most colonial of all colonial societies, where the deepest wrong was done, the effects of the process of colonization and the creolization which accompanied it, have—like the subject peoples themselves—been marginalized."[1] This is a concise way of saying that the cultural identity of the region's indigenous peoples needs to be understood on its own terms as well as being a vital component of the region's culture. Since 1975 the main focus on the identity of the region's indigenous peoples has been on their insertion within nation-building either before or after political independence. Examples include Gullick (1985, pp. 5–24) for the Caribs of St. Vincent; Honychurch (2000, pp. 213–222) for the Caribs of Dominica; Forte (1999) for the Caribs of Trinidad; Palacio (1995) and Sanford (1975) for the Garifuna of Belize; and Sanders (1987, pp.185–204) for Guyana.

While these studies have taken place among informants within their own communities, there has been hardly any work among those who migrated to urban communities.[2] As in other parts of the world, indigenous peoples in the Caribbean have often relocated to towns and cities, where they could have better access to jobs, health care, education, and a higher quality of life. Within the Caribbean the Garifuna have been the target of most studies within their migration destination, mainly in the United States (Gonzalez, 1979, pp. 255–263; Gonzalez & Gonzalez, 1979, pp. 18–20; Palacio, 1992, pp. 17–26). The focus of this chapter is a study of Garifuna rural folk, who have relocated from Barranco, a village in southern Belize, to Belize City, with emphasis on the transition of their cultural identity.

Who Are the Indigenous Peoples of Belize?

According to the 2000 national census there were almost 39,000 persons from a national population of 240,000, who identified themselves as K'ekchi (Maya), Mopan (Maya), Yucatec (Maya), and Garifuna, the four sets of indigenous peoples in Belize. Together they constitute 17% of the national population, the highest percentage of indigenous peoples in any Circum-Caribbean state; and in Central America, the next highest to Guatemala. They are spread over the country with the largest concentration at a high of 72% in the Toledo District. Generally, there is a high proliferation of small rural communities with population hovering less than 1,000 each. Only the Garifuna predominate in urban communities.

The Garifuna (formerly called Black Caribs) are at the center of this chapter. At slightly more than 14,000 they are the largest indigenous nation, making up 6% of the country's population. They are black, showing extensively the results of the blend between their two sets of ancestors, the Island Caribs and Maroon African slaves, which took place in the Eastern Caribbean island of St. Vincent (Gonzalez, 1988).

Like the other indigenous peoples, who now call Belize home, the Garifuna suffered violent persecution at the hands of the Europeans. But none came as close to them in paying the ultimate price, namely genocide, for their homeland in terms of the scale of persecution and the relative proportions of their dead (Craton, 1982). Only about a quarter of the original population in St. Vincent arrived in Roatan, Honduras, having survived the extermination that the British executed. The final ignominy facing them was being unceremoniously unloaded in 1797 on the inhospitable island of Roatan, Honduras, which was then disputed territory. According to the British, it was to be their final death blow (Gonzalez, 1988, p. 41). The sheer determination to survive as a people during their first century in Central America motivated the Garifuna to travel all along its Caribbean coast looking for livelihood. By 1802 they had arrived in Belize.

In adjusting to their new home they have brought to Central America their Antillean component of the Great Amazonian cultural tradition (identified by the use of cassava tubers and their complement of food preparation implements together with other traits) to an area that had been the heartland of Mesoamerica. Such intermixture has accentuated the cultural heterogeneity of the Circum-Caribbean region.

Recurrent persecutions in Honduras together with the demand for cheap wage labor in Belize have always pushed Garifuna immigrants to Belize. It is being repeated at this time with new arrivals from Honduras and Guatemala, as part of the historical cycle of migratory wage labor that has conditioned the life of Garifuna everywhere. Traveling within Central America and to the US has long been an essential part of their livelihood patterns (Gonzalez, 1979, pp. 18–20). One of the results has been their concentration in urban communities in Belize. As many as 50% live in Dangriga, 30% in Belize City, and the rest in four villages. The heavy influences of urban living have placed the youth in doubt with respect to their Garifuna identity. It is much more acceptable for them to follow the predominant Creole cultural lifestyle. Being painfully aware of this precipitous slippage, the Garifuna—both young and old—have expressed strong efforts at cultural revitalization (Palacio et al., 2003, pp. 25–51).

The Study

I drafted the survey instrument for the study entitled "Survey of Belize City from Barranco Village." The topics included biography, household, cultural identification, settlement, livelihood, and community activities. The four fieldworkers who did the interviews were villagers resident in Belize City and had previous experience in doing surveys. They did the work within two months in June and July 1989.

The selection of respondents proved not to be a difficult task. As villagers, the fieldworkers and I knew everyone who had left the village and lived in Belize City. We were able to locate all the addresses and ended up with 100% of our target sample. The person interviewed was either the head of the household or spouse, whoever was the villager. There is a justification for using the term "villagers" for the immigrants: the term they used among themselves was *Barranguna*, "native of Barranco," no matter how long ago they left the village. In most cases both the household head and spouse were villagers and we interviewed the one available, usually the female. We interviewed a total of 60 persons. With an average of four persons for each household, the total number of persons represented within all the households was about 240.

The motivation to do the study came from academic and personal reasons. Having done my doctoral dissertation fieldwork in Barranco in 1979–1980, I was aware of the presence of several Barranguna in Belize City. As a resident of Belize City I met many of them frequently. The study gave me an opportunity to know how they were adjusting to city life. Between 1989 and 1991, I represented the University of the West Indies School of Continuing Studies in a joint urban planning study of Belize City with McGill University. While the McGill faculty and students did the urban planning component, we focused on community extension, using our knowledge of groups within the city. This survey added information about one group of immigrants, among others, in the city. After the fieldwork we ran frequency distribution tables including percentages and cumulative percentages of the variables.

Migration and the Garifuna

Before delving into the narrative of the study, it is necessary to see the movement of rural Garifuna to Belize City as part of a larger scale of migration for them in Central America. Following Gonzalez's chronological sequence of Garifuna migrations (1988, p. 173), the first phase was extensive traveling along the Caribbean coast stretching from Nicaragua to Belize as hired hands on boats or on their own as traders. In the latter case, their women no doubt also joined on the trips to trade their own agricultural produce. Gonzalez (1988, pp. 171–172) attributes these early travels to the tradition of excellent boatmanship, which the Garifuna had used for the purposes of warfare and trading in St. Vincent.

The second phase, which also started as early as their arrival in Central America, was going on seasonal wage labor lasting for the greater part of the year to woodcutting camps along rivers in Honduras and Belize. The third phase started as early as 1910 (M. Palacio, 2002) and picked up momentum after World War II (Gonzalez, 1988, p. 173), when men left for towns and cities within their home countries as well as port towns in the US, some staying permanently. This overview shows that travels by both men and women have always been a way of life for the Garifuna. Where they ended up and what they did depended on opportunities that became available to them, while being completely beyond their control.

The first reference to the Garifuna in Belize was the debate at the Magistrates Meeting[3] on August 9, 1802, to prevent them from coming to the Settlement, in case they committed the same "atrocities" for which they were "well known" in Grenada and St. Vincent (Cayetano, n.d., p. 25). Obviously, this resolution did not stop them from returning to Belize and in 1811 the Magistrates further directed that the Garifuna should not remain in the Settlement (at that time dominated by Belize Town) for more than 48 hours (Cayetano, n.d., p. 30).

These restrictions applied to Garifuna men and women, who came on their own as traders and certainly not to those whom the woodcutters brought as laborers to work on their camps dotted along the rivers in the hinterland. The repeated official proscription, however, left a strong impression affecting the free movement of Garifuna to what was eventually to become Belize City. The folk belief became embedded for generations that the Garifuna did not belong in the city and that those, who came to live there, were shedding away their "Garifunaness" to become Creole[4] townsfolk. The words of the following song, translated from the Garifuna, elaborate,

> Tila, my older sister
> You are the only one I hear about from Belize City
> They say you now have a Creole man.

> You can't even say "Good Morning,"
> So, what will you tell him, Tila, my older sister? (E. R.
> Cayetano, 1993, p. 91)

The singer is decrying her sister's presumptuous behavior not only to come to live in Belize City but also to live with a Creole man, when she cannot even speak the man's language.

Having moved extensively within Central America, the US became the next destination for Garifuna migration at first for a few but gradually taking massive proportions from 1960 (M. Palacio, 2002).[5] Notwithstanding the economic gains forthcoming from the US, the difficulties of migrating there made it a less attractive option over closer destinations. The travel cost—far beyond the budget of villagers—had to be met either through savings over a long period of time or by relatives already in the US. Many arrived initially as visitors and remained illegally running the risk of being caught by the authorities. There was prolonged separation from one's children and older relatives, who might need close attention. For the Garifuna in Belize, internal migration to local towns and Belize City became a more affordable option with fewer risks; besides, one could more easily return home in case of emergencies.

The village has traditionally been the incubator for Garifuna culture since their arrival in Central America a little over 200 years ago. On the other hand, the city—and more especially Belize City, which up to 1970 was the capital of the country—was the source of governance, cash, imported goods, Western religion, and education, all of which influenced every aspect of daily life in the village. The village and the city have been geographically separated not only in distance but also from the difficulties of primitive sea transportation, making the social and cultural gap between them even more profound. Indeed, the process of transition from two diametrically opposed environments presents an unusually rich backdrop to observe how people transform their identity.

Barranco and Belize City in the 1980s

The Garifuna people arrived in Central America as defeated exiles from St. Vincent 1797, a little short of 200 years when I did the fieldwork. Their fault had been to fight off efforts by the British to take over their lands to subdivide among speculators for sugar plantations. Indeed, their resistance was no different than the reaction of any indigenous people to the usurpation of their lands, the destruction of their political/military infrastructure, the total disregard of their kinship system and distinctive cultural traits, the killing of their women and children, and the wanton destruction of their homes, farms, and boats (Fabel, 2000, pp. 162–205). Since their arrival and self-resettlement in Central America, the Garifuna have been subjected to extreme forms of colonial exploitation in Honduras, Nicaragua, Guatemala, and Belize. But they have not given up efforts to take possession of lands for their dwelling and farms, to retain community organizations based on kinship, and to retain their cultural diagnostics—notably language, music, dance, spirituality, and acquiring livelihood through farming and fishing. Besides, they have not forgotten their common origin in St. Vincent. In all of these regards they are a people indigenous to the larger Caribbean region, who have reconstituted their traditional culture wherever they find themselves.

It is not known when the village of Barranco, located along the southernmost coast of Belize, was first settled by the Garifuna.[6] The first recorded settlement started in 1862. The site of the village made it attractive for settlement. It was well drained and provided easy access for good fishing and fertile lands for farming; furthermore, it was far enough from the center of British influence in the capital city to limit the interference of colonial administrators into daily life. Yet it was near enough to sources of wage labor in Belize, Guatemala, and Honduras.

The time of the highest economic prosperity in the village took place from 1900 to 1940, during the banana production period. Since then there have been efforts to revive agriculture and fishing for home consumption and the national market but to little avail. Wage labor migration started as early as the first settlement and became most pronounced between 1960 and 1975 in response to the deteriorating economic conditions in the village.

Notwithstanding the early reliance on wage labor migration the village retained an inwardly oriented Garifuna culture. The diagnostic cultural traits, as listed above, flourished. The kinship structure was the basis for domestic organization, village community solidarity, and the rights to land. There was an outward orientation to sources of wage labor. To succeed in that market children did well in the primary school, which maintained standards as high as those found in other parts of the country. As in the case of other Garifuna villages, Barranco became well known for its teachers, who worked far and wide within the country. From the teaching profession they moved into other careers in the public and private sectors. The respondents in our survey were first generation settlers, joining hundreds from other rural parts of the country coming to Belize City after 1970. Previously, there had been a heavy emigration of Belize City residents to the US from 1960 (Woods, Perry, & Steagall, 1997).

In anticipation of political independence, which came in 1981, the government undertook changes toward a more inclusive national culture. Political leaders gave assurance that the previous "divide and rule" practices of the British would be superseded by a new multiculturalism, encompassing all of Belize's ethnic groups, including those from the south—the Maya and Garifuna—who had been traditionally overlooked. As evidence of such a shift, artistic performances, including items by these two groups, began to be shown in Belize City, revealing a previously untapped source to be accommodated within the national culture. The revitalization of the arts came after political parties had actively recruited their membership from all ethnic groups throughout the country.[7]

The political leaders of nationalism did not impose the iconography of the Ancient Maya, as the first peoples of Belize, to lead the renewed effort at building an overarching multiculturalism. In this case there was a difference with the overt use of Taíno symbolism in Puerto Rico to build its national culture, overlooking the African as a founding culture (Duany, 1999). Honychurch referred to efforts by politicians in Dominica also to use the image of the Caribs, which he described as a "type of idyllic proto-nationalism" (2000, p. 215) as a rallying point for the island's new national culture.

Another cultural groundswell came with the onset of a Black Nationalist movement in Belize City from 1965, which attempted to bring to the forefront the previously unmentioned significance of black people in Belize's historical and current society (Shoman, 1994, pp. 241–256). The cathartic influence of this "revelation" was to encourage closer ties between the two black groups in the country, the Creole and Garifuna.

Simultaneously, the Garifuna were consolidating their own *Garifunaduo* movement in the 1970s. Spearheaded by young returning university graduates, *Garifunaduo* promoted investigation into roots and the application of the results to revitalize the culture. Examples included popularizing the use of the term "Garifuna" in English, replacing "Black Carib"; the use of Garifuna first names instead of traditional Christian names; and, the use of artifacts as decoration, in many cases uplifting them from the traditional kitchen to the modern living room. One of the several offshoots of *Garifunaduo* was the quest to rediscover the strength of African and Amerindian roots in the formation of the culture in St. Vincent.

Garifunaduo, therefore, prepared the way for the Garifuna to accept both black Creoles as well as the indigenous Maya as their brothers and sisters. Toward both there had been more than ambivalence. Taylor recounts the animosity of one of his informants in the Garifuna village of Hopkins against the Creole (1951, p. 39). Garifuna prejudices against the Maya have also been well known. They derived from the position of "bearers of enlightenment" they held as teachers recruited by the Roman Catholic mission to work among the "heathen Indians." The Maya did not take lightly to this imposition into their communities and reacted with ill will against the Garifuna. In hindsight the ambivalence across ethnic groups was the fruit of both British colonialism and Western religion, whittled away with some measure of success by the pre-independence nationalist movement.

The review of these currents in cultural resurgence is important to understand the Garifuna coming from the villages and being met by several kinds of cultural influences within the city after 1970. The city was no longer the bastion of anti-Garifuna sentiment, about which they had heard from their parents. Garifuna urbanites displayed more pride and self-assurance than the Garifuna villagers had anticipated. Furthermore, there was greater scope for acceptance of the Maya and other peoples with whom they interacted as fellow Belizeans. Urban Garifuna thus experienced the rise of the new inclusive multicultural Belize that symbolized the onset of independence in 1981. The importance of this study arises from Belize City being the third-largest concentration of the Garifuna, according to the 1991 census. The two communities superseding Belize City in Garifuna population were Dangriga and Punta Gorda. The population of the country was 186,000.

Survey Results

In describing the results of the survey I place the respondents within wider frameworks of interaction starting from the household and ending with the wider urban community.

The Informants and Their Households

Under this subheading I include gender, household headship, type of family, persons who frequent the households, and leisure activities. Among the informants 25 (42%) were males and 35 (58%) females. I did not include age in the questionnaire to limit the sensitive nature of the questions for the respondents; besides, with the help of the fieldworkers, I was able to arrive at an approximate age range. The respondents were a mixed group. About one-half were men and women 35 years old and older with their children and grandchildren. The remainder was younger men and women living with their spouses and their children. Many of the households were female-headed 29 (48%). Finally, in 39 of the households there were conjugal families and in 21 extended families. In conjugal families the relationship of members to the head is that of spouse or parent. Following the definition of Hammel and Laslett (1974), in extended families there is a wider framework of additional relations with the head. They include consanguineal, i.e., sibling and cousin as well as affinal, i.e., mother-in-law, son-in-law, etc.

The questionnaire asked how members extended their relations beyond the household. The primary group included persons who "dropped by" frequently and those who visited regularly. In the first category I referred to close relatives, infants being cared for either through reciprocity or for a fee, boyfriends/girlfriends, and so forth. There were up to five persons per household and they were mainly relatives and friends from the village. In the second category, namely visitors, they were mainly Garifuna including others not from the village.

The significance of the household as the focal point of activities came forward in response to questions about leisure activities for younger and older members. For the former they were almost all indoor activities, such as reading, listening to music, and watching television. There was minimal mention of outdoor sports. For the latter they were socializing at home with friends, drinking, having parties, or watching television. Occasionally they went to dance at a discotheque.

Location and Livelihood

The majority lived in the Southside of Belize City,[8] where they clustered in parts of the St. Martin de Porres, Port Loyola, and Lake Independence areas. All of these were newly built up areas reclaimed from the wetlands surrounding the older part of the city. Another four lived in the village of Ladyville located 12 miles from Belize City. As in the case of the Southside of Belize City, it was a newly cleared area. The other 10 lived in households in Northside Belize City, where there was a cluster of five along Victoria Street, with the rest scattered in the newer parts of that area of the city.

In summary, the vast majority lived in areas where house lots were more easily available than in the older parts of the city. The land was waterlogged and became easily flooded during the rainy weather, making access difficult. Although they had electricity and piped water, the streets were not paved, becoming alternately dusty and muddy. The houses were substandard, many lacking indoor plumbing. Finally, most of the dwellers were renters. There were a few living in better housing in the Northside but they were also renters.

I asked about three previous addresses to get some idea about the scale of movements within the City. Most had moved at least once but remained within the same general area, with only a few venturing into other parts. Previous renters gave information about their dwelling to others, resulting in the circulation of the same housing within the community of villagers.

In most cases the household head and other members of the household had jobs, half of which were employed in lower-level blue-collar jobs. Examples included construction trades, security, gardener, factory worker, and lower-level health workers. There were 11 (18%) white-collar workers, such as teacher, nurse, and banker. Among the remaining, seven belonged to the uniformed services either as soldier or police officer. Nine were self-employed. In this group there were women who cooked food to sell or did laundry, while the men were electricians, mechanics, or engaged in other trades but worked for themselves.

In summary, most of the persons in the sample were working in lower- and middle-class types of jobs. They were living in rented dwelling, while a few already owned a house in one of the newer parts of the city. To do this they would have lobbied their member of parliament or the government minister responsible for lands and housing loans. Alternatively they would "capture" (i.e., squat on) land with the hope that they could eventually own it legally and that the city infrastructure of streets, drains, and sewerage connection would reach them sooner or later. They clustered near each other where they lived and passed information to newcomers.

Links with the Home Community and the Belize City Garifuna Community

Older persons in our sample started leaving Barranco in 1943 but the outflow picked up from 1965. The median year of departure was 1970 but the median year for arrival in Belize City was 1980. Belize City became the final destination among others in the chain of migratory wage labor for the villagers. Many had worked for some time in the timber, citrus, and sugar industries in different parts of the country.

It did not seem that many were planning to leave for the most popular destination for Belizeans—both Garifuna and non-Garifuna—the US. In casual discussion they gave the impression that they regarded Belize City as a distinct improvement over previous destinations in their wage labor sojourn. By and large they might have weighed the risks and costs of going to the US as against the relative security of staying in Belize City. As one told me, "I feel fairly comfortable here. It would not be possible for me to take the chance to go to America through the back [i.e., by road illegally]. Besides, I am closer to my sick mother at home."

The trips they were making home, however, were not that frequent. About half said that they went home only rarely. The infrequency of visits did not mean breaking contact with relatives. Almost two-thirds were helping to maintain their relatives by sending cash regularly. There was not much reciprocal exchange of relatives sending gifts from the village. Only a quarter said that they received some food items from time to time.

They mentioned that they missed being at home. Almost a half said that they missed the food together with acquiring it through fishing and farming. The food items mentioned included cassava, other root crops, plantain, fruits, and fish. Next in order of frequency were relatives and friends and finally the physical and social environment. By physical environment they meant the sea, seafront, beach, landscape, and the land. The following fall under the category of social environment—peaceful life, warmth and cooperation of the people, village quietness, and the "good old days." The focus on the sea and its parts refers to the extended view of the sea, which stretches to the horizon east of the village. The seafront is the area closer to the beach, where people swim; and the beach where fishermen arrive with their boats and sell fish. These functions associated with parts of the marine and coastal environments remained in the mental imagery of the villagers.

If they could not be in the village, the respondents selected friends and visitors from among fellow villagers and other Garifuna. They attended Garifuna cultural events regularly. They were also aware of a primary institution in the city that promoted Garifuna cultural awareness. Without any prompting the vast majority identified the National Garifuna Council as such an organization.

As expected, the issue of links between themselves and their home community brought a heightened degree of ambivalence among the respondents. At one level, there was still some nostalgia about certain aspects of village life. At the other level, they knew that there was not much future there, given its state of economic stagnation and the lack of prospects for the future. In answer to the provocative question whether they thought that the village was dying, as many as three-fourths said yes. Most attributed this to the lack of jobs, driving away the villagers to places like Belize City. Notwithstanding the bleak prospects, a little more than half said that they planned to return there to retire.

Links with the Non-Garifuna Community

The questionnaire revealed information about the relations of the respondents with their non-Garifuna neighbors, coworkers, and the larger community. Since they had changed addresses in Belize City, I wanted to know the extent to which they were relying on sources within the larger community on the availability of housing. In answer to the question, "Who helped you to locate the addresses where you have lived?" more than half said that it was a Garifuna person.

The friendliness of their neighbors was an important quality they looked for within their neighborhood. Unfriendly neighbors were a main reason for disliking a neighborhood. Another reason for their displeasure was the filth of uncollected garbage, clogged drains, and bushy yards.

There were questions probing how much they participated in neighborhood groups. At that time there were community organizations in some of the areas where they lived, designed to assist with participatory community development projects (Palacio, 1990, pp. 52–67). Most of them had not heard of any. This could be more the result of the community organizations not promoting themselves widely. There was a difference in participation in well-known institutions. For example, almost one-half said that they attended church—mainly the Roman Catholic Church—regularly. The churches were located in their neighborhoods.

Another component of daily life in which the informants necessarily interacted with non-Garifuna was at work. As in the case of locating their dwelling, I asked who was most helpful to them in getting their job. Almost three-quarters said that they looked around and found it on their own. This contrasts with locating the dwelling, where their fellow Garifuna were most helpful. The next question asked who had been helpful to the other household members in getting their jobs. Again, they had helped themselves.

There was a question that tested the level of comfort the respondent had on the job, given the tradition of discrimination against the Garifuna in Belize City. The question asked, "Has any working member of the household been discriminated against on the job?" The vast majority (81%) said no. The indication is that they found their jobs on their own and worked in non-threatening situations within a predominantly non-Garifuna environment.

In terms of economic ties with the larger community, I asked about their relations with the neighborhood grocer and savings institutions. Only 17 said that they maintained an account with their neighborhood grocer. Only 17 said that they saved in a "syndicate."[9] They had greater interest in more formal savings institutions. As many as 33 (55%) said they maintained accounts in commercial banks and 37 (62%) in credit unions. Their use of savings institutions also depicts a savings ethic that they brought from the village, according to my field investigations. During fieldwork in 1979–1980 I observed several children going to save in the credit union every Sunday, bringing along a few coins each, and making the practice as much a ritual as going to the Sunday church service.

Within the overall framework of economic relations, the respondents were able to rely on themselves to obtain a job, the main reason for leaving the village. The reasons no doubt stem from a large enough labor market and their comparative advantage. In the latter case they came with a sound primary school educational background from the village. Furthermore, they had acquired a wealth of prior work experience in various places. For the blue-collar occupations of security, construction trades, machinists, etc., their experience in the Army and Police Force was helpful. Similarly, those who engaged in white-collar jobs as teachers, clerical and administrative public officers, and nurses had received secondary- and tertiary-level education.

Having acquired their jobs, they worked conscientiously enough to ward off any discrimination that the non-Garifuna might have wanted to levy against them. From their salary they saved not so much in the informal syndicate but more in the formal credit unions and banks. These are indicators of a group with a progressive economic profile, attempting to achieve main goals they had set for themselves while in the village.

Cultural Identification

If the respondents were doing fairly well within the limitations of housing and jobs available within the city, I wanted to know what their opinions about cultural identity were concerning themselves and their children. Formulating survey questions about cultural identity can be difficult. Fortunately, I had observed from the pilot questionnaire that informants felt comfortable introducing the topic using language as a cultural marker. Among diagnostics, language seemed to attract the most attraction as the definable trait. So the first question on the topic in the final questionnaire draft was "Do you speak Garifuna to members of your household?"

I knew that all of the respondents spoke the language having grown up in monolingual households in the village. It was not surprising that three-fourths said that they spoke the language within their household. The answer to the next question showed less use of the language among young persons (i.e., younger than 20 years of age). Fewer than half (40%) said that young persons spoke the language. Having visited several households, my own impression is that even this figure is exaggerated, as there is a general defensiveness among parents about the use of their language by their children. As part of this defensiveness they would say, "Well, they don't speak the language but they understand it." In most instances this was not true. On further probing they would say, "You know they need to speak Creole to fit into Belize City. So we don't discourage them from speaking it. Besides, we don't have the time to teach them Garifuna." In reality language use was becoming limited among older family members, who increasingly found themselves talking the Creole vernacular to their children.

The following question went directly to the question of self-identification. It asked whether the respondent thought that the younger members of the household identify themselves as Garifuna. As many as 84% said yes, although, according to them, only 40% spoke the language. The next question probed further why the respondent thought they so identified. The answers took the following patterns. The highest percentage (42%) said that it was heredity; next came "the use of the language" at 32%; then "being proud to be Garifuna" at 16%; and finally "practicing their culture."

The answers need elaboration. Heredity means being born Garifuna. In some cases, the respondent would refer to his or her parents, namely the grandparents of the child in the following manner, "I am Garifuna as well as my own parents, so my child is certainly Garifuna." It is worth noting that claims of heredity had higher value as a marker of identity than being able to speak the language. The last two responses—"proud of being Garifuna" and "practicing the culture"—actually stand for "not being ashamed of being Garifuna," in my view. The reference is to the need for the Garifuna not to hide in shame, fearful of exposing themselves to the threat of discrimination. One hears many examples of Garifuna years ago hiding from others in Belize City so as to not speak the language in public. They had been trying to "pass for Creole" and could not be heard talking the language.

Indeed, the final question validates what should the Garifuna display as part of his or her identity, apart from language. The attributes in order of preference were music and dance 52%, food 15%, spirituality 12%, and attire 8%. Another interpretation is that these are the traits that need to be preserved, according to the respondents. The National Garifuna Council (NGC) has had some success in promoting awareness among the Belize City Garifuna in these and other traits.

A registered NGO since 1991, the NGC has as its main aim the preservation of the Garifuna culture throughout Belize. It has branches in all rural and urban areas, where there are sizable Garifuna communities. The main activities for which NGC is known take place around the 19th of November, which commemorate the arrival of the first pioneers from Honduras to Belize. A public and bank holiday, the day is celebrated throughout the country to share with the Garifuna what the culture has to offer. After that day, however, nothing is heard from the NGC until the following year. In the public perception of other Belizeans, it exists as an institution that promotes the culture, primarily as a form of large-scale celebrations. From time to time there are efforts to move into areas of other concern, such as community development and interactions with regional cultural organizations but there is little consistency in this regard.

Transition and Identity

Transition into urban society is a complex process, which depends on variables such as the skills or academic qualifications one has at the point of entry, age, gender, the length of time at the destination, and so on. From the nature of the survey instrument we applied it was not possible to bring all of these into perspective. In attempting to analyze the extent of transition in the following discussion, I supplement the cryptic data of the survey with my awareness of life in both the village and the city.

Juxtaposition to other Belizeans on a permanent basis for the first time made cultural identity a topic deserving special attention from the villagers. While at first speaking the language was enough to distinguish themselves from the Creole, their children were losing the ability to do so. As language lost its function as a marker, the villagers were substituting heredity and the ability to demonstrate competence in select traits, such as music, dance, spirituality, and wearing traditional attire. Besides, the displays were no longer as spontaneous as they had been in the village; they were to be held through the aegis of the NGC at specific times. Identity, which previously had been taken for granted in the village, was going through a systematic organization led by the villagers with minimal support available from the larger urban society. The lack of strategic support in this process from state funding sources has made Garifuna revitalization a small scale and grassroots effort.

The household was probably the unit that was most transformed in the transition in terms of the family structure and the household function. In the village during 1979–1980 there were 16 conjugal and 31 extended households (Palacio, 1982, p. 24), while in the city survey there were 39 conjugal with 21 extended. Furthermore, the conjugal unit was clearly the ideal in terms of the fluidity of members, who could come and go leaving behind the wife and husband. The interdependence of these two roles coincided with the need to adjust to the demands of city life. The household exists not only for the benefit of family members; it is also a very important place to entertain visitors and to extend some of its functions to others from the larger community. These functions include baby-sitting and offering paid meals or laundry services for a few people. Among our respondents there was selectivity among visitors and to whom these services were provided. The group was small, including close relatives and/or friends, with whom there was reciprocal exchange. The relative openness of visiting and extending household services that took place in the village was limited in the city.

Another major change came from expectations that the cash economy of the city generated. As we have seen from the review of the village as sending society, the villagers were no strangers to the cash economy. The difference was that in Belize City they were living within it far more intensively than in the village. One has to work in the city to be able to meet all household needs, including paying the rent. Besides, one has to be a conscientious worker, avoiding the possibility of blame from the supervisor within the context of an interethnic work environment. One has to save to be able to build the family home, one of the highest priorities for the respondents. All the prerequisites, including getting a lot and the actual construction means entering into relations with several persons, from politician, to plumber, to painter. The stories from the respondents invariably pointed to deceit and the pitfalls of relying on contractors. To many the exercise became a traumatic awakening to urban society. One trait that enabled them to survive was the ethic of savings they brought from the village. Despite my expectations, they saved more in the formal systems of banks and credit unions than among themselves.

These experiences are part of what make up *ibagari balici* loosely translated as "life in the city." By this the villager is referring to the web of Creole culture and society, which consumes everything one does. It includes getting accustomed to the neighborhood, school system, the cycle of ceremonial events, the weather, the high rate of theft and burglary, etc. At moments of difficulty, village aesthetics loom larger in preference—the landscape, sea, the quietness, and the relative orderliness. These are not available in the lower-class neighborhoods, that surround our respondents, especially since they know that there are better parts of the city that are beyond their reach. Being confined within the stratification system of the city was a major source of dissatisfaction for the respondents.

Cultural Identity and the Garifuna as Indigenous People

There is a tendency to regard the cultural identity of indigenous peoples as immutable and self-supporting. Indigenous peoples themselves often refer to attributes as proof of their current rights, ignoring the tendency of people to invent their own identity (Hobsbawm & Ranger, 1992) or to project what they might have imagined as being a fact (Anderson, 1991). In this study we see parents overstating the competence of their offspring in the mother tongue, demonstrating how defensive one can be about cultural identity. This chapter makes the twofold argument that the identity of indigenous peoples changes over time and that the trajectory of change is determined by the social setting in which they find themselves. Such perspective is helpful at a time of overwhelming social forces impinging on the Caribbean and by extension its indigenous peoples. It is further helpful for placing the person within a group as a prime actor within that setting. The primary group in this study is the household.

The Garifuna arrived as indigenous peoples in Central America with an identity severely chastened by their catastrophic experiences in St. Vincent. By the time their descendants settled in Belize City after 10 generations in 1990, the culture had changed a great deal; but should it be possible for their St. Vincent-born ancestors to visit, they would recognize several aspects of their culture.[10]

The village had provided an auspicious setting for the maintenance of kinship ties, which in turn determined family membership, community solidarity, and rights to land. Inroads from beyond the village, such as cash returns from wage labor and primary school education, were internalized to function for the well-being of the community, generating fertile ground for the retention of music, dance, spirituality, worldview, and methods of farming and fishing.

The villagers could not bring the village with them to the city, which became the final destination in their wage labor migration. Instead they brought from it many traits that eased the trauma of their transition. The traits included the close ties among family members, a work and savings ethic, aesthetic imagery of the village landscape, and whatever they could apply from time to time from their traditional food, music, dance, spiritual rituals, and attire.

Practicing these traits became a momentous addition to the multiculturalism that Belize City was concurrently experiencing. The wave of nation-building cultural policy was reaching a crest. Furthermore, a Black Nationalist movement was generating a reassessment within Belize City, the largest concentration of black people in the country, of the strength of its African roots. Among the Garifuna themselves their *Garifunaduo* movement was simultaneously widening among them a sense of their African and Native American origins. There was a convergence of strong cultural movements with people who could participate in and contribute toward them.

Nevertheless, the urban social setting generated its demands that needed critical response from the villagers. They had to modify the structure of their household so that men and women could coordinate their contribution to the responsibilities, which the extended family would have handled in the village. Gonzalez (1979, pp. 255–263) reported a similar constriction in family types among immigrants in New York. Not only were there more conjugal families, there were more men and women formally marrying. Besides, there were far fewer visitors than in the home village.

Most importantly, the issue of promoting cultural identity among children became a task to be added to the mounting household responsibilities. It was a case where the village was no longer there to help raise the child. Because of the difficulty to retain fluency in Garifuna, partly due to the overlapping workload in the household, it no longer became a prime marker for identity. There was a shift toward the more demonstrative and celebratory aspects of the culture, which took place not in the household but within the public domain. One's heredity became important and even more so the need to publicly display it.

Change did not mean that the Garifuna culture had lost its indigenous base. Rather, it was been modified to accommodate the social changes overtaking the Garifuna people. Earlier we saw the generational decline of fluency in the spoken word. Concurrently, Garifuna songs were becoming popular, with music amplified in pulsating rhythms using electronic musical instruments. The birth of the *punta rock* genre took place and became a popular dance not only in Belize but also throughout coastal Central America and the American diaspora. As language declined in use, music as another form of communication rose in cross-cultural popularity.

Conclusion

What is the cultural identity of a people? One can answer this question by listing traits and grouping them into an order showing their significance. This kind of response is inadequate much more for indigenous peoples, among whom identity is invariably a convoluted question of historically denied rights.

In this chapter I have attempted to show that it is possible to analyze not only the identity of an indigenous people but also how it has changed when moving from a village to an urban area.

While so far there has been emphasis in this discussion on the cultural changes that the Garifuna have made with their identity, there has not been a corresponding focus on the social and economic needs of the Garifuna as indigenous people. The study shows that villagers have stayed in Belize City and not followed the inexorable urge to proceed to the US. The expanding economy, geography, and cultural renewal taking place in Belize City enabled them to acquire socioeconomic benefits not available in the village. The National Garifuna Council, despite its strong cultural presence, could not help with the additional problems that they faced. They include revitalizing rights to their traditional lands along the coast and some cayes in southern Belize; special health problems in the high incidence of hypertension, diabetes, and glaucoma; endemic poverty in their communities; and the continued deterioration of home villages from depopulation. Within the city, sectors of their community have mechanisms to advocate for redress. Workers—both blue-collar and white-collar—have their labor unions. Subscribers to credit unions and commercial banks have statutory regulations to protect their welfare. However, there are no government approved organizations with similar functions on behalf of the Garifuna as indigenous people. Such neglect counters the spirit and letter of ILO Convention 169 passed in 1989.[11] Indeed, the lack of any state recognition of the Garifuna and Maya as indigenous peoples is conspicuous within the legal and juridical structures of Belize.[12]

Finally, the approach by the Garifuna to embrace their African and Native American roots introduces a welcome addition to the spotlight on identity among the indigenous peoples of the Caribbean. There is palpable discomfort within the region to accept black-skinned people as being indigenous (see the chapter on the Caribbean Organization of Indigenous Peoples in this volume). The volume edited by Haslip-Viera (1999) discusses this issue within Puerto Rico, especially the contribution by Duany (1999). In the English-speaking Caribbean, on the other hand, there is a bias toward the Africanist position, mainly in terms of being black skinned, which similarly provides minimal scope for those having Native American heritage. Within extremes of one or the other racial pole, several people in the Caribbean fall through the crack. The story of the Garifuna in this chapter leads the way to spotlight others, who have both African and Native American origins.

Notes

1 I acknowledge with gratitude the support of Professor Jeanne Wolfe of the McGill University School of Urban Planning, who provided support in doing the fieldwork for

this study; Mrs. Myrtle Palacio, Director of Glessima Research and Services, whose company did the data entry and tabulation for the field data; and Max Forte for his encouragement.

2   There are few studies on the Garifuna residents in towns in Central America. One example is Khan (1981).

3   The Magistrates Meeting was a form of local government dominated by mainly white landowners.

4   In Belize "Creole" refers to the ethnic group which results from the mixture of former African slaves with their British masters. Their language is also called Creole.

5   Gonzalez and Gonzalez (1979) estimated that there were about 15,000 Garifuna in New York. There were additional thousands in other cities, notably Chicago, Los Angeles, and New Orleans.

6   Data on the village comes from oral history and other primary sources, including church records.

7   For a discussion of the sociopolitical integration of Belizeans within the nationalist movement, see Shoman (1994, pp. 199–225).

8   Belize City is cut into two parts by a tributary of the Belize River. The Southside is poorer and has more ramshackle housing than the Northside.

9   The syndicate is an informal revolving savings group popular among Belize City residents.

10 With respect to language, Taylor (1951, p. 38) mentions that "the dialect of St. Vincent already differed considerably from" the Dominican language in Fr. Breton's dictionary, which his informants in Hopkins could understand "with the proper phonetic adjustments." Taylor's conclusion needs a critical review from linguists.

11 In fact, only Dominica among Anglophone Caribbean territories has endorsed ILO Convention 169.

12 In 1998 the government set up a commission to review what changes should be introduced to the Constitution. A representative of the National Garifuna Council on the commission argued that there should be added a statement acknowledging the presence of indigenous peoples and their basic rights, within the spirit of the ILO Convention 169. The other members of the Commission vigorously rejected the suggestion. It is worth asking whether the members of the Commission reflected the popular sentiment of the majority of Belizeans on this issue. If it is the case, then a massive reeducation effort needs to be implemented to uplift the nation's consciousness on the rights of indigenous peoples.

References

Anderson, B.R. (1991). *Imagined communities: reflections on the origins and spread of nationalism*. London: Verso.

Cayetano, E.R. (1993). *The people's Garifuna dictionary*. Belize: National Garifuna Council of Belize

Cayetano, S. (n.d.). *Garifuna, language, and culture*. Belize.

Craton, M. (1982). *Testing the chains: resistance to slavery in the British West Indies*. Ithaca, NY: Cornell University Press.

Duany, J. (1999). Making indians out of blacks. In G. Haslip-Viera (Ed.), *Taino revival: critical perspectives on Puerto Rican identity and cultural politics* (pp. 31–56). New York: Centro de estudios puertorriqueños, Hunter College, CUNY.

Fabel, R.F.A. (2000). *Britons, Native Americans, and Caribs (1759–1775)*. Gainesville: University Press of Florida.

Forte, M.C. (1999). Reviving Caribs: recognition, patronage and ceremonial indigeneity in Trinidad and Tobago. *Cultural Survival Quarterly*, 23(4), 35–41.

Gonzalez, N.L. (1979). Garifuna (Black Carib) settlement in New York. *International Migration Review*, 13(2), 255–263.

———. (1988). *Sojourners of the Caribbean: ethnogenesis and ethnohistory of the Garifuna*. Chicago: University of Illinois Press.

Gonzalez, N. L., & Gonzalez, I. (1979). Five generations of Garifuna migration: the final chapter? *Migration Today*, 7(5), 18–20.

Gullick, C.J.M.R. (1985). *Myths of a minority: the changing traditions of the Vincentian Caribs*. Assen, The Netherlands: Van Gorcum.

Hammel, E.A., & Laslett, P. (1974). Comparing household structure over time and between cultures. *Comparative Studies in Society and History*, 16, 73–110.

Haslip-Viera, G. (Ed.). (1999). *Taino revival: critical perspectives on Puerto Rican identity and cultural politics*. New York: Centro de Estudios Puertorriquenos, Hunter College, CUNY.

Hobsbawm, E, & Ranger, T. (Eds.). (1992). *The invention of tradition*. Cambridge, UK: Cambridge University Press.

Honychurch, L. (2000). *Carib to Creole: a history of contact and culture exchange*. Dominica: The Business Centre.

Khan, A. (1981). Garifuna women working: street vendors in La Ceiba. Paper presented at the Annual Conference of the American Anthropological Association, Los Angeles, California, December 2–6.

Palacio, J.O. (1982). Food and social relations in a Garifuna village. PhD dissertation, University of California, Berkeley.

———. (1990). The rise of local area community organizations in Belize City, Third Annual Studies on Belize Conference. Belize City: SPEAReports 6.

———. (1992). Garifuna immigrants in Los Angeles: attempts at self-improvement. *Belizean Studies*, 20(3), 17–26.

Palacio, J.O. et al. (2003). Why are some Garifuna students underachieving in primary and secondary school? *Belizean Studies*, 25(2), 25–51.

Palacio, M. (1995). Redefining ethnicity: the experiences of the Garifuna and Creole in post-independent Belize. M.Sc. thesis, University of New Orleans.

———. (2002). Dangriga BZ or USA: out-migration experiences of a Garifuna community in post-independence Belize. Paper presented at the University of West Indies School of Continuing Studies Belize Conference, Belize City.

Sanders, A. (1987). *The powerless people*. London: Macmillan.

Sanford, M. (1975). From the bottom looking up in a developing country. Paper presented at the Annual Conference of the American Anthropological Association Meeting, San Francisco.

Shoman, A. (1994). *Thirteen chapters: a history of Belize*. Belize: Angelus Press.

Taylor, D.M. (1951). *The Black Carib of British Honduras*. New York: Wenner-Gren Foundation for Anthropological Research.

Woods, L.A., Perry, J.M., & Steagall, S.W. (1997). The composition and distribution of ethnic groups in Belize: immigration and emigration patterns. *Latin American Research Review*, 32(3), 63–88.

※ CHAPTER TEN ※

Disputing Aboriginality: French Amerindians in European Guiana

Gérard Collomb

Opposing the intrusions of capitalistic ventures on their territories for gold mining or timber exploitation, the indigenous people of the lowlands of South America are at the same time questioning the nation-state structures that resulted from Western expansion, trying to win acceptance for an aboriginal vision of the world, and for a specific way of living in society, distinct from the vision of the world embodied by modern nation-states. The global expansion of capitalism is the expansion of Western social patterns, and aboriginal struggles are also symbolic struggles for the recognition of non-Western social patterns within the institutions of the states in which history has placed them. In struggling for recognition of non-Western social patterns, Amerindians are thus to some extent in the core of the global-local dialectics that lie behind the process of globalization (Appadurai, 1996; Friedman, 1999).

The situation of the Amerindians in French Guiana[1] represents in this respect an interesting case, given the social, political, economic background in which it fits and which shaped the Amerindian movement in a somewhat specific way compared to other aboriginal movements throughout the continent. The integration of Amerindians in French Guiana into the French nation in the 1960s placed them within an assimilationist constitutional framework, a priori unfavorable to specific claims by aboriginal peoples.[2] The Amerindian movement strove to adjust this status, mainly by challenging the state from within the international area, and by relying on nongovernmental organizations (NGOs) and on United Nations (UN) working groups. This has resulted in legitimation of the concept of "indigenous people" within the national and regional arenas, thus allowing Amerindians to begin to free themselves from the bonds of French colonial history.

At the same time, however, these developments opened the way for new questionings, and partly shifted the debate away from France and toward the regional/French Guianese political stage. It is on this latter stage that we are witnessing growing ferment by local Creole leaders in pressing claims for autonomy, and even independence for French Guiana. In this context of competing claims for autonomy (national and aboriginal), the Amerindian claim for a specific status grounded on "aboriginality" is seen as an attempt to contradict or to obstruct the development of a nationalist idea, which is itself grounded in an idea of the shared "indigeneity" of the main "historical" components of the Guianese population—Amerindians, Maroons, Creoles. Today, the official discourse of the aboriginal organizations is focused on political "resistance" against the hegemony of the French state, resulting in the pronouncement of a heroic statement of history. There is no doubt that this statement speaks of a first step of the modern political history of the Amerindians in Guyana, but the situation is now more complicated. However, if one tries to "resist resistance" (Brown, 1996) and to get a more subtle analysis, one can consider that the main feature of the "aboriginal resurgence" in French Guiana lies in the attempts of the Amerindians to find a way between two risks of being denied as a specific people—whether as "French citizens," or as "Guianese citizens," and, finally, their will to take part in the political process leading to a future *Guyane* as a national entity, whatever may be its political and constitutional shape.

The Colony of Cayenne

French Guiana was established as a French colony in the middle of the 17th century, as a locus of small-scale plantations. It did not experience the development of the large sugar plantations that characterized the economies of the Caribbean islands or that of the colony of Suriname. During the four centuries of its existence as a colony, this territory experienced a succession of plans for colonial development, all of which led to failure for not having taken into account local realities (Mam-Lam-Fouck, 1996). In the second half of the 19th century, prospecting for gold in the rivers of French Guiana became the principal economic activity, diverting most of the population from agricultural activities. The same period witnessed the establishment of penal institutions, which gave French Guiana an image that it still finds difficult to change.

In 1946, the colony of French Guiana (*Guyane*) became (with the islands of Guadeloupe, Martinique and La Reunion) a so-called *département d'outre-mer* (DOM—Overseas Department), i.e., a territorial and administrative entity that is an integral part of the French nation.[3] This status contrasted with that of the other French possessions—in Africa in particular—which remained colonies, but which took the path of independence during the 1960s. The new status instituted for French Guiana a complete legal assimilation into the situation of continental France and opened the way for the application of welfare policies that were developed in France during this time.

Kourou, a rocket launch site for space missions, was created in 1964 to take advantage of the equatorial position of French Guiana. The colony's status as a "French Department" also conferred an aura of political and economic stability. This launch site represents, even today, the main economic sector of French Guiana, less by direct employment, than by the tax resources that it generates for the local authorities and by the activity that it causes in the subcontracting companies, or in the sectors of construction and trades. However this space-oriented activity is likely to be threatened in the medium term since it is dependent on technological developments that have decreased interest in the equatorial position of the site as well as new competition for the hosting of space launches that has arisen in various places around the globe. Gold mining, which had strongly marked French Guiana at the end of the 19th century, has seen dramatic growth for a few years now, causing a gold rush that is attracting many people from neighboring countries. However, even though the social and political consequences of this gold rush are important, the economic impact of the gold mining activities remains modest compared to Gross Domestic Product (GDP). In the 1980s, the creation of another administrative and territorial level, the *Région* (or region, hereafter), stimulated local activity and contributed to a form of local economic wealth mainly due to the installation of new bureaucracies and the construction of education, health and transport infrastructures.

The status of "Overseas Department" and the specific economic assistance packages it provides, still grants French Guiana some prosperity. But this prosperity is largely artificial and remains fragile: whereas the imports of goods increased appreciably during recent years, the deficit in the balance of trade with continental France remains at a very low level, around 20%, with the difference being made up for by financial transfers undertaken by the state. Such a situation masks important social differences, particularly in the cities, between the French population and the immigrants who can hardly benefit from the system. Yet despite these disparities, French Guiana benefits overall from a much more comfortable standard of living than that of neighboring countries.

Today this system is faced with difficulties stemming from depressed growth in Western economies and from the important increase of the population of French Guiana. During the last 20 years the number of inhabitants has almost tripled with the arrival of the migrants, mainly from Brazil, Suriname, Guyana and Haiti, and by a strong increase in the birth rate, linked with these migrations. Thus, in the medium term, French Guiana's privileged situation may become more uncertain. Yet, this subject is hardly debated within the regional political community—apart from conventional discourses about the need for thinking of "sustainable development for French Guiana." Overall, the population seems not to be too concerned with the difficulties to come: on the one hand, the status of a French Overseas Department, and the social and economic advantages which are linked to it, continue to protect most of the French population; on the other hand, the immigrants, who do not have access to all these advantages, find nevertheless that French Guiana is attractive enough to justify tearing themselves away from the conditions of hardship which they knew in their countries. The history of the Amerindian movement in French Guiana has to be understood within this history of the territory itself, and within the frame of its specific economic and social configuration.

"French Citizens!"

Current estimates place the Amerindian population of French Guiana at approximately 7,000 out of a total of more than 200,000 inhabitants for the Department as a whole.[4] The six indigenous ethnic groups belong to the three great language families of South America: the Wayãpi and the Teko (also called Emerillons) speak languages of the Tupi-Guarani group; the Pahikweneh (generally called Palikur) and the Lokono speak an Arawak language; and, the Wayana (with the Apalai, recently come from Jari) and the Kali'na[5] speak Carib languages. During the colonial era an increasing differentiation occurred between natives settled on the coasts (Lokono, Palikur, and especially the Kali'na), which had been involved in exchanges early on with the colonial populations (Collomb & Tiouka, 2001), and those which, settled in the forest, to the upstream of the main rivers (Wayana, Emerillon, Wayãpi), remained in relative isolation until the 1970s. When the colony had been converted into a French Department, this gap increased: since the 1960s the Kali'na and the other peoples on the coast directly underwent the policy of assimilation instituted by France, whereas the majority of the Amerindians settled in the forest experienced only in the last few years the effects of their incorporation into the Guianese and French political and economic systems. This difference remains strong today, even if the villages of the forest are now fully impacted by the effects of development policies and the opening up of the interior, even with the considerable changes that occur with their incorporation into a consumerist economy, and with the first generation that attended school now achieving adulthood.

The transformation of French Guiana into a Department in 1946 removed the colonial distinction between "French citizens" and "indigenous peoples," but it was only in the beginning of the 1960s that the state allotted French citizenship to the Amerindians (and to the Maroons[6] settled in the French territory since the 19th century, i.e., the Aluku). This was the first step toward a policy of cultural and social integration, by grouping previously isolated families and resettling them into large villages, and by the schooling of children within the framework of boarding schools managed by the Catholic clergy. Their integration into an expanded France had especially important economic and social effects by granting Amerindians the right to access the welfare system, which would eventually represent for these resettled families a new and important source of income, with serious consequences for Amerindian economies and social systems (Hurault, 1972).

Such a situation opened the way to the Amerindian protest movement in the early 1980s. In French Guiana, the Amerindians had been maintained for a long time on the margins of a colonial society within which the socio-racial hierarchy allotted to them the status of a "primitive population." From the 1980s this image started to change when a new generation of Amerindians began to enter politics, following Western models. The Kali'na, the first aboriginal people to have been exposed to French school education, have been the initiators of this movement which led to the formation in 1981 of the *Association des Amérindiens de Guyane Française* (AAGF—Association of Amerindians of French Guiana), a vehicle for the new struggles underway. If other Amerindian voices are now heard, with somewhat conflicting or critical voices coming occasionally from other groups, the Kali'na continue to provide the cadre at the foreground for the Amerindian movement in French Guiana, and continue to be its main spokespersons.

The *Rassemblement des Amérindiens de Guyane Française* (Assembly of Amerindians of French Guiana), organized by the AAGF in 1984 in the village of Awala, outlined the political framework that Amerindians would seek to develop during the following years. The organizers had invited the Guianese elected representatives—most of them belonging to the Creole[7] community—as well as representatives of the state in French Guiana. A broad part of the participation in the assembly was Kali'na, but other Amerindian populations from French Guiana and from neighboring areas of Suriname areas also sent representatives. A lot of people, Creoles or Whites, had also come to attend what they thought would be a festival with song and dance. On the last day, the event acquired a different character when Felix Tiouka, the young president of the AAGF, made a speech in which he launched into a vigorous criticism of French policy with respect to the Amerindian communities, asking for more rights and recognition: "We want recognition of our indigenous rights, i.e., recognition of our territorial rights, our right to remain Amerindian, and to develop our own institutions and our culture." This speech created something akin to a scandal and caused the immediate departure of the representative of the state.[8]

The 1984 Amerindian assembly thus symbolically marked the arrival of aboriginal peoples onto the local and national political stage from which they were hitherto excluded; it was a landmark event, a founding moment, one that is constantly referred to in French Guiana. During the following years, the Amerindian movement in French Guiana tried to seek recognition by the state, its institutions and its administrative machinery, of the principles that had been stated at the time of the assembly in 1984. It was a question of negotiating an adjustment of constitutional law so that the Amerindians could be granted a specific status, particularly with regard to the recognition of the right of Amerindians to secure their own territory.

Territory and Community

Today, the threat which stems from the competition for land, and contesting visions of how land should be used, is often seen as an issue of remote concern for most of the Amerindians of the interior who still have use of sufficient lands for hunting and for shifting agriculture. Nevertheless, strong pressures are now being exerted even in interior zones, especially by gold prospectors who intend to exploit rivers in the "Indian country," often with dreadful medical and social consequences.[9] The situation is appreciably different on the coastal littoral, where the Kali'na and the other Amerindian peoples have been confronted much more directly and for much longer, with the competition of other populations (especially Creole and Maroons) encroaching on their hunting and cultivating zones and on places available for the settling of the villages.

Amerindian land claims received their first response in 1987 when the French state recognized for the "communities of inhabitants who traditionally get their subsistence from the forest" collective rights of use on lands that they occupy. These rights were given "for hunting, fishing and, for the exercise of any activity necessary to the subsistence of these communities." This decision had been understood as a solution to the problem of Amerindian land dispossession, but in fact it did not grant straightforward legal recognition of the occupation of land and did nothing but tolerate a precarious and revocable use. In addition, its implementation remained bound by the agreement of the "communes" (the smallest administrative districts in France) of the territory on which the lands in question were located. These communes are, as a whole, under the political control of the Creole majority of the population, who did not intend to accept the idea of granting these rights to the Amerindians. This is understandable on the part of the Creole majority, but the consequence is that 15 years after the state's timid response to Amerindian claims, few requests for native title have been considered, and some of those that received approval are today disputed. The lands that have been given to the natives settled in the urbanized coastal littoral zones are now invested with other economic, social or institutional logics, and are thus claimed by other sectors of the Guyanese population. Amerindian land claims, which for a long time had been a core issue in relations between the indigenous communities and the state, seem today to be at a kind of dead end, the state not too keen to make a decision in favor of the Amerindians against other groups, especially those that are politically more powerful in the regional area.

The 1987 decision made a restrictive and literal interpretation of the claim for lands and took into consideration only agricultural or hunting uses—what gave force to this argument, which is still resorted to at different times, is that Amerindian populations that are settled on the coast, particularly the Kali'na, derive their subsistence less and less from the forest. But the political discourse on this question, that Amerindian leaders articulated for 20 years, went beyond land claims: this discourse was built in reference to a model of social and political space, considered as specifically Amerindian and distinct from the European one, a model that the political leaders speak of as the "community."[10] This notion was still lurking in the background at the 1984 meeting, and was foregrounded thereafter. A case in point is the declaration of the leader of the Amerindian village of Kourou in response to a decision of the town council that aimed to delimit places where Amerindian families were settled and to let them have these parcels for free, but as private lands. He declared that this is "a principle which is completely opposed to our tradition, to our customs, to the very bases of our community based on the common possession of the lands by all of the inhabitants of the same village. If we agree to respect the French legislation, it is necessary that this legislation also respects our ancestral and territorial rights, as well as our customary law."[11]

A fundamental feature of the history of Amerindian struggles for land has been the history of the Amerindian movement in French Guiana to validate a more fundamental claim, from which these land claims proceeded: that of the recognition of the specific cultural and political presence of the Amerindians, and of their capacity to manage their society according to rules different from those found in the wider global society. This is a question that has been shaped in a particular way in France where the debate on the place of minorities and indigenous people in the "nation" has been avoided for quite some time, or at least has not been easily formulated. France has long been a model of the nation-state for the West, a model which relies on an integrationist and homogenizing national idea,[12] erasing the legitimacy of identity constructions based on particularistic cultural and social forms, and thus leaving very little space for the claims made by these subaltern cultures.

Whereas recognition of "the Amerindian question" was taking place in contexts which might appear to be in close proximity, examples being North America and to a certain extent Brazil or various Andean countries, this recognition obviously faces difficulties in emerging in French Guiana, where the state did not intend to give legal and constitutional answer to the cultural and social claims of the Amerindian communities. Set up as "French citizens" some 30 years earlier, the French Guiana Amerindians have labored since then to achieve a specific or particular status, which the French state did not want and could not grant to them. Their weak demographic weight in French Guiana prevented them from playing a significant electoral part, except in some local polls, and made illusory any form of physical resistance. Amerindians therefore lacked the clout to influence, as much as they would wish, the unfavorable political balance of power that binds and subjects them to the state.

A new path has thus been sought by developing a program of action within a larger political and institutional space from which it would perhaps be possible to put more pressure on the state. In 1992 the AAGF was transformed into the *Fédération des Organisations Amérindiennes de Guyane* (Federation of the Amerindian Organizations of French Guiana, FOAG), a shift that aims to widen the political horizon of the indigenous movement, particularly by including more closely the peoples from the forest of the south—the Kali'na remaining nevertheless, as they have been for 10 years, the main actors of the organization at the forefront of the movement. At the First Congress of FOAG in 1992, the Kali'na leader Felix Tiouka recalled that the "Amerindian question" had hitherto not received any satisfactory response from the state. FOAG thus proposed to carry the struggle to the international level and to make claims supported through regional indigenous solidarity networks.

From "Minorities" to "Indigenous Peoples"

Since the creation of the AAGF, Kali'na political leaders had become aware of the place which the indigenous ethnic movement had acquired in the political and cultural life of Canada and the United States and contacts have been made with some North American aboriginal communities, with the Innu of Quebec in particular, whose use of the French language facilitated communication with Amerindians in French Guiana (Chalifoux, 1992). These relations have, to a large extent, been the primary basis for the international presence supporting the Amerindians of French Guiana. In 1992, FOAG was invited to take part in the development of the Charter of the Indigenous and Tribal Peoples of the Tropical Forests in Penang (Malaysia). The same year, French Amerindian leaders attended the Conference of Indigenous Peoples on Territory, Environment and Development, held at the same time as the Earth Summit in Rio de Janeiro (May 1992).

The same strategy was pursued in following years, with the participation of Amerindian leaders in meetings linking the indigenous organizations of the subcontinent, in particular within the *Coordinadora de las Organizaciones Indígenas de la Cuenca Amazónica* (COICA—Coordinating Body of Indigenous Organizations of the Amazon Basin),[13] which FOAG joined at the end of 1992. Participation in working groups on indigenous peoples, with experience obtained in Geneva within the framework of the UN, represents a new stage in achieving an international presence for French Guiana's Amerindian movement. Since 1997, representatives of FOAG have been working within the various commissions that are discussing the text of a universal declaration of the rights of indigenous peoples. With this international presence, with their entry into aboriginal political organizations of the Amazonian region, and by their participation in the working groups of the UN, they formed new transnational ties of solidarity—"Amerindian" or "Amazonian" solidarities—and appreciably extended their networks, thereby facilitating their access to information and to training, concerning legal questions in particular.

Moreover, this international strategy has opened up the social and symbolic space from which the French Amerindians have been shut out for quite some time. Their presence in the international arena has made it possible for them to utilize a large repertoire of representations, and to regain the capacity to define the "Amerindian question" for themselves, within the political and social space of French Guiana. They thus succeeded in transcending an exclusive relationship with France and with the state, shaped through the colonial era. The leaders of FOAG found in new concepts worked out by international authorities the possibility of reassessing their status in contemporary French Guiana, by laboriously producing and controlling the meaning of their social place.

Whereas the Amerindians had hitherto thought of themselves as "minorities" in the French nation, they could now rely on concepts such as "indigenous people" or "aboriginal people," built on the basis of the universal values conveyed by international institutions, particularly through reference to international texts in which they ground these concepts. Examples include the *Universal Declaration of Human Rights*, the 169th International Labor Organization Convention, and the works of the UN Human Rights Commission. This semantic shift gave another dimension to the Amerindian identity claim in French Guiana. The Amerindians could now join the large worldwide indigenous community: "We are a people. We are Kali'na, Teko, Lokono, Pahikweneh, Wayapi, Wayana. We have our own territories. We form an organized aboriginal society and we are a part of the community of indigenous peoples on a worldwide scale. We are the first inhabitants of our country, we occupied it and have had our own governments since time immemorial."[14]

From this point onward, the target of FOAG is not only one of being opposed to the state, and of denouncing the supervision imposed on Amerindians. The intention is also to take part in a regional political area, which is today dealing with a new question: how, and on which bases, could an "imagined community" (Anderson, 1991) be founded which would be shared by most of the ethnic components of French Guiana?

French Guiana and the "Guianese People": Which Place for the "Natives"?

The history of modern French Guianese society has for a very long time been treated as interchangeable with the history of Creole society, which began to take shape within the system of slavery and continued to develop gradually after emancipation in 1848, and then proceeded by integrating immigrants who came in large numbers with the gold rush in the 1860s (Jolivet, 1982). All through the first half of the 20th century, there prevailed an ideology of assimilation to French values and culture, constructing a social hierarchy which distinguished the Creole group (numerically dominant) which was on the way to assimilation, from the other groups settled for a long time in the Guianese space—Amerindians and Businenge ("Bush Negros")—regarded as "primitive" because they remained on the margins of the assimilation process (Jolivet, 1990).

Creole culture was, for most of this period, thought of as being *the* "Guianese culture," and French Guiana was, like Martinique and Guadeloupe, considered a "Creole" country. The transformation of French Guiana into an Overseas Department in 1946, and the so-called administrative "decentralization" occurring after 1982, opened a regional political area[15] in which the Creole component of the Guianese population continued to play a major role.

During the 1970s and the 1980s the relationship between the Creoles and the other components of the Guianese population began to change. First, the Guianese social and political landscape has been modified by the public resurgence of the Amerindians and the Maroons, both experiencing an important demographic revival,[16] and both of which had been kept apart for a very long time. They entered the regional political scene, intending from then on to play a more important role. In the meantime, the creolization process, which formerly succeeded in merging a heterogeneous population, experienced increasing difficulties in integrating migratory inflows (coming mainly from Brazil, Haiti and Suriname), which increased considerably during the economically prosperous years, in particular as a consequence of the construction of the launch site in Kourou (Mam-Lam-Fouck, 1996). In 30 years, these transformations, and the overall demographic effect of the arrival of migrants, tripled the population of French Guiana and considerably increased the cultural diversity of the country.

This new situation forced the various groups to redefine the relations that they had maintained with each other prior to these last 30 years and to position themselves in facing the newcomers. One of the major consequences has been that the demographic, but also cultural, preeminence of the Creoles has weakened, even if they remain politically dominant. Their status gradually changed from one of majority to that of principal minority within the Guianese population. For a long time, Creoles saw themselves alone as the embodiment of what they call "Guianity" (*guyanité*). Following these transformations, Creoles now have to look for other referents to define their identity, on a basis larger than the Creole community alone. Thus the regional political debate has changed. Since the 1970s, this debate addressed the question of the historical bonds linking French Guiana to France. Added to this debate has been a new interrogation about the nature of an "imagined community" that could be an answer to the increasing cultural heterogeneity of French Guiana, which represents a new problem for Guianese political leaders who readily denounce "the risks of a spatial and cultural *balkanization* of French Guiana" (a recurring topic in regional political debates today).

In response to these challenges, another political path has been explored by Guianese leaders in the last few years, in an effort to draw the contours of a new "imagined community." In this country, demographically unstable and now culturally heterogeneous, arises thus an image of a "Guianity" based on the core of the history of French Guiana, assembling the three "indigenous" ethnic groups—the Creoles, the Amerindians and the Maroons—and gradually opening to the more recently settled groups which did not yet experience the creolization process. Diversity would, henceforth, no longer be thought of as an obstacle to be reduced, but as a source of enrichment.

According to this reading, "Guianity" would no longer be built on adhesion to the French/Western cultural model, but on a representation of "national aboriginality," when up to then the only people who could pride themselves of being called aboriginal were those labeled as "primitives" by the dominant society. Clamoring for recognition of their own aboriginality, a more "radical" aboriginality one might say, the Amerindians are thus facing a new configuration: in such a context this claim is today understood by the Creoles as heralding factionalism, and as a demonstration of a "communitarism" anchored in the past, which should, on the contrary, be dissolved into a new Guianese national history that is being written. Thus, the Amerindian claim for a specific status, the assertion of an unyielding ethnic identity, are seen as an attempt to oppose the construction of the nation and to block the way for political independence which may possibly be forthcoming.

This concept of "aboriginality" thus became a major symbolic stake in the relationship between the various populations of French Guiana and in the relationship they maintain with the state and its institutions. The political weight of the Amerindians in French Guiana remains modest indeed, but they carry an important symbolic weight in debates that engage concepts of aboriginality and identity. One will not be surprised to discern a dialectic of construction and refutation: on one side, efforts to validate a concept considered as underpinning Amerindian specificity, and on the other side efforts to deny it, and to reintegrate the Amerindians in a shared history and territory. The debate is not a mere semantic play; it is grounded on the production of accounts of history, produced and diffused by both Amerindian and other actors. In reaction against an Amerindian discourse that underlines the non-autochthonous origin of the populations resulting from the slave trade and the colonial system, Creole accounts strive to establish an equal allochtony of contemporary Amerindians, at the very least by stressing the fact that Amerindians today are largely "mixed" populations. Such Creole accounts thus ensure the return of the Amerindian to a common colonial history in which they themselves also underwent the effects of colonialism:

> America is not a continent where man occurred. Its first human inhabitants, the Amerindians, came from Asia at time when the continents were connected by straits. The European colonial conquests and their mercenary attitude resulted in massacres of Amerindians, the draft of Africans into slavery.... Thus, this land of America mixed distresses and desires, misfortunes, miracles and illusions of men and women who came from the four cardinal points of the Earth.[17]

Behind the terms of such a debate, which takes place today in French Guiana, one could easily recognize a situation which prevails under other latitudes, for example the dispute between the "first nations" of Canada, the Federal Canadian state and the separatist movement in Quebec.

A New Political Space?

Throughout the past 30 years, Amerindian communities in coastal French Guiana lost relative political and social autonomy that they had been able to maintain hitherto on the margins of colonial history. Today the French nation has absorbed them, and they have become an integral part of a regional unit—*la Guyane*—a unit that is concerned with considerable demographic, social and impending institutional changes. The classical forms of the Amerindian polities of the Guyanas, and especially those of the Kali'na communities, had already experienced deep changes throughout the four centuries of the colonial period. However, this situation never really challenged the bases of their society, which were focused on their kinship system and shamanic practices. The changes which one observes today are deeper, drawing other configurations and joining more and more the Amerindian polities with the state, in its global and local forms. For the natives, politics represents an increasingly diversified and autonomous field, a local form of the general process of transformation of Amazonian political systems resulting from their historical confrontation with the white world, what Brown (1992, p. 312) called "the disembedding of social systems," resulting in the emergence of new leaders.

The struggles undertaken by Amerindian organizations throughout the last decades could be interpreted, in a heroic mode, like a progressive reappropriation by the natives of a capacity to produce their own history. Disputed and discussed, but installed within the core of Amerindian identity, the reference to "aboriginality" thus contributed to opening a new political space that the Amerindians can henceforward try to maximize. In 1998, in gathering to set up a "Customary High Council," Amerindian leaders drew the outlines of this space: "As indigenous people, we have rights to community property consisting of our traditional lands and in quantity sufficient for the conservation and the development of our forms of life.... We reaffirm with insistence that the social, legal and spiritual order is under the authority of the Chief and his customary council" (Declaration of Bellevue-Yanu, 1998). This reference to customary authority, which until now had been seen as a mere legacy of the colonial system of indirect rule, today serves to give Amerindian society a ready-made institutional form that can be put forward in dealing with institutions of the state. The "community" is thereby validated as a political locus distinct at the same time from the French nation and its institutions, and from French Guiana (a nation under construction). Reliance on a concept of aboriginality has helped French Guiana's Amerindians to open up a horizon which colonial history and the "Gallicization" process had closed by imposing progressive assimilation and integration within an undifferentiated national unit. Yet, if a conclusion is sought, one will perhaps be tempted to draw a more moderate picture.

Such a reading, as above, is undoubtedly not false, but it does not exhaust other possible interpretations, and it especially does not make it possible to understand what seems to be looming on the horizon. French Guiana is consumed with increasing social and economic difficulties, resulting in the questioning of the postcolonial situation where France obviously bears the burden of guilt. The Amerindian populations, like many of the other populations of French Guiana, are confronted with the difficulties that the process of the globalization of capitalism precipitates. Everyday life still remains relatively easy or simple for a majority of the Amerindians, where the new socioeconomic difficulties emerging in the territory are masked by the facilities provided by French Departmental status. But the future will probably be written for the younger Amerindian generations in terms of social degeneration, based on their immense challenges in being inserted economically, culturally and socially into the Western world and their acute school failure rates. Yet, in the meantime, these younger generations of Amerindians carry aspirations of consuming the signs of a life of ease and luxury that the West leads them to believe is accessible. In addition, these youths are already settled at some remove from the cultural, spiritual and communal social forms that still provide a sense of orientation and belonging for their elders.

Brought forth with determination since 1984 by two generations of political militants, the "Amerindian question" in French Guiana today confronts economic and social processes born of globalization, which cross ethnic identities to create within Guianese society new class stratification. The situation is certainly not specific to French Guiana, nor of course to Amerindians, but it is undoubtedly strongly exacerbated here by the strong contradictions born of the simultaneous membership of French Guiana in the European developed world and in the South American world of underdevelopment.

Notes

1. Editor's note: direct translation from French into English can cause some confusion where French Guiana is concerned. In French, the territory is referred to as "Guyane" which, if translated as Guyana would cause readers to confuse it with modern day Guyana (formerly British Guiana). For this reason, "Guyane" and "Guyane français" are translated as French Guiana, and "guyanais" is translated as Guianese. This chapter was jointly translated by the author and by Maximilian Forte.

2. The French Constitution recognizes only French citizenship, and ignores ethnic or religious affiliations, as is stated in its first Article: "*La France est une République indivisible, laïque, démocratique et sociale. Elle assure l'égalité devant la loi de tous les citoyens sans distinction d'origine, de race ou de religion. Elle respecte toutes les croyances*" (France is an indivisible Republic, secular, democratic and social. It ensures the equality in front of the law of all the citizens, without distinction of origin, race or religion. It respects all creeds). In that context, indigenous claims cannot be accepted in reference to an ethnic affiliation, providing specific rights, but can only be understood as a claim from any group of citizens.

3. Territorial administration in France is organized according to three principal levels, in ascending geographical and demographic importance, with different administrative responsibilities, each one having an elected assembly: the municipal "commune," the "department" and the "region." The history of French institutions in the DOM (overseas departments), made "department" and "region" cover the same geographical territory. A reform in preparation should melt two entities into only one administration in each DOM.

4. The estimate of the number of Amerindians compared to the total population of French Guiana is an object of controversy and represents a political stake. In the absence of official data (censuses by ethnic origins are not accepted by the French law), Amerindian political leaders advance the number of 10,000 Amerindians; 6,000 to 8,000 people appears closer to reality. If "the Amerindian vote" represents less than 3,000 persons in French Guiana, the concentration of a large part of Amerindian voters in some districts nonetheless grants them a significant weight in certain local polls.

5. Today, the Kali'na, or "Galibi" as they have been called for a long time by the French, remain one of the most prominent Amerindian people on the coast of the Guyanas, settled in areas from Brazil to Venezuela, as populations of unequal size that colonial history linked to different cultural arenas (Spanish, English, Dutch, French), but which jointly preserved the use of their native language and certain cultural features.

6. Some of these Maroon groups, descendants of escaped slaves of the Surinamese plantations during the 18th century, were established in French Guiana or on each side of the border of the Maroni River. The recent civil war in Suriname brought to the French bank of the

River thousands of Maroon refugees. After the end of the war, many of them remained settled in the rural periphery of the boroughs and the small towns of western French Guiana.

7   The word "Creole" refers in French Guiana to the population made up of descendants of slaves released in 1848, with which were mixed populations from diverse origins (West Indies, Europe, Asia, and South America) which arrived since the end of the 19th century, forged by the process of "creolization" into a more or less homogeneous culture and society, similar to that of the French West Indies. The Creole population has been for a long time been a large majority in French Guiana, and the politically dominant group. Today, however, the arrival of immigrants has changed the demographic ratio, but the Creoles remain the holders of the local political power and the carriers of cultural legitimacy. Up until recently, the Creoles referred to themselves as "guyanais" (Guianese), and the Creole culture was regarded as co-extensive with a Guianese culture.

8   F. Tiouka, Chairman of the Association des Amérindiens de Guyane Française (AAGF), "*Adresse au gouvernement et au peuple français,*" December 9, 1984.

9   The progressive sedentarization of Amerindian settlements—for medical, school, economic reasons—makes this an increasing threat today, as the families cannot any more choose the traditional strategies of moving their villages.

10 If this concept covers here various forms of social organization, it refers overall to an Amerindian social model that prevails in the Guianese area, founded on parenthood, co-residence and a common use of resources and territory.

11 *France-Guyane*, daily local newspaper, November 16, 1993.

12 Louis Dumont (1991) pointed out that in Western societies citizenship has been historically related to the flowering of modern political forms, in which individualistic representations of the social prevail. In France, he added, these representations are particularly strong, shaping an idea of the nation in which membership as a citizen occupies a central place in the definition of a collective identity.

13 See the organization's website at <http://www.coica.org/>.

14 Final declaration of the 2nd Congress of the Federation of the Amerindian Organizations of French Guiana, December 1996.

15 A reform of the state in 1982 gave to the French "Regions" greater autonomy in making decisions and in social and economic management in various fields of the public life, without granting them a legislative capacity.

16 The Kali'na, for example, were at their demographic minimum in the second half of the 19th century; the population began to grow at the beginning of the 20th century and experienced an important development in the years following "départementalisation," with more efficient medical coverage implemented in the 1960s.

17 Declaration of Christiane Taubira, representative of French Guiana in the French National Assembly, to *France-Guyane*, the local daily newspaper, July 14, 2000.

References

Anderson, B. (1991). *Imagined communities: reflections on the origins and spread of nationalism*. Rev. ed. London: Verso.

Appadurai, A. (1996). *Modernity at large: cultural dimensions of globalization*. Minneapolis: University of Minnesota Press.

Brown, M. (1992). Facing the state, facing the world: Amazonia's native leaders and the new politics of identity. *L'Homme*, 126–128, 307–326.

———. (1996). On resisting resistance. *American Anthropologist*, 98(4), 729–734.

Chalifoux, J-J. (1992). Ethnicité, pouvoir et développement politique chez les Galibis de la Guyane française. *Anthropologie et Sociétés*, 16(3), 37–54.

Collomb, G., & Tiouka F. (2001). *Na'na Kali'na. Une histoire des Kali'na en Guyane*. Pointe-à-Pitre, Cayenne: Ibis Rouge Editions.

Dumont, L. (1991). *Essais sur l'individualisme. Une perspective anthropologique sur l'idéologie moderne*. Paris: Le Seuil.

Friedman, J. (1999). Indigenous struggles and the discrete charm of the bourgeoisie. *Journal of World-System Research*, 5(2), 391–411. Retrieved September 1, 2004, from http://jwsr.ucr.edu/archive/vol5/number2/jwsr-v5n2.pdf.

Hurault, J. (1972). *Français et Indiens en Guyane, 1604–1972*. Paris: UGE.

Jolivet, M-J. (1982). *La question créole. Essai de sociologie sur la Guyane française*. Paris: Editions de l'Office de la Recherche scientifique Outre-mer.

———. (1990). Entre autochtones et immigrants: diversité et logique de positions créoles guyanaises. *Études Créoles*, 13(2), 11–32.

Mam-Lam-Fouck, S. (1996). *Histoire générale de la Guyane française*. Pointe-à-Pitre, Cayenne: Ibis Rouge Editions.

※ REGION ※

The Transnationalization of Caribbean Indigenous Resurgence

Organizing and connecting on a transnational level has proven to be a central component of the resurgence of indigenous Caribbean communities. The Caribbean Organization of Indigenous Peoples (COIP) was the first, and thus far only, regional indigenous body. Joseph Palacio, the first Chair of the body, explains how COIP came into being, its main achievements, and how it grew to encompass the Garifuna of Belize, the Caribs of Dominica, St. Vincent, and Trinidad, as well Amerindians in Guyana. He also reflects on its eventual demise, offering insights for activists who should be wary of repeating similar errors. Other significant developments in the regionalization of Caribbean indigenous revival efforts have been conferences and gatherings, such as those organized in Cuba by José Barreiro, titled Indigenous Legacies of the Caribbean, with a history spanning eight years. The gatherings in Cuba served as a great cultural exchange mechanism, allowing indigenous participants from across the region and North America to share many expressions of personal narrative, ceremony, musical presentations, roundtable discussions of political concepts, historical analysis, spiritual and literary explorations, and sharing food, agriculture and medicinal applications still present from their common indigenous legacy of the Caribbean. Much more "up in the air" is the impact of the Internet for the reproduction and articulation of Caribbean indigeneity, as discussed by Maximilian Forte, himself a webmaster for Trinidad's Carib Community. Central to the article are the ways that the Internet has been used for challenging the myth of Taino extinction, for enhancing a sense of home and indigenous identification for members of the Caribbean diaspora, and for building linkages with non-Caribbean indigenous bodies. As Forte argues in the chapter, the process is one that is both novel and in motion, and it may be that the Internet will become to indigenous resurgence what the printing press became for Europe's early nationalists.

CHAPTER ELEVEN

Looking at Ourselves in the Mirror: The Caribbean Organization of Indigenous Peoples (COIP)

Joseph O. Palacio

At a conference on the island of St. Vincent in August 1987 representatives of indigenous peoples from four English-speaking Caribbean countries saw their fellow regional brothers and sisters for the first time. The descendants of Maya, Arawaks, and Caribs, who had roamed the Circum-Caribbean freely before Columbus, expressed a mixture of joy, surprise, and sadness in being able to share in this historic event. Delegates came from Belize, Dominica, and Guyana, joining those in the host country, St. Vincent. Here I use the analogy of self-reflection in a mirror to describe the event in St. Vincent as the removal of shadows that had been hiding the region's indigenous peoples from each other. The process of gradually seeing each other more sharply continued throughout the five-year lifespan of the Caribbean Organization of Indigenous Peoples (COIP). Notwithstanding the growing reality of closer collaboration, another set of shadows emerged, bringing about the demise of the COIP in 1993. The chapter describes what took place at the conference, gives a synopsis of the beginning of COIP and the several tasks it undertook, and ends with an analysis of the factors that eventually brought about its demise.

The Conference

Preparations

The office of the Canadian University Services Overseas (CUSO) in Kingston, Jamaica, undertook the initiative for a conference of the indigenous peoples of the English-speaking Caribbean. The initiative received a boost from the visit in the mid-1980s to communities of indigenous peoples within the region on the part of Chief Tom Mackenzie of the Federation Saskatchewan of Indian Nations (FSIN) and Professor Bill Logan from the Department of Continuing Education/Extension of the Saskatchewan Indian Federated College (SIFC). In early 1987, Selena Tapper, the officer in charge of the Kingston CUSO office, started planning for the conference to take place in St. Vincent in August of the same year. Her office provided financial and technical support with additional amounts forthcoming from Oxfam Canada, Oxfam USA, and Oxfam UK. These funds covered, among other things, the travel expenses of delegates from the three countries of Belize, Dominica, and Guyana.

In St. Vincent, Nelcia Robinson led much of the preparatory work. The government provided technical support. The members of parliament for the Carib areas addressed sessions of the conference. Nongovernmental organizations (NGOs) and community organizations worked, especially at the several communities the delegates visited. It was obvious that the larger Vincentian society saw the conference as an opportunity to display to the visitors its pride in the island's indigenous peoples, the Caribs, also called locally the Callinago.

CUSO extended invitations to persons who were in leadership positions among indigenous peoples in the four countries. In the case of Belize and Dominica there were already organizations that represented indigenous peoples. In Belize there was the National Garifuna Council representing the Garifuna people and the Toledo Maya Council representing the Maya Mopan and Maya K'ekchi. In Dominica there was the Carib Council, the elected local government body in the Carib Territory. These organizations selected two representatives to be their delegates. In Guyana there was no organization representing its nine nations. CUSO selected the following persons: Desrey Fox, Ian Melville, Philip Duncan, and Sister de la Rose. From St. Vincent delegates came from the northeast of the island, the central portion, and the southeast, all areas where Carib descendants are still to be found.

CUSO also invited persons and agencies with interest in indigenous peoples and rural community development from the region and abroad. They included delegates from the FSIN and from regional NGOs. I was invited to give the keynote address, summarizing the current state of the region's indigenous peoples and prospects for the future. In doing the analysis, I used my long-term anthropological interest in indigenous peoples in the region and my own roots as a Belizean Garifuna. In addition to the above, scores of persons came on their own from within the island to participate in several events.

Activities

The meeting included public events in the capital city of Kingstown as well as in Carib communities. These events varied from official receptions to community displays, featuring music and dance. In the villages, the visitors saw historic sites marking events during the Carib Wars that took place from 1765 to 1796. The working sessions were limited to the delegates. The main part was discussing the state of their peoples, using reports that they had compiled in their respective home countries before coming to the conference. There followed small group sessions that allowed delegates to focus on thematic issues affecting them, such as land rights, gender, and cultural identity. The subsequent plenary sessions provided opportunities for the larger gathering to insert its input. The overall aim was that by the end of the conference there was thorough exposure of the state of the region's indigenous peoples together with some consensus on follow-up actions.

There is a need to elaborate briefly who are the indigenous peoples, who were the focus of the St. Vincent conference. In the late 1980s there were about 100,000 persons, who self-identified as indigenous according to the government censuses in the four countries. The largest number was in Guyana, where they totaled 41,000 within a population of 756,000; next came Belize with 26,000 within a population of 146,000; St. Vincent had 6,000 within 113,000, and Dominica with 3,000 self-identified Caribs within a national population of 74,000 (Palacio, 1995, pp. 25–40).

Using archaeological, ethnohistoric, linguistic, and biological data, Rouse (1992, p. 46) ends his synthesis of the origins of indigenous Caribbean peoples saying, "the ancestral cultures have been traced back as far as the Orinoco Valley, and the ancestral languages, to the center of the Amazon Basin." In Guyana nine nations speaking Arawakan, Cariban, and Warauan languages are found. The first two are the more numerous and are found in most parts of the inhabited interior (Forte, 1988). Without the extensive lands available in Guyana, the people in Dominica and St. Vincent are concentrated in smaller geographical areas. In St. Vincent the Caribs are found in the northeast, central, and southeast areas. In Dominica the Carib Territory is in the northeast.

In Belize, the Garifuna, originally exiled from St. Vincent by the British in 1797, numbered about 12,000. They are found in urban and rural communities from Belize City south to the border with Guatemala. The other nations in Belize—the Mopan, K'ekchi, and Yucatec represent the Mesoamerican tradition and together total 14,000. In numerical order from the largest, they are the K'ekchi, Mopan, and Yucatec. All live mainly in rural communities spread throughout the country. What some would see as the more "traditional" communities, those of the Mopan and K'ekchi, they are concentrated in the extreme southwest of the country bordering with Guatemala.

While the previous description has stressed traditional diagnostics, there is fluidity among all of the nations. There is heavy erosion of cultural traits, notably language, leading many to no longer self-identify, although phenotypically they appear "Amerindian."[1] There is a fair amount of intermarriage across nations and with nonindigenous peoples. There is considerable migration away from communities into other parts of their states or across the border, as in Guyana and Belize.

A significant component of the conference was set aside for delegates to expose the basic social and economic problems they experienced. Almost all communities lacked the basic utilities of electricity, telephone, and potable water. These, however, pale in significance compared to the actual details coming from the delegates. In terms of public health they ranged from the unavailability of immunization shots, to the recurrence of vector-borne diseases like malaria and dengue, to the lack of proper disposal for human and solid waste, and nonfunctioning health centers. In terms of education they included poor conditions of primary school buildings, lack of trained teachers, unavailability of books and basic equipment, the lack of transportation to reach school buildings, and the lack of adult education. The result was low levels of literacy and high attrition in school attendance.

Delegates complained about the lack of jobs and opportunities for their people to generate incomes. Even if they engaged in agriculture, they had difficulties in transportation to reach markets; besides, they were afflicted by either heavy rains or protracted periods of dry spells. Closely linked to these issues was the issue of land rights. The government could move them from lands that they claimed as theirs; besides, the government had not delivered titles, even after promising for years to do so. There was difficulty of transportation, especially in areas of Guyana and Belize, where communities relied on water transportation.

There was discussion on the abuse of human and civil rights. The examples of perpetrators included employers, government officers, and agents of the army and police. The abuse extended to women and children by the outsiders, especially in remote communities.

The delegates were aware that within their countries there were other nonindigenous co-citizens living in similar deprivation. However, they were also aware that their own people suffered even more because of their "Amerindian identity."[2] Indeed, the topic of identity came up as a major problem that most delegates mentioned. The concern was to transform the attitude of their co-citizens toward them, while assisting Amerindians to improve their self-esteem. One way to accomplish both objectives, they argued, was to help Amerindians mount projects in heritage tourism as a basis for income generation.

The above problems were especially grave in Guyana and St. Vincent, but during the presentations delegates nodded in agreement as they could identify with each other's situations. The delegates were men and women between the ages of 30 to 45. Many had jobs as teachers, researchers, community development workers, and public officers, but they were all from rural Amerindian communities. The litany of problems did not dampen their optimism that this gathering would help them and their communities to progress toward "development." They were especially happy about the camaraderie among themselves, which became even more pronounced in visiting the local communities. Within a day or so they were calling themselves, "my long-lost sister or brother from...."

Toward the close of the conference, a list of 16 points that summarized what specific actions should result from the conference was produced. I place them under the following subheadings:

Cultural Retrieval: Language and Folklore. Symbolic activities with high media value within the states: identifying heroes; special indigenous display at the Caribbean Festival of the Arts (CARIFESTA), the regional artistic event; declaring Caribbean Indigenous Peoples Day August 14 to commemorate this first conference; and holding a contest to select a queen of all indigenous peoples' queens.

Regional Exchange. To have persons/groups from different countries visit each other.

Promote Opportunities for Education and Training in Technical Skills.

This list does not mention solutions to the grave basic needs that many of the delegates had identified at the local level. Instead it identified possible actions at the regional level that were not directly development oriented. Obviously, it was not the intention of those involved in drafting the list to disrespect the indigent situation of many communities. Yet the list did betray some mixed signals concerning what needed to be done as against what others would have wanted done, as the COIP began to take shape.

Historical and Socioeconomic Contexts of the COIP Territories

A brief sociopolitical overview shows that the St. Vincent conference took place at a time coinciding with the final stages of transition from colonialism to political independence in Belize, Dominica, and St. Vincent. Guyana was already in the postindependence era, when the state had instituted structural adjustment programs to meet the need to pay for its debts. In both cases—the states prior to independence and the one already independent—indigenous peoples did not occupy high national or social priorities. For Belize, Dominica, and St. Vincent the priority was to build new nations, in which all ethnic groups would blend within a predominant Creole national culture,[3] into which the Amerindians would become fully assimilated. In the case of Guyana, the state needed to take advantage of all opportunities to earn foreign exchange. Natural resources together with the cheap labor services of Amerindians were made available to predatory multinational companies.

The movement toward full independence was predicated on each citizen participating in public affairs. Indeed, the introduction of adult suffrage—in Belize 1954 and Guyana 1953—had marked the first time that all their citizens were able to select their own government leaders. However, neither universal adult suffrage nor participation in the nationalist movement struggles toward independence could erase the historic disadvantages that indigenous peoples had long endured within the social fabric of these states.

The disadvantages faced by Amerindians emerged from the means by which they were inserted into European colonial enterprises. The degree of long-term disadvantage depends on the duration of Amerindian colonial status, the nature of White-indigenous peoples' relations, and the methods by which other groups became intertwined within these relations. At one extreme, the Europeans waged wars to wrest control of the lands of indigenous peoples. Afterward they exiled the survivors hundreds of miles away from their homeland. The St. Vincent Caribs suffered this fate, finding themselves bedraggled and demoralized and having to start life anew in Roatan, Honduras. Fabel (2000, pp. 162–205) discusses the extreme cruelty of the war and its mismanagement resulting in the loss of more lives than was necessary.[4]

Examples of generating conflicts among indigenous peoples, in line with the principle of "divide and rule" came from Dutch Guiana, before it became a British colony. Having described a series of incidents in the 1750s when the Dutch had played one tribe against another, Alvin O. Thompson stated, "it was often the colonists, rather than the colonial authorities, who played off the Indians against each other for their unscrupulous ends and who were also responsible for instances of impassioned invective and armed hostilities between the Dutch and the Indians" (1991, p. 22). With respect to Amerindian-African relations during the same time period, he adds, "without doubt, the European advent multiplied the incidence of warfare within Indian communities, while Indian-European wars, and animosities bred between Indians and Africans due to the use of Indians as slave catchers, added a further dimension to the military factor" (1991, p. 26).

After generations of these and similar practices, the British introduced their policy of trusteeship in 1836, which was designed to place indigenous peoples within a context of enlightened paternalism and supposedly no longer placing them in the role of victims of physical abuse (Menezes, 1977, p. 17). However, such change was in fact another form of imposition, where authorities together with religious missions "supervised" communities for their own welfare. By the beginning of the 20th century the descendants of those who had been integral to the success of earlier European colonial efforts had been reduced to abject poverty, being fully reliant on trade goods for daily living but no longer having access to cash to pay for them. Neither did they have any further role within the periphery of the coercive social structure of the plantation system. The downward spiral of destitution, about which the delegates at the St. Vincent conference spoke, had already become a way of life.

With the onset of the nationalist movement and eventual independence during the postwar period, the Caribbean states discussed in this chapter introduced some basic infrastructure in the form of roads and public utilities, but they did not reach remote communities of indigenous peoples until decades afterward, if any at all. A primary source of development assistance that reached their communities came as bilateral aid from Canada, the US, and the UK during the 1980s. Additionally, NGOs from these countries worked along with local counterparts to offer a variety of financial and technical development programs. In Dominica, the US Save the Children Foundation offered demonstration farms, piped water, training in business accounting, and building of the *Waitukubuli*[5] Karifuna Development Center. With the assistance of Development Alternatives in Dominica, a cultural preservation project featuring oral history, short video, and collection of historical documents was undertaken. In St. Vincent, the Humanistic Institute for Co-operation with Developing Countries (HIVOS), the Interchurch Fund for International Development (ICFID), and Oxfam Canada conducted a survey of Carib communities in 1987 as a backdrop for community development funding. Project Plenty from the United States funded projects among the Garifuna and Maya in Belize.[6]

This brief overview has attempted to explain the historical basis of the socioeconomic conditions of the home territories of the delegates at the St. Vincent conference, as well as their awareness that development assistance came not so much from the state but from outside sources, either directly as bilateral aid, or through NGOs. Obviously, there was great temptation to regard the conference, in which sources of foreign assistance were conspicuous, as ushering another source that would be exclusively for the region's indigenous peoples. However, there were overwhelming problems to overcome in laying the institutional infrastructure for the newly founded organization following the conference.

COIP: Early Stages of Growth

A noteworthy outcome of the St. Vincent conference was the start of a process of familiarization among participants that has continued. All the participants exchanged addresses. Those from within the region have met with each other at various fora since then. More particularly we became contact persons as the aftermath of the conference gained momentum. Another outcome was the determination among all participants—both those from within the region and our visitors from abroad—to form an organization to address the concerns highlighted in the conference. The inspiration came from the deliberations as well as the meetings with communities in St. Vincent.

Another significant outcome was the determination of the primary supporters of the conference to continue extending financial assistance, this time toward the new organization to be formed after the conference. The Jamaica CUSO office and Oxfam Canada made commitments. Through the recommendation of the FSIN delegates, who attended, the Saskatchewan Indian Federated College (SIFC) became a primary supporter of educational assistance.

At the conference we had agreed to form a steering committee that would flesh out the procedures of the postconference consolidation. It met in St. Vincent in January 1988, and confirmed that a Secretariat would be set up with a Coordinator, backed by CUSO's financial assistance for a limited time. I was asked to be the Coordinator and to have the Secretariat based in Belize. I agreed. The position was unpaid and it was assumed that the Secretariat could garner support from the University of the West Indies School of Continuing Studies, which I headed in Belize. The membership of the Secretariat consisted of the following—four persons from Belize, representing the two nations, the Garifuna and Maya; two from Dominica; and two from St. Vincent; and two from Guyana. There was an understanding that St. Vincent needed to ascertain that its members would be representative not only of communities in the northeast but also from the other parts of the island. Similarly, Guyana needed more time to organize its membership and deal with internal issues concerning representation made abroad.

The tentative nature of the structure of the Secretariat extended to the operations of its Coordinator. Keeping in mind the spirit of the St. Vincent Conference and the records of the proceedings, and after discussions with CUSO, I worked out the following modus operandi. My work plan would result from a prioritization of achievable tasks resulting from the conference. I started planning toward a General Assembly of the larger COIP membership, which would include the peoples represented at St. Vincent, and any others from within the region. That General Assembly would become the group to which I would report, while the Secretariat would be the executive arm. I would be in close collaboration with Secretariat members to receive their input on tasks that I carried out. More importantly, my first task was to publicize the COIP extensively and to receive information about funding sources for its operation.

Belize—A Fortuitous Setting

My presence as the Resident Tutor of the University of the West Indies Extramural Department was the reason for locating the Secretariat in Belize. I received permission from my Head of Department, Professor Rex Nettleford, to take up the responsibility, which by and large complemented the program of the Department. The Secretariat brought another target group, the region's indigenous peoples, who had not received many services from the University. Furthermore, the Department had branches in Dominica and St. Vincent that could be of mutual benefit to the COIP as well as the University. The COIP could intensify its networking among its constituents in those countries through the facilities of the University. Besides, the University could more easily support programs directed toward the region's indigenous peoples. This was an unusual opportunity to fulfill one of the goals of the School of Continuing Studies, namely to promote the cultural identity and expression of its constituent groups, especially those traditionally excluded from the mainstream.

Belize's position on the mainland exposed it to the strong currents of the indigenous peoples' movement that were picking up momentum in the late 1980s toward the quincentenary of Columbus. A primary hub was the World Council of Indigenous Peoples (WCIP) office in Costa Rica, which included Belize in several of its regional activities. The close kinship and working relations that peoples in Belize had with their counterparts in neighboring countries became important ties for networking. The Belize Garifuna were intertwined with the Garifuna in Guatemala and Honduras; similarly the K'ekchi with their counterparts in Guatemala. In both cases the Belize based segments were numerically insignificant in proportion to their respective neighbors.

There were other pressures forcing Belize into the mainland indigenous world, coming from the civil strife raging in El Salvador, Guatemala, Honduras, and Nicaragua during the late 1980s. Thousands of refugees were fleeing into Belize, many of them being indigenous peoples (Palacio, 1993; Woods, Perry, & Steagall, 1997). To address their emergency needs the UN High Commission for Refugees (UNHCR) and other agencies sponsored assistance programs. They included training, for which the University of the West Indies' School of Continuing Studies (UWISCS) received funding under my leadership. The training of indigenous peoples and of staff working with them was helpful in the overall projection of the COIP.

In addition to funding on behalf of refugees and their resettlement, I was able to access funding and technical assistance from other sources for the community development program of the UWISCS. They included UNICEF and the Newfoundland/Belize Linkage, a people-to-people exchange program organized with the support of the Canadian International Development Agency (CIDA). As much as possible I inserted indigenous peoples into these initiatives.

COIP benefited from the position of Belize as bridge between the Caribbean and the mainland at the crucial times shortly before the quincentenary and during the periods of war and gradual peace in Central America. In turn, the scope for the participation of the islands and Guyana in the international indigenous peoples' movement widened considerably.

COIP: Task Performance

The COIP Secretariat started functioning in October of 1988 and stopped in August of 1993. In each year several activities took place, which are difficult to summarize because they were often disjointed, taking their own momentum within specific time constraints. Quick decisions had to be made with minimal prior experience, especially in the first two years. Before elaborating on the performance of tasks, it is necessary to describe the setting for the daily operations of the Coordinator.

I was able to arrange that the operations take place at the Secretariat of the National Garifuna Council (NGC) in Belize City, thereby sharing the necessary office support. Such support became the direct assistance of the NGC to the COIP, especially needed during the first few months. As COIP received its own funding, we were able to secure the services of high school and junior college students to work part time on correspondence, filing, manning the telephone, and running errands. The task demanding the most in terms of deadlines was compiling and publishing our newsletter the *COIP Indigi-Notes*. I recruited the services of a junior college English major to help in this regard. Another recurring task was to assist delegates selected to attend workshops and conferences on our behalf. In many cases I had to help them get passports and appropriate visas. Besides, I had to help them write reports about their experiences on returning so there could be information on file to share within the region.

Breaking the office routine were occasional visits of representatives of organizations to work along with us. There was need to help with their local travel within the country, many times accompanying them to given communities.

The main event that tasked our logistical skills was hosting the COIP General Assembly in November 1989, one year after starting the office. We divided the list of tasks into those taking place beforehand, during the Assembly, and afterward. Unfortunately, the same two or three persons had to do everything. One of the greatest difficulties, however, was communicating within the region, especially reaching prospective delegates in remote communities in Guyana, Dominica, and St. Vincent. Also problematic was for delegates to secure US in-transit travel visas, as it was necessary to travel through Miami to reach Belize.

Coordinating the work during the Assembly meant securing conference rooms, public address systems, lunches, session presenters, and recorders not only in Belize City for the main working sessions but also for communities within the country where the visitors stopped during their field trip. Inevitably we ended up having to pay for services, including those for which we had not planned. On the other hand, we received many voluntary contributions from several individuals and groups. In the end, the success of the General Assembly came from the work of many Belizeans, who wanted to display their commitment to the cause of indigenous peoples within their country and those coming from the region and farther abroad.

The work of the COIP, identified in the St. Vincent conference, consisted of building linkages, forming an administrative structure, and making it operational. The targets of the linkages fell within the following order:

- Connecting indigenous peoples with each other across the participating countries;
- Connecting indigenous peoples with each other within the same country;
- Connecting indigenous peoples with arms of the government and civil society in their respective countries;
- Connecting COIP with the CARICOM Secretariat and regional civil society organizations;
- Connecting COIP with counterpart organizations in Central America, the Caribbean, and other parts of the Americas; and
- Connecting COIP with branches of the United Nations, OAS, and other multilateral organizations.

The linkages were instrumental in locating sources of funding for the operations of the Secretariat, for training opportunities for COIP members, as well as securing support for local projects. The linkages also helped in the overall consolidation of the COIP.

Within the same month of assuming the Coordinator position, October 1988, I undertook a regional familiarization tour of the COIP participating countries, in which colleagues from the St. Vincent conference hosted me.

Apart from seeing the conditions of daily life in many communities, I assessed possible sources of financial and technical assistance and other forms of collaboration that were available locally in each of the countries. I introduced the COIP to appropriate ministers of government and their technical officers as well as to arms of the civil society. Besides, I used the media, mainly radio and print, to broadcast news about the COIP. The response was generally positive and cooperative.

In 1989 the SIFC followed the earlier path of the FSIN in assisting with the formation of COIP. It sent a high-level team, headed by the President of the College to visit with me during late May and early June. To intensify their linkages the visitors went to several indigenous communities in Belize. Later in June there was a return visit to Regina, Saskatchewan, by the COIP Secretariat, which included Ian Melville from Guyana, Pat Frazier from St. Vincent, and myself. The aim was to finalize the package of exchange that would take place between the SIFC and COIP, which focused on training, research, and donation of schoolbooks and equipment.

The three COIP delegates had discussions to update ourselves, being the first time we had met since the St. Vincent conference. From Pat Frazier I learned that the Council for the Development of the Carib Community (CDCC) in St. Vincent, which had been formed to become a nationwide organization for all Caribs in St. Vincent after the 1987 conference, still remained focused on communities in the northeast. From Ian Melville I heard about the formation of the Guyanese Organization of Indigenous Peoples, as an attempt to cover all of Guyana. These efforts at forming national organizations were no doubt influenced by the St. Vincent conference. It became the practice to have meetings among Secretariat members wherever we happened to find ourselves on our travels, as it was unaffordable to meet otherwise or communicate with each other by telephone. Mail usually took weeks from one part of the region to another.

Apart from coordinating the SIFC visit and the return to Regina, I was busy spreading information worldwide about the COIP in its first year of life. In response, representatives of indigenous peoples' organizations and agencies that assist them wrote or dropped by to visit, while in Belize. Armstrong Wiggins and a team from the Indian Law Resource Center in Washington, DC, came. The UNESCO representative for the Caribbean, based in Jamaica, also came to our COIP office. In response to our letter of solicitation, the Montreal-based Development for Peace organization assisted with funds for support to the Secretariat. Development for Peace, CUSO, and Oxfam were the main sources of financial assistance to the Secretariat.

Through our solicitation, delegates started attending conferences and workshops in various countries, mainly in Central America and Mexico in 1989. COIP became better known in the following years and invitations came to us to attend numerous events at home and abroad. The delegates were more often persons representing communities in Belize because of geographical proximity and the difficulty of two-way communication between Belize and the other COIP countries. Reports of these visits became regular features in the *COIP Indigi-Notes*.

The primary event for the Secretariat in 1989 was the General Assembly, whose significance rested on the fact that it was the first meeting of COIP after the St. Vincent conference and enabled us to take stock of subsequent developments. The Inter-American Foundation (IAF) from Washington, DC, assisted with funding specifically for the General Assembly. The total cost came up to US$45,000, which included paying airfare for six delegates from the region together with their subsistence for the five-day duration of the meeting.

The very attendance at the General Assembly was one event that was able to satisfy a number of the aims of COIP. Participants from the region and beyond heightened their awareness of their counterparts in Belize. Similarly, Belizeans were able to see and speak with their counterparts to exchange ideas on matters of mutual interest. The tour of delegates to several communities within the country widened the exchange possibilities. The familiarization extended to holding discussions with resource persons, who came representing their organizations, including UNESCO, the International Labour Organization (ILO), IAF, CUSO, and WCIP. The aim was to facilitate familiarization and exchanges leading to funding local projects.

I had requested the General Assembly delegates, before leaving their home countries, to work on a three-year plan for their respective organizations that would be budgeted with specific outputs. I did the same for the Secretariat. I also requested that delegates bring reports of what they had done within their communities in keeping with the spirit of the St. Vincent conference. The result would be that the Secretariat could combine all the reports to produce a comprehensive planning package for both the Secretariat and its member organizations. Unfortunately, only one organization worked hard enough on its deliverables, as I had requested.

A major item on the agenda for the Assembly was to discuss the content of a charter for the Secretariat that I had drafted. The aim was to arrive at a document that would legalize the Secretariat and COIP, thereby progressing from what had been an ad hoc method of operation to one that had the protection of the law in all the participating countries, if possible. The delegates agreed that they needed to study the document. They took it home to discuss in detail and to deal with it at the next meeting of the General Assembly that would take place in Dominica in 1991.

The momentum of linkages increased considerably after the first General Assembly. I will mention just a few examples. The Secretary-General of CARICOM responded to my letter introducing COIP. He acknowledged the organization and promised that CARICOM would include COIP within its programs on cultural and social issues. Subsequently, I received invitations to nominate representatives to attend several CARICOM activities. In the following months similar letters of introduction went to the Caribbean Network for Integrated Rural Development (CNIRD), Caribbean Policy Development Center (CPDC), and Collaboration for Ecumenical Planning and Action (CEPAC), an arm of the Caribbean Council of Churches. As in the case of CARICOM, their response was positive and followed with invitations to workshops and training sessions. The subsequent difficulty was to get delegates mobilized to follow up on these invitations. Again, many obstacles got in the way of effective communication. Many times, potential delegates would not confirm whether they would attend or not; and when they did attend, they would not send reports that could be shared with the larger membership.

The efforts at generating exchanges among the region's indigenous peoples remained a high priority for my office, for a main problem discussed at the St. Vincent conference had been the mutual ignorance between indigenous peoples even within the same country. I was happy to arrange the first formal meeting between the National Garifuna Council and the Toledo Maya Council held in Dangriga, Belize. Five young people from St. Vincent came to spend some weeks with Garifuna families in Belize. In 1990 and 1991 delegates from St. Vincent and Dominica attended Garifuna-language workshops in Belize as part of the compiling of a Garifuna-language dictionary. The invitation went in response to concerns in both countries around the objective of learning Garifuna as part of their own cultural revitalization.

The highlight of such interconnection among indigenous peoples came in 1990 as members of the Secretariat from Dominica, St. Vincent, and Guyana met, while attending a CNIRD meeting in Trinidad and Tobago, with the Caribs in Arima. The Arima Caribs had heard about COIP and asked for formal membership. The Secretariat members explained the benefits of membership and agreed to welcome the Santa Rosa Carib Community as a member organization. COIP had thus broadened its base to include Trinidad.

Receiving funding from external sources to meet the expenses of the Secretariat and the General Assembly was itself a strong form of external validation for COIP. So were the scores of letters and telephone calls coming from all over the world. The highest level of validation, however, came from COIP's acceptance into the World Council of Indigenous Peoples, which had its head office in Ottawa. The acceptance of our letter for admission came at the 1990 General Assembly in Tromso, Norway. A delegation representing the Secretariat traveled to that Assembly. At a meeting I had with the WCIP President Donald Rojas later that year, he explained to me that he wanted to make the organization truly global in scope. For that reason he was happy to have COIP as a member organization. At the next WCIP General Assembly in Guatemala

1993, the WCIP created a new regional seat on its Executive Council to accommodate the Caribbean. COIP was appointed to have oversight over indigenous peoples not only in the English-speaking Caribbean but also in Suriname and French Guiana.

While civil society was the primary point of reference for the COIP Secretariat, we paid high regard to government officers. The Minister of Foreign Affairs of Belize gave the feature address at the 1989 COIP General Assembly. In my travels in the region, I asked to see the ministers of government with responsibility for indigenous peoples' affairs. The government of Trinidad and Tobago, however, deserves special mention for the unusually high support it gave to COIP. Before the 1992 CARIFIESTA (Caribbean Festival of the Arts), the Permanent Secretary in the Ministry of Culture held discussions with me to maximize the contribution of the region's indigenous peoples to the event. He especially wanted to highlight the significance of survival 500 years after Columbus. Indigenous peoples came as part of delegations for their respective states during CARIFESTA. In the following year the government of Trinidad and Tobago sponsored an event exclusively for indigenous peoples. It was the Second Gathering of the Indigenous Peoples of the Caribbean, lasting from August 29 to September 5, 1993.[7] Indigenous Peoples from throughout the region, including Venezuela, met in festive events and displayed music, dance, foodstuff, crafts, and spirituality. There was also a symposium featuring papers and discussions of a more academic nature.

The climax of enthusiasm among member organizations of COIP took place at the 1989 General Assembly. Afterward, we continued running the Secretariat in anticipation of the 1991 General Assembly to take place in Dominica. It did not take place. Instead, the demise of the Secretariat took place in August 1993. It deserves some elaboration further below.

A very important tool for information dissemination was *COIP Indigi-Notes*. Starting as a brief bulletin in 1989, it became a newsletter later that year. Between 1989 and 1992 there were six issues, starting with 6 pages in the first and ending with 11 in the last one. Collecting the materials for each issue, selecting them, and eventually putting them together were tasks that I supervised.

Each issue had an editorial, in which I informed readers about the latest development within the Secretariat. Then followed a more extensive feature about the activities of the Secretariat, items of interest taking place within participating countries, and others from the larger world of indigenous peoples. There was space for letters from our readers and for creative pieces, notably poems. We recorded information about sources of financial and technical assistance and encouraged readers to follow up. The newsletter demonstrated the large amount of information available (at that time before the Internet) about indigenous peoples. Copies of the newsletter were sent free of charge throughout the region and to our supporters further beyond. Many persons appreciated receiving it.

Reflections in the Mirror

I continue the analogy of the mirror to show how the COIP experience cleared shadows and enabled the region's indigenous peoples to see themselves more clearly. The clearing started at the St. Vincent conference in terms of physically seeing each other.

The five-year lifespan of the Secretariat presented ways to see ourselves more clearly within a variety of modes. Here I refer to activities that members by and large undertook. These included fund-raising from agencies, about whom we were learning for the first time; attending workshops and conferences with indigenous peoples from other parts of the world; entertaining regional counterparts within our homes and communities; and receiving acknowledgment from CARICOM and the WCIP. All of these were comparable to multidimensional screens reflecting back to us what was our inner strength. By the end of the five years, were we going to revert to the previous days of darkness in which our ancestors had been groping for centuries?

To answer this question we need to explore what caused the demise of COIP, when it seemed to have been on a positive trajectory. In hindsight there were several points of tension that were militating against the success of COIP. First, there was too strong a push to form an organization not knowing what parts would form the whole. One cannot assume that all indigenous peoples are alike and that they want to form an organization to work together. Earlier we saw briefly the historical distrust toward each other that had been part of their experience under colonialism, i.e., between tribes and along color lines if one group was perceived to be "Black." The fact that there were black people in COIP, namely the Garifuna, who regarded themselves as indigenous, brought considerable unease to people in Dominica, St. Vincent, and Guyana to whom Amerindian racial purity remains a major tenet of their identity.[8]

Second, there was a split among the membership concerning what the appropriate focus of COIP should be. From the St. Vincent conference it was plain that the indigent conditions of many communities needed urgent development assistance. On the other hand, there were others who were convinced that building a Secretariat and having it operational were the first priority. These two positions were complementary, for without a Secretariat COIP could not rally support for the benefit of its constituents. The complementarity needed to be explained to those desperately wanting immediate solutions to their basic needs, and it should have been done by their local leaders. On the other hand, the leaders themselves might not have seen the dichotomy as clearly as I am explaining. Furthermore, some local leaders might have taken advantage of this "ambivalence" of the COIP leadership to spread their own misleading information to their followers.

Indeed, while I was busy building alliances at the interregional and international levels, I had no power to ascertain that national leaders were similarly engaging in solutions toward the needs of their local communities. There was minimal response to my request for copies of reports of activities and projections of plans for the future. A major gap in the organization of COIP was the lack of articulation between my office, the intermediary role of local leaders, and the base communities, who ultimately should have been the primary beneficiaries of COIP. In the end, the clearing away of shadows was being seen by only a few of the COIP leaders, leaving behind the vast majority of the region's indigenous peoples.

Third, there were unusual expectations placed on my office to make COIP a reality with minimal institutional support at the beginning. The tendency in such situations is to personalize matters, a temptation that I resisted. Members of the Secretariat might have seen this differently and interpreted the functions of the Secretariat as part of personal largesse. Given the aura of suspicion and rumor that is rampant within our communities, it is possible that misinterpretations were being disseminated by some local leaders.

One or more of these points of tension could have led to a gradual drop in the enthusiasm of the membership toward COIP. Resorting to these speculations in itself is a reflection of the lack of corporate structure that characterized the Secretariat and by extension COIP. By the end of the first year and with the help of legal counsel, I had drafted a charter, which I gave to the Secretariat members at our first General Assembly. The charter spelled out the rights and obligations of membership in the Secretariat. In hindsight there should have been beforehand a pre-charter, a contract, that bound members to minimal levels of obligation, once fund-raising started on behalf of COIP when I took over the Secretariat Coordinator role. The contract would have stipulated measures to resolve internal conflicts, thereby preserving the integrity of the embryonic COIP. This was not done and in the vacuum there arose conflicts that were not properly ventilated, making their solution even more problematic.

So, it was not too surprising that Chief Auguiste informed me that a group from the Secretariat had agreed to have the Secretariat move to Dominica. Although it broke the gentlemanly agreement in which we had handled matters of the Secretariat, I felt obliged to hand over the files of the Secretariat to him, if it was the decision of the majority. I did so in August 1993. According to conclusions at the 1989 General Assembly, Dominica was to be the venue of the next General Assembly in 1991. Unfortunately, it did not take place; besides, Dominica was not being too forthcoming as to why they could not host the General Assembly.

Whatever the reasons for the transfer of the Secretariat from Belize, it was most unfortunate that no acknowledgment came from Chief Auguiste as to what he would be doing with the files. This was the beginning of absolutely no communication about COIP and the sadly creeping realization that it was coming to an end. A momentum that had taken so much energy, funding, and anticipation dissipated. Within the analogy of the mirror, the reflection froze and the ultimate losers were the people, who had seen a ray of light about which they could rally.

Conclusion

The difficulties of forming organizations among indigenous peoples and maintaining them over time are probably some of the most pressing in terms of attempting to solve their myriad problems. However, such topics are rarely broached either among the indigenous peoples themselves or their funding agencies. Rather, the tendency is to list the problems and to keep adding more. There is a growing need for indigenous peoples to reflect where they themselves have gone wrong in the past and to learn from their mistakes. This chapter, hopefully, will be seen as an attempt to begin this effort.

Notes

1 I use the term Amerindian when referring to how indigenous peoples are called throughout the West Indies.
2 For a discussion of the fear Arawaks have to approach other Guyanese because of a tradition of discrimination, see Forte (1988).
3 Honychurch's analysis of the use of the term "Creole" (2000, pp. 16–18) in the English-speaking Caribbean and his addition to it in terms of the cultural traits of the indigenous peoples is helpful for this discussion.
4 For additional information on the nature of the mismanagement, see Thomas' assessment using parliamentary records (1991).
5 *Waitukubuli* is the original Carib name for Dominica.
6 The source for this information comes from field visits I did in 1988.
7 The first gathering had been the St. Vincent 1987 conference.
8 For information on Black/Indian relations in Dominica, see (Owen, 1980), Guyana (Sanders, 1987), and St. Vincent (Gullick, 1985).

References

Fabel, R.F.A. (2000). *Britons, Native Americans, and Caribs 1759–1775*. Gainesville: University Press of Florida.

Forte, J. (1988). Guyanese Arawaks today. In Janette Forte (Ed.), *Proceedings of the Conference on the Arawaks of Guyana, October 14–15, 1987* (pp. 51–59). Guyana: Amerindian Research Unit, University of Guyana.

Gullick, C.J.M.R. (1985). *Myths of a minority: the changing traditions of the Vincentian Caribs*. Assen, The Netherlands: Van Gorcum.

Honychurch, L. (2000). *Carib to Creole: a history of contact of culture exchange*. Dominica: The Business Centre.

Menezes, M.N. (1977). *British policy towards the Amerindians in British Guiana 1803–1873*. Oxford: Clarendon Press.

Owen, N. (1980). On conflict relations between Afro-Dominicans and Caribs. *Social and Economic Studies*, 29(3), 264–278.

Palacio, J.O. (1993). Social and cultural implications of recent demographic changes in Belize. *Belizean Studies*, 21(3), 3–12.

———. (1995). Aboriginal peoples—their struggle with cultural identity in the CARICOM region. *Bulletin of Eastern Caribbean Affairs*, 20(4), 25–40.

Rouse, I. (1992). *The Taínos: rise and decline of the people who greeted Columbus*. New Haven, CT: Yale University Press.

Sanders, A. (1987). *The powerless people*. London: Macmillan.

Thomas, J.P. (1991). The Caribs of St. Vincent: a study in maladministration 1763–1773. In Hilary Beckles & Verene Shepherd (Eds.), *Caribbean slave society and economy: a student reader* (pp. 28–35). Jamaica: Ian Randle Publishers.

Thompson, A. (1991). Amerindian-European relations in Dutch Guyana. In Hilary Beckles & Verene Shepherd (Eds.), *Caribbean slave society and economy: a student reader* (pp. 13–27). Jamaica: Ian Randle Publishers Ltd.

Woods, L.A., Perry, J.M., & Steagall, S.W. (1997). The composition and distribution of ethnic groups in Belize: immigration and emigration patterns. *Latin American Research Review*, 32(3), 63–88.

※ CHAPTER TWELVE ※

A Bridge for the Journey: Trajectory of the Indigenous Legacies of the Caribbean Encounters, 1997–2003

José Barreiro

The germ of the Indigenous Legacies of the Caribbean Conferences,[1] held in eastern Cuba from 1997 to 2003, emerged during an overnight conversation between Alejandro Hartmann, historian of Baracoa, Cuba, Panchito Ramirez, cacique of Caridad de los Indios, Isabel Lautin, culture specialist, and this writer. November 12, 1995, was a night of heavy rain and only hours earlier, after a quiet visit to Panchito Ramirez's old bohío, a flash flood had washed away our jeep. We were lucky to be alive, everyone thankfully uninjured, and laughed heartily in unison when the old man of the mountain, Panchito, put it this way: "The mountain licked you, but she did not eat you."

Young men from the hill had made human chains in the raging flood waters to rescue several of us from the washed away jeep. Panchito's Indian people of the mountain not only saved us but also fed and warmed and hosted us in humble, dirt-floored, thatch-roofed homes during the long, rainy night. We had not only just survived the rushing waters; we were coming from a wonderful first conversation and visit with Panchito and Reyna Ramirez at La Ranchería where the most documented indigenous folk in Cuba had reasserted, "We are here. We did not die out. Our parents were Indian and so are our grandchildren."

It was very powerful testimony, centering a reality we could all easily see and endorse, based on years of common research on the survival of enclaves of Cuban Amerindian populations, particularly in places of the eastern mountains of the island. Isabel, Alejandro and I shared a passion for the indigenous roots of our Cuban culture. That night, as we each offered pieces of family, regional and academic knowledge on elements of Cuban indigenous legacy in our transcultured Cuban experience, we were able to contemplate the various areas and disciplines where researchers and practitioners are exploring and/or living these connections. The question, beyond our interest in self-identified, documented Caribbean Amerindian populations, was about the indigenous cultural legacies in every possible thematic—from traditional healing, medicinal herbal knowledge and applications, indigenous influences in topography and language, music, religious beliefs, to literature and national identity currents among the Cuban and Caribbean peoples and in Cuban and Caribbean life.

Names of kindred spirits began to surface immediately and by the time we all returned to our respective homes, Professor Angel Graña, managing coordinator of the Foundation of Nature and Humanity in Havana, quickly became a partner; Dr. Antonio Núñez Jiménez (d. 1999), then president of the same foundation, was a strong mentor of the idea, also lent his important support from early on. Other welcomed early partners surfaced within Cuba: Dr. Manuel Rivero de la Calle, dean of Cuban Anthropology (d. 2001); Dr. Eliades Acosta Matos, now director of the José Martí National Library, but then the director of the Santiago de Cuba Ateneo (cultural center); Cuban author scholar José Antonio García Molina, among other scholars in Cuba. In the US, Ingrid Washinawatok el-Issa, the Menominee Indian leader, later martyred in Colombia, lent her immediate attention. Ingrid was then director of the Fund of the Four Directions and very supportive of helping the cultural emergence of Amerindian peoples of any country in the hemisphere. Ingrid's enthusiasm for Cuba was electric and her active nudging set in motion the reality of the first conference in January 1997. An academic and cultural planning group included Dr. Hartmann, Dr. Graña and Ms. Washinawatok, among the more active.

The conferences would be held in the Cuban eastern region, at the invitation of the Nature and Humanity Foundation through Baracoa's office of the city historian, as coastal Baracoa, with a couple of excellent hotels and several humble but functional meeting venues, was chosen as the right center for the gatherings. A main purpose was that the encounters should be nongovernmental, and include as many indigenous peoples as possible, notably community folks from Caridad de los Indios and Amerindian-descendant families from the vicinity of Baracoa to the easternmost Point of Maisi. We all agreed that the main purposes of the events were 1) to recognize the communities of origin, and to celebrate their survival and their knowledge and 2) to gather good-minded people who could consider the importance of the effort to identify our Caribbean indigenous legacies. We proceeded then to invite researchers working independently in these areas of interest, both from within Cuba and internationally, to join us for the encounters. I served in the role of curriculum coordinator for the seven annual sessions (1997–2003) of the Indigenous Legacies encounter, always with the participation of dozens of key scholars and other participants.

By way of intellectual precept, the working group agreed to reconsider and challenge the concept of "extinction," which is almost uniformly applied when describing the fate of the indigenous peoples of the Caribbean. In reviewing the many methods used by colonial apologists to attack the Native American world, the casual denial of identity and existence has been the most constant. Perhaps the majority of historians, anthropologists and archaeologists writing on the Caribbean region have accepted the fallacy of extinction. Significantly, two of the most renown, José Juan Arrom and Irving Rouse, both Yale professors emeritus and authors of classic Caribbean scholarly works, point to the survival of indigenous Caribbean populations. Arrom grew up in eastern Cuba, and asserts the reality of surviving Amerindian descendants of the eastern Cuba communities. Arrom was an early mentor of the work of Indigenous Legacies.

Active for over a decade, in New York City and Puerto Rico, the Taíno Nation of the Antilles has gathered dozens of Puerto Ricans (*Boricua-jivaros*) and Cubans (*Guajiro*) who originate in families from regions where the native people concentrated in order to survive. The Taíno Nation folks showed interest immediately in the Legacies encounters and established a presence in the early sessions. International entities seeking connections to Cuban research bases, including the Smithsonian Institution, the Toronto Royal Ontario Museum, the University of Essex and Cornell University, fielded scholars early into the Legacies process. Canadian, European and American foundations sent personnel. Americans are generally prohibited by their government from most philanthropic activities in Cuba, but Canadian and European foundations can fund favored projects and are out front in securing the confidence and good-will of Cuban people. Several groups and individual US citizens, including high school students, attended the conference with licenses from the US Treasury Department.

Launching on a Current

The idea of a conference process to explore the surviving indigenous presence in Cuba and the Caribbean was noticeably out of the mainstream of Cuban academic currents in 1997. Initially some local and regional government officials rejected the petition to hold such a conference in the Oriente area, particularly in Baracoa. There were misgivings aplenty among these local officials, some considering talk of contemporary "indios" potentially divisive. The popular notion of "extinction" was applied to the request and local constabularies even challenged the authority of Panchito and his folks to proclaim their indianness. Concerns about ethnic separatism confronted the topic of ongoing indigeneity. The validity and potential issues in indigenous cultural assertions were analyzed by various people and groups, including the Cuban Communist Party, in Cuba, and the working group, in Canada. On the one level, the concept of "indigenousness" for the Cuban population can be a great source of nationalistic pride; on the other hand, this pride can be considered dangerous for the country if any group contends a separatist political notion. Political discussion leading to action is notoriously elliptical in Cuba. Challenge can come from many corners. Cuban indigenousness, we came to learn, enthused most Cuban grassroots intellectuals, many eastern regional academics and some high-level political thinkers; however, it can cause discomfort among other political and academic authorities at various levels and for myriad reasons.

Thus, from its inception, the Indigenous Legacies of the Caribbean encounter series necessarily dived into a broad and increasingly intense polemic—introducing a new/old way of perceiving our insular history and culture while some oppositional actors watched in controlled alarm, some with direct or dissimulated challenges, some with outright hostility. Conversely, those interested in the subject of the indigenous Caribbean, but based in the US, were immediately drawn to the myriad requirements of their government relative to travel and research in Cuba. The geopolitical context of Cuba-US relations for nearly half a century has left behind acute mistrust of organizations connecting even academic topics much less people-to-people projects with Cuba. Nevertheless, the Cuban people are hungry for contact and exchange with North Americans and vice versa. Several groups of US high school students (from Missouri) obtained the US Treasury license to participate in the conferences. The open-society concept of discussion, as consistently practiced by the Legacies encounters, brought forth many well-joined, even contentious, dialogues.

The lively discussion was still in full swing in Cuba as the first conference group arrived in January 1997. The program's cultural tour simply (and openly) projected the "Indigenous Caribbean" topic as an ongoing discussion encounter within a travel package. No one had said no, but no one had said yes either. Thus we came into the country to hold a cultural encounter at the open and legal invitation of several Cuban institutions, but without the full affirmation of the academic and political circles that may officiate over such themes and activities. This early, perhaps inevitable, dissonance required the commitment and courage of the full circle of early collaborators to overcome in good faith all around, at the same time assuring the minimum of discomfort to the group already in-country. Finally, the elderly Dr. Antonio Núñez Jiménez, in declining health but a man of still considerable influence in Cuba, weighed in with the government to approve the conference. He succeeded in opening the needed doors and the event went forward.

Dr. Núñez Jiménez, scientist and revolutionary figure from the anti-Batista movement, was an early writer on indigenous legacies in the Cuban people and had a particular sympathy for Cuba's Taíno origins. Dr. Núñez Jiménez, who passed away just prior to our third encounter, was a major and controversial figure in Cuban politics and science. An ardent naturalist from an early age, he had explored the eastern mountains firsthand in the 1940s and met several of the Amerindian families from Yateras. He even wrote about the elder generation of Yateras Amerindians in a 1945 article. During the Castro revolution, Núñez Jiménez joined the rebel cause as a captain under the famous Ché Guevara and was later Minister of Culture, founder of various academies and ambassador to Peru and other countries. The cycle of Legacies events became anchored by the foundation that continues to carry his name (Antonio Núñez Jiménez Foundation for Nature and Humanity, Havana). The work of the foundation is government sanctioned but independent in its scientific research and documentation work, as befitting the scholarly reputation of its founder, who published more than 50 volumes, before and after the revolution. Dr. Núñez Jiménez's resolute support for the topic of Indigenous Legacies during the first two years of our effort, sporadic due to his declining health, helped significantly to guarantee their acceptance.

In time, the factual pattern pointing to the existence of the Indian community at Caridad de los Indios and other descendant populations in the mountains, overarched as a reality experienced by sufficient people and with clear enough historical record that it obviously qualified as a subject worthy of scholarly conferences. Additionally, the "Cubanía" at the core of the Legacies process was evident right away, both in its academic context and in the expression of the mountain people, whose patriotism is without blemish. This was evident as well in the research and study conducted on the life and works of the Cuban Apostle, José Martí, whose own involvements with American indigenous peoples and his final trajectory in the area, among Cuban Amerindians, in 1895, became a signal part of the curriculum. Nevertheless, the core group of involved scholars necessarily engaged the discourse of indigenous survivals in various forums, within and outside of Cuba.

A second major figure from Cuban academic circles to support the early conferences was Dr. Manuel Rivero de la Calle, whose persistent studies in Caridad de los Indios during the 1970s lent precious attention to the subject. Rivero passed away in 2002, but he attended the sessions twice and provided his research.

Seven Encounters

The cycle of seven encounters that began in January 1997 and closed in 2003 constituted the first phase of the Indigenous Legacies of the Caribbean (ILC) meetings. The initiative in cultural and educational tourism was intended as an exploration and study program on the legacies of indigenous cultures and peoples of the Caribbean, with special emphasis on the areas of cultural preservation and recovery, healing arts and medicinal plant use, indigenous *conuco* (permacultural) food self-sufficiency and forest conservation. The educational encounters also explored the legacies theme in music, history and literature, museumology, reforestation, permaculture and use of medicinal plants, environs of the town of Baracoa and a range of schools, museums and other knowledgeable people in the Guantánamo-Baracoa region of Cuba.

The initiative was the culmination of many years of quiet building of trustful relationships with dedicated people in a wide range of fields. Initially and always a mission of friendship with the Cuban Amerindian community at Caridad de los Indios (Guantánamo Province, Cuba), the ILC project partnered with several Cuban, Canadian and American institutions, regionally and nationally. These institutions included the Fundación de la Naturaleza y el Hombre (Havana), Comisión de Cultura (Guantánamo), and Museo Matachin (Baracoa). In Canada, Plenty Canada, the Six Nations International Development Agency (SNIDA), Indigenous World Tours (Six Nations, and in New York, Flying Eagle Woman Fund), and my own research and publishing workshop project at Cornell University during those years, Akwe:kon Press/*Native Americas* journal, which served in strategic planning and curriculum development. Over time, *Native Americas* journal would carry several articles on the Legacies cycle and its general subjects. Numerous sessions on Cuba and the indigenous legacies of the Caribbean were organized out of Akwe:kon Press in various colleges and universities.

Participants and presenters, collaborators and fellow explorers who took the Legacies journey, once or more, these past seven years will hopefully forgive me. What follows is limited by my own minimalist memory, if fueled by profound attachment. The early years of the encounters sometimes are a blur of overlapping activities. I expect we will do more in the next few years to collect and preserve both essence and record of those unpredictable and yet lovingly produced encounters.

Baracoa I (January 1997): A Dialogue Joined

On the first encounter, if truth be told, we all held our breath and jumped into the abyss. A small group of 17 people from the US, Canada, England, Spain, Dominican Republic and Puerto Rico gathered in Toronto and elsewhere for flights to Santiago de Cuba—several presenters and participants—to be met at the Antonio Maceo Airport by the delegation from Baracoa and Havana—Alejandro Hartmann and Angel Graña, and our tour organizers for the first two years (Eleggua Travel, Toronto), with a small tour bus for motoring to the Balcón del Caribe Hotel, overlooking Santiago's coastline. An exciting first evening saw the group gather for a ceremonial welcome and a short history of José Martí, Santiago de Cuba and the aboriginal peoples in the ethnogenesis of Cuba.

On that first ILC meeting we honored the work of Dr. Manuel Rivero de la Calle, dean of Cuban anthropology. The elderly and much-beloved "Manolo," a true gentleman-scholar of the traditional Cuban school, led several teams of scientists and students up the trails to Caridad de los Indios for the most detailed studies to date of the Amerindian population of the mountains. It is Rivero, along with archaeologist Dacal Maure, who estimated the "Indio" population of Caridad de los Indios at some 1,000, perhaps more (c. 1975). Rivero lectured on the history of Cuban anthropology and archaeology and provided generous impromptu commentaries.

Two excellent papers, by Cuban scholars José Antonio García Molina (on the blending of the Taíno *areito* and spiritist ceremonies in the 1840s in Bayamo) and Alejandro Hartmann (setting the record straight on Cacique Guamá) are memorable. These were complemented by ongoing work by Joan Borel on Taíno agricultural legacies in the contemporary Caribbean. The ensuing discussion revealed a wonderful reality: Panchito, Reina and other elders from Caridad hold a copious amount of knowledge on medicinal properties of plants and animals in the region. This welcome contribution quickly extended to various researchers and green medicine practitioners in the region, who presented, formally and informally, in every conference from that year forward. Dr. Peter Ferbel spoke on indigenous Taíno elements in the popular culture of the Dominican Republic. René Marcano (Çibanakan) spoke of the Taíno legacies of Puerto Rico and the revitalization of the Taíno Nation of the Antilles. Ingrid Washinawatok spoke about the developing indigenous circle at the UN and of the role of Caribbean basin countries in processes involving international representation by indigenous peoples.

Pedagogical themes were strong in that first session of Legacies. Several educators, two from Puerto Rico, one from the Dominican Republic and two from the US, shared classroom and curriculum ideas and experiments, on the ethnographic and multicultural work of recovery and depiction of native themes at various educational levels. Dr. Peter Ferbel spoke memorably on the politics of Taíno heritage in the Dominican Republic while educator Hector Alvarez, a Puerto Rican teaching in the Dominican Republic, analyzed the thematic within that country's national curricula. Indigenous origins as a topic elicited energetic discussion among students from the Greater Antilles. The question of indigenous identity quickly took center stage, as both local and other participants pronounced various family histories and shared traditional folk healing practices, utilizing animals and plants indigenous to the region.

The group from Caridad de los Indios could not join the tour the first year, not for the first week. Fuel shortages curtailed public transportation from their mountainous area. A few of us stayed behind, including the Taíno Nation representatives and Ingrid Washinowatok's group. Finally, Panchito and his group arrived. It was the first encounter between the Puerto Rican descendants and the Cuban descendants from the mountains. There was great joy, with much music, dance and prayer. Ingrid witnessed it and blessed it with her wonderful smile.

Ingrid Washinawatok, most of all, understood what was at stake in the Legacies encounters. Ingrid, who studied in Havana in 1980–81, was keen on encouraging Cuban people to speak about their origins and especially the indigenous origins of Cuban nationality. She came with a couple of excellent companions, and would return for the second encounter, before her work in Colombia took her precious life.

Baracoa II (November 1997): Amerindian to Amerindian

From the beginning, the tour/cultural encounter grew by its context and its contacts. The beauty and ancient aura of the eastern Cuban mountains and the sunny and majestic drive along the coast, from Santiago to Baracoa, provided an immediate sense of being in place. Along the way to Baracoa, many places of historical and cultural significance set the stage and elicited talks on rich realities from the times of sole Taíno inhabitation to the later epochs of Spanish conquest, colonial transculturations, wars of independence, wars of liberation and the impacts of a socialist revolution over 40 years of conflict with the US. The travel by tour bus established a pattern that would repeat over the years. In what became tradition, the groups would stop for a visit at the coastal village of Playitas de Cahobabo, where José Martí landed in 1895, just six weeks before his death in battle against the Spanish army. This sacred spot in Cuban history boasts a small museum, a two-room school and a garden planted with dozens of native species of medicinal and other plants noted by Martí in the meticulous diary he kept during his final days in his beloved Cuba. In Santiago, we deposited an honor wreath at the Tomb of the Apostle, at the San Efigenias Cemetery, while primary students from a nearby school, the Jose Marti School #7, sung the Cuban National Anthem in his honor. They pledged to our group that they would prepare a theater production if we promised to return the following year. We promised.

The encounters in Baracoa grew apace. The first three-day session, held at the Matachin Museum in Baracoa in January 1997, drew a local audience of several dozen people. During the second Legacies encounter, held in November of that same year, the local crowd tripled so that the sessions outgrew the space available at the Matachin. The remote region of Cuba offered then and still does an everyday culture of hospitality that opened many invitations to private homes and to community-wide civic celebrations as well as to spiritual ceremonies. A bond developed between the encounter groups and local families that has persisted.

At the second (November 1997) conference, where the discussion of indigenous identities in the Cuban and Caribbean consciousness persisted, Cacique Panchito and several of his people arrived early and stayed throughout, causing much interest among people in Baracoa and calling out the attention of local radio and newspaper reporters. José Antonio García Molina, research associate at the José Martí National Library (Havana), spoke on indigenous themes in Cuban letters, focusing on indigenist poetry during the 19th century Cuban literary movement called *Siboneyismo* and particularly the work of the *independista* poet known as Cucalambé. Peter Hulme, professor at the University of Essex, spoke of novels and other literature at the turn of the turn of the 20th century, depicting Cuban Amerindian communities. Joan Borel, anthropologist from Key West, spoke on the Taíno language and its legacies in the contemporary Spanish of the islands.

We requested access that second year to visit Caridad de los Indios as a tour conference group. Permission was not granted.

Baracoa III and IV (January and November 1999): Caribbean Confabs

The year 1998 passed without a conference. There were two in 1999. A growing range of American Indian peoples joined the conference cycle that year from North and Central America and—most significantly—from other parts of the Caribbean. Several North American teachers and professors also joined. The encounter among native people, particularly practitioners of herbal medicinal healing, expanded. By now the groups were of 30 to 50 travelers from outside the country, representing various viewpoints and constituencies.

In 1999, the tour/encounters came together with a great range of people and papers. More than a dozen Cuban scholars, historians, archaeologists and anthropologists came out to present their work. Interestingly, a substantial range of well-trained, local Cuban historians, particularly from the eastern provinces of Camagüey to Bayamo and Guantánamo, and including Hartmann in Baracoa, were independently working on similar lines of research. Locally driven research on the Amerindian origins of family lines and long-term Amerindian settlement among the incoming Spanish and African people surfaced. Amerindian social existence into the late 19th century was being more clearly documented. In 1999, too, several Canadian First Nations were represented in the Legacies, as Algonquin, Cree, Iroquois and Métis delegations, several singers and presenters, as well as representatives of governments and research centers attended.

In March of 1999, Ingrid Washinawatok was assassinated in Colombia. Baracoa and all who had known her mourned her tragic passing. In the fall of 1999 session, the Guama statue in Baracoa was rededicated in honor of Ingrid Washinawatok. It was a fitting tribute as the conference that year gathered more native leaders than ever and was rich in Caribbean lore.

A Carib cultural leader from Dominica (Prosper Paris) and a Garifuna scholar from Belize (Dr. Joseph Palacio, a contributor to this volume) attended that conference, as did Chief Ricardo Bharath Hernandez from the Santa Rosa Carib Community of Trinidad (also a contributor to this volume). All three important Caribbean indigenous leaders spoke eloquently of their historical and political situations. Prosper Paris is a noted herbalist among the Dominica Caribs and shared many informative sessions with Panchito Ramirez. They shared stories and compared words in each other's languages (*tocayo*, name; *teti*, small, lunar-driven fish; *himagua*, twins, etc.), as well as herbal and medicinal practices. R. Teni, Kekchi-Maya, a traditional daykeeper or healer from Guatemala, attended that year. His people extend to the Caribbean coast, where they are settled along a coast they share with Garifuna of Guatemala.

In Santiago de Cuba that year, the students from the José Martí School #7 presented a theater piece, acted out by some 20 students, from a little-known drama by Martí called "Indio de Guatemala." They performed it in three acts for the assembled touring group. The enthusiasm and public skills of the children, at Martí #7 and at Playitas de Cahobabo, impressed all travelers. Guantánamo historian José Sanchez Guerra lectured at length about the history of the Hatuey Regiment—the contingent made up of Yateras Indians who fought against the Spanish in the 1895 Cuban War of Independence. Maya delegate R. Teni expressed the wonderment of all at the studiousness of the children and the dedication of the teachers in urban and rural Cuban schools.

Most significantly, two presenters from the Smithsonian National Museum of the American Indian, in their lecture on US federal repatriation laws, informed the conference that their institution holds a number of human remains of Cuban Taíno origin. Later, in conversation with Panchito Ramirez, the Cuban Indian cacique indicated a willingness to rebury and give respectful rest to the ancient remains, removed by archaeologist Mark Harrington in 1916. In November 1999, the Cuban Amerindian group that joined the conference numbered 22 people. They brought their old Amerindian music and the more recent but traditional *changüí*. There was excellent camaraderie among scholars, participants and community people. By the second conference, the custom of bringing medicinal and educational materials to donate to hospitals and schools was firmly established. Two US high school teachers brought students with US Treasury visas. The students, while critical, experienced a different world firsthand, previously only media described. They became prized travelers and presented, in Spanish, their perceptions of Cuba, indigenous traditions and medicinal knowledge.

Cuban authorities, not normally given to spiritual ceremony in their public occasions, nevertheless provided respectful space to the activities of the tour that developed in that direction. Not a few functionaries ultimately participated in the ceremonies, regularly held around the statue of Guamá, on a hill overlooking Baracoa Bay, where various native spiritual leaders from throughout the Americas usually led by the Cuban elders, sang their traditional songs and made burnt offerings of tobacco and copal. At Baracoa's House of Culture, several local painters and sculptures offered a wide-ranging exhibition on Cuban indigenous themes. That November 1999, Navajo journalist Valerie Taliman, based in Albuquerque, New Mexico, conducted a live radio interview with three Caribbean Amerindian leaders, for the daily satellite radio show, *Native America Calling*, which broadcasts to over 50 American Indian reservation radio stations in North America. The Cuban national newspaper, *Granma*, carried a news article on the conference that year, and local radio affiliates of Radio Rebelde conducted interviews with some of the attendants.

The Indigenous Legacies Conference projected no politics relative to Cuban international policy, by the US or any other country. The conference respects the fact of Cuban sovereignty belonging in Cuba, and nowhere else.

Baracoa V (January 2001):
To La Ranchería and the Toa River Watershed

For Baracoa V in January 2001, themes relating to natural medicines, healing practices and music were extended. The Cuban system of complementing Western with traditional herbal and other remedies and healing methods caught up with the conference and many researchers and practitioners came to present on their work. Cuban researchers as young as 12 years old presented at that year's event, which also featured the national director of Cuba's alternative medicine program, plus the noted Cornell University natural medicines researcher, Dr. Eloy Rodriguez, who met with several local doctors engaged in fascinating new research with animal and plant medicines. The Iroquois clan mother and noted herbalist Jan Longboat exchanged thoughts and information with community herbalists.

Just as Cacique Panchito and the other elders of Caridad de los Indios gained in public profile as a result of the Legacies conferences, a consciousness of their river valley also emerged. From Panchito's Ranchería communities near the trickling headwaters of the Toa River to the wide and voluminous Toa that flows to the sea just seven kilometers west of Baracoa, this majestic Cuban watershed includes the last, free-standing original tropical forest left on the island of Cuba. The Toa River and its watershed, flowing north from the

Sagua-Baracoa Mountain range, encompasses an area of 1,053 km². The Toa River flows over some 120 km and is known as Cuba's most productive "water factory." This dense Amazonian type forest collects annually as much as 3,500 mm of rainfall and is the most voluminous river in Cuba, with a flow of 30 m³ of water per second. The quality and quantity of fauna and flora is substantial, including some 1,700 species, of which some 54% are endemic to Cuba. The ecological region hosts over 85 bird species, among them many types of parrots and "cateys," minute "Bee" hummingbirds and the endangered *gavilán* or *guaraguao* hawk. Some 40 reptile and amphibian species, numerous endemic plant and insect species persist in the region. With about 100 species currently endangered, serious attention is required in the area to protect the treasures still living there.

On behalf of his community and circle of elders, Cacique Panchito has made a strong call for the preservation and protection of the River Toa watershed, the reforestation of the mountains against erosion and other projects. Thus the community endorsed a partnership between Indigenous Legacies (Six Nations, Canada) and the Cuban Foundation for Nature and Humanity to seek ways to help the protection and preservation of the mountains and watershed of the Toa River.

The region of Baracoa-Guantánamo is under the watchful stewardship of a group of well-recognized natural science Cuban foundations and research entities, which enjoy the good graces and cooperation of many activists and intellectuals, including an ecology-minded retired general of the Cuban Army (Francisco Gonzalez), who has appreciated and supported Panchito's call for ecological protection.

General Francisco (Pancho) Gonzalez is known in the mountains as an ardent protector of ecological integrity. He has directed the major reforestation and anti-erosion projects in the watershed and holds the line of protection against encroachment into the pristine forests just north of Baracoa. In 2001, General Pancho assisted in securing the major breakthrough of the tour, the permission to visit the Amerindian community village at La Ranchería.

As the large group gathered around the fire at La Ranchería, continuities in the message of the Legacies conferences became apparent. Panchito intoned a heart-rending, authentic indigenous prayer in a tobacco burning ceremony that brought the intellectual process in step with cultural people-to-people continuities. General Pancho participated, smoking the sacred *macuyo*, or Amerindian cigar that the cacique gave him and then intoning a serious lecture on the effort to preserve the Toa River Valley for future generations.

It is not an easy journey up the mountain. Open-backed army trucks carried the group up the rutted mountain roads for the 35 km to the community. The general guaranteed it but not a few local government functionaries complained. The phenomenon of nearly 50 foreigners visiting the area was unique and somewhat scandalous. La Ranchería is way off the beaten path, in a restricted mountain area, not far from the US base at Guantánamo, which creates extra security tensions around the immediate region. That the Legacies conference of 2001 succeeded finally in visiting La Ranchería is a tribute to the openness that was developing in Cuba after some years of relative calm between the US and the socialist island. Our consistent message in this context was that these cultural and scientific tours in Cuba provided a tremendous bridge to growth, both for visitors and for the Cubans whom we met and engaged all along the way. The highly intensified climate of hostility since 2000 has frozen and reversed this trend, instead fueling the most retrograde attitudes on all sides.

But that year, at the top of the mountain, the people of La Ranchería fed us and danced with us. Oscar Montoto, publisher of Ediciones Catedral, presented the personal testimony book, *Panchito: Cacique de Montaña*, the first book-length document to emerge from the Legacies project. At the conclusion, as the encounter gathered for farewells in Santiago, came word from Havana of an official invitation to the Amerindian people of La Ranchería, to lead the opening of the International Festival of Cuban Havano (tobacco). This constituted a major de facto recognition on a national level for the long-ignored mountain community.

Many participants in the Legacies encounters have continued to express interest and support for reforestation and other ecosystemic projects in the Cuban mountains. The elders of the Ranchería *yucayeque* (extended-family community) of Cacique Panchito Ramirez are spiritual and cultural advisors to the initiative. These native elders are traditional conuco farmers from the Cuban mountains and deeply conversant on natural world themes. Native agriculture and natural knowledge was the backdrop for developing an educational program for both local community and foreign students in these important ecosystemic economic and production projects. Cuba-based American filmmaker, Estela Bravo, screened her new film, a biography of Cuban president Fidel Castro, bringing a focus from the Cuban media to the conference.

Baracoa VI (January 2002): A Mission Emerges

The January 2002 tour group was small. The tragic events of September 11, 2001, drastically reduced international travel that season. There was a suggestion to cancel the tour but organizers took the moment as a challenge not to let the tour fall ("que no se caiga la gira"). It was a quality group that included a keynote lecture on indigenous survivals from Mexican author, Jesús Serna Moreno, and a substantial workshop presentation on indigenous international themes by José Zarate, a Quechua development specialist. Both substantially framed the Caribbean cultural and identity recovery currents within the broader hemispheric indigenous movement. Noted Cuban photographer, Julio Larramendi, opened his exhibit of photographs taken among the folks of Caridad de los Indios. A group of high school students from Kansas City, Missouri, traveling with three teachers, gave the tour the feel of a traveling classroom and the ongoing discussion created an "ambulatory *tertulia* (chat)," as volunteer translator Mario Llorente called it.

Once again, the touring group visited Caridad de Los Indios and ate lunch at La Ranchería. Several elders spoke extensively on herbal uses and the group toured Panchito's conucos, hearing from our favored lecturer on the uses of tobacco, and the indigenous meaning of the conuco companion planting system.

Negotiations between the Smithsonian Institution's National Museum of the American Indian (NMAI) and various Cuban institutions were resumed around the potential repatriation to Cuba of Taíno human remains held in the vast NMAI collections. Tim Johnson, James Pepper Henry and Nicolasa Sandovál, from NMAI, and Dr. Angel Graña, from the Cuban Foundation of Nature and Humanity, were instrumental in achieving the repatriation agreement between officials of the two countries.

Baracoa VII (January 2003): A Mission Fulfilled

The trip in January 2003 was the culmination of a full cycle of seven conferences over seven years. More than mere academic conferences, these encounters across cultures and political frameworks to explore the indigenous roots of our contemporary existence in these Caribbean islands became an active network of relations.

A mission had emerged for that year: to witness, as a group, the repatriation and reinterment of human remains of Taíno people, disinterred and transported from funerary sites in Cuba to New York's Museum of the American Indian (see Fig. 9).

The theme of research and indigenous peoples became an obvious one for the final encounter in the series. One memorable discussion ensued during a visit to the Guantánamo Museum, where a new Taíno exhibit was inaugurated. The exhibit featured two cases that depicted actual Taíno remains— skulls and bones of arms and legs, even the tiny bones of hands and feet— arranged as found. As the tour in part was in Cuba to witness the proper reburial of excavated and removed human remains—this done in most solemn ceremony—the shock of seeing the skeletal displays exploded a heated exchange on the propriety in design of museum displays using indigenous human remains. Themes on intercultural understanding, spiritual respect for ancestor's remains, and the analysis of colonialist patterns that linger in all national cultures and within the scientific method itself were presented in a dialogue that involved most of museum staff and all of the tour group. Panchito, local cacique and welcomed authority, helped settle the distinctions finally by strongly celebrating the return of the long-ago-taken remains, and the manner of their reburial, while approving the displays in the Guantánamo Museum. He approved of them because they were done respectfully, he asserted, in collaboration with his own community and with the intent of educating more of his own people about their own origins. "I don't know how it is in other places," he said "but here, we need this type of idea because we have been so out of sight."

Figure 9: Traveling group crosses stream to the cemetery at Caridad de los Indios, to witness reinterment ceremony, January 9, 2003. Photograph courtesy Millie Knapp.

About the repatriation, as reported in *American Indian Magazine*, the cacique had said in 1998: "We would want to bury the ancestors. We will receive them properly and reintegrate them to rest in peace on their own land." After five years of visits by scholars and other officials from institutions in Washington and Havana, all were satisfied that a primary objective of the NMAI—the return of human remains for proper reburial by a "community of relatives"—would be achieved by accepting Panchito's request. On June 19, 2002, the remains were delivered to Cuba, into the hands of Mrs. Lupe Velis de Núñez, President of the Cuban Foundation for Nature and Humanity by NMAI Director W. Richard West. Later, at Panchito's request, they were delivered to Dr. Alejandro Hartmann, historian of Baracoa, to be held until their final journey to Panchito's mountain for the reburial.

On January 9, 2003, as final official act of the Indigenous Legacies of the Caribbean Conference cycle, all participants took the long and still rutty ride up the mountain to the cemetery at Caridad de los Indios and witnessed the actual reception ceremony and the placement of the ancestors in their final funerary urn. The reburial of the long-ago-taken remains, with singing and a traditional dance was simple yet significant. No one will ever forget the re-encirclement dance put up by the community elders of La Ranchería. It was a tradition born of them. A North American reporter stationed in Cuba for two years, called the ceremony the "most genuine public event I have witnessed in Cuba."

The Legacy of "Legacies": Positive Results

The Indigenous Legacies of the Caribbean tours and cultural encounters were held annually for seven years. The annual event became more than just another conference; it generated a growing web of people that continue to interlink. The purpose is mutual learning and to be of help to one another, to break down barriers so that the hostility relative to Cuban sovereignty internationally may be tempered by direct contact, sharing information and a respectful sharing of perspectives. The ILC initiative approved of the Cuban policy of support for the indigenous-descendant families in this area to emerge and be recognized as genuine bearers of Caribbean indigenous culture.

An informal network of people dedicated to assisting the Cuban grass-roots communities has formed. Out of some 120 people who joined the tours over the years, some 70 stay in direct contact with conference organizers. More than 50 have returned on two or more occasions. As a result, in a decentralized but informed manner, small projects have developed that have generated a range of friendship and assistance for a population passing through a difficult economic and political moment. For example, various of the participants have organized the collection and shipment of four dialysis machines for remote clinics; donated dental and medical equipment; linked up Cuban schools with schools in Puerto Rico and Canada that have donated school supplies and established workshops for sharing curricula; facilitated medical operations for cataracts for two elders and provided reading glasses for over a dozen people, amongst other forms of support. One couple provided adequate medicine for several young girls with a very difficult skin condition. The ILC encounters opened a range of partnerships in Cuba that can support programs in permacultural farming, forest preservation, reforestation and medicinal farming, in the context of living/learning within a population whose lifestyle incorporates many such skills.

Despite their many years under an ostensibly agnostic political system, the Cuban people and especially the native population are highly spiritual. There is a great deal of ceremony. People on the tour were able to share in this reality.

Figure 10: The old-style thatched-roof bohíos have been replaced by a group of 11 solar-powered houses in the village of La Ranchería, Guantánamo, Cuba. Educational programs, music and news are finally available. Noticeably, the cacique's old bohío, at the right, has been preserved as an "altar house," where sacred ceremonies are held. Photograph courtesy Millie Knapp.

Most gratifyingly, the main native community itself, Caridad de los Indios, is working on small development projects of their own choosing. One in particular concerns the documentation and propagation of natural medicines in the mountains. Conversely, many people in remote areas of the embargoed island met and engaged Americans and other foreigners, many of them for the first time. The La Ranchería community is an Amerindian *caserío* of 11 houses that is the home village of Panchito Ramirez's clan. The Legacies project provided a forum for Panchito and several other knowledgeable and eloquent community elders to present their knowledge, which is extensive, free of intimidating and uninviting strictures, whether academic or governmental. Panchito and his community gained in increased recognition and strength, particularly relative to the local and regional milieu of political and cultural players, as a result of the conferences. Their national projection as a genuine culture/music group was fortified as a result of their invitations and participation in the Legacies tours. A national and international network of friends who are willing to help also came together. One of these contacts carried the word to cultural personalities in Havana and elsewhere who championed the small community. One result of the proper identification of the Caridad community was the building of 11 new solar-energy generating units in the various wooden homes (see Fig. 10). Over a dozen families from Panchito's clan who have migrated for lack of housing are exploring ways of repatriating to their beloved mountain community.

Note

1 This article presents a brief narrative of the seven-year conference cycle, Indigenous Legacies of the Caribbean, held in Baracoa, Cuba, from 1997 to 2003. A comprehensive, cooperative archiving project is being conducted by the Office of the City Historian of Baracoa and by the Indigenous Legacies Project (Berkshire, New York).

※ CHAPTER THIRTEEN ※

Searching for a Center in the Digital Ether: Notes on the Indigenous Caribbean Resurgence on the Internet

Maximilian C. Forte

"I went on the Internet to find out who I am." These words of a Trinidadian resident in Canada were offered as part of an explanation of how she came to probe her own aboriginal ancestral origins as a person who once saw herself as being only of "mixed" descent, in a family where some relatives preferred to label themselves "French." She went on the Internet in 2003 and encountered the website of Trinidad's Santa Rosa Carib Community (SRCC),[1] which I designed and maintain as the webmaster of the SRCC. It is not an entirely unique story. Many Trinidadians, especially those residing overseas, possibly longing for the place in which they truly fit in as persons at "home," seeking to gain knowledge of their home, longing for a sense of rootedness, and using the technology at their disposal, have come to re-identify as Amerindian descendants in their adult years. This is a heavily loaded bundle of partial explanations, yet one that largely resonates with what I have distilled from over six years of correspondence with dozens of Trinidadians online, and from what I have witnessed from the feedback provided to various sites by expatriates of the Dominican Republic and Puerto Rico.[2]

The Internet, in and of itself, has no creative agency—it is simply a medium. These are not "Internet Indians," as if the Internet possessed some agency to create identities and senses of belonging, as if the Internet somehow elicited identity positions that individuals and groups never had before. The Internet is a medium that conveys certain possibilities to those who are already predisposed, to some degree, to position themselves and rearticulate their identities as Amerindian descendants. The plethora of websites by Caribbean Amerindians, especially Puerto Rican Taínos, stressing the message, "we are not extinct," has served to build a new field of possibility and a new space for identity which older media, often monopolized by more conservative scholarly interests, left largely closed (see Forte, 2002). Thus far, it is admittedly the case that I have reduced a complex phenomenon to a simple and unequivocal search for one's identity using a special medium, as if it were a fast-food outlet, immediately delivering a consumable good on demand.

Some difficult questions need to be addressed, therefore, if we are to more fully appreciate the Internet as a new platform in the contemporary international resurgence of Amerindian identification. My intention is to focus on the practices of building a Caribbean indigenous presence online that aids dispersed individuals and groups in further developing a sense of belonging to a home, in the process of articulating their own representations as indigenous. In my attempt to realize this intention, I will raise two questions. First, to what extent has the Internet been useful in furthering Caribbean indigenous goals of self-representation, regional organization and actual change "on the ground"? Second, what are the challenges facing Caribbean indigenous utilization of the Internet that limit their presence or the character of their representations?

The reason for asking these questions, and not other perfectly valid and interesting questions, is not an indication of an attempt to secure a premature closure of inquiry. The primary purpose of these questions is to explore and chart Caribbean indigenous cultural practice through engagements with Internet media on personal and collective levels. This is by no means the only angle by which we can appreciate the flourishing growth of Caribbean indigenous websites, but it is one way of arriving at an understanding of the relevance that Internet media have for the forms of practice and organization that we refer to under the heading of the *resurgence* of the indigenous Caribbean. These novel means of communication impose certain constraints even while they open up new opportunities for self-representation. We need to understand the nature of those limitations in addition to the ways Internet media are used and engaged.

What Is "New" about Indigeneity Online?

The Internet provides a qualitatively new and contemporary arena for identification as Amerindian, whether Carib or Taíno as the cases tend to be. First, in those cases involving solitary persons using the Internet to document, verify, or give new voice to their self-identification as indigenous, one may detect a certain degree of individuality in search of a community. On the other hand, the Internet serves as yet another membrane for collecting stories and images of the tribe, transmitting these directly, even if not face to face, to the newest members of a tribe that is constantly in the process of reproducing itself. The Internet serves as "screen memories" (to borrow Ginsburg's metaphor), helping to encode and establish presence where presence is precisely what has been under threat: "indigenous people are using screen media not to mask but to recuperate their own collective stories and histories...that have been erased in the national narratives of the dominant culture and are in danger of being forgotten in local worlds as well" (Ginsburg, 2002, p. 40).

Second, while speaking of deeply personal needs for belonging, the online mode of interaction often proceeds without face-to-face interaction and without a shared geographic locality for the interactions, though the latter is not always true of course. As some have already observed in studying interpersonal relations on the Internet in broader terms, the Internet "enables two qualities that individuals can find empowering: anonymity and intimacy" (Doheny-Farina, 1996, p. 65). Through the Internet, some individuals may come to perceive themselves as indigenous with the aid of others engaged in the same process. I will return to this issue in the seventh point below.

Third, the Internet arena for this identification is substantially wider in spatial terms, extending well beyond the Circum-Caribbean, and is shaped by the acceleration of communication in temporal terms. This dimension of the internationalization of Amerindian identification speaks to a uniquely contemporary situation that is not only indicative of the fact that there is a resurgence of this identification, but it can also show us the extent to which wider spheres of this resurgence can occur in and through the Internet.

In line with the last point, one can see that the Internet has increasingly become a significant vehicle in the propagation of a transnational, indigenous Fourth World (Prins, 2002, p. 72). As Prins recognized, the Internet "enables tribal communities and individuals to represent themselves and to do so largely on their own terms and according to their own aesthetic preferences" (2002, p. 70). The question of "transnationalized indigeneity," to the extent that one can meaningfully speak of this, represents an important paradox of indigeneity: seemingly free floating whilst emphasizing local rootedness (see Clifford, 1994). As Dávila (1999, p. 25) explains, Taíno groups and associations "have tended to conceptualize themselves not so much in nationalist as in diasporic terms." In addition, Dávila found that most of the Taíno revivalists were either born or raised in the US, with most residing there, and it was in the US that "most of the Taínos recouped their indigenous identity" (1999, p. 19). It seems that for many of the individuals I encounter both online and in person, identification as indigenous is developed and defined, in part, in and through a transnationalized network of representation. Returning to the case of the Trinidadian woman who spoke at the outset of this chapter, she had also accompanied Canadian aboriginals in various protest marches, had studied Canadian aboriginals in various texts, and had "traveled" across a spectrum of indigenous websites until she found her way back home, so to speak, in examining Trinidadian aboriginal websites. Clifford's paradox can be seen in two different ways: individuals in the diaspora, seemingly free floating, while home remains in place where they left it; or, individuals are rooted wherever they are, and home is symbolically lifted from a place and appears to be free floating over members of the diaspora.

Fourth, there are important parameters conditioning, even constraining, this phenomenon of indigenous resurgence practiced via the Internet, which I very loosely refer to as "Internet indigeneity," that is, indigeneity partly conceptualized and practiced in and through the Internet. By and large, only very few indigenous Caribbean communities have been in the position to make significant and sustained use of the Internet, apart from the Garifuna of Central America. We can thus discern a spectrum of representation from the Greater Antilles to the Mainland in terms of the *decreased* occurrence of what we might call critiques of "extinctionist" discourse (i.e., emphatic repetition of the thesis that no Amerindians remain in a given territory), proceeding through the region from north to south. At the same time, we see the *increasing* dominance of the number of websites by Caribbean Amerindians as we move back from south to north. Most websites are by self-identified Taínos from Puerto Rico; the fewest are by Guyanese Amerindians. Significantly then, the theme of disputing extinction makes its presence felt heavily in the narratives of these websites of the Greater Antillean diaspora. In an attempt to underscore Amerindian survival, some websites have seemingly taken revenge against older scholarly orthodoxies that asserted extinction, by stressing, maybe even over communicating in some cases, the degree of social and cultural continuity. For my part, I do not lament the polemics that result from the clash of two extremes, given that they serve to admit the fact that there is a debate to be had (e.g., Borrero, 1999) and that older orthodoxies merit intense critical scrutiny (see Barreiro and Guitar, Ferbel-Azcarate and Estevez, this volume).

Fifth, like previous media, use of new media such as the Internet are tied up with issues of power. Both Turner (2002) and Alia (1999) observed how involvement in film and television production, as well as journalism, among the Kayapo of Brazil and the Inuit in northern Canada, offered a means for some to graduate to higher political status within native communities, helping them to become more prominent as political leaders, or simply cementing their claims to authority through media use. As Turner observed with the Kayapo: "political acts and projects, such as a young leader's claims to chiefly authority, that in the normal run of Kayapo political life would remain relatively contingent and reversible, can be represented by video in ways that help establish them as objective public realities" (2002, p. 87). To a limited extent, this may also be true of some of the Taíno websites, insofar as claims to communal and intercommunal leadership are made most forcibly, and visibly, through the Internet. Indeed, the Internet can be used in those cases for organizations to indirectly contest each other's claims to authority.[3]

Sixth, the Internet has gone a long way toward enabling some Caribbean aboriginals, especially those who are best positioned to make use of it, to affirm self-determination in their own self-representations. As Turner found in the case of video, new techniques of representation may empower persons to transform their stock of social and cultural forms (2002, p. 80). The very practice of representation helps to establish the reality being recorded on Taíno websites, for example (see Turner, 2002, p. 87).

Seventh, unlike previous media, the Internet provides the basis for new ways of building and expressing community, for bringing the solitary "surfer" back home. As Jones explains, resonating with the declaration at the start of this paper, "we are struck, as we use the Internet, by the sense that there are others out there *like us*" (1997, p. 17, emphasis in the original). Being on the Internet is a time to be alone and yet with others (Jones, 1997, p. 17). Community is experienced imaginatively, even by the solitary surfer, in the surfer's process of establishing relevant and potentially meaningful connections in the process of navigating across related websites: "the World Wide Web, exists as a set of connections from one text to another, providing for choice in navigation from text to text" (Jones, 1997, p. 28). Connections are also developed by more communal means. Indeed, there is already a significant range of literature pointing to the emergence of communities online, no less "real" than offline communities: "community exists in the minds of the participants; it exists because its participants define it and give it meaning" (Fernback, 1999, p. 213). As Fernback extends this argument, if communication is at the heart of "community," then, "community is real whether it exists within the same physical locality or half a world away via the telephone wires" (Fernback, 1999, p. 213). The development of indigenous community online is not any more imaginary than the development of other mediated forms of collectivity, including nationalism (see Anderson, 1991). In fact, given the pronounced degree of interactivity of these new media, where the allegedly passive and solitary media consumer of the past has largely vanished, communities mediated by new media may be far less fictive than established forms of nationalism. Though it may be practiced through a nonplace such as the Internet, online indigeneity is place oriented: Trinidad and Puerto Rico, for example, still figure prominently in the minds of online site producers and associated visitors as respective locations of Carib and Taíno cultures.

In other words, we see the development of a community of webmasters, discussants, and correspondents, some of whom may have little interaction with each other off-line, especially where geographically dispersed. The centrality of the role of the Internet in this new phase of indigenous resurgence in the

Caribbean is that a much broader, transnational set of associations and linkages can be built, gathering disparate individuals and groups, in both the homeland and the diaspora, into one "web" of mutual recognition and self-definition. Home is thus both a place and a practice. The Carib-descended Trinidadian web surfer is producing home by seeking it. The online community to which that Trinidadian may find herself gravitating toward may not be locale dependent, but it certainly is locale oriented. At the foundation of this community is the presence of common symbolic meanings, ultimately of greater importance than mere co-presence in one geographic point (see Cohen, 1989).

Representing Caribbean Indigeneity on the Internet

The first question I posed at the outset was "To what extent has the Internet been useful in furthering Caribbean indigenous goals of self-representation, regional organization and actual change 'on the ground'?" There are three distinct elements to this question, all focused on the ability to realize some of the positive potentials of the Internet, from the viewpoint of furthering and deepening Caribbean indigenous resurgence.

Beginning with self-representation, the Internet is allowing relatively marginalized groups to recover a history and identity that colonialism, in large part, helped to erase or distort, an absence which dominant social science has unfortunately helped to inscribe. The online assertions of survival are able to attain visibility precisely because the off-line realm places many more constraints on the dissemination of these assertions. Indeed, this becomes painfully evident given the fact that there are no professional historians or anthropologists who are Caribbean indigenes apart from the few who contribute to this very volume—otherwise, Caribs and Taínos, by and large, are spoken for, and spoken about, by others, with agendas that only infrequently emerge from within these communities. The Internet allows for a reversal of that history of asymmetrical power in that now Taínos, for example, can engage in their own self-exploration and self-expression, utilizing historical resources, artistic expressions, and contemporary images to produce a Taíno discourse of presence. It is important to note that, even in cases where they have contracted non-Taíno webmasters, websites such as those of the United Confederation of Taíno People, the Jatibonicu Taíno Tribal Nation, the Taíno Nation of the Antilles, and especially those sites completely crafted by the site owners themselves, such as those of Baramaya, Biaraku, and Valerie Nanaturey Vargas' Bohio Bajacu, Taínos themselves have full control over content creation, image composition, and communication with visitors.

This is a remarkable turn of events, more than may be realized at first: for the *first* time in *written* history, those identifying themselves as Taíno Indians are able to speak directly to the wider world. Histories of the Taínos featured the latter largely as mute spectators to their own destruction; no wonder then that contemporary history written by Taínos is so disturbing to some that they prefer to believe these are somehow "fake" Taínos. The Internet, as a "technology of representation," has also played a revitalizing role, "as a self-conscious means of cultural preservation and production and a form of political mobilization" (see Ginsburg, 2002, p. 41). With the advent of the Internet, one may witness a considerable degree of reversal of previous invisibility and distorted representations, along with a certain increase in intergroup communication. The creation of websites, by and for the region's aboriginal communities and descendants, has helped to emphasize themes of cultural survival, to outline current organizational efforts and practices centered on the revitalization of traditions on a regional scale, and such sites have aided in directly challenging age-old colonial stereotypes of the "cannibalism" of the Caribs, or the "extinction" of the Taínos, at least to a greater extent than before the Internet's rise. Taínos in particular have been steadfast and diligent in tracking down sites that continue to misrepresent their ancestors, or their current situation, and have worked their way into various editorial and other contributing positions on diverse open source websites. They have also attracted the interest and support of numerous agents behind American Indian websites, many of which list Taíno organizations as respected and recognized entities that they view as members of a joint, pan-Indian struggle. An American Indian newspapers, such as *Indian Country Today*, has also carried stories and editorials on the Taínos that have been made available online (see www.indiancountry.com).

In helping to promote the visibility of peoples long believed to have been extinct, or ignored for being minorities, the Internet also helps to *embody* and *embed* groups facing difficulties in gaining offline acceptance as "indigenous." It simultaneously facilitates mutual online and offline recognition between these groups, thereby lending further authority and authenticity to any given group in its respective off-line context(s). It is also true that activities on the Internet continue the overall communications efforts that accompany the Taíno resurgence, for example, the 13 years in which the Taíno Nation of the Antilles has been printing its bulletin, or the various conferences that have been organized (see Barreiro, chapter 12).

There is a growing network of interlinked, mutually referring, Taíno websites that now build on each other's online presence. In the case of these Taíno networks on the Internet, we can delineate patterns of association and commonality. Via regular exchange (electronic newsletters, e-mail petitions, mailing lists, listservs, newsgroups, message boards, chat rooms, and individual e-mail messages) these sites build common interests (e.g., affirming Taíno survival, seeking recognition as Taínos). They do so through related content (commonly reproduced essays on Taíno history and culture, and common links to similar archaeological sites and language resources, etc.), shared perspectives and symbols (petroglyphic icons, zemis,[4] animal figures seen as sacred symbols in Taíno cosmology). By cross-referencing, the granting of awards, hyperlinks, webrings and the like, they form boundaries of mutual advantage. More than that, they are demonstrating Taíno culture by putting it into practice in one particular arena.

The observation that the Internet has aided some Caribbean indigenous groups in better representing and projecting themselves externally, while aiding them in collaborating and communicating internally, that is, among themselves, seemingly conflicts with the fact there is no single representative association uniting all of the disparate groups, nor any one website to which all the rest act as tributaries or derivatives. We have therefore arrived at the second element of the first question from the opening of this article, involving regional organization. As indicated by Palacio (this volume), the biggest effort yet at fostering some inter-island indigenous unity, has largely collapsed, at least for now, that being the Caribbean Organization of Indigenous Peoples (COIP). The COIP never had a website of its own, and indeed went into decline before the Internet arose in most of the COIP member territories. Even now, the presence of the Internet in the indigenous communities that constituted COIP is quite uneven, in some cases nonexistent. The Garifuna, both in the US and in Central America, have been at the forefront of developing some astoundingly comprehensive, well designed, and richly informative websites. Only in the months before this article neared completion, did the Santa Rosa Carib Community in Trinidad obtain one single computer, with a dial-up Internet connection, and this is used solely for downloading. The diversity of interests between island and mainland groups, the former acutely concerned with identity politics, and the latter possibly more concerned with material politics (such as defending rights to land), makes single and unified collaborative projects very challenging.

At least at the academic level, the Internet has allowed for the formation of an "invisible college" in the form of the Caribbean Amerindian Centrelink (www.centrelink.org) and *Kacike: The Journal of Caribbean Amerindian History and Anthropology* (www.kacike.org).[5] Indeed, this very volume is an expression of that collaboration between contributors who, in most cases, have yet to meet face-to-face, and who have worked on both the Centrelink and *Kacike* (including Barreiro, J. Bulkan, Collomb, Estevez, Ferbel, Guitar, and myself). Given the absence of "competitors" online, by default a certain degree of "centrality" has been achieved, one that in many ways has aided in spreading recognition of Caribbean indigenous peoples among the broader Internet public.

This then takes us to the third element considered here, that being the degree to which one might argue that activities on the Internet have helped to promote change "on the ground." On one level, it may be true for others, like it was for myself until the late 1990s, that we knew of no contemporary Taíno people until we saw them on the Internet. Indeed, this "first encounter," between the non-aboriginal Internet visitor (like myself) and those representing themselves as Taíno (for example) can produce results unwelcome to the Taínos. The medium of the encounter can produce an unconscious biasing effect: "I only saw them online, because they only exist online. These are Internet Taínos, not *real* Taínos." This is not speculation either, though the statement itself is a fictitious example: one need only consult the many postings in various newsgroups hosted by Google to see that this bias is shared by a number of individuals. Then there are those who look to see where some of these Taíno organizations are "based." They will find, as in the case of the Jatibonicu Taíno Tribal Nation, that it is headquartered in New Jersey. This produces a second bias: "As they are based in New Jersey, they are fake Taínos, because Taínos are indigenous to the Caribbean." Indeed, this reference to New Jersey is also not speculative: fused with malice, vulgar accusations of fakery abound online, famously focused on "New Jersey." The consideration that indigenous people, *like other people*, are often forced to move, is simply not entertained. Instead of thinking of Taínos *in* New Jersey, detractors recast them as "New Jersey Taínos," meant to ridicule, of course, as Taínos are not indigenous to that state. The "New Jersey Taínos," which would be the equivalent of "Maryland Maasai," are meant in such constructions to be seen as "out of place," thus rendering their pronouncements "out of line."

We might pause to ask why anyone would wish to "fake" being a Taíno? After all, it is not as if there have been any proven material rewards associated with this identification. This is an issue that hostile critics fumble over repeatedly, producing contradictory and unsubstantiated assertions, clearly rooted in prejudice, and often expressed in forms of juvenile literary excreta, e.g., (a) the aim is to get a casino (Who says so? Where is such a casino to be located? In New Jersey? Are there not American Indian nations in that region who might have something to say about immigrant Taínos claiming their lands as indigenous peoples? A casino back in Puerto Rico then? How would that work, as they apparently reside in New Jersey?); or (b) they are trying to evade their "Blackness" (Can anyone cite a representative number of examples to support the assertion? If Indians with "one drop" of African blood are evading their "Blackness" by proclaiming themselves Indian, then what do we say of Africans with "one drop" of Indian blood who proclaim themselves African?). Indeed, "Black" is taken as the "normal," "natural," and unquestionable default identity of Caribbean peoples in such arguments, and anyone claiming a distinct history must be motivated by a sinister, separatist or racist agenda. That many indigenous cultural traditions, and even the Island Carib language, have been retained and brought forward by one of the most visibly "Black" populations of the Caribbean—the Garifuna—must come as a complete shock to some. Lurking in the background of these anti-Taíno criticisms are unexamined and thus unquestioned attachments to outdated ideas of assimilation and evolution, better suited to the era of scientific racism than the postcolonial period.

These "first encounters" on the Internet can therefore produce unforeseen outcomes, especially where viewers are in the grips of antiquated pseudoanthropological assumptions that Indians do not change, do not marry non-Indians, do not move, do not use the Internet, and are supposed to remain poor. This is a burden of biases that is uniquely applied against indigenous peoples, a burden that the Internet may not mitigate, but *may* ironically reinforce. This may be especially true in cases of individuals for whom valid and reliable knowledge is that which appears in print and which precedes the Internet. In these instances, the Internet may be seen as more telephone than library, meaning a tool that anyone can use, and one that every "con artist" will use.

Countervailing tendencies can also be witnessed, that is, where online visibility has helped to embody groups who otherwise might not have been noticed or distinguished and who, given this virtualized visibility and embodiment, subsequently gain recognition. More than that even, the Caribbean indigenous persons and groups representing themselves online can help to attract and encourage many in the diaspora to overcome previous stigmas attached to aboriginal ancestries, i.e., stigmas of poverty, ignorance, backwardness or "cannibalism." In this case, the Internet is more like a register and a library.

As the webmaster for the Carib Community in Arima, Trinidad, I have created venues for online visitors to express their opinions, having accumulated in the process a number of electronic "guest books" filled with interesting ethnographic data that were voluntarily supplied. I printed out these many entries, along with individual e-mail messages, and passed them along to the leadership of the Carib Community. What struck all of us was the emotional intensity of the messages, as if a burden of repressed associations had been lifted, allowing some to finally express their desire to proclaim their Amerindian ancestry; the fact that many of these Trinidadians abroad were proudly proclaiming their Amerindian ancestry, together constituting a number much larger than the numbers involved in the Carib Community in Arima; and, their apparent patriotism. One representative example of a statement sent by a Trinidadian resident in California was the following: "My grandmother's grandmother was Carib and I have cousins in Arima who are married to pure Carib Indians. We do have to keep *our* culture alive and there's no better way to doing it than through this medium" (emphasis added). In this case, the author of the message is identifying with Carib ancestry, referring to Carib culture as her own ("our culture"), and in fact praising use of the Internet for promoting cultural survival and recognition. As another correspondent wrote, "it is wonderful to see that our original culture has moved into the new age." Others clearly indicate, echoing the quote at the opening of this chapter, that materials on the Internet have aided them in their personal process of re-identifying with their Carib heritage and overcoming past stigma: "At one point in time, I would never have...thought to reveal my heritage. I felt that most people viewed us as being extinct, thanks to one-sided history books. Now, whenever I am approached, or someone assumes that they know my background, I am very pleased to proclaim who I AM. I appreciate the fact that this site exists." Some Trinidadians abroad indicate that they look to the Internet, at least in part, for information on their Carib roots: "I would like to learn more about my Carib roots from Trinidad, where I was born." Affective ties to their Trinidadian home are also expressed by self-identified Carib descendants abroad: "knowing about my homeland means a lot to me."

The presence of Trinidadian Carib materials on the web has also attracted very interesting feedback from individuals across the Caribbean and its diaspora. Messages have been received from self-identified Amerindian descendants, or from those related to them, from places about which little knowledge of such populations is available. Examples include the following: "I live in Anguilla, BWI (a British possession). Most of our island's native inhabitants (including my in-laws) were born of the union between Irish Settlers and Arawak Indians"; from Curaçao in the Netherlands Antilles, one person wrote, "my grandfather was an Arawak Indian"; from a young woman in Guadeloupe, a French Overseas Department, "my grand-mother who is now 96 years old is part Carib. She was born on the island of Marie-Galante"; and, from St. Thomas, in the US Virgin Islands, one wrote, "my family on my father's side are from Nevis. My grandmother would tell us when we were little that she was Amerindian and that our people lived in Nevis for centuries and centuries. In the words of my aunt they always lived there. When the Europeans began coming and bringing slaves, they moved to the mountains." Some authors of online postings also seek to use the medium as a means of communicating with other Caribs, for example: "I am a Vincentian Carib living in America. Would love to hear from other Caribs."

There are no apparent material or political agendas that surface from such messages, which instead seem to focus on affective ties and self-knowledge. "Race" or "physical appearance" is possibly of limited importance to such online Trinidadians and other Caribbean nationals. Though this is not a scientific survey based on a representative sample, a voluntary guest poll for anonymous users (safeguarded against repeat votes from the same computer) was hosted on the Carib Community website for five years. The results are interesting, and open to multiple interpretations. In defining what it is that makes a person "indigenous," only 19% chose "race, physical appearance."

The same number chose "it's all subjective." The overwhelming majority responded with a combination of "proven aboriginal ties to the land" (37%), "the persons *say* they are indigenous" (7%), and "observable cultural difference" (17%). With such polls one cannot know for certain that Trinidadians or other Caribbean nationals posted the votes. However, given consistent traffic statistics for the sites concerned over several years, a majority of visitors are from Trinidad and Tobago itself, the rest being from Canada, the US, and the UK, and it therefore seems likely that these visitors posted most of the votes.

Feedback from individuals in the Dominican Republic has also been forthcoming in response to articles posted in the online journal, *Kacike*. Expressions range from pride and gratitude for making available information on indigenous cultural survivals in the Dominican Republic, especially through a special issue edited by Lynne Guitar. Some visitors feel encouraged that their own ideas on indigenous cultural survival have been furthered and deepened, or simply articulated, by what they have read online: "I never realized how much of my own lifestyle has survived from my Taíno heritage.... American textbooks had me in fooled in thinking that we Dominicans were just symbolizing a culture that was 'extinct.' I grew up in *el campo* [countryside] and much of what was in [the] article applied to my vocabulary, cooking style, and cuisine." Similar responses have been received from Cubans: "I thank you for publishing these enriching articles and I agree with the fact that the indigenous presence in Cuba is not extinct, as it is evident in our diet, several traditions, and words that enrich our language." The "extinction" theme appears to have been increasingly eroded, and references to print sources that endorsed this theme are looked back upon as having been misleading.

Taíno tribal organizations have also received considerable feedback as recorded in their online guest books. The United Confederation of Taíno People (www.uctp.org), as just one example, received responses that are primarily focused on pride, self-knowledge and genealogy, rather than any overtly material- or politically oriented messages, like the anti-Taíno critics would have us expect. Illustrative of these comments are ones that state, "let's all get together and share our pride by helping each other with informative material," which again affirms the role of the Internet in this collective knowledge-sharing enterprise. The Internet acts as a bridge between what visitors had already learned off-line, in many cases, and what is now given new voice online: "Thank god for this site; my grandmother would talk to me about my Indian background and it's good to finally see some of it on the web. I was born in New York, but like all the rest of us 'Newyoricans,' I am always holding on to my *Boricua* heart." Websites such as those of the UCTP thus allow some to develop a sense of an indigenous home that is rooted, not in the US, but in Boriquen, the indigenous name for Puerto Rico: "if it were not for them [the UCTP] I would have been lost. I am now home with my own kind." As another visitor expressed this sense of belonging: "I was so alone...to realize that there are people somewhere in the world just like me and to finally put meaning and a sense of stability to all those nameless yearnings is quite overwhelming," a comment that was affirmed by another visitor, "I always wanted to know about my native roots, now that I have a computer I don't feel like a freak anymore." This sense of belonging to a larger community, finding a sense of home, was condensed in one emotionally striking message: "All I can do is read and cry not really knowing why I'm crying but finally finding my place in the world. Thank you for helping me find my identity as a human being." For some, the Internet is clearly the means through which they explore themselves as Taíno and find their way back to a symbolic homeland, in communion with others online: "I am a Taíno descendant that, regrettably, has lost his way.... That's about to finally change." Having experienced a past when the stigma of shame was attached to Taíno identity—"as a child my grandmother told us we were Indians. My father unfortunately was ashamed of his ancestry, so he never spoke of it or his childhood"—sites such as that of the UCTP help some to overcome this stigma, to feel "more proud than ever now knowing that the new generations are learning about their roots," as another visitor explained. While websites such as the UCTP are likely not creating anything that was not already present offline, what they do is provide some inspiration and encouragement: "I plan on soaking in every last drop of knowledge available and embracing my ancestry. I think this site, along with others devoted to Taíno/Carib heritage and history, will become an excellent starting point in my journey. Keep up the great work, as your site may inspire others to do the same!"

Also critical is the fact that members of other indigenous communities in the Caribbean now have a means for engaging in exchange with Taínos in the US, by first making contact through the Internet. Indeed, this new means of networking that renders distance immaterial has afforded the UCTP the means for a considerable expansion of its web of ties and connections, as noted on the front page of the site where they list all of their affiliated partner communities across the Caribbean. This, when supplemented by the extensive travels of the head of the UCTP, Roberto Mucaro Borrero, enables the creation of inter-tribal linkages that have not been possible for a large part of the history of the Caribbean since European conquest. Likewise for the Santa Rosa Carib Community, the development of their online presence since 1998 has attracted the attention of journalists, researchers, and other indigenous groups, with the apparent result of a significant increase in their networking and exchange activities. What we have then, at least as some likely results of the Internet, are stronger senses of self-identification as indigenous, coupled with increased regional networking, even in the absence of a central organizing body such as COIP.

The Limits of Indigenous Resurgence via the Internet

The second question I raised at the start of this chapter concerned the challenges facing Caribbean indigenous utilization of the Internet. In speaking of the practice of indigenous resurgence by way of the Internet, we must, at least for now, respect the fact that there are practical, material constraints on Internet access, and Internet use, for indigenous communities in the region. Sometimes groups in North America will attempt to aid in expanding the communication facilities of those in the Caribbean, one of the most notable examples that I am aware of being the UCTP's gift of a fax machine to the Santa Rosa Carib Community, which has been put to very intense use. Nevertheless, there are no Carib websites that emerge directly from communities in Dominica, St. Vincent, and Trinidad (see Forte, 2003), even when they have actual Internet access.

The fact remains that there is far more information on the Internet *about* Caribbean aboriginals than there is *by* them. In addition, amongst the indigenous population of the Americas as a whole, there is differential representation on the Internet, with websites from Latin America and the Caribbean far outnumbered by those from Canada and the US, even though the latter two nations have an indigenous population that is only a fraction of that of South America. This trend suggests that primarily North American representations of aboriginality, and issues and debates peculiar to North America, become the dominant representations, even if not exclusively so.

Further study is needed to understand why indigenous persons and organizations with Internet access, in Dominica and Trinidad, for example, have not used those resources (thus far) to create any of their own websites. Indeed, one very common feature, widely remarked upon by many of us outside of those territories, is that the Caribs of Dominica simply use their machines as download devices. This is also true, for now, of the Santa Rosa Carib Community. E-mails sent to these communities are never returned. Websites have been downloaded in these communities, extensively and painstakingly in some cases, making copies of each and every page of sites that sometimes have dozens of pages, but no independent production of their own has been forthcoming. One has to hope that this is not a sign of new media, like previous media, being absorbed into a cultural mode of spectatorship.

Conclusions: Centering Indigenous Identities Online

A less-than-cheerful assessment of the impact of the Internet might call attention to the fact that while indigenous practices on the Internet have been successful in encouraging and shaping indigenous self-representations, amongst those who are already predisposed to identify as indigenous, representations to hostile segments of the external audience have been less successful. It is impossible for contemporary Taínos to explain their identity to individuals who refuse, in advance, to admit that they could ever be speaking to Taínos. All the Internet has done, seen from this vantage point, is to make the debate public, and to transform the debate into two separate monologues. As a number of observers have recognized, "cultural biases that exist offline can be made manifest online in a variety of ways; therefore, the net is rarely a refuge from those biases" (Doheny-Farina, 1996, p. 65; see also Nakamura, 2002).

Cyberspace—a nonspace on its own—is being adapted to individual and group strategies for creating a sense of place that incorporates a wide variety of geographically dispersed persons. Without that sense of place, there can be no idea of roots, no vision of a home, and no basis for self-identification as indigenous. That is not to say that the Internet is the sole or primary means by which that sense of place and associated identifications are being created. The Internet does not have any power to create identity positions that individuals and groups never possessed before. What the Internet does provide is a vehicle, convenient to those who have access, to coordinate and communicate ideas of indigeneity and plans for organization. What the printing press was to European nationalists, the Internet is to aboriginal activists. The Internet will, I believe, eventually be regarded as the primary communication medium of the ongoing indigenous resurgence that has been taking place in multiple locations around the planet.

Caribbean indigenous peoples with an online presence have developed a web of mutual recognition and self-definition. In the process, individuals who conceptualize their indigeneity by multiple paths are called to belong to a vision of home, one that is both place and practice. Taíno activism on the Internet has enabled the recovery of a history and identity that had been marginalized, reduced to a symbolic category without a living reality, and treated at best as something to be commemorated rather than experienced personally. From this vantage point, the Internet has afforded the means for reversing previous invisibility while aiding intergroup communication between a variety of Caribbean indigenous peoples. As the vehicle for a collective knowledge sharing enterprise, the Internet has been important for networking of a qualitatively different order, as well as enabling self-definition on terms chosen by participants. This medium has played an important role in fomenting a broader resurgence of indigenous self-identification. As Ginsburg noted, "media practices are part of a broader project of constituting a cultural future in which their [indigenous peoples'] traditions and contemporary technologies are combined in ways that can give new vitality to [indigenous peoples'] life" (2002, p. 43). By allowing indigenous participants to self-determine their own representations and write their own histories, presenting images of themselves as *present*, one might agree with Prins in noting the "current relief from visual imperialism afforded to indigenous peoples by the web" (2002, p. 72). We must also be cautious and admit that conclusions made about a "moving target," a process in motion, may simply be invalidated by future developments.

Notes

1. The SRCC website can be found currently at http://www.kacike.org/srcc/.
2. This chapter does not pay sufficient attention to the range of topically expansive, community embedded, Garifuna websites that exist—not because they do not merit attention, but only because I encountered difficulty in trying to integrate voluminous empirical data. I am forced to mention, only in passing, that Garifuna websites worthy of note include the Garifuna Network (www.garinet.com), Labuga Livingston Garifunas (www.labuga.com), the Official Website of Seine Bight Village (www.seinebight.com), and Felene Cayetano (www.wadigidigi.com). For a concise overview of these Garifuna websites, readers should consult Figueroa (2005).
3. See, for example, the websites of the Jatibonicu Taíno Tribal Nation at http://www.tainotribe.org, and the United Confederation of Taíno People at http://www.uctp.org.
4. Usually carved from wood or stone and not much bigger than can be held in a hand, these are seen as containing spirits and are often associated with shamans and chiefs, sometimes depicting skeletal yet fertile representations of shamans.
5. The term "invisible college" is now widely used with reference to scientific exchange across locales, especially through electronic circuits of communication. The term has been in use for some time as reportedly coined by Robert Boyle for referring to a small cluster of intellectuals in 17th century England. See also Crane (1972).

References

Alia, V. (1999). *Un/covering the north: news, media and aboriginal people*. Vancouver: University of British Columbia Press.

Anderson, B. (1991). *Imagined communities: reflections on the origins and spread of nationalism*. Rev. ed. London: Verso.

Borrero, R.M. (1999). Rethinking Taíno: a Taíno perspective. In Gabriel Haslip-Viera (Ed.), *Taíno revival: critical perspectives on Puerto Rican identity and cultural politics* (pp. 109–127). New York: Centro de Estudios Puertorriqueños, Hunter College, City University of New York.

Clifford, J. (1994). Diasporas. *Cultural Anthropology*, 9(3), 302–338.

Cohen, A. P. (1989). *The symbolic construction of community*. London: Routledge.

Crane, D. (1972). *Invisible colleges: diffusion of knowledge in scientific communities*. Chicago: University of Chicago Press.

Dávila, A. (1999). Local/diasporic Taínos: towards a cultural politics of memory, reality and imagery. In Gabriel Haslip-Viera (Ed.), *Taíno revival: critical perspectives on Puerto Rican identity and cultural politics* (pp. 11–29). New York: Centro de Estudios Puertorriqueños, Hunter College, City University of New York.

Doheny-Farina, S. (1996). *The wired neighborhood*. New Haven, CT: Yale University Press.

Fernback, J. (1999). There is a there there: notes toward a definition of cybercommunity. In Steven Jones (Ed.), *Doing Internet research: critical issues and methods for examining the net* (pp. 203–220). London: Sage.

Figueroa, R. (2005). A guide to Garifuna websites. *The CAC Review Web Log*, April 9. Retrieved April 16, 2005, from http://cacreview.blogspot.com/2005/04/guide-to-garifuna-websites-by-tony.html.

Forte, M.C. (2002). 'We are not extinct': the revival of Carib and Taíno identities, the Internet, and the transformation of offline indigenes into online 'N-digenes'. *Sincronía*, Spring. Retrieved May 28, 2004, from http://sincronia.cucsh.udg.mx/CyberIndigen.htm.

———. (2003). Caribbean aboriginals online: digitized culture, networked representation. *Indigenous Affairs*, (2), 32–37.

Ginsburg, F. D. (2002). Screen memories: resignifying the traditional in indigenous media. In Faye D. Ginsburg, Lila Abu Lughod, & Brian Larkin (Eds.), *Media worlds: anthropology on new terrain* (pp. 39–57). Berkeley: University of California Press.

Jones, S. G. (1997). The Internet and its social landscape. In Steven G. Jones (Ed.), *Virtual culture: identity and communication in cybersociety* (pp. 7–35). London: Sage.

Nakamura, L. (2002). *Cybertypes: race, ethnicity, and identity on the Internet*. New York: Routledge.

Prins, H. E. L. (2002). Visual media and the primitivist perplex: colonial fantasies, indigenous imagination, and advocacy in North America. In Faye D. Ginsburg, Lila Abu Lughod, & Brian Larkin (Eds.), *Media worlds: anthropology on new terrain* (pp. 58–74). Berkeley: University of California Press.

Turner, T. (2002). Representation, politics, and cultural imagination in indigenous video: general points and kayapo examples. In Faye D. Ginsburg, Lila Abu Lughod, & Brian Larkin (Eds.), *Media worlds: anthropology on new terrain* (pp. 75–89). Berkeley: University of California Press.

※ CHAPTER FOURTEEN ※

Conclusion: "Before, We Were Asleep: Now We Must Awake from Our Sleep and Move Forward"*

Arthur Einhorn

Attempting to write anything about the Circum-Caribbean of the past half millennium is a daunting challenge, and certainly events of the last two centuries have made it even more complex with the abolition of slavery, new technologies, decolonization and globalization. The rise of neo-nationalism during the last 50 years also compounds the equation even more, as several of the essays in this volume illustrate.

The American Mediterranean

A long-ignored, almost forgotten, region until the post-World War II era, expanding commercial airline services and luxury ocean liners spurred growth of tourism with its ancillary industries of hotels, beaches, fishing, souvenirs, casinos, renovated forts, historical buildings, ecotourism, tax-free emporiums, haute cuisine restaurants, tropical drinks, pan music, and carnivals—all of them enriching sun-filled days of leisure spent in a tropical "Shangri-La." Obviously, it wasn't always as the image presented today, while even some of what is currently seen may be largely a facade created by Madison Avenue for tourist board ads and TV commercials.

For most North American and European visitors who in past decades ventured into this wedge of paradise between the continents, the colorful potpourri images of its "West Indian" peoples, cultures and lifestyles must have

---

* The title is taken from the words of the late Hilary Frederick, former Chief of the Carib Territory on the island of Dominica.

seemed exotic and alluring, as indeed it was and still is. What few outsiders see or perceive beyond the majority African Creole population and defunct sugar industry, are the hidden-in-plain-sight vestiges of its original pre-Columbian indigenous inhabitants or the transformational blend of traditions born of Native American, African, East Indian, and the various European nations that colonized the region. Few tourists knew, or know, anything about the history of the islands or adjacent mainland areas, save for perhaps lurid tales of voodoo zombies, cannibal Caribs, blood-thirsty pirates, sunken Spanish treasure ships, sugar mills and other romantic notions derived from novels and Hollywood films. The very name, "West Indian," became a catch-all term—like "American," "European" or "Asian"—that could mean almost anything or everything to unfamiliar outsiders. Prior to the rise of mass tourism and vacationers, the islands were and remain ports of call to wealthy American and Canadian yachtsmen, joined in recent years by various Europeans, Latin Americans and nouveaux riches Arabs. In a manner of speaking, it has become America's "Mediterranean playground."

The Caribbean in an Era of Globalization

Long before, in the Age of Exploration, the process of the region's exploitation had already started with trade in exotic spices, peltry, timber, precious minerals, slaves, salt, sugar cane, whale oil, bird plumage, dried cod fish, ivory and so much else; even the land itself was peddled off by insensitive speculators for quick profits. Though the sordid story goes back well before biblical times, when populations were smaller and exploiting resources was a slow labor intensive chore, its driving motive hasn't changed to this day: bottom line profit-driven greed, pure and simple.

Conquest of the Indies and the American mainland after 1492 was only midpoint in a global process that began thousands of years earlier far to the east, and in the following centuries would continue on far to the west in the Pacific basin and Australia, only to start over and regenerate the process again through South Asia, Africa and back to the Americas.

From the 16th century onward the "Indies," as the Caribbean islands and known mainland areas were then called, became synonymous with the opportunity for quick wealth waiting to be taken by the daring and venturesome. Spain made the first incursions, and for nearly a century held a monopoly on the "New World" by securing the Greater Antilles (the alternate name used for Puerto Rico, Hispaniola, Jamaica and Cuba), Mexico, Central America and Peru. Their "shock and awe" confrontations using horses, crossbows, and firearms along with duped Indian allies were as effective in subjugating resisting Indian groups, as had been the tactics of Roman Legions 1,500 years earlier. In Mexico, the Spaniards were "shocked" by the Aztec's wholesale sacrifice of captives to their gods, and at once "awed" by the magnificent city of Tenochtitlán. This revulsion and admiration from a band of untutored Iberian vagabond cutthroats, who knew nothing of their ancient Roman colonizers, or the human slaughters in the Coliseum, or its links to the bull fights in which they reveled. Not even their "Christian" faith held them back from wholesale slaughter on the battlefield or outrageous acts of torture to learn sources of gold. However, we must remember they were "civilizers" bringing "enlightenment" and "god" to the pagans. As expected, all the lands were claimed for Spain's empire, the Indians baptized whether willing or not, the lands awarded to outstanding conquistadors, slavery or indenture imposed on the resistant or rebellious natives, and resources—mainly gold and silver—shipped back to Spain. The shouting echoes of Rome and other conquest empires are deafening here.

Not to be outdone, in quick succession England, France, Holland and several Scandinavian countries joined the fray of exploration, seeking a short passage to the riches of the East; not as aggressively as Spain to be sure but just as determined. Portugal had already reached India and acquired Brazil via the Papal Demarcation Line of 1493. Blocked by two continents, these later interlopers settled for outposts on the coast of both Americas where they traded for peltry, exotic plants or whatever would turn a profit for their backers in Europe. While they were at it, they kidnapped Indians here and there to be sold into slavery. Envious of Spain's purloined gold, most of those later followers anxiously looked for gold near their landfalls, one so obsessive as to dig on an Arctic island. When the search for a fabled "Northwest Passage" appeared elusive and futile, the latecomers entrenched themselves in their various coastal outposts to take pot luck, with fur trading in North America or sugar production in the Caribbean and South America. These semi legitimate diversions did not stop some of their more adventuresome compatriots from raiding the "Spanish Main" and robbing Spain's annual treasure fleets. Their rationale, apart from their own greed, was a simple one: Spain took the Indians' gold and they were merely stealing from the greater thieves. England's Sir Francis Drake stands out among many others from that period; Drake was successful in both hijacking Spanish treasures and circumnavigating the globe, the second to achieve the distinction after Magellan.

The "Extinction" Problematique

Amidst all this convulsive turmoil in the Circum-Caribbean of the 16th and 17th centuries, we find the Amerindians struggling to survive culturally while beset with slaughter, enslavement, disease and potential "extinction."

In the first half of the 16th century, tens of thousands of Taíno (Arawak) Indians had seemingly "evaporated" from the Greater Antilles due to pandemics caused by various imported European diseases against which they had no natural immunity. In addition equal numbers died in resistance battles, mass suicides, or the males were taken off as slave labor to mainland Mexico during the conquest. There was also a growing population of *mestizos* sired by Spanish men with Indian wives and concubines. By then the island supply of Indian slave labor had diminished so drastically, at least this was the oft-repeated claim, that African slaves were imported to fill the alleged gap. At some point before 1550, it was recorded that all of the island Amerindians were extinct, a base line misleading statement oft quoted thereafter by historians up to the present day. Despite such official pronouncement, many small pockets of Taíno people survived in mountain retreats of Cuba, Hispaniola and Puerto Rico. They, and their half-Amerindian kin residing in the Spanish settlements, constituted a living and surviving population. A recent survey in Puerto Rico for example, of mitochondrial DNA revealed that more than 60% of the population had a Taíno ancestor. Similar tests for the Dominican Republic and Cuba will likely reveal similar results in greater or lesser percentages.

The Eastern Caribbean (Lesser Antilles), stretching from the Virgin Islands all the way to Trinidad and the South American mainland, was not impacted as bluntly or disastrously as the larger islands. The many small islands of the archipelago were occupied by the Carib (Karaphuna) people who had impressed the Spanish with their ferocity and highly skilled seafaring mobility; they were thus nominally left alone at first. Besides, the Spaniards saw no profitable mineral (gold or silver), resources there worth bothering with when easier sources had been found in Mexico and Peru.

However, Spanish reluctance to dominate the Lesser Antilles left the door open to other European contenders for New World real estate, namely the Dutch, English and French. By the 17th century, all of them had laid claim to one or more islands, and with the recently imported sugar cane plant from India, were establishing plantations to harvest an alternate source of wealth. The Spanish also started sugar production on the larger islands. Many islands were denuded of native forests to accommodate huge sugar cane fields, while thousands of Africans were shipped in to provide the intensive labor. Driven off certain islands, many Caribs amalgamated on other mountainous islands to stay free. Those few who were enslaved either pined away, committed suicide, or managed to escape. Overseer opinions of the day considered Caribs to be unsuitable as slaves. Not unexpectedly, the English and French intermittently made war to acquire the other's sugar rich islands. Both would enlist Caribs as mercenaries, with the resulting mortalities helping to decrease the Carib populations. Diseases also took their toll.

Colonialism: Caribbean-North American Parallels

If sugar became the "gold" of the Caribbean—the "gold" of North America was in its beaver peltry, harvested by Iroquois and Algonquian Indians to take product with at trading posts from the St. Lawrence River to Chesapeake Bay. The harvesting was so intense in the first four decades of the 17th century that vast areas of eastern North America were totally stripped of beaver. This led to intense tribal rivalry over trapping grounds in the west, fostering tribal alliances with the Dutch, Swedish, English and French during their various conflicts to oust each other. The Dutch eventually swallowed up the Swedish settlement on the Delaware; the English subsequently wrested away the Dutch holdings centered in New York, which stretched from Connecticut to Delaware; and finally Britain conquered French Canada and its West Indies possessions by 1760. At the negotiating table to sign the peace accords at the "Treaty of Paris" in 1763, France bargained away all of Canada (save two small coastal islands as fishing stations), to regain its two prized sugar islands in the Eastern Caribbean—Guadeloupe and Martinique. Clearly, the sugar trade was more valuable than the fur trade on a huge continental land mass. France's Louisiana territory was turned over to Spain in that Paris Treaty.

For the latter half of the 18th century and early 19th century the subsequent ebb and flow in the colonial wars of empire would eventually moderate to keeping what had been gained. Competition for Africa was yet to come. Beyond the Americas Britain was in full control of India, Australia, New Zealand, Capetown, and various Polynesian archipelagos; Holland was ensconced in the East Indies (now Indonesia); France gained a foothold in Indo-China (now Vietnam); Portugal held Brazil, Goa in India, Macao on the coast of China, and various enclaves around the African coast; while Denmark had Greenland and several Caribbean sugar islands. It was a game of global monopoly that enriched Europe while their colonies were forbidden to play or share in the wealth.

Focusing back to the Circum-Caribbean, Britain was entrenched on the "Mosquito Coast" (what became British Honduras and now Belize), and held Jamaica as well as a whole string of islands from the Bahamas and Virgin Islands to Trinidad. On the South American mainland, England had British Guiana (now Guyana) and Canada as noted above. France and Holland both had a piece of the Guiana coast (now French Guiana and Suriname), along with various sugar islands scattered through the Caribbean area.

Until 1821, Spain was still in control of her American mainland empire, including the Greater Antilles, and the Philippines in Asia. However, during the Napoleonic era, Napoleon managed to squeeze a negotiated transfer of Hispaniola from Spain to France, which was renamed Santo Domingo, and returned Louisiana to French jurisdiction. Napoleon had a dream to rebuild a

French empire in America, using Hispaniola as a staging point. In this venture he voided the African emancipation that had been granted earlier as a result of the French Revolution's "Liberty, Equality, Fraternity" ideology. Returned to slavery by decree, the masses of Africans revolted under such leaders as Toussaint L'Ouverture, thus Napoleon sent in Polish troops from Danzig to quell the revolt. They were quickly decimated by tropical diseases, dysentery, ambushes and winter uniforms ill suited to a hot and humid climate. With the loss of Hispaniola and mounting debt from his unending European wars, notably with Britain, Napoleon's Louisiana dream ended by its sale to the infant US for $15 million dollars. In New Orleans the Spanish flag had barely been replaced by France's tricolor when the Stars and Stripes were hoisted. In all this kaleidoscopic hustle and bustle of commerce in slaves, cotton, sugar, rice, indigo, peltry, exotic lumber and shifting colonial administrations, there had to be some Native Americans watching and wondering what was going on, and perhaps as confused about it all as a novice visitor to today's stock market. All of it was available like commodities for the right price, even the land and the Indians themselves.

All through the 19th century and into the 20th the various European colonies in the Circum-Caribbean continued to grow in population, mainly among the Creoles, while the White colonial segment generally remained small. The volume of exports increased with the advent of steamships and greater trade opportunities. Following British emancipation in the 1830s, freedmen acquired small farm plots, expanding settlements into the interiors of the larger islands and the mainland possessions. Many of the freed peoples refused to work for their former owners; thus, Tamils and other South Asians were imported to fill the labor gap. With these changes came new administrative regulations directed at land ownership and usage. The century also brought greater missionary activity and with it a focus on minimal education and a directed history about the mother country, and especially a cultivated patriotism for it. For Creoles and Amerindians alike, their cultures and histories sublimated to virtual nonentities.

Amerindian Transformations

Amerindians dwelling in the remote interior regions of mainland colonies or isolated sections of various islands were largely unaware and unaffected by much of the changing processes in operation, at least for a while. Nor would they understand, when finally confronted with threats to their land bases, that someone far away in Europe determined they did not own the lands they lived on. The absurdity and arrogance of it all is astounding, even allowing for the colonial mind-set of those times.

As the collected papers in this volume brutally demonstrate, God, King, Country and entrepreneurs determined who would benefit from the land and its resources. For most Amerindians and communities of mestizos, even many African Creoles, life centered around a given neighborhood of natural resources and farm plots, and were largely self-sustaining communities. Some never visited the world outside from cradle to grave, though likely were well aware it existed. Within such village communities and enclaves, many traditions were maintained that had roots in their Amerindian past. These ranged from language survival in whole or part, mythology, culture heroes, food preparation, craft technology, farming and fishing practices, song and dance, respect for the dead, place names, sacred places, village social organization and headmen, etc. Often too some African traditions were incorporated from African Creole influences via marriage or proximity of residence.

With the imposition of colonial administration and justice, however, internal control was diminished, whereby only elected headmen and councils were recognized by the colonial governments. While very democratic on the surface, such change disrupted traditional formulas for leadership and created internal factionalism. The net effect was to create, in some cases, puppet pawns willing to work with government for special considerations, usually at the expense of their own people's best interests.

A Crashing Civilization

One of the long-term critical problems that faced the human species and its groups during the last 10,000 years has been population growth, weighed against available resources for sustenance. Early on, growth was checked by median life spans, high infant mortality, disease, fatal encounters, wars, or accidents, low birth rates, and infanticide for a whole range of reasons. Groups moved around to supply their needs, or found ecological niches that sustained them year-round. The development of agriculture has long been considered a factor in the explosion of population: a dependable food source that required attention, leading to sedentary villages with decreased natural mortality. Up to a point, this paradigm is reasonable, and explains the spurt of classic centers of "civilization" in Africa, the Middle East, South and East Asia, and in Mesoamerica. However, the hypothesis overlooks sizable populations that mushroomed in places where agriculture was absent or only a marginal factor, such as the Northwest Coast of North America, Polynesia, and the Greater Antilles. The three regions had an abundant source of seafood, the latter two having marginal agriculture to supplement the diet. Europeans who first encountered them estimated some groups numbering in the hundreds of thousands—even millions in a few instances. Except for the Northwest Coast, the East Indies, Polynesia, and the West Indies, were for the most part insulated by the sea from serious competition. This of course did not preclude internal feuds or competition within their limited spaces, especially in the extreme case of Easter Island.

With sedentary life came specialization. Production of excess goods for trade was the incentive—we should add greed—to go beyond a group's territory in search of raw materials in order to create even more trade goods. Mere sustenance and subsistence was no longer the chief factor in one's survival and existence. Trails, rivers, later roads and rails facilitated such human expansion, and along such access routes new settlements mushroomed and with them new expanding populations.

Well established in the New World of Pre-Columbian Indians, this process was long operative in the old world; when the "new world" was reached the process started anew with the Indians as pawns in a larger enterprise. Though oceans were no longer a barrier, in the Americas the various mountain ranges, dense forests and jungles did present some containment for several centuries until new technologies made penetration easier, and so harvesting resources continued unabated. More people, more goods, more exploitation. In the 100 years since development of the internal combustion engine, applied to land, water and air conveyances; the chain saw; factory fishing ships; satellite mapping of subsurface resources; instant communication technologies, and globalization, more long-term damage has been meted out to the earth's fragile ecosystems than the combined human efforts of the last 10,000 years. Not only that, but humanity's now enormous population has taken on the geometric progression of rats, or a metastasized cancer consuming everything in its path. Despite all the warning signs of an impending ecological crash, mindless theologians and the untutored faithful propagate on and on with no thought for tomorrow or the generations ahead. These heedless masses seem to be hard wired by a blind faith in the myth that "god will provide," and failing such succor, "it was god's will." Such naive fatalism, along with "god helps those who help themselves," will be the banana peel on which all of humanity will fatally slip.

Amidst this background of greed and population expansion it is remarkable tribal peoples have survived anywhere to the present day in more remote regions of the world, and even more incredible that any indigenous Amerindians managed to confront the 21st century knowing who they were. They had to be tenacious. Keeping that thought in mind—tenacity—I will return to it in discussing identity below.

Challenges to Amerindian Survival: Comparing the Caribbean and North America

The articles in this volume have demonstrated Amerindian survival in many areas of the greater Caribbean. Though their voices were sublimated, yet smoldering for centuries, a phoenix-like renaissance has been emerging almost everywhere. The general movement, often home grown, but certainly inspired as well by American Indian resurgence movements in the US and Canada since the 1970s, has taken on a life of its own. Yet many of the obstacles facing such indigenous groups in the Circum-Caribbean, who strive to reassert identity and reclaim land rights, have striking parallels to those that confronted Indian movements in North America, in the past and currently.

While the US and Canada have slowly come to terms with their respective Indian Nations, revalidating old treaties, land rights and accommodating semi-sovereignty (note the creation of Nunavut and Nunatsiavut in Canada's Arctic), the newly independent island and mainland nations of the Caribbean region have been caught up with neo-nationalism in their efforts to establish a unique identity as sovereign states. In so doing they have pursued a homogenizing policy with their citizens often disavowing aboriginal minority rights and even their very existence. This thrust is especially visible in dealing with aboriginal land rights. Any noble motive about "nation building" aside, the reality is economic survival of the new nation in the world economy, and profit for the few who manipulate the land and its natural resources.

The Mainland

This especially can be seen in the chapters dealing with countries on mainland South and Central America. However, even the tiny insular nations of the Eastern Caribbean have their paranoia over minority rights and resources. Eugenia Charles, former Prime Minister of Dominica, some years ago voiced this fear publicly: "We cannot have a nation within a nation!" The sentiment likely was/is shared by other leaders in the region, who yearn to homogenize the citizens and solidify power. The fear of cultural and political pluralism is striking, given most of the new nations were born of adversity and cultural diversity over hundreds of years, and their present image epitomizes that past. One hopes they all don't stumble through similar failed policies, mistakes and tragedies aboriginal peoples experienced in North America, yet some of the papers here describe glaring examples that they unfortunately have done so or are doing just that now.

England's Crown policy of a patron–client relationship with Indians in Guiana (Guyana); of reserving forests for the Royal Navy's use; its attaching of "trust status" to Indian lands; and later Guyana's "Relocation" program to move Indians off the coveted lands, are virtually identical to policies executed in 18th century colonial North America, and subsequently by the US and Canada. Even Guyana's Lands Commission of 1976 is comparable to the US Indian Claims Commission of 1948—both attempting to erase former land confiscation via monetary compensation while voiding claims.

In French Guiana we can hear echoes of US/Canadian policy (fortunately now ended), whereby Amerindian children are taken from the home and forcibly installed in religious boarding schools to make better "French citizens" of them, while smothering their culture, identity and language. Also comparable is France's effort to impose a program of "free land grants" carved from Amerindian territory—it echoes the 1887 Dawes Act whereby the US Congress unilaterally broke up most of the reservations in Indian Territory (Oklahoma), allocating each head of household 640 acres, thus dismembering corporate ownership by the tribes. Never a viable colony economically, French Guiana progressed from a timber source to gold mining, penal colony, and now a rocket launching site. Her policies with possessions in the Pacific play much the same tune, despite decolonization having occurred all around the region. Although technically designated "Departments of France," that is merely legal jargon to maintain political control of areas that are still colonies in reality. Unfortunately, the US played a similar game earlier with Hawaii, Samoa and Guam.

When the Netherlands declared independence for Suriname, it seemingly walked off, much as Belgium did with the Congo, leaving the Amerindians and Djukas to the mercy of Creole entrepreneurs and their schemes to generate wealth at the expense of native peoples who lived on the land. Age-old agreements and treaties made with the Dutch were scrapped as Suriname's leaders flexed their political muscle. Interior lands have been opened up to wholesale gold mining by impoverished Brazilians, while forests are clear-cut by Chinese interests. In both instances, the Amerindians have been dispossessed of their lands and exposed to poisonous environmental hazards as well as sexual diseases. This deplorable rape of land and people mirrors the unbridled greed and destruction meted out to the natives of California, starting in 1849, by Americans and others from around the world. The scars yet remain.

Belize (former British Honduras), despite its many problems, has been a far safer haven for Amerindians than the volatile conditions prevailing in neighboring countries. Land rights have been addressed as well, but the dilemma of identity looms large for many individuals—as the nation presses its homogeneity efforts.

"To be, or not to be," that is the question Belizeans are forced to face about their indigeneity. In the US, since 1970 many North American Indians faced that question with resolve; money and fame awaited them if they re-indigenized, because Indians were "in" with the general public's approval.

Therefore, out they went from cities to their reservation homesteads to learn —or relearn—what they had shunned or ignored previously. However, they were not "old time" Indians, nor did they envision a return to pristine utopian happy hunting grounds (a few may have), as their future. Armed with education and business savvy, many used the media, the law, the entertainment industry, literature, and public protest to make substantial changes for all Indians nationwide. In so doing, they validated their rights and identities, and reinforced the salvaging of many indigenous traditions. Whatever the degree of re-indigenization with many North American Indians, most now proudly project the "dual identity"—a modern human being who lives in an alien cultural milieu, but who happens to be Indian. Fortunately this process and option seem easier to achieve in the US and Canada, but not as readily in the older race-oriented nations of Latin America or newly independent ones asserting "national identity."

The census declarations that seemed to say the Miskito "disappeared" into the general population run counter to what has happened in the US—in the last census indigenous numbers swelled enormously, coming from many with only a fraction of genetic ancestry and barely a feather's worth of cultural inheritance, often claiming descent from an "extinct" tribe—they just wanted to declare their "Indianness" officially for the public record.

The Greater Antilles

Cultural revitalization among people of Taíno (Arawak), descent seems to have taken a slightly different twist in the Greater Antilles (Cuba, Hispaniola and Puerto Rico), than in the other areas under discussion here. In Cuba there is a viable community led by Panchito, an elder who has carried on a tradition of "Indianness" on his isolated mountain retreat in eastern Cuba. Though but a fragment of the once teeming population of 500 years ago, they carry on with tenacious, almost religious, dedication. Alejandro Hartman, running around with pencil and notebook seeking genuine Taíno survivors invoked memory of Frank G. Speck, who nearly a century ago tirelessly sought remnants and fragments of New England's Indians and other coastal Algonquin speakers long thought to be "extinct." They were there in plain sight all along. No doubt, agrarian rural isolation was responsible in large part for such conservative survivals to be sustained, but we also must consider outside bigotry and racism as having served as a shielding buffer zone, insulating such small groups from outside influences. The marginalized members of such enclaves found strength in each other and with it the comfort of language, ceremony, and custom was nurtured and maintained over time.

In addition to the surviving native Taíno community, there are the many Cubans who likely are of Indian descent but who are not aware of it or deny it.

In addition, we now know a Calusa presence in Cuba, in the late 17th and early 18th centuries, was much more substantial than previously thought. These people apparently were driven out by Creeks moving south into the Florida peninsula, rather aggressively it would seem. The Calusa, quite interestingly, used catamaran canoes in their exodus to Cuba. I think this Calusa presence so late in Cuba's history must be factored into the "survival equation" of Taíno as the Calusa are also defined as "extinct."

For the Dominican Republic (Hispaniola), the indigenous revival is more open, if slanted a bit differently. Overall, despite the contemporary Taíno revival and heritage pride, the Dominican Republic's general population seems to retain a compulsive urge to promote the Iberian part of their identity while—if not rejecting Taíno identity entirely—paradoxically it lionizes the precontact Taíno-Arawak past and at once denies the existence of "survivors" in school texts, museums, and national identity. Yet once Dominicans land in New York City, an amazing transformation ensues; the "diaspora" populations in New York City and elsewhere have affiliated with established North American Indian groups as well as organizing their own groups as Taínos.

Reappraisal of the *encomienda* system as it operated in Hispaniola, the tenuous Spanish hold on the island, the inflated records and reports, etc., all tend to paint a much different picture of conditions there during the first century after Columbus—and subsequent history as well. The Hispanic cultural umbrella that cast a shadow over the Greater Antilles for half a millennium certainly wilted many cultural aspects in that time—but I suspect something like Mexico's dual Indian-Hispanic identity will eventually emerge from the current revitalization stimulus. The nation will come out of denial and accept itself for what it is—not a European/Iberian bastion in the Caribbean, but an American original. Puerto Rico and Cuba likely will follow suit.

In reviewing this collection, I was glad to see comparisons drawn with several North American Indian groups, especially the Mashpee of Cape Cod who have experienced similar identity dilemmas and confusions in shedding marginalization or "text book extinction." Further north along the St. Lawrence River there are many Iroquois and Algonquin communities (formerly Catholic Missions, now Reserves), where the populations are well-mixed genetically with French, English, Irish, Scottish, Welsh, Belgian, Slavic and "others"—with plenty of phenotype confusion arising from blue/gray eyes, blond/red hair, and light complexions and Euro surnames—yet surprisingly have retained language, ceremonies, customs and culinary traditions. More importantly, they are...Indians. Ironically, the above condition may have been preserved by the very mission system dedicated to de-indianizing the people. The failure of the system in Hispaniola somewhat explains what happened in the Greater Antilles, but it seemed to have worked elsewhere in Hispanic America, e.g., California, the Southwest, Mexico, Central America, the Andes, etc. Missions may have served as unwitting cultural insulators, as where they succeeded, the Indian cultures, languages and customs survived rather well.

It is unfortunate this volume lacks a paper focused on Puerto Rico, but from independent observation and experience, it is safe to say the pattern described for the Dominican Republic would fairly be representative for Puerto Rico as well.

Before descending southeast to the Lesser Antilles, it might be useful to briefly mention the Bahamas, another forgotten backwater of former Indian occupation where Columbus met his first "Indians." Though largely dominated by an African Creole population today, there are pockets of Indian heritage that survive on various islands. Several can trace their origins back, not to Arawak, but Seminole, Creek, and African Seminole refugees who fled Florida in the early 19th century. It is known generally that certain Indian traditions have been maintained into the present.

The Lesser Antilles

For many decades scholars and the literature in general, accorded recognition to the Carib people of Dominica as the "only survivors" of the combined Arawak/Carib Indians of the West Indies. Recent research has proven this assumption false, but most telling for this high visibility has been their recognized land base: a "reservation." Established in 1903 by then governor Sir Hesketh Bell, it gave the Dominica Caribs a distinction and unique advantage in maintaining their identity. Having that special recognition fostered a self-awareness among them that was enhanced by the presence of the late Douglas Taylor, an anthropologist, who permanently resided with them from 1930 until his death in 1979. His inquiries and interest in their language and traditions, leading to many publications over the years, reinforced Carib awareness and self-respect for their culture and history. Perhaps second only to Hesketh Bell, Taylor fostered a sense of dignity for the Caribs as a people.

The special status of the Carib people in Dominica has naturally incurred envy from the Creole population, much of it focused on their inalienable reservation land. This envy, coming as much from the uninformed as from the greedy, mirrors attitudes and statements encountered among some US citizens who resent any special privileges enjoyed by Indians in the US; fortunately they are a minority voice in a country that has tried to rectify the injustices of the past during the last 40 years.

Despite the current impasse over a model village for tourists, a problem clearly born of the government's inept procedures in planning the project, the Carib people will continue to move along as they always have and doing things in their own way. They might take heart by looking into similar model village ventures in the US.

Indian-owned and operated model villages and museums are relatively successful in the US, e.g., the Cherokee Village of "Oconaluftee" located on their reserve in North Carolina amidst the Great Smoky Mountains, and the Seminole Village of "Ahtahthiki" located in Florida at the Big Cypress Reserve. Both are going concerns, and there are others around the US and Canada doing as well.

Language and cultural history have been the focus of Carib revivalists in recent decades; both are currently intensively pursued by Indian groups in the US and Canada in an "11th hour" reawakening. The Carib remark—or general feeling—that they will manage to survive Dominica's current economic crisis mirrors the remark of an Onondaga Clan Mother 40 years ago in New York State. She viewed the potential collapse of cities due to a depression or war as having little affect on the reservation. They had their gardens and had survived the 1930s Depression and other crises many times over; tenacity and self-sufficiency were the answer. In a similar fashion, one can presume Carib gardens will always provide "provisions," that is if they have the will to put in the effort. There are other native peoples in the US and Canada who have become so addicted to luxuries and the "good life" they scarcely know how to survive any differently now, and worse, know little about themselves. Nevertheless, such people are now becoming the exception in the ongoing revival.

St. Vincent's Carib community almost equates with Dominica's but for lack of a legally recognized land base. The St. Vincent cultural resurgence and the controversial question of building a "traditional Indian dwelling" to attract tourist revenues, certainly mirrors the account of Dominica's "model village" situation; as does the general Carib feeling of being "second class citizens," and their remote inaccessibility on the windward side prior to road improvements. It also seems the non-Carib majority still views Caribs as "creatures of the wild," but now more romantically than formerly it would seem.

Emotional ties to the land in both the spiritual and physical sense would seem to be a common theme among most Amerindians on both continents, born in part by their forced removal and alienation from it historically, but also from their belief the ancestors' spirits yet dwell among trees and rocks, in addition to burial remains and sacred places. The concept of land ownership in the European sense was also alien to most Indian cognitions of the ordered world they viewed.

The land question controversy brought the situation into focus for St. Vincent's Caribs. Parallels might be drawn with the Mohawks of St. Regis (Akwesasne), in northern New York. The reservation was in limbo only 50 years ago and the community divided by politics, religion (several Christian sects, Roman Catholic and traditional), conservative and progressive, well-off and dirt poor. Two things unified the entire community in the years since: education and threats to the land, the latter being the stronger of the two.

Since then, many factors contributed to their emergence as a moving force in North America's Indian resurgence.

In the March 1985 St. Vincent *Unity* news article entitled, "Chatoyer's Community Farm," I saw a literary articulation of protest that is at once an idealized reflection of the past coupled with its use to address a present dilemma. While a threatening call for action, it gives slack for government to rectify things. In the US during the 1970s and '80s, many archaeological digs were attacked and disrupted by angry militants. Their vandalistic endeavors finally led Congress to enact NAGPRA (Native American Graves Protection and Repatriation Act) in the early 1990s. The militants' original move to action was in some measure inspired by Vine Deloria Jr's published writings about injustices to Native Americans, including grave robbing, displaying burials in museums, public disrespect for sacred places, hunting and fishing restrictions, ad infinitum. A problem arising at any reservation nationwide became a magnet for Pan-Indian protest from scores of tribes. Indian patriots of the past were lionized in Indian papers while their images were blazoned on posters, T-shirts and jacket backs.

It was noted the once "strict" rule of marrying within the tribe has broken down, much as it did in Dominica. On islands with limited choice of partners, or travel beyond, mixing is inevitable. For mainland Indians, especially in North America, travel access is easier and partners often meet via inter-tribal powwows, at work, or at political gatherings. It's not uncommon today to find individuals with descent from Cuna, Yaqui, Sioux, Chippewa, and multiple other ancestors. It's easy to be Pan-Indian with such a background, yet be enrolled with only one tribe. Marriage to non-Indians of every shade has become common in urban areas, but the Indian identity seems to take precedence.

Using the Danes as the whipping boy for the latest neo-colonial oppression, the "Ice Men" provoked somewhat of a spiritual alliance between the Caribs and the St. Vincent majority. In some instances a few decades back, here in the US, certain well-publicized Indian issues created considerable non-Indian public support; e.g., the Mohawk armed takeover of land in the Adirondacks in 1974, RAIN (Right for American Indians Now), was a non-Indian organization that mushroomed overnight with support in cash, food, equipment, publicity, media conferences, etc. The state was finally forced to concede and transfer land to the Mohawks by 1977. Unusual situations sometimes make strange bedfellows, especially in the politics of group survival.

In Trinidad we see the same, almost ubiquitous attempts at homogenization found elsewhere, with a slight twist similar to that found in the Dominican Republic. The "Indian" is lionized as a heroic figure in the nation's folklore, history and museums, a footnote artifact to romanticize about, but heaven forbid to believe he/she might still be around in the modern population. Yet, there exists, with ample new recognition, from both government and the general populace, a Carib enclave. But there are those in Trinidad who still would brush them off as Creoles pretending to be Indians. Such naysayers usually are uninformed or base their assumptions on physical (phenotype), features, color, and or other "idealized" notions. Interestingly, in the case of the Iroquois people in the US and Canada, genetically and phenotypically they are about as mixed as any ethnic group could get, yet despite that and adherence to various Christian ideologies as well as traditional beliefs, "Iroquois" bubbles to the surface with pride and few should dare say "Creole" or "extinct" to their faces. I venture to say there are some right wing politicians who would like Indians to be just a "national memory," but individual and group tenacity has frustrated that ethnocidal dream—like it or not—they are "still here."

Amerindian Identity since 1992

Before the Columbian quincentennial in 1992, I am sure many people in the area of our discussion gave their "Indianness" little thought. Then suddenly, as gala celebrations were being planned or enacted, Indian people in general felt a sense of outrage that the year was marking a signal event that led to their collective misery over the 500 years since. Even some Creoles with a family legend of an Indian ancestor many generations back felt some indignity over the proceedings and media hype.

Whether legitimately enrolled or registered with a recognized band, tribe, nation, or not, identity will always be in the mind of the individual, never uniformly in the eyes of beholders. Who is legally what nowadays is often determined on criteria established by central governments for specific agendas, but in the end, who is culturally what largely rests with opinion at the community level and in the mind of the individual.

Many years ago the late Peter LaFarge (son of the famous Oliver LaFarge), composed a folk song honoring the Indian resurgence, which he sang at a New York City powwow. The opening lyrics were:

> There are drums beyond the mountains,
> There are drums which I can hear;
> There are drums beyond the mountains,
> And they're getting mighty near...

They said so much, and continue to say much, about the reawakening and moving forward we now see.

※ CONTRIBUTORS ※

José Barreiro, Taíno, senior editor at *Indian Country Today* and founding editor of *Native Americas* journal, has for nearly 20 years helped to forge the American Indian Program at Cornell University, where he served as associate director and editor-in-chief of Akwe:kon Press and its journal *Native Americas*. A member of the Taíno Nation of the Antilles, Barreiro was instrumental in remodeling *Indian Country Today* into the United States' leading American Indian news source. Barreiro has edited several books on indigenous American topics, including *Indian Roots of American Democracy*; *View from the Shore: American Indian Perspectives on the Quincentenary*; *Chiapas: Challenging History*; *Panchito: Cacique de Montaña*, a testimony narrative; and, most recently, with Tim Johnson, he edited *America Is Indian Country*. He is author of the novel, *The Indian Chronicles* (Arte Publico Press–University of Houston, 1993). For 25 years, Barreiro has worked on development of communications networks among indigenous peoples of North, Central and South America and the Caribbean. He has been an advisor to several Native nations and a consultant with the John D. and Catherine T. MacArthur Foundation, the Canadian International Development Agency, the Smithsonian Institution's National Museum of the American Indian, and the Council on Indigenous Peoples' Economies. Barreiro was chosen as one of the most influential 100 Latinos in the US in 1993 for his work in ethnic literatures. He holds a PhD in American Studies from the State University of New York at Buffalo. He is also a member of the editorial board of *Kacike: The Journal of Caribbean Amerindian History and Anthropology* (www.kacike.org).

Ricardo Bharath Hernandez has been the President of the Santa Rosa Carib Community of Arima, Trinidad, since 1976. Bharath Hernandez has been a central figure in the revitalization of the Arima Carib Community, following his return from living in Detroit, Michigan, during the early 1970s. He has served four terms as an elected representative on the Arima Borough Council, with responsibility for culture, and has recently been appointed Deputy Mayor. His primary activities have been the annual preparation of the Santa Rosa Festival and the maintenance of Carib traditions in processing cassava and in weaving, which he also teaches to school children. Bharath Hernandez has also been responsible for building a wide network of exchange and solidarity with numerous Amerindian communities and organizations across the Caribbean, South America and North America. His work in representing Arima's Caribs has taken him to indigenous gatherings in Canada, Cuba, Dominica, Guyana, Belize and as far away as India.

Arif Bulkan has practiced as an Attorney-at-Law, specializing in Criminal Law as well as Human Rights and Environmental Law. At present, he is a PhD candidate at Osgoode Hall Law School, York University, Toronto. In the past, he has worked with the Government of Guyana as the Assistant Director of Public Prosecutions, and was on contract with the Ministry of Amerindian Affairs in Guyana as the lead Legal Consultant on the revision of the 1951 Amerindian Act. Arif Bulkan has also been on staff at the University of Guyana as a part-time lecturer, where he lectured on Human Rights Law. He has published on Amerindian land rights in Guyana in the *Guyana Law Review*.

Janette Bulkan is a doctoral student at the Yale School of Forestry and Environmental Studies. She is an anthropologist by training and has work experience in social forestry, participatory community development, teaching and diplomacy. Her most recent full-time job was as Senior Social Scientist with the Iwokrama International Program for Rainforest Conservation and Development in Guyana (March 2000–2003) where she coordinated various projects in participatory resource management, sustainable livelihoods, Makushi linguistics, environmental education, monitoring and evaluation, and cultural diversity awareness and protection. She has published on forest peoples and broader forest issues in Guyana, including in publications and reports issued by *Social and Economic Studies* (1990), UNDP Program for Forests, PROFOR (2001), *Tropenbos* (1998, 1999) and *New West Indian Guide/Nieuwe West-Indische Gids* (1999).

Gérard Collomb obtained his doctorate in Anthropology from the Sorbonne in 1973. He is currently a researcher at the Centre National de la Recherche Scientifique (Laboratoire d'Anthropologie des Institutions). His present research deals with three main questions: the political organization of the Kali'na Amerindians in French Guiana and Suriname; the making of a collective identity; and Amerindian self-representation. Collomb has published in numerous French-language journals, including *Journal de la Société des Américanistes*, *Recherches amérindiennes au Québec*, *Ethnologie Française*, and *Socio-Anthropologie*. With Felix Tiouka, an Amerindian leader in French Guiana, he authored *Na'na kali'na: une histoire des Amérindiens Kali'na en Guyane* (Ibis Rouge Editions, 2000), and has published a chapter in the book *Zoos Humains, Mémoire coloniale*, edited by N. Bancel, P. Blanchard, G. Boëtsch, S. Lemaire and É. Deroo (Editions La Découverte, 2002). He is also an editor with the *Caribbean Amerindian Centrelink* (www.centrelink.org) and a member of the editorial board of *Kacike: The Journal of Caribbean Amerindian History and Anthropology* (www.kacike.org).

Arthur Einhorn has had a life-long interest in the indigenous peoples of the United States as well as the Caribbean and further afield. Formerly director of the Lewis County (New York) Historical Society and Museum, Lewis County Historian, Chair of the History Department at Lowville Academy (one of the oldest schools in New York State, and where he introduced the first anthropology courses for high school approved by the state of New York in the 1960s), he was also an Associate Professor of Anthropology at Jefferson Community College (Watertown, NY), and taught briefly at the State University of New York at Buffalo while studying there. He served as Associate Director for an Institute on Indians in higher education at St. Lawrence University (Canton, NY), for three years. In 1974 Einhorn was elected as a Fellow in the American Anthropological Association. Einhorn's fieldwork, spanning a half-century among Amerindians, has taken him to the Cree and Algonquin of the Sub-Arctic under the aegis of the Canadian National Museum, and all the way to visiting the Carib people of Dominica in the Eastern Caribbean. His major work, however, has been with the Iroquoian peoples of New York and Canada. During the early 1970s he was a consultant to the New York State Assembly Sub-Committee on Indian Affairs relating to laws for protecting Indian burials from collectors, an early effort that eventually led to the Federal Native American Graves Protection and Repatriation Act (NAGPRA) legislation in 1990. His ethnohistoric research over the years has uncovered unexpected links during the colonial period between Amerindians of Northeast North America and the Caribbean. Amongst his other research interests has been a devotion to indigenous traditional technology, with the aim of fostering its revival and maintenance. Einhorn's publications have appeared in major journals, as well as the *Encyclopedia of Anthropology*, the *Dictionary of Canadian Biography*, the *American Indian Art Magazine*, and most recently in the *Encyclopedia of New York State*. Although officially retired now, he continues research and publishing.

Jorge Estevez, a Taíno from the Dominican Republic, is Participant Coordinator of Public Programs at the Smithsonian National Museum of the American Indian in New York. Estevez's contact information is one of the first passed on by those "in the know" to anyone who is seriously interested in research about the Taíno or, better said, to anyone who has any questions at all about the Taíno of the past or present. Estevez gives dozens of presentations about the Taíno and their culture each year to school groups in the state of New York and abroad as a special lecturer, including a visit to the Dominican Republic in 2003 to address an educational conference on indigenous revival. He is a frequent contributor to the Smithsonian Museum's magazine, and has written for *Native Peoples* as well as for the soon-to-be-published *Encyclopedia of Caribbean Religions*. He is also an editor with the Caribbean Amerindian Centrelink (www.centrelink.org) and a member of the editorial board of *Kacike: The Journal of Caribbean Amerindian History and Anthropology* (www.kacike.org).

Pedro J. Ferbel-Azcarate earned his PhD in Interdisciplinary Archaeology from the University of Minnesota in Minneapolis; a master's in Anthropology/Archaeology from the University of South Carolina; and a BA in Psychology from the University of Michigan. He is an interdisciplinary archaeologist, an independent scholar affiliated with the Archivo Histórico de Santiago, Dominican Republic, and currently teaches in the Department of Black Studies at Portland State University, Oregon. A dynamic speaker, Ferbel-Azcarate has presented talks and directed workshops on the Taíno, archaeology, anthropology, and related topics at different venues in the US, the Dominican Republic, and Cuba. For four years he was the director and principal field researcher, project coordinator, instructor, advisor, public speaker, and curator for historical and cultural projects at the public archives of Santiago, Dominican Republic. He has published articles in *La Información* and *El Siglo* newspapers, in *Acta Americana* and the *Boletín of the Museo del Hombre Dominicano*, and is coauthor of *The Practice of Colonial Archaeology in the Dominican Republic* and *The Ancient Caribbean: Research Guides to Ancient Civilizations*. Ferbel-Azcarate is an editor with the Caribbean Amerindian Centrelink (www.centrelink.org) and a member of the editorial board of *Kacike: The Journal of Caribbean Amerindian History and Anthropology* (www.kacike.org).

Maximilian C. Forte is an Assistant Professor in Anthropology in the Department of Sociology and Anthropology at Concordia University in Montreal, Canada. Forte, a Permanent Resident of Trinidad and Tobago, lived and studied in Trinidad for almost seven years, with most of those years spent in Arima researching the Santa Rosa Carib Community. He has also conducted limited field research in Dominica. He obtained a PhD in Anthropology from the University of Adelaide in 2002. His dissertation research focused on practices of representation by and about the Caribs of Trinidad and the cultural politics of indigeneity. Related research foci included ethnohistory, colonial political economy and globalization. He has published aspects of his research in *Cultural Survival Quarterly*, *Indigenous Affairs* and *The Indigenous World*. He is the founding editor of the Caribbean Amerindian Centrelink (www.centrelink.org) and the current senior editor of *Kacike: The Journal of Caribbean Amerindian History and Anthropology* (www.kacike.org). Forte also serves as the webmaster for the Santa Rosa Carib Community and has posted numerous research essays online. A book, based on his research in Trinidad, titled *Ruins of Absence, Presence of Caribs: (Post) Colonial Representations of Aboriginality in Trinidad and Tobago* was published by the University Press of Florida in 2005.

Lynne Guitar, a Fulbright Fellow, earned her PhD in History and Anthropology from Vanderbilt University in Nashville, Tennessee, as well as a Master's in history from Vanderbilt, and two BA's from Michigan State University (one in history and the other in anthropology). She is an independent historian and anthropologist in Santo Domingo, Dominican Republic. She has taught at El Colegio Americano de Santo Domingo, guiding educational tours, and writing two series of books about the Taíno, one for children and one for adults, among other diverse projects. She is currently the Resident Director of the Council on International Education Exchange's program in Spanish and Caribbean Studies at Pontificia Universidad Catolica Madre y Maestra in Santiago de los Caballeros, Dominican Republic. She is an editor with the Caribbean Amerindian Centrelink (www.centrelink.org) and a member of the editorial board of *Kacike: The Journal of Caribbean Amerindian History and Anthropology* (www.kacike.org), where she has also served as the guest editor of an immensely popular special issue on "New Directions in Taíno Research." Guitar is a gifted lecturer, who has spoken on the Taíno and Dominican popular culture across the US, in Europe, the Dominican Republic, Jamaica, Martinique, and Mexico. Her publications include articles on the Taíno and Dominican history and culture for a wide variety of encyclopedias, for an upcoming collection edited by Jane Landers titled *Slaves, Subjects, and Subversives: Blacks in Colonial Latin America*, to be published by the University of New Mexico Press, in *Native Peoples*, and academic journals including the *Boletín of the Museo del Hombre Dominicano*, *Revista Interamericana*, *Ethnohistory*, and *Colonial Latin American Historical Review*. Guitar and her work were recently spotlighted in *Deep Sea Detectives*, a documentary aired on the History Channel.

Fergus MacKay is a human rights lawyer trained at the California Western School of Law. He is an expert in indigenous rights and has written a number of books and articles on the subject. He has worked as an attorney for indigenous peoples in Alaska. As legal adviser to the World Council of Indigenous Peoples, he worked with indigenous organizations throughout the Americas and the Pacific and was actively involved in the development of the draft United Nations Declaration on the Rights of Indigenous Peoples, the draft Organization of American States Declaration on the Rights of Indigenous Peoples and other international standard-setting exercises pertaining to indigenous peoples. He presently acts as Coordinator of the Three Guyanas Programme, working with indigenous and tribal peoples in Guyana, Suriname and French Guiana, and Coordinator of the Human Rights and Legal Programme of UK-based non-governmental organization, the Forest Peoples Programme. He is also attorney of record in two cases involving Suriname Maroons before the Inter-American Court on Human Rights. Recent publications include, with E-R Kambel, *De Rechten van Inheemse Volken en Marrons in Suriname* (2003) and *The Rights of Indigenous Peoples and Maroons in Suriname* (1999). He has published for the International Work Group on Indigenous Affairs, in *American University International Law Review*, in *Human Rights and the Environment: Conflicts and Norms in a Globalizing World*, and in *Cultural Survival Quarterly*.

Joseph O. Palacio, a Belizean Garifuna, recently retired (2004) from the University of the West Indies, where he served as Resident Tutor, reaching the level of Senior Lecturer. His main responsibility was designing and implementing several continuing studies programs as well as fielding degree-level programs originating from the University. In 1982 he received his doctorate in Social Anthropology from the University of California at Berkeley with a focus on the Caribbean/Central American subregion, food studies, and development. During his tenure at the University of the West Indies he did research on indigenous peoples, migration, and rural community development. He has published several articles and monographs on these topics in Belize and within the Caribbean and Central America. In 2005, *The Garifuna, A Nation Across Borders: Essays in Social Anthropology*, a volume edited by Palacio, was published by CUBOLA, Belize.

Kelvin Smith is currently completing a PhD in the Department of Sociology at the University of Essex. His research looks at the economic and political positioning of the indigenous community of Dominica, and how it has been affected by the initiatives of the global finance and development organizations. Funded by the European Social Research Council, he conducted fieldwork during 2003 in the Carib Territory. He also teaches part time within the Anthropology pathway at the University of East London.

Paul Twinn studied Ancient History and Social Anthropology at University College London, 1973–76. After a long period in management he returned to university in 1994 to complete an MSc in Social Anthropology (with distinction). Since then he has been conducting research in St. Vincent and the Grenadines, has made four field trips to the island, and currently holds citizenship there. He has been visiting Tutor at Goldsmiths College and Tutorial Assistant at University College London. At present he is an Associate Lecturer with the Open University based in London.

INDEX

• A •

ajoupas, 121
Akuriyo. See under indigenous peoples of the Caribbean
Algonquin, 243, 281, 282
Amerindian Peoples Association, 13, 137
Anthropologists: academic knowledge base, 37; anti-indigenous trend amongst, 5; biological ancestry, 55; ethnic identity, definition of, 53; extinction thesis, 9, 10, 60–61, 108, 237; indigenous anthropologists, 258; neglect of indigenous peoples of the Caribbean by, 2, 4; resurgence ethnography, 15
Anguilla, 7, 263
Apalai. See under indigenous peoples of the Caribbean
Arawak Mountain Singers, 62
Arawaks, 2, 22, 24, 25, 30, 112, 119, 148, 215, 263, 273, 281–283; French Guiana, 200; Suriname,156
Arawakan languages, 15, 24, 123, 200, 217
areitos, 27, 241
Assembly of Amerindians of French Guiana, 201
Assembly of First Nations (Canada), 3, 14, 127
Assembly of Manitoba Chiefs, 3, 127
assimilation of indigenous peoples
    French Guiana: 197, 200–201, 206–208, 280; international presence and solidarity, 204–205; national aboriginality, 207; reaction to assimilationist policy, 201–202, 203–205, 209
    Suriname, 157, 169
    Trinidad and Tobago, 110, 115
Asociacion Indígena de Puerto Rico, 13, 62

Association of Amerindians of French Guiana, 201
Association of Indigenous Village Leaders in Suriname, 156

• B •

Baramaya, 258
batey, 22
benab, 121
Bharath Hernandez, Ricardo, 7, 118, 119, 120, 121, 123, 125, 127, 244, 287
Biaraku, 258
Black Caribs. See under Caribs: St. Vincent, Garifuna: Belize
bohíos, 22, 30, 31, 36, 41, 235, 251, 258
Boriquen (Puerto Rico), 264
Borrero, Roberto Mucaro, 5, 265

• C •

Caciques, 31, 48, 116, See also Enriquillo; Hatuey; Hyarima, Chief; Ramirez Rojas, Don Francisco (Panchito); Rojas, Celestino; Rojas, Ladisalo
Calusa: migration to Cuba, 282
Carib Model Village. See under tourism: Dominica
Caribbean Organization of Indigenous Peoples (COIP), 2, 13, 215–233; Belize as Secretariat, 223–224; cultural retrieval, 219; demise, 230–233; early stages of growth, 222–223; membership in the World Council of Indigenous Peoples, 228–229; origins, 215–221; support from Trinidad and Tobago, 229; task performance review, 224–240; widening membership, 228

Caribs
    Dominica: Carib Reserve, creation of, 75–77, 76; Carib Territory, 69, 71–72, 74, 77–79, 82–84, 216–217; cultural identity, 72; cultural revitalization of, 283; identity, creation of, 75–76; land, Carib relationship to, 12, 76, 77; self identification, 75; tourism (see under tourism: Dominica)
    French Guiana: assimilation, 200, 203, 208; competition with other populations, 202; protest movement, 201, 204, 205
    St. Vincent, 90, 100, 104, 284–285; architecture, 94; artifacts, alienation from, 93; Black Caribs, 90, 100, 104–105, 105n3; Campaign for the Development of the Carib Community, 101; Chatoyer, 99, 100, 285; land, Carib relationship to, 89–106; Orange Hill Estates, controversy resulting from Danish purchase of, 97–105; Sandy Bay, 91–92
    Suriname, 156
    Trinidad and Tobago: Amerindian cultural influence, 110–113; cultural interchange, 13, 124, 125, 127; cultural preservation, 13, 259; cultural reclamation, 13, 125; cultural retrieval, 13, 107, 109, 121, 123, 124, 125; historical emergence, 113–119; international recognition of, 127; maintenance of traditions, 13, 14, 116, 119, 120; Mission of Santa Rosa de Arima, 113–117; national recognition, 285–286; revival of traditions, 119–125, 127; Santa Rosa Carib Community, 2, 13, 69, 108–109, 113–127, 228, 244, 253; Santa Rosa Festival, 109, 110, 115, 117, 118, 121, 123, 124, 126, 127; state support, 125–126; traditions, 120–125; translation of traditions, 13, 124, 125
Caridad de Los Indios (Cuba), 19, 21, 25–26, 28–30, 235–236, 239, 240–243, 245, 248–251
changui music, 22
chin-chin, 21, 37, 60

cimarrones, 45, 47, 48, 51
conquest and colonialism: Caribbean, 271–273; North American parallels, 275–276;
conucos, 29, 32, 240, 247, 248
Coordinating Body of Indigenous Organizations of the Amazon Basin (COICA), 14, 204
Creek: migration to Caribbean, 283
Curaçao, 7, 263
curanderos, 22, 35

• D •

de las Casas, Bartolomé, 24, 31, 41, 43, 47, 48
diaspora, indigenous
    Caribbean diaspora, 14, 213, 255–256, 258, 262, 263
    Caribs: St. Vincent Carib diaspora, 100, 103
    Garifuna, 193
    internet, role of, 213
    Taínos: Dominican Republic Taínos in the Unites States, 282; Puerto Rican Taínos in the United States, 7, 42
    transnationalized indigeneity, 255
DNA studies. *See under* Taínos: Dominican Republic, Taínos: Puerto Rico

• E •

Encomienda system, 41, 47, 49, 59, 282; protests by the Dominican Order of Friars, 47
Enriquillo (cacique), 47
Extinction thesis, 1–4, 10–11, 12, 15, 273–275;
    Caribbean/North American parallels, 279
    Cuba, 19, 26, 27, 29, 30, 237,
    Dominican Republic, 41, 42; census records, 45; de las Casas, Bartolomé, 41
    internet challenge to, 213, 256, 259, 264
    paper genocide, 11, 59
    Mashpee of Cape Cod, 282

Puerto Rico, 54
Taínos, 54, 59, 60–62, 65
Trinidad and Tobago: Caribs, 108–109, 110, 114, 115

• F •

Federation of Saskatchewan Indian Nations (FSIN), 3, 216, 222, 226
Federation of the Amerindian Organizations of French Guiana (FOAG), 204, 205
Forestry industry
  Guyana: forestry on Amerindian lands, 150–151; indigenous knowledge and labour, colonial use of, 146–147; Ministry of Amerindian Affairs, 137, 150, 288; state lands and forests, 142–146; timber industry and Amerindians, 147–150

• G •

Garifuna, 217
  Belize: Barranco, 182; Barrangunas in Belize City, 179, 184–194; cultural identification in Belize City, 177, 189–194; expulsion from St.Vincent, 178, 181; Garifunaduo, 13, 183, 193; language loss, 189–190; migration to urban communities, history of, 175, 177, 178, 179; 180–194, 217. See also National Garifuna Council
Garifunaduo, See under Garifuna: Belize
Globalization, 64, 148–149, 197, 209–210, 271, 278
guajiros, 1, 19, 22, 24, 27, 29, 237
guatiáo, 46
Guadeloupe, 7, 198, 206, 263, 275
Guyanese Organization of Indigenous Peoples, 13, 226

• H •

Haiti, 7, 41, 52, 60, 199, 206
Hatuey (cacique), 31
Hatuey Regiment (Cuba), 30–32, 244

human rights
  French Guiana: international recognition of indigenous rights, 204–205
  Suriname: health and education, 158; nonrecognition of rights, 156–157
  See also land rights
Hulme, Peter, 1, 75, 81, 243
Hyarima, Chief, 107, 124

• I •

indigeneity vs. nationalism, 54, 279–280; Dominica, 78–79; Dominican Republic, 54; French Guiana, 198, 206–210, 280
Indigenous Legacies of the Caribbean Conferences (1997–2003) (Cuba), 21, 213, 235–252
Indigenous peoples of the Caribbean
  Akuriyo (Suriname), 156
  Apalai (French Guiana), 200
  Garifuna. See Garifuna
  Kalinya. See Caribs
  Lokono. See Arawaks
  Pahikweneh (French Guiana), 200, 205
  Taínos. See Taínos
  Teko (French Guiana), 200
  Trio (Suriname), 156
  Wai Wai (Suriname), 156
  Warao (Venezuela), 121
  Wayana: French Guiana, 200; Suriname 156, 162
  Wayapi (French Guiana), 200
indigenous resurgence, 2, 3, 5–6, 9
  Caribbean, 6, 13, 14, 213, 279
  Caribs: St. Vincent, 284; Trinidad and Tobago, 117, 118, 125, 127
  demographic resurgence, 14
  Garifuna: Belize, 184
  French Guiana, 198, 206
  Greater Antilles, 281–283,
  Guyana, 12, 133
  internet, role of, 213, 254–259, 266, 267
  Lesser Antilles, 283–286
  North America, 279, 285, 286
  St. Vincent, 284
  Suriname, 133
  Taínos, 5

transnationalization, 2, 13
Indigenous survival: Caribbean and North America, comparison of, 279–286
indios de la montaña, 24
Interamerican Commission on Human Rights (IACHR). *See under* land rights: Suriname
Interamerican Court of Human Rights (IACtHR). *See under* land rights: Suriname
Internet presence of indigenous peoples, 3, 14, 213, 253–268
   building and expressing community, 257–258
   Caribbean Amerindian Centrelink, 260
   Caribs: Trinidad and Tobago, 253, 257, 258, 260, 262–264, 265, 266
   Dominican Republic, 264
   Garifuna, 256, 260–261
   Jatibonicu Taíno Tribal Nation, 258, 261, 268n3
   Kacike: The Journal of Caribbean Amerindian History and Anthropology, 260
   Puerto Rico, 256, 257, 264
   self-representation, 258–260
   Taíno Nation of the Antilles, 258–259
   Taínos, 256, 257, 258–260, 261–262, 264–265, 267
   Transnational Indigenous Fourth World, 255–256
   United Confederation of Taíno People, 258, 264–266, 268n3
Iroquois, 243, 245, 275, 282, 286

• J •

Jamaica, 7, 24, 51, 215, 222, 226, 272, 275
Jatibonicu Taíno Tribal Nation. *See also under* Internet presence of indigenous peoples

• K •

Kali'na. *See* Caribs: French Guiana
Kalinya. *See* Caribs: Suriname
Karifuna Cultural Group (Dominica), 81, 84n2
Karina Cultural Group (Dominica), 81, 84n2
Karina (Dominica), 81, 84n2
Karina Cultural Village (Dominica), 84n2
koudmen (work party), 76, 85n7

• L •

land rights
   French Guiana, 202–203
   Guyana: Amerindian Act, 144, 145, 150, 288; Amerindian dispossession, 135–137; Amerindian Lands Commission, 144; Amerindian Ordinance, 144; land, indigenous societies' relationship to, 137–138; land rights, 137–154; land takeovers, resistance to 138–141; state lands and forests, 142–146
   Suriname: Buskondre Dey (Interior or Bushland Day) Protocol 2000, 163–164,165; domestic courts, failure of, 165–166; the Gran Krutus, 164–165; international scrutiny, 166–167, 169; nature conservation areas, negative impacts of, 162; N'djuka village, forcible relocation of, 161; Peace Accord of Lelydorp, 163–164; Redan and state lands commissions, 164; resource exploitation, 158–162; rights to territories and resources, nonrecognition of 160–162, 280; Saramaka Maroons case, 167–169; Wayana environment and subsistence resources, threats to, 162
language issues: 36, 81, 120, 127, 182, 189, 205, 219, 236, 244, 260, 264, 277, 280–284; language, loss of, 109, 141, 189–190, 218
languages: Arawakan, 15, 24, 123, 200, 217; Cariban, 15, 114, 174, 200, 217; Garifuna, 189, 228; Island Carib, 123, 261, 228; Taíno, 243; Tupi-Guarani, 200; Waruan, 217; Wayuu, 24
Lokonos. *See* Arawaks

• M •

Maisiti Yucayeque Taíno, 62

manare, 121, 122
Mashpee of Cape Cod, 53, 282
Maybury-Lewis, David: extinction thesis, 1
mouina (huts), 72

• N •

Nanaturey, Valerie, 258
National Garifuna Council (Belize), 13, 187, 190, 194, 195n12, 216, 224, 228
nationalism, 14, 43, 52, 54–55, 63, 69, 81, 98, 107–108, 110, 120–121, 126, 177, 183, 198, 220–221, 238, 255, 257, 271, 279, 280–282
nonindigenous tribal peoples
  Suriname: 156; Aluku, 156; Kwinti, 162; Matawai, 156; N'djuka, 161; Paramaka, 156; Saramaka, 156, 157, 167–169

• P •

Pahikweneh. See *under* indigenous peoples of the Caribbean
parranda, 122
Pocaterra, Noeli, 24

• R •

Ramirez Rojas, Don Francisco (Panchito), 19, 21–24, 26, 28–37, 38, 235, 243–252
Reproduction of indigeneity, 2, 5, 9–12, 14, 15, 69, 111, 213
Resurgence ethnography, 15
Revival, 6, 8, 10, 42, 61, 64, 109, 119, 121, 123, 206, 213, 255, 282, 284
Rojas, Celestino, 28
Rojas, Ladislao, 30, 31, 32

• S •

Sahlins, Marshall: extinction thesis, 1, 5, 11; reproduction of indigeneity, 9
Salvage ethnography, 9, 15

Seminole: 284; migration to Caribbean, 283
Survival, 3, 4, 6, 8, 10, 19, 26–29, 34, 37, 42, 45, 52–55, 58, 63–64, 108–110, 112–113, 117, 119, 133, 157, 229, 235–237, 239, 247, 256, 258–259, 263, 264, 277–279, 281–282, 285

• T •

Taíno Nation of the Antilles, 62, 237, 241, 289. See also *under* Internet presence of indigenous peoples
Taínos
  Cuba: 19, 21–40; cultural revitalization, 281; La Ranchería, 21–22, 25–26, 28–29, 235, 245–248, 250–251; spirituality, 32–35; survival, documentary evidence of, 26–30; La Virgen del Cobre, 24–25, 34; War of Independence, participation in, 30–32; Yateras Indians, 24, 26, 27, 28, 29, 30, 31, 239, 244. (See also Indigenous Legacies of the Caribbean Conferences, 1997–2003)
  Dominican Republic: biological cultural heritage, 55–59; cultural heritage, 56–59; cultural revitalization, 282; critiques of authenticity, 5, 10; DNA studies, 42, 56, 61–62; depiction of, 42, 52; ethnic authenticity, 52–55; ethnic identity, 53–59; extinction thesis, 41–43, 59–64; indigeneity vs. nationalism, 54; race, 52–53, 54–55; population censuses, inaccuracies in, 48–51; revival, 62; spirituality, 42–43; survival, evidence for, 42–43, 44–52, 63–65
  Puerto Rico: authenticity, critiques of, 5; culture, 62; DNA studies, 274; revival, 42; survival, 3, 15; Taíno symbolism, nationalistic use of, 183
Teko. See *under* indigenous peoples of the Caribbean
Tiouka, Felix, 201, 204
Tourism
  Caribbean, 12, 271–272

Dominica: 69, 71–74, 77–84; Carib Model Village, 72, 78–84, 283; heritage sites, 71
Dominican Republic: heritage tourism and identity, 55
heritage tourism, 218, 240
North America: model villages and museums, 284
St. Vincent: 93–94, 284
Trio. See under indigenous peoples of the Caribbean

• U •

United Confederation of Taíno People, 5; internet presence, 258, 264–265

• V •

La Virgen del Cobre, 24; legend of, 25, 34

• W •

Wai Wai. See under indigenous peoples of the Caribbean
Wallerstein, Immanuel: extinction thesis, 1–2
warap, 121
Wayana. See under indigenous peoples of the Caribbean
Wayapi. See under indigenous peoples of the Caribbean
World Council of Indigenous Peoples, 14, 223, 228

• Y •

Yateras Indians. See under Taínos: Cuba

www.ingramcontent.com/pod-product-compliance
Ingram Content Group UK Ltd.
Pitfield, Milton Keynes, MK11 3LW, UK
UKHW022238230426
12048UKWH00018BA/1326